Women, Insecurity, and Violence in a Post-9/11 World

Gender and Globalization
Susan S. Wadley, *Series Editor*

Women, Insecurity, and Violence in a Post-9/11 World

BRONWYN WINTER

Syracuse University Press

First Edition 2017
17 18 19 20 21 22   6 5 4 3 2 1

∞ The paper used in this publication meets the minimum requirements of
the American National Standard for Information Sciences—Permanence of
Paper for Printed Library Materials, ANSI Z39.48-1992.

For a listing of books published and distributed by Syracuse University
Press, visit www.SyracuseUniversityPress.syr.edu.

ISBN: 978-0-8156-3502-4 (hardcover)   978-0-8156-3525-3 (paperback)
978-0-8156-5402-5 (e-book)

Library of Congress Cataloging-in-Publication Data
Names: Winter, Bronwyn, 1955– author.
Title: Women, insecurity, and violence in a post-9/11 world / Bronwyn
    Winter.
Description: 1st Edition. | Syracuse, NY : Syracuse University Press,
    [2017] | Series: Select titles in gender and globalization | Includes
    bibliographical references and index.
Identifiers: LCCN 2016049535 (print) | LCCN 2017005768
    (ebook) | ISBN 9780815635024 (hardcover : alk. paper) | ISBN
    9780815635253 (pbk. : alk. paper) | ISBN 9780815654025 (e-book)
Subjects: LCSH: Women—Social conditions—21st century. | Women's
    rights. | Terrorism.
Classification: LCC HQ1155 .W56 2017 (print) | LCC HQ1155 (ebook)
    | DDC 305.42—dc23
LC record available at https://lccn.loc.gov/2016049535

Manufactured in the United States of America

In honor of the resilience and courage of feminists everywhere who continue, obstinately as only feminists can, to make sense in the face of the most horrific nonsense

Contents

Preface

Gelibolu

D uring the night of April 25, 1915, the newly formed Australian and New Zealand Army Corps (ANZAC) landed on a beach on the western side of the Gelibolu (Gallipoli) Peninsula. Thus began the Gallipoli campaign of World War I, one of the worst-planned military operations in the history of modern warfare. By the time the campaign ended in early January 1916, more than 100,000 soldiers, the overwhelming majority of whom were Ottoman, had died, and some 250,000 had been wounded. The operation, which was planned as a means to open up a land route for the Allied forces to attack Germany by its Turkish "back door," was a colossal failure, as had been the sea-based operation in the Dardanelles Strait that preceded it.

Yet, despite this defeat, which should have marked yet another ignominious moment in the history of that bloodiest of wars, ANZAC was subsequently celebrated as a defining moment in the formation of the very recently federated and very recently independent Australian nation. The date April 25 is now ANZAC Day: a national public holiday. As I write these words in April 2015, almost exactly one hundred years after the start of the Gallipoli campaign, centenary fever is much in evidence. Australia even has a national military biscuit (cookie): the ANZAC biscuit, a staple in the traditional Australian culinary canon and the stuff of school fetes and local fairs. The name "Gallipoli" itself has for most Australians only a vague association with a place in Turkey, outside pilgrimages to the ANZAC memorial and cemetery there, to which tour operators

ix

routinely organize visits. Gelibolu is now forever Gallipoli, forever ANZAC, and forever Australia.

Even for feminists, ANZAC memorialization became a focus when second-wave feminists formed antiwar groups throughout Australia and lay wreaths and flowers at war memorials in memory of all women raped in wars in all countries. In doing so, they attracted accusations of disloyalty and treason, arrests, and some legal sanctions preventing them from disrupting ANZAC Day marches or memorial services (Lake and Reynolds 2010). ANZAC, as the anthology on it edited by Marilyn Lake and Henry Reynolds underlines so clearly, became the consolidating moment for the militarization of Australian history—even though soldiers, nurses, engineers, and others from the various colonies of what was not quite yet Australia had also participated in the Crimean and Boer Wars. Anyone contesting the ANZAC version of history was a traitor, at least symbolically, and thus not considered worthy of belonging to the nation. The latter is, however, a moot point because feminists protesting against the glorification of war were unlikely to *want* to belong to the nation.

Three days after the beginning of the Gallipoli campaign, on April 28, 1915, a group of feminist pacifists began a three-day meeting at The Hague in the Netherlands, which resulted in the creation of the Women's International League for Peace and Freedom (WILPF) (Rupp 1997). Jane Addams, the founding president, was, like her Australian counterparts many decades later, considered to be a treasonous individual. Most famously, J. Edgar Hoover, founding director of the Federal Bureau of Investigation, reportedly dubbed her "the most dangerous woman in America."

War defines nations, defines history, and defines our place in it. Over at least the past century, feminists have challenged those definitions and have almost systematically been labeled traitorous, disloyal, and so on. Such accusations, far from deterring feminists, are almost always celebrated as evidence that the protests are having an impact. "Not in our name" rang out in April 1915 as it rang out after September 11, 2001 (9/11) and at many other moments during the twentieth century as the militarization of nations and their history continued unabated. Nations have armies. They have, throughout recorded history, come into being through territorial, colonial, and anticolonial wars. Even if Australia, outside armed resistance by some of its Indigenous population, did not "come into being" through war (federation being a largely peaceful affair), it has defined itself through war for at least the past century. To be Australian is to be a symbolic ANZAC.

Since 9/11, Gelibolu has taken on a new dimension, at least for some. In launching a book by a young scholar in Sydney in March 2015, Australian sociologist Raewyn (R. W.) Connell alluded to Gelibolu and paused dramatically before telling the audience, "Remember, we were fighting Muslims then, too." This statement—made at a time when both anti-Muslim racism and other forms of prejudice as well as recruitment of young Australians to fight for Daesh (Islamic State) or al Qaeda were being much discussed in political, media, community, and academic fora—was greeted with nods and assenting murmurs. I found myself, however, troubled by its sweeping ahistoricity, not to mention its gratuitousness, for the book being launched had nothing to do with either war or Muslims. The "Muslims" being fought in Gelibolu in 1915 were the conscripted soldiers of a crumbling Ottoman Empire, and the ultimate military target for the Allied forces was in fact Germany. Turkey was simply a means to an end, for the Allies as much as for Germany. The Muslimness of the Turkish soldiers stationed on the Gelibolu Peninsula was irrelevant for most Allied participants. Perhaps more important for some then and certainly for many now was the Ottoman state's arrest, the night before the Allied landing at Gelibolu, of more than two hundred Armenian intellectuals, which began a genocide that the international community is still attempting to hold Turkey to account for a century later.[1]

On the Turkish side, the Gelibolu victory was a rallying moment for the "sick man of Europe," as Ottoman Turkey was characterized at the time (a comment attributed to Czar Nicholas I of Russia) because

---

1. For a recent comprehensive account of the Armenian genocide, see Suny 2015.

of its financial woes and loss of all of its European territories during the 1912–13 Balkan wars. The commander at Gelibolu, Mustafa Kemal Atatürk, was less than a decade later to become the leader of the newly independent Turkish Republic. So for Turkey also Gelibolu became in some ways a nation-building, if not necessarily nation-defining, moment. The nation that was subsequently built, however, in part thanks to the military and political experience—and political ambition—of Atatürk was at the time and still is today one of the "whitest" and most Westernized Muslim countries in the Middle East, at least in the urban centers of its own Western regions.

It thus seems odd to 9/11-ize the Ottoman Turkey of 1915, even if Turkey does enter the post-9/11 conversation in other ways. The fact, however, that Connell swept the failing Ottoman Empire of 1915 into the Muslim Otherness of a post-9/11 world is indicative of the pervasiveness of what I call "post-9/11ism" in this book. Just as the ANZAC centenary is a reminder of how much militarism has been woven, since long before 9/11, into our lives in all sorts of big and small ways and has shaped our collective consciousness, whether we want it to or not. Seen in this light, 9/11, however much it may have shaken "the world," is simply another step in the militarized march of "world" history. How big a step, in which direction, with which consequences, and for whom are more complex matters to investigate. But let us try.

Acknowledgments

First, I thank the many feminists, whether activists or intellectuals or both, who have provided me with knowledge, insights, understandings; who have engaged in conversation across the divides of nation, race, and class; and who have been generous with their time, their energy, their enthusiasm, their wisdom.

Second, I am most grateful to the countless colleagues and students in various parts of the world who have provided feedback and encouragement of various forms over the years it took me to put this book together. I am also indebted to the reviewers of the first draft of this book, whose detailed feedback helped me make the book as good as it can be. It may never be good *enough* for the things I would like it to be able to do, but that is nobody's fault but my own.

Third, my heartfelt thanks to the editorial, copyediting, marketing, and administrative staff at Syracuse University Press, in particular Deanna McCay and her successor on this project, Suzanne Guiod, and Kelly Balenske, as well as to freelance copy editor Annie Barva and the indexer, Cathy Goddard, whose careful work has brought this book to publication readiness. My first experience with the press in publishing *Hijab and the Republic* was a very positive one, and this second experience has lived up to the promise of the first.

Finally, I am as always hugely appreciative of the friendship and support of Véronique Delaunay, who has always steadfastly believed in my capacity to make some feminist sense of the world through my writing and has read and commented on innumerable drafts of various chapters.

Abbreviations

9/11	September 11, 2001
AKP	Adalet ve Kalkınma Partisi (Justice and Development Party, Turkey)
ANZAC	Australian and New Zealand Army Corps
ASEAN	Association of South East Asian Nations
BJP	Bharatiya Janata Party (People's Party, India)
BRIC	Brazil, Russia, India, China (emerging powerful economies)
BRICS	Brazil, Russia, India, China, South Africa
CIA	US Central Intelligence Agency
CSL	Cooperative Security Location
Daesh	al-Dowla al-Islaamiyya fii-il-I'raaq wa-ash-Shaam (Islamic State of Iraq and Syria)
EU	European Union
FGM	female genital mutilation
FIS	Front islamique du salut (Islamic Salvation Front, Algeria)
FLN	Front de libération nationale (National Liberation Front, Algeria)
FOS	Forward Operating Site
GDP	gross domestic product
IGLHRC	International Gay and Lesbian Human Rights Commission (former name of OutRight Action International)
IM GLAD	Initiative and Movement for Gender Liberation against Discrimination

JDP   Parti de la justice et du développement (Justice and Development Party, Morocco)

LGBT(I)   lesbian, gay, bisexual, transgender (and intersex)

MENA   Middle East and North Africa

MILF   Jabhat Tahrir Moro al-'Islamiyyah (Moro Islamic Liberation Front)

NATO   North Atlantic Treaty Organization

NGO   nongovernmental organization

O&M   operations and maintenance (budget line in military spending)

OAS   Organization of American States

OECD   Organization for Economic Cooperation and Development

OFW   overseas Filipino worker

R2P   Responsibility to Protect (United Nations doctrine)

SIPRI   Stockholm International Peace Research Institute

TBA   Tri-Border Area (in Spanish: Triple Frontera), between Argentina, Paraguay, and Brazil

UN   United Nations

UNDP   United Nations Development Program

UNICEF   United Nations Children's Emergency Fund

UNODC   United Nations Office on Drugs and Crime

US DoD   US Department of Defense

US DoS   US Department of State

VFA   Visiting Forces Agreement

WEOG   Western European and Others Group

WIB   Women in Black

WTO   World Trade Organization

WW05   Women's Worlds International Interdisciplinary Congress on Women, 2005

Women, Insecurity, and Violence in a Post-9/11 World

Introduction

September, Security, and Sisterhood

In 2009, a young Afghan woman by the name of Gulnaz, then nineteen, was raped by her cousin's husband and then promptly jailed under Afghan law for adultery, having sex outside marriage. Being raped in such circumstances remains, at the time of writing this book, one of several "moral crimes" on the Afghan statute books that are punishable by prison. Others include leaving an abusive husband or running away from a forced marriage. On December 1, 2011, President Hamid Karzai pardoned Gulnaz after considerable international pressure, and on December 13 she was transferred to a safe house with her daughter, the child of the rape, to whom she gave birth in prison. The safe house was organized because it was feared that her brothers would murder her in the name of "honor." By marrying her rapist, however, she would give her child a "normal" family and save this "honor," thus protecting herself from death, as she explained in an interview with CNN in 2011 (CNN 2011). At that time, it was far from sure that her brothers would agree to this plan. In the same interview, Gulnaz reported asking President Karzai to have her brothers sign a document guaranteeing that nothing would happen to her or to her rapist and would-be husband, himself still in prison for the same crime at the time (that is, sex outside marriage, not rape; he ended up serving two and a half years). Gulnaz had no education, no money of her own, and thus few options. A decade after 9/11, her case was not unique. She and her child ended up living with her new husband, his first wife, and the first wife's five children. In 2013, a

UK Channel 4 news report described the atmosphere in their house as "glacial" (Channel 4 2013).

In 2001, the administration of George W. Bush (Bush II) proclaimed the liberation of Afghan women one of the moral justifications for bombing and invading this already much-ravaged and extremely poor country (Delphy 2002). In 2004, on the occasion of International Women's Day, the US Department of State (DoS) proclaimed how much things had improved for women in a now Taliban-free Afghanistan, a statement that flew in the face of demonstrable fact (Winter 2006b).

As for Iraq, a little more than three years after President Barack Obama declared the country "sovereign, stable and self-reliant" and thus ready to be left to its own devices (Obama and Obama 2011), he was requesting from Congress an Authorization for the Use of Military Force in Iraq against Islamic State—also known as Islamic State of Iraq and the Levant or Islamic State of Iraq and Syria or Daesh, the acronym for the latter's Arabic name (al-Dowla al-Islaami-yya fii-il-I'raaq wa-ash-Shaam), which I use in this book. In the wake of the Daesh attacks on Beirut and Paris in November 2015, there was media speculation that these attacks and French president François Hollande's call for a US–France–Russia coalition against Daesh might push Congress to finally approve Obama's request. At the end of January 2016, however, Congress remained divided on the issue, and the matter had been stalled for almost a year.

A few days before sending his request to Congress in February 2015, Obama had angered the Christian Right by making a reference to the violence done in the name of Christianity during the Crusades and slavery (see Obama 2015); it is believed that the reference was also an indirect criticism of the Bush II administration's actions in Iraq, which are largely responsible for the current catastrophic situation there. On September 16, 2001, on the South Lawn of the White House, Bush had said, "This crusade, this war on terrorism, is going to take a while" (Bush 2001c).

While Congress debates the merits of more intervention and Obama distances himself from the glowing picture he himself painted concerning Iraq in 2011, Iraqi women are facing quite similar day-to-day challenges as women in Afghanistan. Women's status in Iraq has gone from "one of the highest in the region to one of the lowest, in less than two decades" (Ditmars 2015), thus showing a similar disjuncture between US rhetoric and on-the-ground reality to that in Afghanistan. In 2011, at the time Obama proclaimed Iraq's stability and self-reliance, life was, in fact, anything but secure and stable for Iraqi women, who faced violence and persecution from the state and at home and lacked reliable access to minimum infrastructure.

One of the many anthologies published in the wake of 9/11 characterized 9/11 as "the day that shook the world" (Baxter and Downing 2001). A decade and a half later, my book investigates the medium-term implications of this statement for "the world's" women. The book considers what the impacts of 9/11 and its aftermath have been for women, whether these impacts have been the same or of the same magnitude everywhere, and whether they have been significant at all. The premise that 9/11 "shook the world" immediately begs two sets of questions. First, what is "the world" that is being referred to, and how is it conceptualized? Second, how was that world shaken? Was the whole world shaken? Were some bits of it shaken more than others, and if so, which bits, and why? How did the shaking continue (or not) in the wake of 9/11? How did post-9/11 shaking interact with other shakings, such as the global financial crisis of 2008 or the so-called Arab spring of 2011? And how do we know?

In short, what is "the post-9/11 world," and who lives in it? Who are its actors and audience, its actors and acted-upon? Who are its mere bystanders? Further questions arise, of course, within the context of this book. They can be summarized by the feminist question made famous in an international relations context by Cynthia Enloe: "Where are the women?" (1990, 7). How were the world's women affected by 9/11? Were they all affected in the same way? Were they affected at all? Which women and which aspects of their lives have been discussed in the post-9/11 scenario? How, indeed, are impacts on "the world's" women to be assessed, and how do women respond? How do we know? *Do* we know? Have the impacts been primarily material or discursive, or is this point moot because the discursive and the material are interconnected in any case?

It is impossible, of course, to answer such huge questions in the space of one book. For a start, I have nowhere near the amount of knowledge and expertise to judge what impacts 9/11 and its aftermath (hereafter "9/11" for the sake of brevity) may or may not have had on "the world's" women. I know relatively little about "the world" in all its diverse and unequal places and dimensions and virtually nothing about some significant parts of it. Attempting to present a book about the impacts or otherwise of 9/11 on "the world's" women can thus appear to be a foolishly ambitious exercise. My aim is not, however, to document every impact for every woman the world over. It is rather to ask how 9/11 and "the world" that has presumably been shaken by it have been politically framed, by whom, and to what ends. It is to ask what the gendered impacts of those framings have been beyond the most copiously discussed sites of the United States, Afghanistan, and Iraq, even if those sites are necessarily a starting point: How could they not be, after all? But beyond stating the obvious concerning the post-9/11 messes that have been made, most particularly for women in those sites, how has 9/11 shaped our understandings of what "the world" looks like for women?

The very idea of "the post-9/11 world" is ambiguous because it simultaneously suggests a simple relationship of chronology—"after September 11, 2001"—and a far more complex one of cause and effect: "the world is a different place after 9/11 than before it, and this is because of the events of September 11, 2001." This ambiguity then readily lends itself to analyses of the *post hoc ergo propter hoc* type: after this, therefore because of this. It is an ambiguity that is central to this book: 9/11 happened; it had an impact; it became at the very least a temporal marker, arguably the single biggest "world event" in the first decade of the third millennium, although the global financial crisis and the very beginning of the Arab uprisings gave it a little competition during that same decade. In a contemporary world in which temporal landmarks are so frequently articulated in terms of armed conflict, often involving the United States, 9/11 and the wars that ensued have certainly been the biggest acts of international aggression since the most recent major international war—the Gulf War for some, Vietnam or Korea for others, or World War II for yet others.

However one contextualizes 9/11, it has undeniably become a visual and verbal symbol that has marked the early years of this century and that no doubt will, for future historians, become a somber signpost marking the start of the third millennium. The abbreviation 9/11 will never again refer simply to November 9, as this arrangement of figures and a slash (9/11) is normally interpreted by most of us living outside North America. More than ever, even at the level of naming of dates, the date September 11, 2001, events that happened on that day, and the date's graphic and vocal representation in US English force the rest of the world to think like US Americans or "United Statians," as French Canadians and other "Latin" Americans, all also "Americans," call them and as I call them here.

The date September 11, 2001, has supplanted other somber anniversaries in US history. For many on the left in my generation and certainly for Chileans, 9/11 was until 2001 remembered as September 11, 1973, the date of the military coup backed by the US Central Intelligence Agency (CIA) that ended President Salvador Allende's government (and Allende's life when the deposed president committed suicide later the same day, although some continue to believe this suicide was staged) and that introduced eighteen years of dictatorship under General Augusto Pinochet. Nor is September 11 widely remembered as the day in 1609 when Henry Hudson arrived on Manhattan Island, a day of discovery for Hudson and the British, which was to begin the Anglo history of the world's most powerful nation and the concurrent history of dispossession and genocide for Indigenous Americans. Almost four centuries later, an invasion of an entirely different order has all but erased the collective memory of Manhattan's colonization, and, unlike September 11, 1973, or September 11, 1609, the United States and its Anglo power base were this time not the aggressor but the victim.

Given the 1609 antecedent, some may find in 9/11 a cruel irony. It is easy to attribute patterns to coincidences—even though, as this book shows, apparent coincidences sometimes *are* related to patterns. Yet the fact that 9/11 happened in the first year of the new millennium and exposed the world's only superpower at that time as vulnerable in ways that were inconceivable for most—certainly for most US citizens—has generated a symbolism that easily lends itself to hyperbole. "The world" was shaken; "terror" became the enemy of "freedom" and "democracy" as self-cast by the US state and thus must have war declared upon it.

What yardstick, then, can we possibly use to measure the degrees to which the seism of 9/11 reverberated (or not) through nations geographically or politically close to or distant from the United States, Afghanistan, or Iraq and the events that occurred therein between 2001 and 2003 in particular? Other great seisms of history have shown us that impacts can be indirect, diffuse, and spread over time. If one considers, for example, the impact of Nazism and fascism in Europe and of the second world war that came about largely because of them, and if one then links these events with Japan's militarism and imperialism of the time, then it will become apparent that the impacts of World War II continue to be felt in many places. They are felt in the South American countries where Nazi war criminals took refuge and in the ongoing legacy of the Shoah (Holocaust) in Europe. They are felt in Israel and in the Israeli state's ongoing cynical use of the Shoah as a moral pretext for its colonization of Palestine. They are felt in the emergence and relative success of neo-Nazi and neofascist groups and of other extreme-right groups influenced by them throughout Europe from the 1980s on. They are felt in the legacy of the US occupation and US bases in the Philippines and in the ongoing campaign for the Japanese state to apologize and make reparations to the "comfort women" and other women raped by the Japanese military during the war. And so on and on.

So I suspect it will be with 9/11 and its aftermath: the shock waves are still rippling throughout "the world." A decade and a half is a very short time to be able to make any sort of claim concerning impacts, many of which are still being felt and assessed.

Security Talk and 9/11: *Post Hoc Ergo propter Hoc*?

It is a self-evident statement that 9/11 did not suddenly occur within a geopolitical vacuum. "World events," which in traditional international relations analyses generally mean either wars or economic crises, do not happen out of a void but are produced within and by an existing context. Yet the material and rhetorical impacts of 9/11 have been so dramatic, in some parts of the world at least, that the "before 9/11" all but disappears in the ferocious theatrics of "after 9/11." Yet after 9/11 was indeed in the making before 9/11. For example, the US arms buildup and the "security" rhetoric used to justify it were present before 9/11, as they were elsewhere, for instance in Australia in the lead-up to the Olympic Games in Sydney in 2000 (Winter 2007). Similarly, the Southeast Asian terrorism that became the justification for Bush II's post-9/11 military buildup in the region did not suddenly appear in the period immediately prior to or immediately after the 9/11 attacks in New York and Washington. Former Australian foreign minister Gareth Evans has even suggested that "it is probably the case that [9/11's] main impact was to change perceptions rather than realities. The fundamentals of the global security environment . . . remain pretty much as they were" (2004, 34).

Evans was writing in 2004 and may or may not have the same opinion now. But to follow his argument on perception, what 9/11 certainly did was to provide a focus and a framework within which certain actions by the United States—as well as by other Western, some Middle Eastern, and some Asian states—could occur and be justified. The material fuels the rhetorical fuels the material fuels the rhetorical. . . .

The "as well as" qualification in the previous paragraph is important. The plethora of post-9/11 literature on "what we think of America" (to quote the theme of issue 77 of *Granta* magazine [*Granta* 2002]) tends to make us forget that the United States has not been the only villain in a post-9/11 world. I am referring here not to Islamist terrorist villains (although one might do so, and I will) but to other state and nonstate actors, however aligned in the post-9/11 scenario, who are responsible for various acts of aggression or collusion that have made "the world" a more difficult place for a number of people, especially women. Yet it is often in women's name that these same acts have been committed.

Women's rights and security were of concern before 9/11 and continue to be so after 9/11. At the same time, 9/11 affected how those rights and security are articulated and protected—or threatened—by state actions. It is arguable that before 9/11 women's rights and security were mostly of concern only to feminists. Even if state and international institutional actors took some measures to address feminists' concerns, they did so only after the latter lobbied them forcefully, painstakingly, and persistently. After 9/11, the lobbying of course continued, but "women's rights and security" started to be instrumentalized to post-9/11ist ends, such that conversations about rights and equality became subsumed under conversations about security. Even if, again, "security talk" and its capacity to shape the direction of world politics and economics long predates 9/11 (N. Hudson 2010), 9/11 appears to have cemented "security talk" within the everyday.

In a national radio interview to mark the tenth anniversary of an Australian current-affairs periodical, *Griffith Review*, editor Julianne Schultz commented that the theme that had immediately suggested itself for the first issue in 2003 was "insecurity in the new world order": "It was post-9/11, around the time of military incursions into Iraq and Afghanistan. There was a lot of political talk about this 'new world order' which was 'post–Cold War,' then 'post-9/11.' Who knew what it was quite going to be, but it wasn't looking particularly secure at that point and I'm not sure it's looking that much more secure now" (ABC Radio National 2013).

For the tenth anniversary issue in July 2013, the editors of *Griffith Review* decided not to have a particular theme, but among the contributions that came from fiction writers, academics, and journalists "oddly there were themes that suggested themselves. . . . The theme that's come through is one about this notion of security, and it's economic security, personal security, and so on. So a theme emerged even though we didn't seek to do it from the outset" (*Griffith Review* 2013).

"Security talk" is everywhere. We talk about human security, financial security, national security, neighborhood security, income security, food security, environmental security, cyber security. Security talk has even invaded our universities. This invasion has not occurred so much through a proliferation of security studies because this field was already well established and had even experienced a resurgence in the mid-1970s, with a broadening of themes and, according to Stephen Walt (1991), an increased scientific rigor that made the field a "serious player" in academe. But since 9/11, security studies have taken on a heightened research profile. In the wake of 9/11 in Australia, for example, political interference in the Australian Research Council's criteria for funding research projects led to the establishment of four national research priorities, and an applicant was awarded extra points if he or she could justify that his or her work fitted them. One of the four priorities was "safeguarding Australia." Even though one of the subcriteria was the rather vague catch-all "Understanding Australia and the World," most of the subcriteria had to do with security and surveillance and were decidedly part of a post-9/11 scenario. The latter also, for Australia, included the Bali bombing of October 12, 2002, in which Australians were the largest national group among those who died (202 people were killed, of whom 88 were Australian).

Similarly to Gareth Evans, Yee-Kuang Heng (2006) has noted, however, that war had become a US "risk-management strategy" long before 9/11. According to Heng, in many ways Bush II's interventionist politics were a continuation of Clinton's—a continuity where one might have expected discontinuity. Relatively "weak" entities—so-called rogue or failed states—became the new strategic concern for the United States since it had become "the" superpower after the collapse of the Soviet Union. Even terrorism of the 9/11 magnitude did not constitute the "existential survival threat" that the Soviet bloc was perceived to be during the Cold War (2006, 2). War, suggests Heng, is now preemptive, a way of averting possible risks before the event. "Doing war," for the United States, is no longer a matter of Great Powers acting and reacting to sort out their balance of power but a matter of the superpower putting out spot fires, with the aspiration, Heng suggests, of spreading democracy in a world where *global governance* has become the new catchphrase.

Seen through another lens, however, "spreading democracy" appears less an aim than a moral veneer to justify the preemptive risk strategy. It has demonstrably failed in any case, as the current situations in Afghanistan and Iraq demonstrate. Moreover, the safeguarding or spreading of democracy was a justification for US interventionism long before 9/11 and even before Clinton's intervention in Kosovo in 1999: the Gulf War in 1990–91, for example, and the bombing of Libya in 1986, which also failed by the US own professed yardstick because it did not stop terrorist attacks against US targets in Europe and Africa.

Putting aside, however, the genuineness or otherwise of the aspiration to "spread democracy," the idea of "war as risk management" begs other questions: Risk for whom? What, exactly, is at stake? Whose security and whose "democratic rights" are being protected? Among other things, the "security" agenda has necessitated a reconsideration of women's relationship to political and military violence. Although some scholars focus on the problems that female suicide bombers and female army personnel raise for feminist analysis (e.g., Eager 2008), I am more concerned in this book with the double bind of "security." On one hand, women want to be safe and in particular to be able to move safely within and between countries, regions and towns, which in many places implies the presence of some level of armed personnel. On the other hand, the bewildering array of new security measures introduced by many of the world's governments have the perverse effect of making border crossing even more difficult than before. "Security" has become an integral part of the day to day. Even if the globalization of security and surveillance is rooted in a pre-9/11 history, it has become ever more pervasive in the post-9/11 "technosecurity" regime of "unending war" (Mattelart 2008). Another aspect of the "security" dilemma is that the presence of a Western researcher in some of the areas under study in this book potentially creates an extra security risk and certainly security burden for local participants because they feel obliged to look after their guest's safety. This burden usually includes extra financial expense, which is necessarily passed on to the researcher or which in any case the researcher feels morally bound to cover.

Post-9/11ism

All of this "security chatter" is part of what I described as "post-9/11ism" in a short piece I was asked to write in 2011 for the tenth anniversary of 9/11 and within the context of a celebration of the anthology on 9/11 that I coedited with Susan Hawthorne (Hawthorne and Winter 2002; Winter 2011b). I defined what I understood to be the Western (US-driven) ideology of, for want of a better term, "post-9/11ism"—the network of ideology, discourse, and practices that developed following the attacks on September 11, 2001.

The ideology of post-9/11ism has, as I see it, three related elements,

> all of which have manicheanism [extreme, unnuanced dualism] at their core. . . . The first is an escalation of Huntington-esque "clash of civilizations" rhetoric that constructs "the West" and "the Muslim world" as radically incommensurable in terms of values, culture and political philosophy: at best, their presumed antagonism may be minimized within separate-but-equal multiculturalist structures; at worst, each is constructed as desiring the other's destruction. (Winter 2011b, 271–72)

The second element of post-9/11ism is "the political deployment, in the West and among its allies, of 'terrorism,' 'security,' '(democratic) values' and 'women's rights (security, dignity . . .)' as moral alibis for increased state militarism and the passage of legislation that limits civil rights, or indeed, women's rights (security, dignity . . .)" (Winter 2011b, 272).

The third element of post-9/11ism is a renewed imbrication of religion and politics—and this is true outside "the West" as well, as events in Tunisia, Egypt, and elsewhere since late 2010 and in Turkey earlier in the decade have made clear. "The post-9/11 'clash of civilizations' frame has provided a fertile terrain for a revival of religious politics," and history has shown us that women in general and ethnoreligious or sexual minorities in particular are the privileged targets of a religious recasting of the polity (Winter 2011b, 272). "Salvation" sits alongside "safeguarding" within the post-9/11ist mantra. The discourses of the political class—and a significant proportion of media, academic, and civil society commentators—have overflowed with rhetoric that privileges various combinations of religion and security ideologies and imagery. A "just God" helps the US nation and underpins its ideals, but an equally "just God" helps the Islamic fundamentalist nation or its nationalist aspirations and underpins its ideals. On both sides of the "Islam-and-the-West," 9/11ist polarity, salvation and safeguarding, God and our just way are foregrounded, as they are in many other parts of the post-9/11 world. This is the right-wing version of the story, in any case.

There is also, however, a "progressive" version, which Western governments present as more compatible with a "tolerant" or "multicultural" Western self-image. It goes something like this: we now live in a "postsecular" world, one in which we (that is, "we the West") would do well to develop an "awareness of what is missing" (Habermas 2001, 2007). Religious values become recast within a logic of antiracism and inclusiveness, so that criticism and especially lampooning of religions—in particular Islam—are frowned upon (as I discuss in chapter 7). If Jürgen Habermas was referring to the need for religious pluralism combined with an awareness of the "missing" moral dimensions in our secularized world, many on the Western left who have picked up a "postsecularist" position, often combined with concerns about "Islamophobia," have taken this argument a step further.

We have also seen the reinjection of what appears to be "missing" via "moderate" political expressions of Islam in the Middle East and North Africa. Although the causes of the uprisings in many Arab countries of the Middle East and North Africa and the change in government in Turkey in 2002 are not attributable to 9/11 as such, the emergence of an "Islamic democracy" movement in these countries, with explicit or tacit Western support, has been shaped within a post-9/11 context. In a manichean post-9/11 world of Good and Evil, the development of a "good" Islamism—the new friend of the West in opposition to more authoritarian, albeit more secular regimes in the Muslim world—and the responses by Western governments have among other things somewhat disrupted the Us-and-Them equation.

Yet the equation is persistent, with the United States as a key player on both sides, depending on which version of post-9/11 politics one embraces. September 11 is dramatically, irrevocably *about* "America," with the rest of "the world" lined up as allies or enemies, fighting just or unjust wars, depending on one's point of view. The post-9/11 world is one where taking sides appears to be inevitable, and even if one resists taking sides, one will be allocated to a "side" anyway. There is no place for nuance or creative doubt in a post-9/11 world. "If you are not for us, you are against us" is more than ever the catch-phrase. But who is "us"?

States of Emergency and the State of This Book

If women are always living in "states of emergency" (MacKinnon 2002), the noise of emergency has been amplified since 9/11. Yet women, like prey animals who learn quickly to hide their pain so as not to be picked off by the predator, learn to normalize the various "states of emergency" in which they live in an attempt to minimize their effects. Through logics of national, cultural, ethnic, or religious belonging; notions of individual "choice"; internalization of responsibility for damage done to them; or simply a need to get through the next day without major mishap, women learn to downplay the harm done to them on a daily basis. Harm is just what happens.

This book, then, is organized around a consideration of whether or how that harm has been affected by 9/11, for better or for worse, and around some things that women have done to bring it to "the world's" attention in order to eradicate or at least minimize that harm. Some chapters are oriented more around theoretical questions, and some or parts of some chapters are based on case studies, stemming largely albeit not entirely from my own fieldwork in various places over the decade it took to piece this book together. I have no clear or unambiguous answers to the multiple questions I raised earlier in this introduction. This lack of clear answers does not, however, mean that the questions should not be asked. Feminist scholarship, especially feminist international relations scholarship, has so often found itself within the no-woman's-land of the uncertain and the impossible that it is almost a given in this type of work.

Chapter 1 looks at two questions: "What is 'the world'?" and "How was it shaken by 9/11?" The first part of the chapter investigates different ways of understanding "the world" in current international relations. As we will see, none of the various ways of conceptualizing the world, its components, and its power bases is in fact entirely outside the post-9/11ist frame. Nor, however, are these ways all entirely within that frame. Yet what does emerge clearly is that "the world" as we understand it is made up of nation-states or aspirational nation-states, themselves grouped in different ways: regional, religious, economic, and so on. In an attempt to consider how different components of this "world" might be "shaken" by 9/11, I finish chapter 1 with four country/regional case studies: Djibouti; Turkey; the triborder region of Argentina, Brazil, and Paraguay; and China. I knew virtually nothing about Djibouti and very little about China, Brazil, and Paraguay before writing this chapter, so it was a daunting exercise. Only Djibouti had any overt connection to 9/11 because it was the main site of Operation Enduring Freedom, the second phase of Bush II's war on terror. Yet staggeringly little has been written about this tiny country on the Horn of Africa, so strategically important for the United States but so, it seems, unimportant for the rest of the world. Turkey is certainly more copiously discussed in the scholarly literature, including feminist work, but its connection to 9/11 is less direct and less immediately apparent. As for the triborder region, its link to 9/11 is extremely tenuous, and it did not in fact occur to me that there might be such a link before I heard a paper on the subject at a conference in Poitiers, France, to mark the tenth anniversary of 9/11. Intrigued, I decided to dig further, but all was not as it seemed, especially how it was presented in that conference paper. I have retained the section on the triborder region in chapter 1 as an illustration of the pervasiveness of post-9/11ism. Finally, China entered the post-9/11 club via its Uyghur people and its emergence as an economic power to be reckoned with and even, according to some, as the next superpower. In sum, nations and regions as different and distant from each other as those listed here present interesting cases of the material or imagined links between globalization, militarism, and post-9/11ism in countries and regions that may at first appear far removed from post-9/11 concerns.

Having looked at what "the world" is made up of and how various bits of it may or may not be connected to 9/11, I proceed in chapter 2 to examine the question of how this world is managed or how some would like to manage it: namely, "global governance." Global governance has become an increasing post-9/11 preoccupation in both political and academic fora, and—notwithstanding assertions in some quarters that we now live in a post-Westphalian (post-nation-state) world—it remains firmly tied up with ideas of (nation-)statehood. However, attempts to provide other solutions to the "governance" problem in a post-9/11 frame, notably the United Nations (UN) Responsibility to Protect (R2P) doctrine, present other sorts of problems. For women, then, the state of states appears to remain much as it ever was: the state is both an ally that has the power to enact laws that ensure us some measure of safety and a little maneuvering room in our "states of emergency" and an enemy that is frequently the creator of the same states of emergency, either explicitly through laws or tacitly through its failure to protect women. Moreover, the nation-state is a cunning propagandist: it engineers an "us-ness" from which it is difficult to dissociate.

The problem of who "us" is and how one aligns with "us" of course dogged the world's women long before 9/11 happened. When our us-ness as a nation, a class, an ethnicity, a religious minority is called into question, our us-ness as women is invariably shoved onto the back seat, if not into the trunk. In a post-9/11 world, who is "us" for the "world's" women? On one level, this question has no unitary answer. Identity is always multifaceted, as is allegiance. "Us" is always multiple. But in the "world" as we know it, the identification, conscious or unconscious, with an ethnonational grouping is the inevitable starting point, even if the identification is negative: set up in order to better deny. I am an Anglo US citizen, *but* . . . I am a Muslim Arab *but*. . . . Chapter 2 considers this singular post-9/11 endurance, even reinforcement, of the ethnonation or the political nation or both in a world supposedly transnationalized by globalization and examines the implications of that nationalism for women. It also considers why R2P is not necessarily going to help.

This leads to chapter 3, which investigates the pitfalls for feminist activism and research alike created by both the "security" arsenal and official women's rights discourse deployed in a post-9/11 frame and analyzes some of the pre-9/11 history of the relationship between the "security" and "human rights" discourses, notably the development of the idea of "human security." It considers how "security chatter" has been deployed in relation to women and discusses the application or otherwise of UN Security Council Resolution 1325 on Women, Peace, and Security. Has "security talk" served women at all, and if so, how? What of violence inflicted on women outside conflict? How is "the world" doing on women's security there?

Chapter 4 continues this discussion of "security" within the context of links between globalization, militarism, and violence against women that many—but certainly not yet enough—feminist scholars have studied. Its starting point and, indeed, the starting point for this entire book was the occurrence of two events on opposite sides of the world in 2005, the United States and the Philippines, as well as these events' indirect links to globalized militarism, the associated accumulation of wealth and the poverty of racialized women, and men's violence against these women. In asking the question "What does Hurricane Katrina have to do with the Subic rape case?" chapter 4 thus attempts to connect some post-9/11 transnational dots and their pre-9/11 contributing factors. In doing so, it seeks to demonstrate that women's lives are linked transnationally in ways that are often not immediately apparent. These links matter not only symbolically through a sense of transnational feminist solidarity but also materially in the consequences of globalized masculinist militarism for all of us.

Chapter 5 considers the material operation of feminist activism in this transnational context, notably in relation to the post-9/11 politics of religion, which is imbricated with anticolonial struggles and ideas. The chapter is not intended as a canvassing of women's transnational activist responses to 9/11 but rather as an investigation of the difficulties of dealing with the complexities of transnational feminist solidarity. It takes as its point of focus a feminist population that has always been at the forefront of transnational peace activism in particular yet has been strangely silenced within it: lesbians. The chapter draws on my personal experience of this issue at two different international conferences, one of which was activist centered (Women in Black conference, Jerusalem, August 2005), whereas the other was more academically oriented (Women's Worlds conference, Seoul, June 2005), although activists also participated. Through discussion of incidents at and following both events, the chapter looks at how lesbian rights have been strategically silenced within transnational feminist activism and, conversely, strategically mobilized and manipulated within the lesbian, gay, bisexual, transgender (and intersex) (LGBT[I]) grouping by imperialist states anxious to demonstrate their "progressive" credentials. Unfortunately, states' cynical co-optation (in this chapter I refer primarily to Israel) feeds a certain perception that the fight for lesbian visibility and rights is yet another iteration of white, Western, middle-class privilege. Yet nothing could be further from the truth. Lesbians are, as the saying goes, everywhere, and everywhere they are as disproportionately victims of violence as they are "disproportionately" present in transnational feminist peace activism.

When I showed a draft of this chapter to a friend, she responded: "This is really an 'insider' chapter, isn't it? Intended for feminist activists and scholars rather than a wider public, as the other chapters are?" In some ways it is indeed. It is part of a conversation among feminists about how we "do" transnational feminist work and about ongoing heterosexism within the women's movement. It is also, however, intended as a taboo breaker and as a refutation of the assumptions that somehow lesbians' rights are less important than heterosexual women's rights and that the violence to which lesbians are subjected is somehow less systematic and urgent than that experienced by either straight women or gay men. If we are to talk seriously about women's rights in the international sphere, then the conversation needs to be about all women. This chapter is thus also for anyone, "insider" or not, with an interest in the subject matter and themes of this book.

Chapters 6 and 7 deal with a post-9/11 Western cognitive dissonance about the politics of religion in connection to the Muslim world. Chapter 6 explores this question with relation to the so-called Arab spring (a term that is not used in the Arab world), focusing on Tunisia in particular. The symbolic commencement of the "Arab spring" was in the Tunisian town of Sidi Bouzid on December 17, 2010, when a street vendor, deprived by the authorities of his tools of trade, self-immolated. (Hence, the name "Sidi Bouzid revolution" is used in Tunisia.) The "Arab spring" events are also, however, connected to a political process of religion-based oppositions to authoritarian states that began earlier that decade in other parts of the Middle East—Turkey in 2002, Morocco in 2007—and, indeed, well before 9/11: Algeria, the Muslim Brotherhood, and Khomeinism all being cases in point. The chapter discusses both "postsecularism" and Islamist parties' use of the idea of democratic "legitimacy" to justify their actions, often with Western explicit or tacit support. The impacts on women have been disastrous. Tunisia is an interesting case because at the time of this writing it represents the only real success story of the "Arab spring" or at least the beginnings of such a story, and feminist activism has been a significant contributor to the relatively successful outcomes there to date.

Chapter 7 is a last-minute addition, commenced after the killings in Paris on January 7, 8, and 9, 2015, and augmented following the attacks that occurred on November 13, 2015. I decided to add the chapter because the debates that followed these assassinations are so typical of aspects of the cognitive dissonance I discuss in chapter 6. I begin the chapter by discussing the history of the concept of

"Islamophobia," in particular the idea of defamation of religion that has come up in political and legal conversations in both national and international contexts since 9/11. The intense debate in early 2015 about "being Charlie (Hebdo)" or not was in many ways so emblematic of post-9/11ism that it became a necessary and perhaps fitting final chapter. The chapter's appropriateness has only grown since November 13, 2015. Not only were the debates of earlier in the year repeated, at least in part, but there are now also the added dimensions of the security politics of the French state, which have met with widespread concern about civil liberties and have provoked some high-profile exits from the government; the Syrian refugee crisis; and the military strategies that France and its allies are adopting in relation to Daesh.

In the conclusion, I return once again to the Philippines and to activism. If I am not always hopeful that transnational feminist activism, with all its internal debates and all the material obstacles it faces, can move the masculinist mountains of international politics, I do know for certain that it is the only thing that will.

1

Where Is the "Post-9/11 World"?

One might have thought that answering the question "Where is the 'post-9/11' world?" would be a fairly straightforward exercise. Usual norms of definition, based on sovereign states and UN-organized regions that are roughly equivalent to widespread consensus about what and where continents are, will surely provide some clarity, even if one does not necessarily accept these norms' premises—from a transnational feminist viewpoint, such premises are difficult to accept uncritically. Yet even these norms do not give us 100 percent clarity on what "counts" as part of "the world" shaken by 9/11 and on what criteria this "world" should be divided into components (or not). The "Muslim world versus the West" division is succinct and thus a convenient shorthand for many on both sides of that particular divide—however that divide may be conceptualized in both hegemonic and oppositional discourses—but it is nonetheless unsatisfactorily simplistic and dualistic (Winter 2011b). Moreover, in becoming the dominant conceptual framework for the post-9/11 "world," this representation excludes large chunks of the actual world as defined in UN or US geopolitics—virtually the whole of Latin America, large parts of Asia and Africa, some of Europe, and practically all Pacific island states. Neither the UN norms, with member states, world regions, voting blocs, and Security Council memberships, nor the post-9/11 Muslim–West scenario, with its monolithic Them-and-Us-ness, seems adequate in helping us conceptualize the "post-9/11 world."

Moreover, the norms of "world" definition, however articulated, are problematic from a feminist point of view. First, our relationship with the sovereign state has always been ambiguous. The state is both ally and enemy, both protector (sometimes even creator) of rights and often, even usually, the primary agent of undermining or curtailing them (Winter 2002a), especially for women. If nothing else, the state of the post-9/11 world (double entendre intended) has amplified this paradox (as discussed further in chapter 2).

Second, the post-9/11 world continues to be strangely devoid of women even as it is discursively hyperpopulated with us through the marketing of "women's rights, security, dignity," which serves as moral veneer for actions taken by the US state and its allies, among others (Delphy 2002; Winter 2011b; see also chapter 3). We know that the flesh-and-blood, ordinary women are there somewhere, beyond the powerful Condoleezza Rices, Hillary Clintons, Angela Merkels, and Gloria Arroyos; beyond the weeping women mourning the deaths of husbands and children; beyond the veiled Everymuslim-woman; beyond the antiheroic figures of Lynndie England at Abu Ghraib in 2005 and the female suicide bombers of al Qaeda, Daesh, and Boko Haram; even beyond the women attacked as they demonstrated in Tahrir Square, at once the collective agent of their liberation and collective victim of its denial. All these images of women have been deployed symbolically in many post-9/11 conversations as exceptional, culturally codified cases to prove some political point concerning women (and concerning our rights, security, and dignity). Yet the women "beyond"—those nonsymbolic, nonexceptional women "out there"—remain largely silent and invisible except in feminist writing, which is an infinitesimal part of all post-9/11 literature, whether institutional, journalistic, activist, or scholarly. That same feminist literature has taught us that those invisible and inaudible women are more than bystanders in masculinist international politics: they are also actors and figures acted upon (Enloe 1990, 2010). Indeed, masculinist international politics depends on women's participation at the same time as that participation is constructed as nonexistent or irrelevant, which Cynthia Enloe pointed out so clearly well before 9/11:

> Women's experiences—of war, marriage, trade, travel, factory work—are relegated to the "human interest" column. Women's

roles in creating and sustaining international politics have been treated as if they were "natural" and thus not worthy of investigation. Consequently, how the conduct of international politics has depended on men's control of women has been left unexamined. This has meant that those wielding influence over foreign policy have escaped responsibility for how women have been affected by international politics. (1990, 3–4)

Women are used symbolically to serve masculinist agendas, and they certainly have been used this way in a post-9/11 context. At the same time, women as symbols in a discursive context are not the same as women as actors in a material context, although the symbolism does shed light on how gender is manipulated within masculinist international relations.

In this chapter, then, I consider how "the world" is constructed geopolitically and framed discursively in a post-9/11 context. In doing so, I also attempt to step outside the usual well-worn post-9/11 paths that go from the United States to Afghanistan via Iraq and Israel and instead consider some of the other, less-discussed players in the "world" that was presumably "shaken" on September 11, 2001, to see if everyone got all shook up in the same way or indeed at all.

Constituting "the World" I: What Is a State and Why Does This Matter?

If one subscribes to the so-called realist view that remains dominant in international relations theory, the basic components of "the world" are states. One then immediately faces the task of deciding what a state is. I thus start with a brief overview of the politics of state creation and state identification. The specific interactions between women and the state and the concepts of the nation and national sovereignty in global governance are treated in chapter 2.

There exist two main sets of criteria for deciding whether a political entity is a state or not. The UN and other international and supranational organizations take the constitutive view, which requires recognition as a state by at least one other formally constituted and internationally recognized state. The other view is the declarative one under the terms of the Montevideo Convention on the Rights and Duties of States (1933). This convention requires that for a state to exist in international law, it has to have a permanent population, a defined territory, a government, and capacity to enter into relations with the other states, but recognition by other states is not necessary: in other words, recognition is not status creating; it is simply status confirming. That is, declarative statehood is a necessary step toward constitutive statehood. There has been much debate since 2015 over whether Daesh is really a state. Following the attacks in Paris in November 2015, there was an increased push to stop referring in English or French to Daesh as "Islamic State" but as "Daesh." This choice does not, however, remove the problem because "Daesh" is simply the acronym for "Islamic State in Iraq and Syria/the Levant" in Arabic. In any case, Daesh can be seen as a "state" in declarative terms, and some political commentators have stressed that the international community should understand this fact and respond appropriately. For example, Faysal Itani, commenting in *Time* magazine in August 2014, wrote: "ISIS is no mere militia; in its territory, it is the state. Its claims to statehood are neither unfounded nor ridiculous. Its control of vast territory and resources make it arguably the most powerful religious militant group in modern history. . . . Unless its rivals understand and treat ISIS as a state, and exploit the vulnerabilities statehood presents, ISIS will continue to outclass them in ambition and sophistication, and it will have its state." Other commentators have contested that view, and the argument continues in international media regarding how powerful or statelike Daesh really is (e.g., Sly 2014; Withnall and Romero 2015). What is certain is that the question of recognition versus nonrecognition—even on a discursive level—of Daesh as a state has significant political and potentially legal ramifications, as it has in the cases of other disputed states and newly emerged states (Starke 1967; T. Grant 1999; Talmon 2004). More on this point presently.

The UN has 193 member states at the time of writing (including the tiny European principalities Monaco, Andorra, and Liechtenstein as well as tax-haven states such as the Commonwealth of the

Bahamas). The most recent addition, thus member number 193, was South Sudan, following secession from Sudan in mid-2011. This secession, however, has not solved the issue of governance among the Sudanese because South Sudan, far from being a united fledgling state, spent all of 2014 in civil war, provoking a significant humanitarian crisis, not to mention governance issues (Amnesty International 2014; UN Mission in the Republic of South Sudan 2014). Two other states have permanent observer status, which confers all access and participation rights except the right to vote: the Holy See (the Vatican, whose seat at the UN has long been a subject of vociferous feminist criticism [see, e.g., Sjørup 1999; Center for Reproductive Rights 2000; Fleishman 2000; Stein 2001]) and Palestine, although the UN has yet to recognize Palestinian statehood formally because its Security Council is divided on the question. Palestine is thus considered a declarative state only, a not-yet state from the UN's point of view, largely because of Israeli and US opposition, although 135 UN member states do recognize it. Nonrecognition by former colonizing or "parent" states or by powerful UN member states (such as the G7 [Group of 7] states or permanent Security Council members) is usually a significant block to constitutive statehood in UN terms. Bangladesh is to date the only state admitted to UN membership without the recognition by the "parent" state from which it seceded (Pakistan). The Sovereign Military Hospitaller Order of St. John of Jerusalem of Rhodes and of Malta, located in Rome, also has UN observer status but does not claim statehood or any territory: it is a "sovereign entity" governed by a religious lay order.[1] This takes the number of wholly or partially recognized sovereign states to 195 plus an "entity."

A handful of other states are recognized by several, even the majority, of UN member states but by early 2016 had not yet been accepted into UN membership or observer status: Taiwan, recognized by 22 member states and the Holy See and also member of the World Trade

---

1. For further information, see the site of the Permanent Mission of the Order of Malta to the UN at http://www.un.int/orderofmalta/.

Organization (WTO); Kosovo, recognized by 108 member states and a member of the International Monetary Fund since 2009; the Sahrawi Arab Democratic Republic, recognized by 84 UN member states; the Republic of Abkhazia and the Republic of South Ossetia, both secessionist states from Georgia but recognized only by Russia, Venezuela, Nicaragua, Nauru, and Tuvalu; and the Turkish Republic of Northern Cyprus, recognized only by Turkey. This takes our running total of constitutive states in the international system to 201 plus an entity.

Another two states are recognized only by non-UN member states: Nagorno-Karabakh in the southern Caucasus and the Pridnestrovian Moldavian Republic (Transnistria), a breakaway state from Moldova. These two states recognize each other and are, no doubt predictably, also recognized by Abkhazia and South Ossetia. Finally, Somaliland, which declared its independence from Somalia in 1991, is recognized by no other state at all. These three states are thus the only ones to fully fit the "declarative" definition. Running total: 204 (or 205 if one counts Daesh) plus an entity.

The final category of constitutive states comprises "substates," such as Niue and the Cook Islands, which are satellite states in "free association" with New Zealand. They have national autonomy in all areas except defense and foreign affairs, which are handled by New Zealand. The UN recognizes them as states although they are not UN members, but they are members of UN agencies such as the UN Educational, Scientific, and Cultural Organization and the World Health Organization.

In addition, there are a number of contested subnational or transnational regions: the Autonomous Region in Muslim Mindanao in the Philippines, to become "the Autonomous Government of Bangsamoro" (which literally means "Muslim Nation") under the terms of an October 2012 peace agreement with the Philippine state, although negotiations were stalled following a violent clash in late January 2015; Aceh in Indonesia as well as Tibet and the Xinjiang Uyghur region in China, all of which are formally constituted as autonomous regions within the parent state; the tribal lands in northern Pakistan;

Kashmir, which is formally spread across India, Pakistan, and China (the Chinese section being largely uninhabited), but over which India and Pakistan are disputing sovereignty; Chechnya, which remains formally part of the Russian Federation; and the Autonomous Republic of Crimea in the Ukraine, which was invaded and annexed by Russia in 2014. Transnational "nation-peoples" include Kurdistan, a name that describes the Kurdish populations living in Iran, Turkey, Syria, and Iraq, with the latter being the only country in which Kurds have semiautonomous status, both during and subsequent to the Hussein regime. Finally, there are semiautonomous overseas territories of Western states such as the United States (Guam, Puerto Rico) and France (including Polynesia and New Caledonia).

In most of these regions, notwithstanding the peculiarities of local histories and politics, populations are divided over the issues of autonomy within the nation versus independence. Claims to autonomy or independence—although politically grounded in material grievances (usually persecution and impoverishment by the central state)—are also invariably built on either ethnic or religious bases or both. In addition, almost all either recently or historically have been subject to armed conflict or the threat thereof within, between, or across states or, at the very least, subject to spasmodic or ongoing violent uprisings and a defined resistance movement. These conflicts often involve the formation of political parties and are often acknowledged within global civil society and even international politics as defending a justifiable cause, even if the means of defense of the cause are not supported. Globally less-controversial, semiautonomous regions such as the Inuit homeland of Nunavut in Canada, Scotland in the United Kingdom, and Catalonia and the Basque region in Spain are also "nation-peoples." These regions have also been the subject of ongoing political debate (leading, for example, to the Scottish independence referendum of 2014) and occasionally of violence (such as in the case of the Basque armed independence group Euskadi Ta Askatasuna [Basque Homeland and Freedom], or ETA, which formally committed to a cessation of violence in 2011), but they remain uncontroversial and low impact in today's global politics.

All of these regions and indeed other populations, such as the Indigenous populations of the United States, Australia, New Zealand, and some parts of Central and South America or the Roma people of Europe, might count as "nations" insofar as nationhood is constructed around a common identity or "imagined community" (Anderson 1983). Such a community is premised on such factors as ethnicity, language, religion, shared history, and others, but they do not count as "states."

Few of the nationhood disputes mentioned earlier, however, have any direct cause-and-effect relationship with 9/11, even where they involve armed conflict. Most of these disputes existed well before 9/11 and are part of a broader scenario of ethnonationalism in relationship to a state seen as oppressive of the ethnicity and/or religion in question. Some of them have nonetheless become part of the global post-9/11 conversation, usually because of their Muslimness or the Muslimness of the states disputing their control. This is the case, for example, for the Bangsamoro in western Mindanao and the Sulu Archipelago because of the presence of Abu Sayyaf and the US use of the Philippines as the main operating base of its "Asian front" in the "war on terror," as discussed in chapter 4.

Whether one applies the declarative or constitutive view of statehood, the nation-state is so much part of the way we see ourselves in the world today that it is considered as "natural" as sex differentiation. Human beings like to herd together within ethnic, religious, and linguistic communities: this herding is frequently characterized not as a political phenomenon but as a defining characteristic of our humanness (A. Smith 1991). States then become the political means we give ourselves to manage these "national" communities, and in consequence states take on some of the communities' supposed naturalness. Imagining a world without nation-states is like imagining a world without gender. Feminists can of course imagine both, but we come up against what is now and for the foreseeable future the incontrovertible reality that our world is and will be managed according to these power structures. Within them, it is as impossible for women to disappear as women as it is for Bangsamoro to disappear as Bangsamoro.

Yet states are arbitrary structures, and the nationhoods that underpin their creation are fluctuating entities: both emerge as the artifacts of political interactions. These aspects are perhaps best revealed through the caricature of the micronation. The micronation may at times fit the declarative view of statehood, but it does not fit the constitutive view; it is often ephemeral, and its citizens may simply be the members of a particular family or small local community. The origins of micronations, like the origins of the nation-states we take far more seriously, are rooted in various combinations of protest, self-aggrandizement, sometimes financial considerations (fiscal evasion being a common basis for a micronation), and simply creative fantasy. British writer-comedian Danny Wallace evinced the latter in his creation of his own country called Lovely in his flat in London, which was the subject of the BBC comedy documentary series *How to Start Your Own Country* (2005). More than half the world's micronations, as it happens, are located in Australia, this vast, largely desert, and underpopulated continent of some 24 million people. The Hutt River Province, a principality created by Leonard George Casley in 1972, is perhaps the best known of Australian micronations. Whether this proliferation of micronations constitutes some sort of comment on the peculiarities of the Australian national context is open to debate, but what the phenomenon does reveal more generally is that the idea of national sovereignty and the political, economic, and territorial rights that go with it are of fundamental importance to individuals and social groups, however constituted, even if the nation is simply an extension of one individual. After all, extensions of individuals are precisely what absolute monarchies were in the past, as the now legendary statement "L'État, c'est moi" (I am the State), attributed to French absolutist monarch Louis XIV, clearly demonstrates. Indeed, some dictatorial or monarchical states remain so today, at least to some extent, with sometimes absurd effects, such as the changing of names of months in Turkmenistan in 2002. January was renamed "Türkmenbaşy" for the man who had himself named president for life. Even in regimes that are politically and structurally constituted as democracies, the personal identification of the elected leader with the nation-state as a whole is invariably strong. States have leaders. Without them, the state does not exist.

Constituting "the World" II: Geopolitical Groupings, Chosen or Otherwise

Discussion of what constitutes "the world" is further complicated by the consideration of "world regions." Within UN politics, "the world" is divided into political groupings—most of which correspond roughly to geographical groupings (African Group, Eastern European Group, and Latin American Group); one of which is politically but not geographically "Western" (the Western European and Others Group [WEOG]); and one of which is both politically and geographically diverse (Asia-Pacific Group, which has members ranging from Saudi Arabia to Samoa). Kiribati and the United States are not members of any group, although the United States is a WEOG observer. Turkey straddles WEOG and Asia-Pacific but votes with WEOG. The Population Division of the UN Department of Economic and Social Affairs, however, classifies the world into "macroregions," each with its subregions: Africa (eastern, middle, northern, southern, western); Asia (eastern, south central, southeastern, and western); Europe (eastern, northern, southern, and western); Latin America (Caribbean, Central, South); Northern America (no subdivision); and Oceania (Australia and New Zealand, Melanesia, Micronesia, Polynesia) (see UN Statistics Division 2013). This is, roughly speaking, a geographical carving up, but it is a carving up that more easily resonates with some local imaginaries than with others. North or West Africans can surely recognize themselves as North or West Africans, although in the many French-speaking countries of these regions and their interlocutors north of the Mediterranean the descriptions "Maghreb" and "Afrique subsaharienne" would no doubt have as much if not more resonance. Latin Americans may easily recognize themselves as Latin Americans, although neither residents of the former British colonies of the Caribbean nor those of African or Indigenous descent in the South American continent are likely to identify themselves as "Latin," and Mexicans will emphasize that their country is actually in North

America. But I have never heard or read any resident of Australia or Aotearoa/New Zealand or of any Micronesian, Melanesian, or Polynesian country or territory self-identify as "Oceanian." The term and its variant "Oceana" appear largely to be products of European and North American colonizing and literary views and not always of the same region that the UN collectively has in mind (e.g., Froude [1886] 2010; Theroux [1992] 2006; see also Jolly 2007). I am sure that if I were to reply to the question "Where are you from?" with the answer "Oceania," you might be excused for thinking I am the fanciful creator of some new Australian micronation.

These observations concerning the "imagined Oceanic" may appear only peripherally relevant, if at all, to my discussion of the post-9/11 world, yet they illuminate that very discussion by highlighting the extent to which the periphery of "the world" is imagined by those within the centers of global power, as in Immanuel Wallerstein's (1974) designations *center, periphery,* and *semiperiphery.* Hegemony has always meant the power not only to decide but also to imagine for others: to construct global discursive frameworks within which all those "other" to the power base must attempt to situate themselves. Even in adopting oppositional positionings, one necessarily accepts the premise of the dialectic, the starting position from which one claims a "not-this-ness." At times, one may even reproduce the very hegemonic formations one wishes to contest, as we will see presently—and, indeed, as has been made painfully evident by the emergence of Daesh. Within such imaginings, "Oceania" becomes a region defined largely by faraway tropical-island-ness, an idyllic yet geopolitically insignificant space, notwithstanding the presence within the group of G20 member Australia. A staunch US ally and major trading partner of, among others, existing Asian hegemonic power Japan and the emerging hegemonic power China, Australia is a would-be and to some extent actual main player in the Asia-Pacific context. Regardless of these (inter)national pretentions, Australia has been defined as "Oceanic" in UN cartography, itself a legacy of colonialist tropicalizing imaginings.

The "Middle East," that region on which the post-9/11 world is ostensibly acutely focused, does not appear at all as a discrete entity in the UN's mapping of regions and voting blocs, although it is an established site within contemporary geopolitics and, indeed, academic area studies, usually under the acronym MENA: Middle East and North Africa. This acronym, among other things, displaces North Africa from its Africanness, a geographical location, into Arabo-Muslimness, an ethnic, cultural, and religious location, and disappears North Africa's Berber and Sephardic populations in the process—as it also arguably disappears other minorities in the Middle East. So where exactly is the "Middle East"? Is it described under the heading "western Asia"? What, then, are we to do with Turkey, with its European aspirations? If Turkey is accepted into the European Union (EU), will our "world" then be reconfigured to shift Turkey from "western Asia" into "Europe"? Would the geoethnic entity of Kurdistan then effectively become not only transnational but also transcontinental, straddling Europe and Asia, as Turkey is already presumed to do with the Bosphorus Strait, which, running through Istanbul, marks the continental border?

Even supposedly oppositional ways of mapping the world present problems. The preference in many feminist circles for the name "Global South" came into decolonial or anti-imperialist fashion to replace the successive unsatisfactory framings—decided from the hegemonic "Global North"—of "underdeveloped" or "developing" countries or the "Third World." The Global South was the part of the world that had been devastated by the Global North's imperialism and the concentration of global political, economic, and cultural power among "northern" countries. Even if this name, like "the West," has been symbolic rather than strictly geographical, it nonetheless poses problems for some other countries that are geographically in the "South" but economically—and often politically and culturally—dominated by people of European ancestry. These countries include not only Australia and New Zealand but also South Africa, where the economic and cultural power of white citizens remains significant in the postapartheid regime, as well as many countries in South America, which have their own issues of race and whiteness that are frequently disappeared in the framing of "Latin America" as part of a Global South bloc. Race and class inequalities are problems in other parts of the Global South as well: India, Pakistan, Afghanistan, and the Philippines, for example, are ruled by highly privileged light-skinned ethnic elites.

Even if some scholars, such as R. W. Connell (2005), suggest a "southern theory" and other alternatives to Global North conceptualizations, these proposed alternatives more often than not simply provide a mirror image of the association of certain ways of thinking with cardinal points on a map (Jolly 2008). As such, they are as totalizing and binary in their logic as anything the Global North dishes out and thus in keeping with the manicheaism/dualism that characterizes post-9/11ism (Winter 2011b). Particularly disturbing in Connell's account, from a feminist point of view, for example, is a by now tiresomely familiar cultural-relativist rejection of anything that is openly and unapologetically feminist and expressed in so-called universalist terms (such as Vandana Shiva's feminist ecology, targeted in Connell's book). Also worrying is Connell's celebration of Islamic political scholars such as the Iranian Jalal Al-e Ahmad, inventor of the concept of *gharbzadegi*—variously translated as "plague from the West," "Occidentosis," "Weststruckness," "Westitis," or "Westoxication"—and principal ideologue of the Khomeinist revolution in Iran (Al-e Ahmad 1982, 1983, 1984; see also Moghadam 1993 and chapter 5 here). "Southern theory" is not a coherent response to perceived "northern" hegemony, particularly when one considers that, geographically speaking, parts of Connell's "South," such as Martinique and North Africa, are in fact in the "North"—that is, north of the equator—and may not self-identify as part of either symbolic hemisphere.

The "Global South," however, is being framed in another way. Some ten weeks after 9/11, Jim O'Neill, head of economic research at Goldman Sachs, published his article "Building Better Global Economic BRICs" (2001), the BRIC in question being Brazil, Russia,

India, and China, a new acronym that would develop a considerable measure of currency (see also Wilson and Purushothaman 2003). The 1990s was the decade of the so-called Asian Tigers' rise and, if not fall, at least stumbling at the time of the financial crisis in 1997 and then again after the global financial crisis in 2008. The 2000s appear to have transformed some of those tigers into BRICs, with an increasing focus on "southern" multinationals and South-South investment, which, according to an Organization for Economic Cooperation and Development (OECD) working paper, was "coming of age" (Aykut and Goldstein 2006). In 2007, the OECD inserted South Africa into its BRIC wall, so that BRIC became BRICS—technically BRICSA, but this configuration would undermine the neatness of the acronym (OECD 2007, chap. 9). BRICS have claimed this grouping as their own, and BRICS summits are now held regularly; the seventh took place in the Russian city Ufa in July 2015.

In his article, O'Neill suggested that there would need to be a realignment of global economic power structures, with the G7 dropping its three Eurozone representatives to one, thus becoming the G5, and then taking on BRIC to become a G9. WTO statistics for 2013 do indeed show that the four-BRIC block is an economic force to be reckoned with, accounting for 18.5 percent of world merchandise exports, in comparison to the 75.5 percent share of the G20 and the 1.1 percent share of the forty-eight countries classified by the WTO and the UN as "least developed" (WTO 2014, 12–13). In 2013, China overtook the United States as the world's biggest merchandise trader and had a trade surplus of 2.8 percent of gross domestic product (GDP) as opposed to the US trade deficit of 4.5 percent of GDP (WTO 2014, 15). Germany comes in third, and Japan fourth. The WTO statistics also reinforce the long-known fact that the world's most powerful economies trade primarily with each other and highlight internal economic and political power discrepancies within supranational or semisupranational trading blocs (the North American Free Trade Agreement, the EU, the Association of South East Asian Nations [ASEAN], the Union of South American Nations, the Southern African Development Community).

Who is or should be in this global economic power game and who is or should be out, however, nonetheless remains uncertain, as O'Neill himself pointed out in 2001. Ten years later, in a brief review of the BRIC decade, he suggested that other rapidly growing economies could be added to the BRIC wall—(South) Korea, Turkey, Indonesia, and Mexico—thus creating the acronym BRICKTIM (or BRICKS(A)TIM if one includes South Africa). He added in relation to Turkey that he could not understand "why continental European countries are not more eager to embrace this country, especially as it would seem like an obvious credible 'model' for some of the dramatically changing nations in Northern Africa and the Middle East" (2011). I return in chapter 6 to Turkey's status as a "model" because this idea recurs in much post-9/11 and post–Arab spring rhetoric.

So, in capitalist economic terms, what and where "the world" is may, in the medium term, end up no longer being what and where we think it is today. That is, it may no longer be defined in G7, G8, or G20 terms and certainly not in post-9/11ist terms. According to O'Neill at least, the locus of economic might will shift away from the G7 stronghold—with very little, if any, of it, according to O'Neill, ending up in the Middle East or in the Muslim world more generally, notwithstanding the wealth of some Arabian Gulf states (Qatar, for example, having the world's highest GDP per capita). Such an analysis thus sits at variance with the Us-and-Them-ness of post-9/11ist rhetoric. However, economic might is framed somewhat differently by the mighty: in contrast to "Us-and-Them" in conflict over differing worldviews and the political, military, or cultural right to assert them, economic might is perhaps better defined as membership in the same club, whether one "likes" one's co-members or not. In any case, whether and how fast the transformation of this club's membership profile will happen and whether it will be accompanied by a corresponding political shift or new politico-military tensions remain open questions at this time.

For example, tensions between Japan and China over the Senkaku/Diaoyu Islands led in July 2014 to the Japanese government's reinterpretation of Article 9 of the postwar Japanese Constitution, which states that Japan "forever renounce[s] war as a sovereign right of the nation and the threat or use of force as means of settling international disputes."[2] The Abe Shinzo government's reinterpretation makes an exception to the renunciation of military force in cases of "self-defense," not only when Japan is attacked but also when an ally of Japan is attacked and for the purposes of international security operations. This interpretation builds on successive Japanese governments' long-held view that Japan is entitled to legitimate self-defense under international law, notwithstanding Article 9, which technically renders such a position unconstitutional. The proposal is welcomed by the United States and by some international commentators in the name of international security cooperation (e.g., Ali 2015) but has also met with fierce opposition, including a number of large demonstrations and one man's self-immolation outside Tokyo's Shinjuku station on June 29, 2014. Abe's ruling Liberal Democratic Party was nonetheless reelected to the Lower House in a landslide on December 14, 2014. More recently, the United States has expressed concerns over China's claiming of maritime territory around its artificial islands on atolls in the South China Sea. The United States tested China's claim, which interferes with shipping lanes in the area, by sending guided-missile destroyer USS *Lassen* into the waters claimed by China, causing a diplomatic incident between the two powers. Whether these Japan–China–US territorial disputes will shift the focus of global military-capital alliances and impede any further US rapprochement with China remains to be seen.

In early 2016, notwithstanding China's economic ascent and Qatar's efforts on the soft-diplomacy scene through hosting or bids to host world sporting events while it allegedly bankrolls Islamist movements behind the scenes, the United States remained the world's hegemon. It did not need the assent of the UN Security Council or of coalition partners to take military action against Iraq in 2003, and

2. The Japanese Constitution is available at http://japan.kantei.go.jp/constitu tion_and_government_of_japan/constitution_e.html (accessed July 25, 2014).

it did not need consent to return there amid the crisis of 2014. Even if rhetorically the United States, in particular the Bush II administration, has deployed the idea of multilateralism, its actions in the international arena since 9/11 have at best instrumentalized multilateralism to belligerent, hegemonic, and thus entirely unilateral ends (Dombrowski 2005).

None of these alternative world maps, then—a UN nation/region, a "postcolonialist" North-South, or an economics-and-business new dynamic South—appears on the face of it to be particularly relevant to a discussion of a post-9/11 world. There appears to be no demonstrable relationship between the fledgling states seeking UN recognition following national disintegrations, secessions, or anticolonial struggles, on one hand, and the events and aftermath of 9/11, on the other. Nor can one posit such a relationship between the emergence of a Global South with its very own "southern theory" and 9/11 because the terminology of the Global South was with us prior to 9/11. As concerns the global economy, the BRICS conversation appears, at first sight at least, as distant from post-9/11ist concerns as does the global financial crisis of 2008 and the Eurozone crisis of 2011.

In fact, try as I might to complicate and extend representations of "the world," it would seem that in the majority of post-9/11 literature all roads lead back to the polarized blocs of "the West" and "the Muslim world" à la Samuel Huntington (1993, 1996). This, by and large, is the "world" that is presumed to have been shaken by 9/11. Or is it? And, again, was every part of each of these imagined "worlds" ("Western" and "Muslim") shaken in equal doses? Are we to divide the Muslim world into the Middle East (or MENA), South Asia, and Southeast Asia? And should MENA then undergo further ethnic and religious subdivisions, separating out what is Jewish, Arab, Persian, Berber, and so on and, in religious terms, what is Jewish, Orthodox, Catholic, Sunni, and Shia (as well as the various traditions and expressions thereof)? Should we carve "the West" up into the Anglo and non-Anglo worlds? Into the G7 countries and the rest? What, then, do we do with such oddities as the miniscule Islamic republic of Djibouti, a site that barely registers on the post-9/11 impact meter yet was identified as an important transit site for terrorist operations prior to 9/11 (United States Institute of Peace 2004) and has been, along with the Philippines, a major operating base for the secondary US "war on terror" that goes by the name "Operation Enduring Freedom"? (The operation was rebadged from its original title, "Operation Infinite Justice," which inspired Arundhati Roy's celebrated essay "The Algebra of Infinite Justice" [2002].) Djibouti's role included controversial involvement in so-called extraordinary-rendition cases during the post-9/11 period (Amnesty International 2006; African Commission for Human and People's Rights 2011), and some have suggested that Djibouti's involvement in Operation Enduring Freedom has served to reinforce the power of a repressive government (Lallemand 2007).

The problematic role of Djibouti or of other ostensibly West-friendly countries such as Saudi Arabia and Qatar on both sides of the post-9/11 "war on terror" prompts me to ask why these regimes are not featured more prominently in post-9/11ist conversations about the "Middle East" or the "Muslim world" that are supposedly so problematic for the West. Saudi Arabia, for example, through both overt actions such as the charitable activities of al-Rabita al-Alam al-Islami (Muslim World League) and more covert ones such as the (relatively) anarchic bankrolling of Salafist extremists by members of the Saudi elite,[3] has been one of the main actors in pulling various parts of the global "Muslim world" to the fundamentalist right.

Clearly, to speak of a post-9/11 world in any coherent way is impossible, just as it is impossible to speak of any unique and global material impact of 9/11 on "the world's women." So the question "Has September 11, 2001, changed the world for women?" invites not only the question "Which women?" but also the question "Which world?" Even if one presumes the "shaken world" of post-9/11 to be primarily the United States, the EU, and their key allies within and

---

3. The observation concerning the important role of Saudi princes acting relatively independently of the government was offered to me by a senior EU diplomat in the Middle East, who for security reasons must remain anonymous.

outside the West, along with the "Muslim world," not all were shaken in the same way or for the same reasons, and for some the "shaking" proved more profitable than not. As I noted earlier, many of the ethnic, religious, and statehood debates mentioned in this chapter, including those involving Muslims, existed before 9/11, even if the post-9/11 climate exacerbated the violence of their expression in some cases (Bangsamoro, Aceh, Kashmir, Uyghur). These conflicts and their impacts on women cannot be attributed solely to 9/11.

The presumed post-9/11 Us-and-Them-ness of "the West and the Muslim world," then, is oversimplistic from whichever side of that discursive divide the opposition is viewed. This may be stating the obvious, but, given the overwhelming impact of post-9/11ist rhetoric, it is worth restating. What 9/11 did show yet again, however, is the importance of both the ethnic and the religious in the construction of the national and the reinforced importance of the latter in the construction of the international. Identity politics, never long absent from the world stage, has returned with a vengeance, and its particular expression in the post-9/11 world, such as it is, is definitely religious.

If "ethnic nationalism" as a means of configuring statehood reemerged as characterizing the post-Soviet decade of the 1990s, with the violent disintegration of Yugoslavia in particular, ethnoreligious identities as a means of configuring international relations appear to have characterized the post-9/11 period. As my earlier overview of a variety of subnational and transnational declarative states suggests, local and transnational politics of identity have become inextricably intertwined with conversations about global governance. What is paradoxical yet not contradictory is that the most significant demonstrable impact of 9/11 throughout the world is that it has become a metaphor redeployed within national and regional—but mostly national—contexts. Indeed, in post-9/11 literature and the actions of various "global actors," it is striking how inescapable the *national* is in our talk of post-9/11 international and transnational impacts and actions.

So we come back full cycle to the question of how we define the post-9/11 world. Much of the literature on 9/11, including feminist literature—where some of my own work is found—focuses predictably and understandably on the United States and its relations with others, on Iraq and on Afghanistan, and to some extent on US allies (see, e.g., Hawthorne and Winter 2002; Winter 2006b, 2007; Riley, Mohanty, and Pratt 2008; Enloe 2010). Much of it is placed, unsurprisingly, within some variation of the post-9/11 discursive frame "US and its allies versus the Muslim world." Interestingly, however, and germanely to our discussion of how we understand "the world" in a post-9/11 context, there is some (not much, but some) material that demonstrates post-9/11 impacts, framings, and responses in countries that are not immediately perceived as being relevant to the post-9/11ist conversation (see, e.g., Alexander and Hawkesworth 2008; Sutton, Morgen, and Novkov 2008; Lutz 2009). Sites as diverse as Morocco, India, Mexico, Turkey, Japan, and the Philippines are covered in this literature. Even here, however, it is difficult to escape the shadow of the US hegemon; contributions to these anthologies discuss various antiterrorist and "security" mindsets and legislation that mimic or are influenced by the decisions taken by the US state in the weeks and months following 9/11.

Outside the Main Frame

In the last part of this chapter, I follow up on these endeavors to consider parts of the post-9/11 world that lie outside the well-worn paths. The sites I discuss in this section are Djibouti, Turkey, the Tri-Border Area of the Iguazú/Guaraní Aquifer in South America, and China. Their positions in the post-9/11 world are somewhat unusual and revealing of the discursive and even material reach of post-9/11ism into sites whose connection with "the events" is not always immediately apparent. These cases also reveal the connections made by a combination of globalization, militarism, and the exercise of and resistance to or competition with hegemonic power. Although the position of women or of feminist activity or analysis within or in relation to these sites in a post-9/11 context is mostly—with the exception of Turkey—not addressed in the available literature (revealing a need for more research and discussion), the scenarios in themselves are eloquent from the point of view of feminist analysis of post-9/11ism.

Djibouti

The Republic of Djibouti is a tiny, multiethnic, French- and Arabic-speaking state of a little more than 800,000 people located in the horn of Africa, an area known in ancient Egypt as Pwenet (Land of Punt) and a major trading partner of Egypt at that time. A semi-presidential, constitutionally democratic, and Islamic state (although its democracy leaves much to be desired), Djibouti is both a commercial and a military hub in the region. There is very little research on the role of Djibouti in the post-9/11 scenario, and most of that research falls within the security studies rubric or emanates from the US Department of Defense (DoD) or Department of State (DoS) or from nongovernmental organizations (NGOs) on human rights abuses by both the US state in Djibouti or by the Djiboutian state against its citizens. The only research on women that I have been able to find is published mostly by the UN's various agencies and other human rights agencies, such as the African Commission on Human and People's Rights, and it focuses mainly on violence against women and the Djibouti state's failure to address it as well as on female genital mutilation (FGM). The paucity of scholarly research on Djibouti is a little puzzling given its importance in the post-9/11 "war on terror" scenario. One could speculate that this invisibility is owing to the republic's tiny size and its marginalization in relation to more visible African crises. It may also be owing to the lack of an internationally audible voice within Djibouti that is opposed to the US presence there. There is, however, a long-standing opposition to the Djiboutian state's abuses of civil liberties and human rights and to violence against women, as discussed here.

In 2002, Djibouti became the site of what is still the only US military base in Africa—although the US participates in joint training and other military exercises in other parts of the continent and thus has an effective ongoing military presence there. In that year, Djibouti leased the former French base Camp Lemonnier to the US government as part

of the latter's Operation Enduring Freedom post-9/11 military campaign. The Djibouti–US Status of Visiting Forces Agreement, which
is similar to the Visiting Forces Agreement between the United States
and the Philippines, discussed in chapter 4, gives the United States
unfettered access to the nearby seaport and airport facilities as well.
Far from being scaled down after the initial post-9/11 belligerence,
Camp Lemonnier has been expanded, with some 4,000 US troops
stationed there in May 2014, when the Obama administration signed
a new ten-year lease on the base, at the annual rate of US$63 million.
Camp Lemonnier falls under the US Africa Command, whose head-
quarters are in the vicinity of Stuttgart in Germany, and is now, among
other things, a launching site for drone strikes against Yemen. The US
DoD's Quadrennial Review in 2014 positions the Djibouti base, without explicitly mentioning it, alongside activities in the Maghreb and
the Sahel, as a high-return, low-investment component in the global
US defense strategy, "further[ing US] national security interests without a large commitment of US forces" (US DoD 2014, 37).

During the years following 9/11, the US state, through the CIA,
operated an extraordinary-rendition and secret detention program for
suspected terrorists. Although Guantánamo Bay has been copiously
discussed in both institutional and scholarly literature, there has been
far less discussion of the continued use of rendition and detention elsewhere, with some exceptions, such as a report published in late 2014
by the US Senate Select Intelligence Committee, which covers all CIA
detention and interrogation programs in the wake of 9/11. Even following Bush II's admission concerning Guantánamo in 2006, which
itself followed a Supreme Court case calling into question the legality
of the CIA's rendition and detention program, and Obama's official
closure in 2009 of the remaining CIA "black sites" (secret detention
sites), "the practice of rendition of detainees to third countries continued" (African Commission for Human and People's Rights 2010,
2; see also Gutteridge 2012). More significantly, and as has been the
case elsewhere (see chapters 3 and 4), the US government and the
CIA were in the process of setting up counterterrorism operations in
the Horn of Africa before 9/11. Rendition and detention of terrorist

suspects dates back to at least 1998, according to an affidavit by Clara Gutteridge, who conducted extensive research in Djibouti in her role as resident fellow with the Open Society Justice Initiative in 2011 and prior to that as deputy director of the Secret Prisons team with the organization Reprieve (Gutteridge 2012, 1–2).

Much of the research on US detention of terrorism suspects in its Djibouti "black site" has centered on the case of Mohammed Abdullah Saleh al-Asad, a Yemeni businessman who was arrested in Tanzania in 2003 and allegedly taken first to Djibouti and then to Afghanistan. In both locations, evidence indicates that he was tortured. In 2005, he was found not guilty of any association with al Qaeda or terrorism operations and released back to Yemen. The Global Justice Clinic of the New York University Center for Human Rights and Global Justice, in collaboration with the NGO Interights, subsequently took al-Asad's case to the African Commission on Human and People's Rights. At its fifty-fifth session in May 2014, the commission ruled that the case was inadmissible because of the unreliability of evidence relating to al-Asad's deportation to Djibouti (Decision 383/10; see Global Justice Clinic and Interights 2010).

On the Djibouti side, ongoing human rights abuses have been well documented and roundly criticized. One of the more recent high-profile cases concerned the arrest of Jean-Paul Noël Abdi, president of the Djiboutian League of Human Rights, in February 2011 following his publication of information on arbitrary arrests of student protesters a few days earlier. Abdi was charged with participation in an insurrectional movement under Articles 145 and 146 of the Djibouti Penal Code. He was released a few days later for health reasons, but the charges remained. He died in Marseilles the following year and was mourned by both Djiboutian and international human rights organizations as a champion of human rights in his home country. The student protests of 2011 had been primarily about the poor quality of education in Djibouti but were also associated with political freedoms in the lead-up to the elections that year. In 2005 and 2008, the opposition parties had boycotted the elections, claiming that the latter were not organized freely and fairly, and some did so again in 2011.

Even the United States calls Djibouti to account for its poor human rights record, which may seem hypocritical in light of the US administration's cozy relationship with the Djibouti regime and its own "black site" human rights abuses. In its Djibouti annual human rights report for 2013, the US DoS characterized Djibouti as having a "strong elected president" (for whom term limits were removed in 2010, allowing President Ismail Omar Guelleh to be elected for a third term) but a "weak legislature" (US DoS 2013, 1). The report documents a series of human rights abuses, the most serious of which is the abridgement of civil rights through harassment, detention, denial of freedom of speech and information, and restrictions on freedom of assembly. It also denounces the use of torture, arbitrary arrest, denial of a public trial, invasion of privacy, restrictions to freedom of association, corruption, discriminations and violence against women (including FGM), trafficking in persons, and denial of workers' rights.

As noted earlier, domestic violence and FGM are the main issues concerning women on which there is any international literature at all (see, e.g., UN Children's Emergency Fund [UNICEF] 2013; United Nations Radio 2013). The National Union of Djiboutian Women, which works in partnership with various UN agencies, runs regular campaigns about violence against women, workplace equality, and so on, but progress is patchy for all the usual reasons: lack of legislation or unenforced legislation; the weight of tradition and shar'ia law; lack of resources; underreporting of abuses (US DoS 2013). For example, an estimated 93 percent of Djiboutian women and girls have undergone FGM, including around 20 percent who have been infibulated, despite the existence of legislation banning FGM, which also provides for punishment of anyone failing to report it. To date, however, no convictions have resulted under this legislation (UNICEF 2013; US DoS 2013), despite the fact that, according to a detailed UNICEF report on FGM worldwide, at least 65 percent of Djiboutian women are opposed to the practice (UNICEF 2013, 54).

On March 25, 2016, in the tense lead-up to the Djiboutian presidential election, ten Djiboutian women from the Comité des femmes djiboutiennes contre le viol et l'impunité (Committee of Djiboutian

Women against Rape and Impunity) began a hunger strike in Paris in protest against the systematic rape of women by the Djiboutian army. They chose to organize the protest outside Djibouti because government crackdowns on any opposition make it impossible to stage a protest there, and the women wished in addition to attract international attention to the high levels of violence against women in their country. In particular, they wished to denounce the hypocrisy of France, which also maintains a significant military presence in Djibouti but "turns a blind eye" to the abuses perpetrated by Djiboutian soldiers in parts of the country identified with opposition to the Guelleh regime. The Committee of Djiboutian Women had documented 246 rapes at the time of the hunger strike, in contrast to the 20 identified by state records. Their spokeswoman in Paris was reported as saying that rape was widespread but that complaints "end up in the trash," and doctors examining victims are reluctant to document rapes out of fear of reprisals against them and their families (Maublanc 2016).

The militarized violence by both Djiboutian and foreign military personnel against Djiboutian women extends—predictably—to prostitution. The US DoS report refers in passing to child prostitution, including via a trafficking corridor along the Ethiopia–Djibouti trucking route (US DoS 2013, 21). The DoS's *Trafficking in Persons Report 2014* elaborates on this scenario, confirming that Djibouti is a transit zone for trafficking of children and women from Ethiopia, Eritrea, and Somalia for domestic labor or prostitution in Yemen and other Gulf countries. This report even makes reference, albeit rather obliquely, to the impact of US military presence via the statement that "members of foreign militaries stationed in Djibouti contribute to the demand for women and girls in prostitution, including possible trafficking victims" (US DoS 2014b, 158). Well, of course they do. Feminist research has long shown the link between the presence of military bases and levels of prostitution. As Cynthia Enloe puts it in her aptly titled book *Maneuvers* in the context of her historical overview of links between militarization and prostitution at various times and in various geographical locations, "Through wartime mobilization, postwar demobilization, and peacetime preparedness maneuvers, sexuality and militarism have been intertwined. They have been constructed and reconstructed together, usually with the help of deliberate policy decisions. Together, ideologies of militarism and sexuality have shaped the social order of military base towns and the lives of women in those same towns" (2000, 51).

Within this masculinist linkage of sexuality and militarism, prostitution has played a central role. Whole cultures of cities—and even the cities themselves—have developed around military bases and their links with prostitution. Those cultures even remain long after the bases close, as the Philippine example I discuss in chapter 4 and that both Enloe and I discuss elsewhere eloquently demonstrates (Enloe 2004, chap. 3; Winter 2011a, 2012b).

How, then, might the lives of women and female children in Djibouti be affected by the significant US military presence there? How might this presence combine with poverty, existing trafficking networks, patriarchal customs, and an abusive national government to render women's lives more difficult? How should we consider the lives of Djiboutian women, about whom the "international community" knows so little, about whom I know so little, within a post-9/11 scenario? To what extent has 9/11 changed the world for them?

Turkey

Fortunately, we have significantly more research at our disposal concerning Turkish women, the Turkish state, and Turkish feminism, including research on post-9/11 militarism. Even so, we still do not often see discussions of Turkey in post-9/11 scholarly work, even feminist work. Again, this is surprising. Turkey was after 2003 one of the main regional beneficiaries of the "situation" in the Middle East, presenting, according to some, the region's clearest example at that time not only of a functioning democracy but also of one that wholeheartedly embraced a European liberal market economy and security imperatives (Oguzlu 2005–6; Bozdémir 2007; Kilinç 2009; Yavuz 2009). It was also a site of post-9/11 militarization in collaboration with the North Atlantic Treaty Organization (NATO). For this and related reasons, Turkey is an important case study within the post-9/11 world, including and perhaps even particularly as concerns women.

A little more than a year after 9/11, the Adalet ve Kalkinma Partisi (AKP, Justice and Development Party) was elected in Turkey and became hailed both in Turkey and throughout the world as an instrument of democratization there. Yet almost six years later, according to Turkish feminist political scientist Fatmagül Berktay, Turkey's main problem continued to be the struggle to achieve democracy (interview, Istanbul, 2008). Another five years down the track, in 2013, protests that began against an urban development in Gezi Park in Istanbul spread across the country, broadening their focus to issues ranging from freedom of speech and assembly to the government's corruption and its attempts to undermine secularism. The AKP, which entered its fourth term in 2015, has certainly not lived up to its promise of a modern Islamic democratic party. It has taken successive turns to the socially conservative right, and several government members have been involved in financial corruption, first exposed in international media in late 2013. It was anticipated that the AKP would be defeated in the June 2015 election, but the election delivered a hung Parliament. Unable to negotiate a coalition government, President Recep Tayyip Erdoğan (AKP) called a second election on November 1, at which the AKP gained a clear majority. The party had been able to take advantage of disarray on the left and of security concerns related in particular to violent conflicts between the state and the Partiya Karkerên Kurdistanê (Kurdistan Workers Party) and to terrorism. On October 10, 2015, not long before the second election, a rally in Ankara calling for a peaceful solution to the Kurdish conflict became the target of a terrorist attack: 102 people were killed, and more than 400 were injured. No one claimed responsibility for the attack, but the Turkish state accused Daesh. By early 2016, the "security" situation in Turkey had become so bad that the International Political Science Association, which hosts the world's largest biennial academic political science conference, decided to move the conference planned for Istanbul in July 2016 to another European city because it deemed itself unable to ensure the safety of the several thousand delegates expected. Feminists inside and outside Turkey found this decision disappointing. As Fatmagül Berktay commented to me by email, "[I] am really disappointed that they are relocating. It's difficult times for us and we do need more solidarity and more courage" (personal communication, Feb. 27, 2016).

Women have been the particular targets of the AKP's increasing moves to the right, with some Talibanesque manifestations: in a speech made on the occasion of Eid al-Fitr on July 28, 2014, Deputy Prime Minister Bülent Arınç condemned "moral corruption" in Turkey, saying that women should not talk too much on their mobile phones or laugh in public and should "blush, lower their heads and turn their eyes away" when men look at them (qtd. in *Hurriyet Daily News* 2014). Turkish women immediately responded by publishing photographs of themselves laughing on Instagram and Twitter under the hashtags #*kahkaha* (laughter) and #*direnkahkaha* (resist laughter).

The World Economic Forum's Global Gender Gap report in 2014 ranked Turkey 130th out of 145 countries, which was worse than in the previous year and, despite some prior improvement, also worse than in 2006. It was the lowest ranking in "Europe and Central Asia" countries surveyed (World Economic Forum 2015). Less than one-third of Turkish women participated in the labor force, and only 17 percent of Turkish members of Parliament elected in June 2015 were women—which was nonetheless an improvement over the 14 percent of 2011. Violence against women continues to be endemic. It attracted attention once again in February 2015 after a minibus driver brutally murdered twenty-year-old student Özgecan Aslan in southern Turkey. The murder sparked national protests by both women and some men and pushed President Erdoğan to take a public stand in favor of the "harshest penalty" for the perpetrator and his accomplices, even as he publicly condemned the protest tactics used by some feminists (*Hurriyet Daily News* 2015b).

Increasingly woman-excluding Turkey is nonetheless the world's seventeenth-largest economy in terms of GDP (US$820 billion in 2014), although it falls in the middle tier in world business rankings (US DoS 2014a). The year before the financial scandal erupted and in the wake of the AKP's return to power for a third term, then prime minister Recep Tayyip Erdoğan announced as part of the AKP's ten-year plan "Vision 2023," the ambition for Turkey to become one of the top-ten economies in the world by 2023 (AK Parti 2012). The plan also mentioned the AKP's strong stance against corruption, which is ironic in light of the scandal in 2013. Turkey's economic growth and its ambitions for 2023 have led some Turkish and international business commentators to frame Turkey as "the China of Europe." For example, an article on the economic aspects of Vision 2023, posted on the CNBC news site in January 2013, used the "China of Europe" metaphor, citing Turkey's high economic growth rate in 2011: at 8.5 percent, it was the fastest in Europe for that year and second only to China among world emerging market economies (Ellyat 2013). Since its first election to power, the AKP has favored the development of a market economy and has had its sights set firmly on EU membership, so much so that it has an EU ministry dedicated to this task.

The United States has taken a strong interest in Turkey's economic and political development, with President Obama ushering in a new phase of economic cooperation early in his first term. In October 2010, the year after Obama announced this new phase, the first meeting was held of the US–Turkey Framework for Strategic Economic and Commercial Cooperation, "a Cabinet-level dialogue aimed at enhancing economic relations and boosting bilateral trade and investment" (US DoS 2014a). These new economic ties, however, were simply an elevation of economic cooperation to the same level as already-existing military cooperation.

As a NATO member since 1952, Turkey has been a US military ally for several decades, but this relationship was upset in 2003 when Turkey voted against both deployment of Turkish forces in Iraq and deployment of US forces in Turkey. One commentator labeled diplomatic interactions between Turkey and the United States at that time "a comedy of errors" (Rubin 2005). Prior to that time, Turkey and the United States had had a checkered military relationship, with Cyprus being a major bone of contention. Following the Turkish invasion of Cyprus in 1974 and the retaliatory US arms embargo,

Turkey suspended activities at US bases, with only one, Incirlik Air Base, remaining in operation. Interestingly, military cooperation was renewed following the Turkish military coup of 1980, and Turkey became a key ally in Operation Desert Storm in Iraq in 1991, with Incirlik playing a major role. According to Ayşe Altınay and Amy Holmes, "It is difficult to overemphasize the importance of the Incirlik Air Base for US power projection in the Middle East, particularly since the early 1990s; for more than a decade, the entire Iraq policy of the United States hinged on Incirlik" (2009, 276).

Post-9/11 pressure on a then indebted and Europe-hopeful Turkey was great; it included US proposals of increased financial aid in exchange for increased military access and Turkey's support for the Iraq War in 2003. Turkey's nonparticipation in that war is thus all the more remarkable. It was certainly not the only country to have participated in Afghanistan but to have stopped short of Iraq: neither France nor Canada joined the Coalition of the Willing in 2003, and many others either subsequently withdrew or gave minimal support. But Turkey's nonparticipation was a blow to the United States, given Incirlik's strategic importance in relation to Iraq. Altınay and Holmes argue that the role of the antiwar movement in Turkey in achieving the "no" vote has been underestimated. They comment on the growth of social movement antimilitarism since 2003, including feminist dimensions, with some demonstrators demanding that Incirlik be closed and turned into a women's shelter (2009, 289–91).

Turkish feminist activism has, in fact, been an integral component of Turkish peace activism for some time. One of the best known of these activists is Pinar Selek, one of the founders of feminist journal *Amargi* and of the Amargi feminist bookshop and café in Istanbul. The Turkish state accused Selek—an antimilitarist feminist sociologist and activist who has for many years advocated for the rights of the poor, women, and other minorities, notably Kurds—of being responsible for a bombing in the Istanbul Spice Bazaar in 1998. She has been sentenced and acquitted four times—with the most recent acquittal, in December 2014, under appeal by the Turkish state in early 2016—and has served time in Turkish prisons. Now living in exile in France, Selek has become a cause célèbre on the international stage, with numerous international human rights defenders calling on the Turkish state to end its judicial harassment of her. She continues to speak out against abuses by the Turkish "deep state"—that is, the authoritarian and militarized state within the state. For example, her book on the Armenian genocide perpetrated between 1915 and 1923 by the Ottoman government, originally authored in her native Turkish, was published in French translation on the occasion of the hundredth anniversary of the beginning of the genocide, thus opening her work to a somewhat wider audience (Selek 2015). No English translation was yet available at the time of this writing.

Incirlik is also a symbolic site in relation to the Armenian genocide. It is one of the foci of an ongoing Armenian American lawsuit against the Turkish state for reparations to the Armenian people. The Turkish government has rejected the claims and has taken umbrage at the EU Human Rights report for 2013, adopted by the European Parliament on March 12, 2015. Article 77 of this report calls on all EU member states to legally acknowledge the Armenian genocide and encourages them and EU institutions to contribute further to its recognition. The Turkish Foreign Ministry slammed the report, and on March 14, 2015, the *Hurriyet Daily News* quoted a statement by ministry spokesperson Tanju Bilgiç, who claimed that "the report interpreted the event with a one-sided approach and disregarded Turkey's realistic and constructive initiatives relating to the matter" (*Hurriyet Daily News* 2015a).

Obama's reinforcement of ties with Turkey includes pushing for further development of the neoliberal economic path on which Turkey is already embarked, including privatizations, encouragement of foreign direct investment, and increasing labor-market "flexibility." As mentioned earlier, Turkey was considered in the years after 9/11 to be the best, indeed the only, example of a working democracy in the Muslim Middle East, and Islamist movements in North Africa have looked to the AKP as a model. The truth, however, is that Turkey remains plagued by many of the same problems that have plagued it for decades: the social, cultural, and economic marginalization of Kurds;

its position on Cyprus; government corruption; and its relatively poor performance in improving the situation of women, an aspect to which I return in chapter 6.

Most recently, the influx of Syrian refugees into already impoverished southeastern Turkey and into the informal economies of the country's western cities, although not as gravely destabilizing as in Lebanon and to a lesser extent in Jordan, has placed Turkey under pressure. That pressure is set to grow with the increase in refugee numbers, which the UN High Commission for Refugees estimated in mid-2015 to be a little more than 4 million, with almost half now in Turkey, currently the world's major host of refugees (UN High Commission for Refugees 2015). Conversely, Turkey has been criticized by Western governments and media commentators for not doing enough to stem the flow of would-be jihadists crossing the border in the other direction, many of them en route from European countries—a claim that the Turkish state has vigorously refuted. These problems and the instability of the region more generally have lowered investor confidence, notwithstanding Turkey's relatively liberal foreign-direct-investment regime. The "dollarization" of the Turkish economy is placing pressure on its currency, and unemployment, officially around 10 percent, is rising.[4] The "China of Europe," then, is not doing quite as well as the analogy suggests and faces some difficult battles, notwithstanding its now apparently cozier relationship with the United States.

The extent to which 9/11 has affected Turkey and to which Turkey has been a "player" in the post-9/11 MENA region and the world merits greater attention within feminist international relations in a post-9/11 context. It warrants that attention all the more because Turkey has undergone the paradoxically positive impact of 9/11 in the generation of increased democratic voice through social activism,

4. See the statistics provided by the Turkish Statistical Institute for 2015 at http://www.turkstat.gov.tr/Start.do;jsessionid=JNS6WNCJkycfylqytvlGPv3vXlz hBg2lH9F3GJksD2mLZdhQpSv9!-181659759 (accessed Nov. 19, 2015).

not to mention the long-standing and internationally known work by Turkish feminist activists, in a context where things are worsening, not improving, for women.

La Triple Frontera (Argentina, Brazil, Paraguay)

One of the less usual post-9/11 sites to be discussed in some of the literature—most of it by the US DoS or DoD or by scholars loosely or tightly affiliated with US defense interests—concerns the Triple Frontera (Tri-Border Area, TBA) at which Argentina meets Paraguay and Brazil. These three countries, along with Uruguay and Venezuela, which joined in 2004, make up the five-country customs union that goes by the name "Mercosur." Mercosur itself joined up with the Community of Andean Nations in 2008 to form Unasur, which is increasingly modeling itself along EU lines as an alternative economic, cultural, and political power bloc to the United States and the North American Free Trade Agreement in the Americas. The TBA has long been an area of concern in the region owing to various arms- and drug-smuggling and money-laundering operations as well as to document fraud. After 9/11, there was some suspicion in the United States of possible terrorist-financing activities in the TBA, leading the United States to become a partner in 2002, ostensibly at the invitation of the TBA countries, in operations to combat these various illicit activities, resulting in the formation of the 3+1 Group on Tri-Border Area Security (US DoS 2010a, 165). In 2003, a detailed US Library of Congress report noted that according to US, Argentine, and Paraguayan intelligence, there was some likelihood of fundraising, arms-trafficking, and terrorist "sleeper" cells in the TBA (R. Hudson 2003, 14–16).

Some defense industry researchers, publishing in specialized journals, subsequently gave weight to the thesis of a TBA Islamist threat. Defense analyst Cristiana Brafman Kittner of the Decisive Analytics Corporation in Arlington, Virginia, for example, claimed in 2007 to have evidence that there had been Islamist terrorist activity in the TBA for several years, although the evidence she presented is weak and circumstantial (see Brafman Kittner 2007). Much of it is, in fact, simply conjecture based on the existence of what she claims to be the four necessary conditions for the establishment of "safe havens" for the development of Islamist terrorism: geographic features; weak governance; history of corruption and violence; and poverty. She argues that the presence of these conditions in themselves in the region, along with the existing presence of the trafficking and fraud crimes and an Arab minority, indicate probability.

In a both chilling and amusing echo of Donald Rumsfeld's infamous "known knowns and known unknowns" comment, Brafman Kittner asserted that to "successfully fight the GWOT [global war on terror], the US, together with its allies, must focus not only on the known and visible threat, but also on those threats that remain unknown" (2007, 325). Rumsfeld's full remark, made at a press briefing on February 12, 2002, in answer to a question on the absence of evidence of Iraq's supplying of weapons of mass destruction to terrorist groups, reads as follows: "There are known knowns; there are things we know we know. We also know there are known unknowns; that is to say we know there are some things we do not know. But there are also unknown unknowns—there are things we do not know we don't know" (Rumsfeld 2002). Brafman Kittner's article, along with other literature supporting the TBA terrorist-cells thesis (see, e.g., Abbott 2004), also cites the presumably Iran/Hezbollah-backed terrorist attacks in Buenos Aires against the Israeli embassy (1992) and the Argentine–Israeli Mutual Association (1994) as evidence of the long-standing existence of terrorist networks in the region, aided by government corruption.

Investigations into the attacks in 1992 and 1994 revealed bribes and apparent involvement of some Buenos Aires police, and the bombing in 1994 has more recently come once again into international headlines. A few days after Alberto Nisman, the prosecutor put in charge of the recent investigation, accused Argentine political leaders, including President Cristina Kirchner, of covering up Iran's involvement, he was found mysteriously dead in his home on January 18, 2015. Gerardo Pollicita, the prosecutor who took up the case following Nisman's death, agreed with Nisman's accusation and pushed for a criminal investigation, but in February 2015 Judge Daniel Rafecas found that the minimum conditions to launch such an investigation had not been met. Meanwhile, a month earlier, in January, President Kirchner had dissolved the Argentinian Intelligence Agency and set up a new one, allegedly—according to multiple press reports at the time—to ensure that it would be staffed by people loyal to her when she would be investigated following the end of her term for tax fraud and money laundering. Large and angry demonstrations against Kirchner, demanding an independent judiciary and an end to corruption, took place in Buenos Aires in February 2015; some demonstrators, echoing the French "I am Charlie" slogans of the previous month (see chapter 7), carried placards reading "I am Nisman."

The thesis of a TBA "safe haven" for terrorists, however, has been well and truly refuted. Even the US DoS considers that there is no convincing evidence of terrorist operations in the area: "The United States remained concerned that Hizballah and HAMAS sympathizers were raising funds in the Tri-Border Area by participating in illicit activities and soliciting donations from sympathizers in the sizable Middle Eastern communities in the region. There was no corroborated information, however, that these or other Islamic extremist groups had an operational presence in the region" (2010a, 165).

The United States has nonetheless been active in the region, notably in the middle of the past decade, although its history of military presence there goes back much further. In particular, in 2005 it commenced a series of thirteen joint military-training exercises with and in Paraguay over eighteen months. The exercises were officially designed to serve both humanitarian and counterterrorism-training purposes: this is a fairly standard official justification for US overseas military exercises. In exchange for the presence of up to four hundred US marines in Paraguay for each exercise, Washington pledged US$45,000 in aid to Paraguay. This military-presence-for-aid exchange is fairly common, as in the Philippines, where the exchange was successful, and in the case of Turkey, where it was not, as noted earlier.

Although US military activity in the TBA did not commence with these Paraguay exercises, the latter sparked considerable controversy, including claims that the United States planned to use Dr. Luis Maria Argana International Airport in Mariscal Estigarribia as the starting point for setting up a permanent military base in the Chaco region. Washington has denied this plan, and a detailed article published by Global Security (2011), a public-policy NGO devoted to providing information about military and defense-related matters, debunks the claim. Among other things, the organization cites information about the infrastructure and runway space at the airport to demonstrate that US military aircraft would not be able to use it. Other concerns, according to a BBC report in 2005, included that the deal was an attempt to break up Mercosur by offering Paraguay its own bilateral free-trade agreement in exchange for a US military base (Obama later set up bases in Argentina and Chile); that there were ploys to destabilize the government of neighboring Bolivia, with an eye on Bolivian gas reserves in particular; and that the deal would add another stepping stone to enhancing US financial interests in the vast freshwater reserves of the Guaraní Aquifer (Elmer 2005).

Access to clean water has become an increasingly politicized global issue. It has long been a humanitarian one: according to the Red Cross, 800 million people across the world do not have access to potable water, and 2.7 billion do not have access to adequate sanitation. This lack of access results in 4 million deaths annually, and children younger than five are the main casualties (Australian Red Cross 2011). With water pollution and chronic drought also affecting sizeable chunks of industrialized or emerging capitalist economies, and with water management increasingly under corporate control, water has become "blue gold," to cite the title of a well-known critique of corporate appropriation of the world's water resources (Barlow and Clarke 2002). As the authors point out, the 800 million cited by the Red Cross do not live in regions geographically distant from the global "center." For example, among the 1.3 million-strong workforce in one of the world's largest and most notorious export-processing zones, the maquiladoras in the free-trade zone on the US–Mexico border, only 12 percent have reliable access to clean water in what Maude Barlow and Tony Clarke describe as a "toxic cesspool" (2002, 51). Water is trucked in; it is not available locally. As Madeleine Baer puts it in her discussion of the Bolivian "water war," the struggle for water is now "at the nexus of the larger battle between states, multinational corporations, international financial institutions, and organized groups of citizens" (2008, 195).

The Guaraní Aquifer, which lies under the four original Mercosur countries (minus Venezuela) and includes the TBA, is one of the largest underground freshwater reserves in the world, covering an area of 1.2 million square kilometers and estimated to contain 37,000 cubic kilometers of water. According to a factsheet produced by the International Atomic Energy Agency (n.d.), the aquifer, which currently supplies water to approximately 15 million people in the region, has the potential to provide sustainable water supply to some 360 million people, which is roughly one and a half times the current population of the four countries. The aquifer is currently managed by the four Mercosur countries with the financial help of the Global Environmental Facility—a joint funding consortium of the UN Development Program (UNDP), the UN Environment Program, and the World Bank, with the World Bank serving as the implementing agency. The Organization of American States (OAS) also participates as co-manager. As the International Atomic Energy Agency notes, the main threat to the aquifer is uncontrolled pollution.

Military activity has long been associated with significantly increased release of toxins into the air and groundwater, so anywhere military operations are happening, the risk of toxic waste is augmented. In particular, the military is the single biggest polluter in the United States and is responsible for more toxic waste than the five biggest chemical companies combined (International Peace Bureau 2002). The US DoS has been the subject of actions on behalf of people having suffered the impact of military toxic waste, one of the most well-known cases being that of the Philippines, but that case has not to date succeeded because of rulings by the US Supreme Court that the US Comprehensive Environmental Response, Compensation, and Liability Act of 1980 does not apply to sovereign states over which the United States does not have formal jurisdiction (Winter 2012b). US military operations in US

Forward Operating Sites in South America have been largely priva-
tized, with Dyncorp being one of the big beneficiaries in Ecuador in
particular (Lindsay-Poland 2009). This, combined with the US record
on military-industrial pollution, gives cause for some, even considerable, environmental concern in the Guaraní region.

US and OAS representatives have dubbed as conspiracy theorists
those who criticize US military interest in the TBA as being linked to
commercial interests in either Bolivian gas or Guaraní water. Among
such "conspiracy theorists" are Argentineans Adolfo Perez Esquivel,
activist and Nobel Peace laureate; Elsa Bruzzone of the Buenos Aires–
based organization Centro de Militares para la Democracia Argentina,
a pro-democracy group founded by retired Argentine military personnel; and the makers of the Argentinian documentary *Sed, invasión
gota a gota* (Thirst: Invasion Drop by Drop) (Hearn 2006). Although
the United States, the OAS, and the Global Environmental Facility
assert that the national sovereignty and transnational cooperation of
the four Mercosur states is being and will be guaranteed, critics are not
so certain. Among those critics are the Guaraní Indigenous peoples
and peasant farmers of the region, who met with other residents and
activists for the first TBA social forum in 2004, held in the Argentinian frontier city Puerto Iguazú. Some 13,000 people attended. A
report on the TBA social forum, published on July 7, 2004, at the
Latin American website of the Unión Internacional de Trabajadores
de la Alimentación (International Union of Foodworkers), referring to
US antiterrorist initiatives in the region from 2002, stated that

> the participants . . . denounced the real objectives motivating these
> ["antiterrorist" and "cooperation"] initiatives of the US government
> in the region. The TBA is a strategic region for the United States, as
> a portal giving access to the Amazon region, as a reserve of freshwa-
> ter—one of the biggest in the world, for its ecological richness and
> biodiversity, and as a strategic territorial space for exercising control
> over the three countries of the region. (Korol 2004, my translation)

The forum focused on the need for peoples of the region and their
respective states to band together in order to protect their sovereignty

over the Guaraní Aquifer, for a halt to militarism, for sustainable development in the region—rather than "aid" trade-offs for US military presence—and checks to tourism development that would represent further incursions into Indigenous Guaraní land. (The Iguazú Falls in the TBA are a major tourism money earner for Argentina and Brazil.)

The questions of indigeneity, peasant rights, and food and water sovereignty are central to Latin American political conversations about democracy, socioeconomic equality, and national sovereignty. The Western imagining of "Latin America" often obscures the persistence of white privilege in many Latin American contexts and its relationships to significant internal divides along lines of class, ethnicity, and urbanness versus ruralness. Popular mobilization around the TBA thus ties the rights of the internally disenfranchised to the broader question of Latin American sovereignty in the face of a greedy and militaristic US state and its corporate entities. The popular pressure represented by the TBA social forum thus targets both internal and external power structures.

The issues that have come to a head around US military and economic incursion in the TBA are not new in Latin America, for there has been US military and commercial presence there for some time, including some questionable transnational corporate water-management ventures in TBA countries (Conca 2006), and food and water sovereignty has been core to much social protest (Robin 2008). That said, 9/11 has once again become the framing mechanism: the pretext for closer US scrutiny of and involvement in the region. Even if the US DoS itself has concluded that the probability of terrorist cells in the region is low, the United States still makes a case for "soft" links through money laundering and document fraud that finance channels for possible terrorist networks based elsewhere. Whether that claim is founded or not, the history of US military and civilian involvement, both state and corporate, in Latin America and of its usually devastating effects for impoverished locals is such that concerns over US interest in controlling water and gas supply in the region do appear well founded. At the same time, as demonstrated in subsequent chapters and case studies in this book, how well the United States succeeds in its aims also depends in part on how cooperative the richer and more powerful local partners are, whether we are talking about the wealthier Latin American countries or the wealthier classes within them. If one is to accept the BRICS thesis, perhaps Brazil, as the new economic dynamo of the region, will be the country to watch in the post-9/11 list TBA scenario. As I write these words in the lead-up to the Rio de Janeiro Olympic Games in 2016, Brazil is dogged by a range of problems relating to the organization of the games, one of which is, interestingly for our conversation here, water pollution.

China

In a post-9/11 anthology on regional security in the Asia-Pacific, former Australian foreign minister Gareth Evans wrote that

> for as long as any of us can remember, and certainly long predating 11 September 2001, Asia has been a laboratory for the analysis of just about every class of security problem with which policy makers have to wrestle: major power tensions; nuclear weapons proliferation; sub-regional and bilateral disputation; internal conflict and state failure. In the case of major power tension, Northeast Asia feels the tectonic plates grinding more than anywhere else on earth as the US becomes ever more assertive. (2004, 30)

That "plate[] grinding," for Evans, consisted in great part of China's growing strength as Japan weakened both economically and politically. Evans considered the impact of 9/11 on "the world" to be overstated but found that one of the paradoxically more positive impacts at that time was to encourage more stable and cooperative political relationships between the United States, Russia, and China as well as between China and India.

In fact, US–Russia relations have soured considerably in the decade since Evans wrote those words, and US–China relations are tense at the time of writing, as noted earlier. Whether the Sino-American warming has been substantial and will endure past the current diplomatic tension is a matter for conjecture and for those more expert on China than I to discuss, but the current hegemon cannot easily ignore what is generally viewed as the emerging one.

In trade, politics, and even globalized education, all eyes seem currently to be on China, which has also become a major economic actor in the Asia-Pacific region. In 2002, a framework agreement was signed between China and ASEAN to launch the ASEAN–China Free Trade Area (which came into effect in 2010). The ASEAN–China Free Trade Area had at that time the world's largest consumer market (1.9 billion in 2009) and was until 2015 the world's third-largest free-trade area in GDP terms. On October 5, 2015, however, the controversial Trans Pacific Partnership, which does not include China, was finally signed. The twelve Partnership members as of late 2015 accounted for 40 percent of the global economy, rendering the Partnership the world's largest free-trade agreement. As for the Pacific, China's aid program has increased immensely, but human rights NGOs have expressed concerns about China's poor human rights record domestically, and its lack of focus on human rights and good governance in its disbursement of aid is distrusted in the West.[5]

In a more specifically post-9/11 sense, the claims of the Uyghur people have come to light in the West, and views vary on the extent to which the Uyghur have identified with the "sleeping dragon's" spectacular awakening to emerge as a significant global player beginning in the 1990s. For Marika Vicziany, "any middle-class Uygur . . . would prefer to play a more meaningful role in the development of a modern China. It has not escaped them that the whole world regards China as an emerging global force. How could they benefit by splitting off from 'the main game in town'?" (2004, 160). For Arienne Dwyer, however, writing on Chinese language policy, the People's Republic of China has covertly belied its officially "egalitarian and accommodationist" policy in focusing since the 1980s "on assimilating Xinjiang's

---

5. See, for example, commentary by the Sydney-based Lowy Institute for International Policy at http://www.lowyinstitute.org/issues/chinese-foreign-aid (accessed March 26, 2015).

major minorities, particularly the Uyghurs, to the dominant Chinese culture" (2005, 2). Dwyer further notes that "accounts of the Xinjiang conflict have appeared with increasing frequency in the international press. While many Western media services have implied that the source of conflict in Xinjiang lies in cultural differences between Uyghurs and Chinese, the Chinese press has recently ascribed almost all dissent to international terrorism" (2).

China did indeed move centrally into the post-9/11 list frame when Uyghurs joined Tibet as an international cause célèbre that highlighted China's poor record on human rights; the organization of the Olympic Games in Beijing in 2008 amplified this international focus. By the time the tenth anniversary of 9/11 came around, China's persecution of Uyghurs had become well documented. At the World Uyghur Congress held in September 2011, the exiled head of the congress, Rebiya Kadeer, stated that "the Chinese authorities found in 9/11 the perfect excuse to crack down on all forms of peaceful political, social and cultural Uighur dissent" (qtd. in *Sydney Morning Herald* 2011). China also appears to have ridden the back of the European terrorist scares of 2015. On November 14, 2015, the day after the Paris terrorist attacks, Reuters news agency reported that Chinese state media were displaying rare photos of Chinese military setting out to storm supposed terrorist enclaves in Xinjiang (Reuters 2015b).

In 2012, an Amnesty International report on death sentences in 2011 noted it was impossible to provide exact figures for China because death penalties are considered a state secret. The report nonetheless estimates that the number of those having undergone that penalty in China in 2011 were in the thousands, notwithstanding a global decrease in the use of the death penalty (Amnesty International 2012). A number of high-profile Uyghurs advocating independence or autonomy are believed to have been executed. Others, such as economist Ilham Tohti, jailed for life since 2014, live under the shadow of a possible death penalty. Uyghurs have also had difficulty obtaining passports, which makes fleeing more difficult and has fueled the development of a black market in fake Turkish passports because Uyghurs are of Turkic ethnicity.

Some media reports indicate that crackdowns disproportionately affect women and children, who are arrested and detained as they attempt to flee (Radio Free Asia 2014). A report by the Unrepresented Nations and Peoples Organization, submitted to the UN Committee on the Elimination of Discrimination Against Women in 2014, indicates that Uyghur women are persecuted by locals because of their religious dress and that Uyghur women and children are trafficked for prostitution, domestic-service work, and factory work in Han regions in numbers disproportionate to elsewhere in China. The Unrepresented Nations (2014) report cites even official Chinese data on the number of Uyghur women who are "relocated." It also cites instances of persecution of women who have attempted to petition the Chinese government for information about male family members who have disappeared and regarding lack of educational and employment opportunities, where Uyghur women suffer sex, race, and language discrimination (see also Kadeer 2011). Uyghurs speak a Turkic language of the same subfamily as Uzbek, but the Chinese state policy of supposedly "bilingual" education has in fact privileged Mandarin and marginalized the Uyghur language (Finley and Zang 2015).

The "Chinese crackdown" has extended beyond China's borders. Uyghurs fleeing China have been arrested in Malaysia, a key transit country for Uyghurs on route to Turkey, and antiterrorism politics and laws have also been invoked outside China against Uyghur nationals in the wake of the emergence of Daesh. In September 2014, four Uyghur nationals carrying false Turkish passports as well as, allegedly, Daesh material were arrested in Indonesia when they were supposedly on their way to meet Indonesian Islamist leader Abu Wardah Santoso. Their trial began in Jakarta in March 2015, and in July each was sentenced to four years in prison (*Jakarta Post* 2015).

Turkey has been a relatively welcoming country for Uyghurs, whom it considers to be part of the Turkic diaspora extending across West and Central Asia. Many Uyghurs have settled in the central Anatolian city Kayseri, Turkey's ninth-largest city, with the closet airport to the famed Cappadocia region. An Al Jazeera report published on February 3, 2015, included a photograph of a Uyghur couple and one of the two children they were allowed to bring with them; they apparently were unable to obtain passports for three other children (Al Jazeera America 2015). Many Uyghurs who have settled in Turkey are poor and live in state housing.

What is most disturbing for me, however, about the photograph published by Al Jazeera, is that neither the wife's nor the husband's face is fully visible. The husband is wearing a balaclava-like head covering that leaves only his eyes visible. The wife is wearing a full black burqa; only her hands are uncovered. It is a familiar image in our post-9/11 world, yet the gendered narrative of the persecution and particularly the resistance of Uyghurs often escapes international scrutiny and analysis. In her discussion of the allegorical Uyghur story of Nuzugum, Kara Abramson (2012) suggests that women have been a pivotal element in both the Chinese state's control of Uyghur people and Uyghur men's construction of identity. Feminists have long pointed out that women's bodies and lives are the terrain of colonial and anticolonial struggles among men: women are the guardians at the gates of culture, both its symbols and its delegated authorities (see, e.g., Mies 1986; Hélie-Lucas 1990; Pettman 1996; Yuval-Davis 1997; Mohanty 2003). As the colonized, women are victims of the colonizing male and invariably end up irrevocably damaged in some way or often dead: in the Uyghur story that Abramson tells, Nuzugum kills herself rather than be forced to marry an "outsider." As resistants to colonization, women literally embody the colonized culture and are charged with passing on its values to both sons and daughters. The colonizing state can also then reconfigure its "intervention" by offering programs that ostensibly enhance women's education or economic empowerment and promote cultural diversity, which the Chinese state claims to have done in Xinjiang (Chinese State Council 2009).

In international concern over the legitimate grievances of the Uyghur people, how are the concerns of Uyghur women articulated? For Rebiya Kadeer, who has become for many the international face of Uyghur women, the oppressor is the Chinese state. But is it the only one? As Abramson (2012) notes, no culture is homogenous, and Uyghur advocacy inside China takes many forms, including with respect to gender. As is so often the case, and as I discuss further in chapter 2, women's voices are time and again either put to the service of the claims of nation and culture or drowned out in the cacophony.

Shaken, Stirred, and All Mixed Up

These four brief sketches—Djibouti, Turkey, la Triple Frontera, and China—reveal that attempts to assess the impact of 9/11 on "the world," let alone on its women, are doomed if not to failure, then to very mitigated success. This is so, first, because we simply do not know enough (I certainly do not), and some places are not seen to matter enough (Djibouti is so small, after all) or are seen to matter for different reasons (BRICishness, for example). But, more importantly, it is so because the events and situations discussed here are not related solely to 9/11. Nor, for that matter, are they solely "about" women.

Yet if one takes as a central premise of feminist political science that everything in international politics is somewhere "about" women or, perhaps more to the point, about masculinist power relations, then one has very sound feminist reasons to discuss a range of issues in international politics, even when they are not ostensibly about women or gender in the first instance. Also, given the very complex and sometimes not immediately visible links between capitalist globalization, militarization, violence against women, and environmental sustainability, feminists investigating the post-9/11 world have sound reasons to discuss such issues as the politics of water and indigeneity and those politics' subtle links to global capitalism and militarization in South America; the relationships between guns and money through promises or withdrawal of aid, among other things, in Turkey; the tacit US support of an authoritarian regime in Djibouti out of military self-interest; and the intricacies of foreign diplomatic and economic dances with and by China.

The events of September 11, 2001, did not cause any of the problems discussed in relation to these four parts of the world. But they have shaped their development in quite specific ways, either discursively, as in the TBA case, or materially, as in the case of the lives of trafficked Djiboutian women. It seems that even the unlikeliest of places or the most underdiscussed in the literature have been shaken in one way or another by 9/11 and stirred to various forms of action through popular protest or political maneuvering or both. In both direct and indirect ways, 9/11, then, trickles through the lives of the world's women. An Uyghur village woman may have no particular sense of the grand debates going on about Muslim minorities in the post-9/11 world, or, if she does, she may feel little personal connection to them, but those debates are influencing policies that in turn will influence her life or that of women who come after her.

This consideration leads us to the focus of the next chapter: the idea of "global governance," a newish preoccupation related to the idea that the 9/11-shaken world is going awry in quite worrying ways and needs better mechanisms to keep it in order. Achieving such governance, however, is an extremely daunting and perhaps impossible task, given the ongoing importance of the nation-state and the endless conflicts between various forms of sovereignty claims. Turkey asserts its sovereign right not to follow the United States into Iraq or to reject Armenian reparation claims; China asserts its sovereign right to deal with its ethnic minorities as it sees fit, and those same ethnic minorities are busily asserting their own sovereign rights; Djibouti's sovereignty is undermined by the US military presence there but is asserted and respected by the United States on a number of other levels. And so on. How can we even begin to contemplate "global governance" of such a huge, diverse, and unruly pack?

2

Woman–Nation–State Revisited

Global Governance

S askia Sassen wrote in 2002 that 9/11 brought to the fore, "with perhaps greater urgency than other events," the need for global governance (106). This observation begs two questions from a feminist perspective. First, what would such governance involve in feminist terms, given that "the world" is constituted of states and would-be states with their attendant ethnoreligious dimensions and claims to sovereignty? Second, how may such governance be achieved in the face of the seemingly insurmountable obstacles that 9/11 also brought to the fore? I attend to the first question a little later in this chapter. As for the second, obstacles to global governance can probably be summarized under the rubric of a "crisis of multilateralism": one economic and military hyperpower (the United States), acting unilaterally and often aggressively; a series of weak(ened) or failed states (their failure often owing in part, albeit not wholly, to US and sometimes other foreign unilateral intervention), in which social anomie and political violence leave a governance void; and a UN that is structurally and politically incapable of performing the key tasks expected of it: maintaining order, keeping the peace, and protecting human rights (Newman 2007; see also Dombrowski 2005). In a post-9/11 world, security and global governance are perceived to go hand in hand, but no one quite seems to be able to identify unambiguously which "globe" is to be governed, by whom, and, most especially, how.

The title of this chapter includes a nod to Yuval-Davis and Anthias 1989.

In this chapter, I use the terms *state, nation,* and *nation-state.* Broadly speaking, the first refers to the political and institutional apparatus that rules over citizens and residents of the national territory and that enters into dialogue, cooperation, or conflict with other states in international relations. The term *nation,* etymologically speaking, derives from the Latin word *nationem,* meaning "birth, origin, race, tribe." The idea of the nation was originally associated with this birthright and the cultural communities and imagined communities (Anderson 1983) that formed around it. That association remains but has been overlaid with the modern sense of the nation as a people: the two terms *nation* and *people* in fact were interchanged in the successive Declarations of the Rights of Man during the French revolutionary decade. In the Declaration of 1789, sovereignty was deemed to reside in the nation; by 1793, it resided in the people, one and indivisible. It has remained in the hands of the people ever since (Constitution of the Fifth Republic, Art. 3) and is exercised through the vote of representatives and referenda. The people, in this modern sense, are constructed as sharing, beyond any question of birthright, a political will to group together as a sovereign nation. The term *nation-state* brings those two entities together: the apparatus of a modern state as well as the "people" and cultural imaginary that the state represents.

Global Governance and State Sovereignty

In his essay on "contesting sovereignty," Samuel Makinda posits "a dialectical relationship between state sovereignty and global governance. That is, sovereignty enables and, at the same time, seeks to undermine global governance. At the same time, global governance is partly constituted by norms, rules and institutions that include sovereignty. Without sovereignty, global governance would be incomplete. Similarly, without global governance, sovereignty would be unintelligible" (2009, 22).

Makinda discusses three types of sovereignty, the first two of which, juridical and empirical sovereignty, originated with the Peace of Westphalia in 1648, which put an end to a series of wars in Europe and created the idea of national sovereignty linked to reciprocal respect among nations for territorial borders. Juridical sovereignty means that the state has no other authority over it but international law, whereas empirical sovereignty is "based on the understanding that states have, or should have, the ability to control the people, resources and institutions within their borders" (Makinda 2009, 23). Makinda calls the third type of sovereignty "popular sovereignty," which is predicated on the Enlightenment notions of equality, fundamental rights and freedoms, and the consent of the people to being governed.

The world's powerful capitalist democracies posit these values as underpinning the principles of both good national and global governance, with "rogue," corrupt, and authoritarian states being seen as falling down in the juridical or popular areas of sovereignty and governance. These failings were held up as added justifications for the post-9/11 wars on Afghanistan and Iraq. The empirical idea of sovereignty, however, is just as often invoked as a justification for nonintervention, as has been tragically observed, for example, in the cases of Rwanda in 1994 and Syria in 2011–14, even if covert Western intervention occurred in both sites at the time through intelligence and financial aid, among other things. The French state, for example, has been clearly implicated in the Rwandan genocide, as shown by the work of the Commission d'enquête citoyenne (Citizens' Inquiry Commission) in France, among others.[1] Yet it maintained an official position of nonintervention, which meant that it did not help the victims at the time.

Just as troublingly, the global economic model of "good governance" to which poorer nations are held to conform in order to obtain debt relief, aid, and so on often compound some of the problems deemed to be the reason for the model's imposition in the first place. These problems include, for example, the requirement to farm export crops rather than subsistence crops or to use income from such farming to service debt rather than to provide food, clean water, sanitation,

---

1. The Commission d'enquête citoyenne has held a number of gatherings and published several reports. It also maintains a website at http://cec.rwanda.free.fr/ (accessed Nov. 20, 2015).

and infrastructure. Peter Dombrowski argues that "sovereignty in the classical, ideal-type sense that flourishes only in academic texts is an unaffordable luxury for all but the most powerful and successful states" (2005, 232). The so-called Washington Consensus on fostering market-driven economic "reform" is consensual only for those with the power to opt in or out. Less-powerful states attempting to opt out are faced with economic and financial ostracism. Moreover, even in more powerful states, with increased state outsourcing to the private sector—including, especially since 9/11, the outsourcing of "security" (see chapters 3 and 4)—the state's ability to control what happens becomes more limited. In post-2003 Iraq, for example, private contractors have not necessarily done the bidding of either the United States or the Iraqi states if they deem conditions too dangerous or the economic benefits insufficient.

At the same time, states invoke sovereignty protectively as the basis for deciding how rights codified in international law are to be translated and applied in their national law. Restrictions on immigration and asylum and on the treatment of immigrants and asylum seekers as not qualified for access to rights and freedoms guaranteed to citizens are one example of how powerful nations' "sovereignty" trumps any ideas of multilateralism in global governance. Such behaviors by states undermine the assumption that international treaties to which those states are parties are legally binding.

Even among citizens, rights and equalities codified by law may be inapplicable or inadequately applied because of other structural, systemic, and ideological factors. Violence against women is a clear case in point: in many countries, there exists some sort of legislative apparatus to protect women from violence. This does not mean, however, that women are free from violence: states usually have other priorities, notwithstanding post-9/11 rhetoric on women's rights (see chapter 3). The existence of global governance structures through law, institutions, trade, cultural globalization, and transnational civil society cannot be assumed to suffice in ensuring that sovereign states abide by whatever the global consensus on rights and freedoms is taken to be—assuming such consensus clearly exists.

Moreover, in many ways sovereign states are not at odds with the forces of globalization but on the contrary are the producers of those forces and their impacts. Most liberal or neoliberal views (what one might call the "left" and "right" wings of global capitalist political economy)—or "alternative" views such as poststructuralist or feminist—of supra, trans-, or extranational relations contain explicit or implicit assertions that the state is no longer the main player in global governance. We supposedly now live in a "post-Westphalian" world (see, e.g., Fraser 2007; Rai 2008). Yet an examination of how global governance works reveals that hegemonic states are still, either by themselves or in concert with other states or transnational entities, calling the shots globally.

Even global corporate capitalism—which supposedly has escaped the state's power, as the earlier example of corporate presence in Iraq suggests—is subject to various national legislations or international treaties: that is, agreements worked out between states. Indeed, states actively regulate in favor of transnational capitalism and are often willing participants in what critics of global capitalism characterize as their own exploitation. The Philippines, for example, vies with India and Malaysia for offshore call-center, information technology and microelectronics business, inviting injections of foreign capital and jobs at better than a teacher's or nurse's salary for its frustrated middle classes. Even if, as many scholars of globalization, global governance, and global security argue, territorial borders have become delocalized, the state is still, outside military invasion and armed insurgency, the main decider of what does or does not get to happen within those borders, delocalized or not. The state's power of decision affects not only business- and knowledge-process outsourcing but also the increasingly automated and globally networked technology involved in international surveillance of the movements of individuals (Lyon 2003).

The crucial importance of states has been spectacularly demonstrated—and I use the word *spectacularly* advisedly to express both degree and a mise-en-scène, a carefully crafted performance—by the global financial crisis, its causes, and its aftermath. Certainly, global financial crises are precisely that: they have an impact beyond the boundaries of the nation-state in a world in which nation-states have become transnationally interdependent, at least in economic terms. This interdependency is not, however, in itself a new phenomenon: it has been the case at least since the Westphalian peace that brought the modern European sovereign state into being in the mid–seventeenth century. What is new is the level of technology-enhanced global networking. At the same time, the lack of national regulation of banks' behavior, notably within the United States but also elsewhere, made the global financial crisis in 2008 possible in the first place. Trading in derivatives was largely unregulated, and in the United States in particular mortgage markets were subject to little watchdog scrutiny that might afford some protection to the vulnerable. Similarly, the existence or otherwise of national legal protections for those most severely affected and other decisions made by states at a national level have either attenuated or exacerbated the impact of the crisis.

Moreover, the credit-rating agencies that are recognized as having the power to rate both corporations and national governments are themselves accredited by governments. The so-called big three, Standard and Poor's, Moody's, and the Fitch Group—the first two of which are US agencies and the third a US- and UK-based subsidiary of a French company—have become so largely through recognition as such by the US state. They are thus empowered by the state to rate the state. The credit-rating agencies in place in the United States have been criticized not only as "in bed" with corporate oligopolies but also as ineffective and inaccurate, notably in relation to the Enron crisis and Freddie Mac: both companies were given top ratings only days before going bankrupt (Crotty 2009; White 2010; Bolton, Freixas, and Shapiro 2012).

To return to the more obvious post-9/11 scenario, it is states that are waging wars, adopting security and surveillance legislation, and punishing or imprisoning "suspects" and other transgressors, including asylum seekers and women—and some men—who do not conform to codes of appropriate gender behavior. Conversely, it is also states that are viewed as carrying primary responsibility for failing to enforce their own laws in protecting those of their citizens persecuted by other citizens, such as women who are subjected to violence by men in the private sphere.

If it is true that states are not the only player on the global stage and indeed never have been, to suggest that their role is no longer decisive is to buy into an illusory logic of powerlessness (of the state) or, conversely, of a false sense of empowerment (of social movement actors). This is so notwithstanding the much-discussed emergence of global civil society, in particular feminist civil society, and its importance as "an answer to war" (Kaldor 2003; see also Moghadam 2005 and Cockburn 2007). Global civil society in its transnational feminist articulations is indeed important. As I have argued elsewhere and explore further later in this book, "radical and subversive transnational feminist networks" are essential if we are ever to have a hope of transforming the global system (Winter 2012a, 31). It is through those networks that we are able to create feminist envisionings of a "beyond" or "other than" the nation-state and its baggage of sovereign authority (Jones 1993; Hawthorne 2002; Kaldor 2003; Rai and Waylen 2008). The existence of global networks that sit outside or across state and interstate institutions as well as such networks' aspirations to something beyond the national do not, however, cancel out the continued decisive role that nation-states play in regulating our lives and, indeed, in regulating the very global apparatus that some of those nation-states have collectively brought into being.

We would also be naïve to underestimate the ideological weight of nationalism: the ideas of sovereignty, rights, and borders; inclusion and exclusion; shared values and shared aspirations. We struggle both against and with this weight as a force external to us but also within us as that which shapes our personal identities and our political behaviors. Much as we might like to divert to feminist idealistic ends Virginia Woolf's observation of the nonrecognition of women as participants in the national conversation, proclaiming that as women we have no country and that our country is therefore the world ([1938] 1977, 125), this assertion is always at some moment undermined by our nationalized habitus (Bourdieu 1980). That is, none of us is entirely free from the national allegiances and values inculcated within us from birth. Whether through some hegemonic assumption of "how things are," how they should be analyzed and acted upon, and what terms of reference we use to do so or through an antihegemonic assertion of "not-this-ness" from the global periphery and semiperiphery, to use Immanuel Wallerstein's (1974) terminology, we are locked within national frames even as we assert transnational values and a sense of belonging to global(ized) communities. All of us are politically, socially, culturally overdetermined by birthplaces (not chosen) and places of long-term residence (chosen or not). As feminists, we like to say that context matters. The nation is inescapably part of that context. Laudable as our being-of-the-world-and-not-the-nation aspirations may be, they remain precisely that: aspirations.

As to whether the state, this ally-and-enemy state, should be the main actor in global governance, the discussion is to a great extent moot. Nation-states are what *are*: they are still the primary agent of regulation of women's lives and of shaping women's thinking, whether we like it or not. That we mostly do *not* like it appears clear, as is demonstrated among other things by feminist political and legal appeals to superstructures such as the UN or the European Commission or the Human Rights Court or even the World Bank (which has the money), to name a few. This apparent unavoidability of nation-states does not mean that one has to resign oneself to a forced embracing of the so-called realist worldview that continues to dominate in masculinist international relations and that has been so roundly criticized by feminists such as J. Ann Tickner (1992). It is simply to recognize that this worldview continues to dominate, as 9/11 and its aftermath have reminded us so painfully, and we can change that fact only by continuing to confront it openly. We are stuck with the nation-state and its assertions of sovereign authority—as well as with varying forms and degrees of global hegemony—for a while to come.

Part of the Nation, Whether We Like It or Not

There is an encyclopedic literature, including feminist, on what nations, nation-states, and nationalism are and are not and on the effects of their construction for women (see, e.g., Yuval-Davis and Anthias

1989; Moghadam 1994; Yuval-Davis 1997; Skidmore and Lawrence 2007), and I will not rehearse here all the arguments made therein. It is nonetheless instructive to return to Frenchman Ernest Renan's lecture "Qu'est-ce qu'une nation?" (What Is a Nation?), given in 1882, because this document is such an enduringly accurate reminder of the ideologies that constitute and maintain modern nations and their nationalisms. For Renan, it is not shared language or race or religion or commerce or territory alone that make up a nation, and none of these elements is indispensable. For Renan, a nation is the combination of two elements: on the one hand, a past of shared experience or collective memory (invented or otherwise, usually both) and, on the other hand, a present will of a group of men (as he puts it) to unite (generally carefully engineered by the ruling class) and to express solidarity toward and make sacrifices for their *patrie* (fatherland). These elements underpin the modern "imagined community" (Anderson 1983) and give nations their already self-evident status that, according to Renan, was the particular "glory" of France through the French Revolution: to posit that the nation "existed by itself." But Renan also reminds us that nations maintain their coherency, their plausibility, and, most important, their unity only through practiced amnesia.

> Forgetting, I would even go so far as to say historical error, is a crucial factor in the creation of a nation, which is why progress in historical studies often constitutes a danger for [the principle of] nationality. Indeed, historical enquiry brings to light deeds of violence which took place at the origin of all political formations, even of those whose consequences have been altogether beneficial. Unity is always effected by means of brutality. (1882, my translation)

Renan nonetheless considers nations to be the "moral consciousness" created by "a great aggregate of men" and necessary for the protection of liberty and the advancement of human civilization. Today, the context of his lecture and his political allegiances to the young Third Republic—that exemplar of modern "political" nationalism (for better or for worse) founded on an anticlerical positivism and the conceit of France's "civilizing mission"—force us to take critical distance. Yet it is unwise simply to dismiss his words as unacceptable French universalist nationalism. For we are still—and clearly not only in the West—living in the imagined communities posited by Renan and are subject to and even participate in their practiced amnesia. We are still living in a world in which "our" national values are there to be celebrated and defended. This is so whether "we" are part of the US hyperpower that is profoundly and collectively convinced, as Wallerstein puts it, of the "less-ness" of the rest of the world (2002, 346)—less free, less democratic, less rights giving, less efficient, less technologically advanced, less rich; or "we" are a Chinese state, emerging as a regional superpower but not quite yet ready to economically arm wrestle the trans-Pacific hyperpower and even less to go to war against it but in the meantime asserting "our" strong, vibrant, and all-encompassing Chineseness against internal and external challengers to national identity and cohesion; or "we" are a not quite yet postwar Iraq in political, cultural, and economic disarray trying to reconfigure who "we" are or should be or have the most muscle to be and whether we have the collective strength and unity of will to successfully resist Daesh.

Renan's words have resonance for those who every year place flowers and messages at Ground Zero—now the National September 11 Memorial—in New York in a public orchestration of grieving in which personal and community sorrow are difficult to distinguish from the imaginary of a wounded nation for which a just war has been fought. They have resonance in the US street celebrations the day Barack Obama announced that Osama Bin Laden had been found and killed, celebrations that I describe elsewhere as "disturbing as much for their naïvety as for their jingoism" (Winter 2011b, 272). Were those US citizens who alternately wept or danced in the streets of New York and Washington, DC, not as conscious as Ernest Renan of the ideas of the nation's collective moral imperative, the collective political will that constitutes it, and the collective sacrifice that ensures its survival and indeed its triumph? Where more than in mourning the sacrificed in battle or in celebrating the combatants' triumph over a threat do we confirm the nation's need to exist?

"What is a nation?" we thus do well to ask still. Is it what we are told to believe it is, or is it what it does? Are we sure that we know the difference? Does that difference matter? And what is the "it" that performs the doing for which nations are then collectively responsible? Do we separate the nation from the state? From the citizen? What individual and collective responsibilities do the answers to these questions imply for feminists? The level of ownership—and level of choice in that ownership—by members of the imagined national community of what the state does in the nation's name is central to discussion of "world-shaking" events such as 9/11 and the "war on terror."

How do we reconcile our transnational feminist aspirations, including with respect to offering feminist perspectives on global governance, with our continued dependence—for well-being, for protection, or even simply for survival—on the state and the nation with which it is inextricably linked? Even for the declarative states and for subnational "nations," those oppositional or not-yet states, both discussed in chapter 1, the state is what ensures the validity of the nation on the international stage. How do we reconcile our distrust of nationalism with its political, economic, and affective centrality with our sense of who we are in the world? How do we grapple with issues of sovereignty and governance in a globalized and militarized world of networked states and their nonstate partners, where the newly aggressive demarcation of borders sits peculiarly alongside the notion that somehow these borders have become irrelevant? How do we reconstitute a workable "moral consciousness" that challenges the consciousness of the "aggregate of men" in their post-9/11 globalized and reciprocal belligerence or, alternatively, in their "realist" deal making?

The nation is what oppresses and constrains, what interferes with our transnational feminist conversations. At the same time, for those of us living or having lived under colonial or imperial domination, the nation is what we aspire to: sovereignty, freedom from an external oppressor. The nation-state is, in this context, the very guarantor of the "liberty" that Renan celebrated more than a century ago. For women from Palestine to the Philippines (or, indeed, Bangsamoro), their "nation" may fall far short of meeting their idea of a collective "moral consciousness," or their state may be not-quite-yet-existent, corrupt, dysfunctional, weak, authoritarian, financially in disarray, or any one of a number of other inadequacies. The sovereignty of that nation and the necessity of the state as a means to obtain or protect it are not, however, ideas we are willing to contest in that context. Because they are the only resource to hand. Right now. In the Philippines, for example, the left-wing anti-US catchphrase or the anti–"war on terror" catchphrase or the feminist antiviolence catchphrase is unambiguously one of national sovereignty (Winter 2011a, 2012b; Lacsamana 2012). The Philippine populace and the Philippine political class may be divided about which nation is to be protected and from what—that is, against which enemy the war needs to be waged—but sovereignty is at the core, and sovereignty is a reason for doing battle.

Even those of us living within the relatively comfortable nation-states of the so-called Global North know that our comfort and, yes, our relative freedom are protected by the nation-state, its customs, its laws, and its borders. We criticize our Western states for their despicable behavior as global hegemons waging war against chimeric enemies because the latter have the oil (or whatever else) we want and as local despots propping up elites at the expense of everyone else. We despise the nationalisms that are constructed and the patriot acts that are perpetrated against others in our names, but we know that "our" sovereignty is never really at issue. We know we are not going to be called upon to take a sovereign stand against the hegemon because we *are* the hegemon. We do not have to deal with the contradictions of sovereignty. We can fight for the sovereignty of others because ours is never in question. Hegemony has its uses, even in dissent. The Ashkenazi women from Israel's "white middle class" who founded the antioccupation movement Women in Black, for example, know this well (see chapter 5).

Yet even here, even as we despise our white male heterosexist warmonger states, we appeal to them to protect our rights and our economic security against both internal and external threats—by men, by "the market," and so on (Winter 2002b). Even we-the-hegemon are

constantly placed in situations in which nations are set off or set themselves off against each other or in a nation that sets itself against "the
world," however defined. We are constantly brought back up against
so-called realist conceptualizations of international politics: "a man's
world, a world of power and conflict in which warfare is a privileged
activity" (Tickner 1992, 25). Much of the post-9/11 literature posits that worldview as inescapable: "the hard currency in the international system remains military might," as Thomas Weiss and Rorden
Wilkinson remind us (2007, ix–x). If the realist political worldview has
been repeatedly challenged—and not just by feminists—since Tickner published her book *Gender in International Relations* in 1992,
it has rarely been challenged from *within* the political class or within
dominant international relations scholarship. Such challenges as do
exist have not fundamentally transformed the way business is done in
world politics. Quite the contrary: many have argued that Hobbesian masculine, muscular nationalism has come galloping back to fill
the post-9/11 space (see, e.g., Young 2003; Winter 2007; Weber
2014). Multilateralism and other configurations of internationalism or
transnationalism and their associated dreams of creating hope out of
despair through some sort of workable global governance have since
9/11 failed us—failed us miserably and failed us repeatedly.

The "hard currency" of international relations instead becomes
the small change of our daily lives in the nation-state: from the militarized can of soup Cynthia Enloe describes (2000, 1) to the "sexed
pistols," those small arms that have too often become the day-to-day
currency of social relations and individual power (Farr, Myrttinen,
and Schnabel 2009), to the social services and local infrastructure that
do not get funded because the state needs to privilege the activity of
warfare (Winter 2007; see also chapter 3).

International Governance

When the great powers of Europe signed the Treaties of Westphalia in
1648, recognition of state sovereignty and clear territorial borders—of
the "good fences make good neighbors" type—was key to the establishment of "world governance." The "world" then, of course, was

imagined rather differently by these modern nation-state makers in a so-called civilized Christian Europe free of the lions, dragons, heathens, and savages that were thought to reside beyond its borders.[2] More than three and a half centuries later, however, questions of sovereignty and borders and of the unknowns (known or unknown), undesirables, and threats beyond those borders are still central to how "the world" organizes its governance. The main difference is that "the (known) world" is much bigger now. It has developed the financial, industrial, and technological means not only to assert and expand hegemony but also to contest it vocally, transnationally, and often violently. Those means also give "the world" the power to destroy itself or large chunks of itself that matter at varying levels and to do so in ways that are not easily foreseeable and difficult to prevent. As 9/11 brought home most decidedly, and as numerous other terrorist attacks in various parts of the world have shown since 9/11, many of those means have become available to transnationally networked nonstate actors who are both *beyond* and *within* (as well as both known and unknown, to pursue the Rumsfeldian imagery). In 2015 alone, attacks by Boko Haram, now affiliated to Daesh, in Nigeria and Chad and Daesh's expansion beyond Syria and Iraq to attack Turkey, Lebanon, and France remind us that governing "the world" has become a seemingly impossible job.

Seventeenth-century Europe's problem, as it expanded its power when the Westphalian nation-states appropriated large chunks of the

2. Medieval and Renaissance European maps and globes of "the world" contain references to or drawings of mythical, dangerous, or unfamiliar beasts (such as dragons, lions, elephants, and snakes) placed on areas of terra incognita, some of them quite close to western Europe. The reference to "dragons" on the famous Lenox Globe of the early sixteenth century ("Hic sunt dracones") is the only written reference, and even there map historians believe that "dragons" is a mistranslation of "Dragoians," a reputedly cannibalistic people from Sumatra (Blake 1999). They have nonetheless become a frequent literary and cultural reference and the default joke for various "idiots' maps" of the world such as "the World according to America" maps of the Reagan and Bush II eras.

unknown and beyond to add to their own political and economic might, was that those territories it colonized also appropriated for themselves precisely the logic and the political and military tools of their colonizers. They asserted their national sovereignty and were prepared to fight for it. In successfully doing so, they became rather less *unknown* and *beyond* (no longer dragons) but not entirely *within* and *known* either (still decidedly heathens). The assertion of a "not-this-ness" while still using these tools of sovereignty and statehood as well as, indeed, modern capitalism and warfare for the most part continues the enterprise of othering-yet-belonging but does so from the place of the othered. We are Other because we want to be (and because we don't want to be like you), yet we assert the right to belong in your world on our terms, on equal footing. These claims for ever greater numbers of national seats at the international table and a voice in international deliberations, in a context of global capitalism where the *others beyond* also claim their participation as *us here*, demanding them through the use of arms if necessary, result in a global situation requiring careful management, even requiring it with some urgency, as Sassen (2002) suggests.

So, to return to the questions posed at the beginning of this chapter: What exactly does "global governance" mean after 9/11? And is that meaning really different from before 9/11? An oft-cited definition comes from US political scientist James Rosenau, who explained global governance in our times as "a more encompassing phenomenon than government," including "activities backed by shared goals that may or may not derive from legal and formally prescribed responsibilities" (1992, 4). Such definitions are not entirely satisfactory because they are at once vague and beg the question of how "shared goals" are arrived at and who decides on them. Writing a few years later but still half a decade before 9/11, Rosenau described "global governance in the twenty-first century" as characterized by the "search for order in disorder, for coherence in contradiction, and for continuity in change" as well as the experience of "hope embedded in despair" (1995, 13). These words ring in retrospect as prophetic of 9/11 and its depressing aftermath. Returning to the original Greek from which the word *governance* derives, as does the word *gouvernail* (rudder) in French, Rosenau placed the emphasis less on who commands and more on "the process whereby an organization or society steers itself, and the dynamics of communication and control are central to that process" (1995, 14). The question remains, however, how governance and government might differ. Even if one accepts that there are a range of political and civil society actors who contribute to steering the world, in order to steer one must nonetheless first have control of the rudder.

In contemporary international relations terms, "governance" remains closely associated with government: it is understood as a set of international rules for public life in a world that is networked not only internationally but also transnationally, primarily through global capitalism. Other networks clearly exist: transnational political formations, grassroots social and protest movements of various sorts, international trade union movements, human rights organizations, international religious communities or ethnic communities, and, of course, terrorist networks. These nongovernmental, noncorporate networks are still not, however, generally recognized as core actors in global governance, notwithstanding the NGOization of civil society—that is, civil society's increased levels of formal structuring, institutional affiliation, and institutional funding. Global governance remains largely understood in masculinist international relations and, indeed, by government and corporate leaders as how transnational capitalism and nation-statehood coexist and organize the world so that status quos are preserved without deleterious impacts on the people who matter, while keeping people who matter somewhat less or do not matter at all contained. This means either placating or curbing the power of those who may present a threat to the status quo, which is achieved by co-optation or combat. It means keeping sufficiently docile those who matter only as instruments of the preservation of global capitalism and state hegemony through their roles as workers, servicers of workers, and reproducers of workers so that they do not join the category of people who constitute a threat. And it means ensuring that people who do not matter at all—nonworkers, nonservicers, and nonreproducers who have no money and live on the periphery of the periphery—remain sufficiently marginalized, controlled, and dispersed so that they cannot conceivably have access to any sort of means that might make them a recognizable group, let alone any sort of threat.

Clearly, such an outline of global governance would not appear in any international relations textbook. But as Susan George ironically points out in her book *The Lugano Report* (1999), global governance today is largely about strategies for preserving global capitalism and the political hegemonies that accompany it in the twenty-first century. In this fictitious report by a fictitious working party to a fictitious commission, George sets out a number of population-reduction strategies that will limit world overcrowding and thus ease tensions within the capitalist system, notably through containing the rage of the poor. Among these strategies is internal warfare ("kill one another"), which also nicely helps the arms trade, a key factor in economic growth: "the most efficient way to increase GNP [gross national product] rapidly is probably to wage war" (George 1999, 8). Getting the bothersome to kill each other needs some psychological preconditioning, which involves careful encouragement of identity politics and hostility to others who do not share that identity:

> Discrimination and oppression targeting particular groups strengthen their sense of self-identity and should, for that reason, be discreetly encouraged. . . . Nor should one neglect a relatively recent force we may call "e-mail," "remittance" or "diaspora chauvinists." Emigré populations frequently possess greater material resources than their former compatriots. They may also harbour guilt feelings at not being in the thick of the nationalist or religious fray "at home" and compensate by promoting extremist strategies from afar. . . . It is worth encouraging them so long as they confine their activities strictly to their former homelands and do not interfere in the politics of their host countries. (93–94)

That "strategy" backfired in September 2001; it has nonetheless continued to be pursued energetically since then. George cites Peace Research Institute Oslo studies from the 1990s that show a high number of wars during that decade (ninety-eight from 1990 to 1996), mostly civil wars. The institute further noted that such wars occur primarily in poor countries where people are still largely dependent on a rural economy, where natural resources are under pressure, where the government is not entirely authoritarian but "semidemocratic," where external debt is high and export income is low or falling, and where International Monetary Fund intervention is vigorous (George 1999, 94–95). More recently, the Department of Peace and Conflict Research at Uppsala University (n.d.) points to twenty-eight ongoing civil conflicts and nine internationalized conflicts for the year 2010 alone.

George's satirical work shows the links between guns and money that I discuss in chapter 4. What George's satire also shows, however, is that "governance" is necessarily tied to both economic and political hegemony. The effective management of "governance" in the interest of preserving the hegemonic status quo depends for its very lifeblood on the ongoing existence of nationalisms of various kinds. Without nationalism, internationalism cannot exist. Without national and international legislative apparatuses to enable it, global capitalism cannot conduct its affairs efficiently. Without states to keep citizens in check, the social regulation necessary to "the preservation of capitalism in the twenty-first century" cannot happen. Without wars, capitalist oligopolic growth is severely limited, even curtailed. Even ultraconsumerism has its limits. Only wars are potentially endless.

Responsibility to Protect?

"Nations," then, are an abstraction, notwithstanding their very material state apparatus and well-policed borders and notwithstanding the extensive material damage done by wars in their name. The essence of a nation, as "existing in itself" (Renan), and its rationale for that existence, whether hegemonic (from the top down) or resistant (up from below), are ideas and no more a unique and inevitable reality than are capitalism or wars. They are ideas produced by men in the interest of the preservation of male dominance (a point George misses), even if some women have subsequently espoused them. All of those battles over sovereignty in the seventeenth century were discussions among men about men's interests, and such battles remain primarily so now. Women were not then considered equal members of the nation and indeed had little if anything to gain by becoming so. They consequently were not considered part of the international conversation on world governance (which is what Woolf meant in 1938). Global governance, whether based on a contest of muscle or on the negotiation of treaties—usually following a contest of muscle—is still considered men's business, even if it is sometimes conducted by "exceptional" women.

Certainly, problems in global governance are seen as affecting women. For example, Sassen (2002) points out in her contribution to the volume *Understanding September 11*, one of the wake-of-9/11 anthologies cited at the beginning of this chapter, that two post-9/11 "governance hotspots [*sic*]" and contextual contributory factors to the 9/11 attacks—the growing debt of Global South states and the "world immigration regime"—have significant deleterious impacts on women. Women bear the social burden of debt and are the majority of those trafficked from South to North. In analyzing the political economy of violence against women, Jacqui True deploys the concept of hegemonic masculinity used by R. W. Connell to paint a picture of a transnationalized corporate and militarized planet that depends on the continued hegemonic construction of reason, mobility, and power—control of the rudder, if you will—as male, while their absence is constructed as female (2012, chap. 3; see also Connell 1987). Like Cynthia Enloe (2000, 2004, 2010), True stresses that violence against women in times of war is not peculiar to the act of war but part of a broader political economy in which violence against women is a constant (2012, chap. 7; see also Winter 2012a).

Women are thus if not centrally present then at least somewhat present in academic conversations about post-9/11 governance, but they are present as those undergoing the effects of bad governance and in need of protection therefrom. In the international relations/ human rights conversation, that protection takes the form of the application of the R2P doctrine. Women are not seen as contributors to governance, whether good or bad—at least, not collectively. In fact, much has been made of the fact that they are excluded from global conversations about governance. Much of the transnational feminist and institutional conversation about that exclusion in a post-9/11 world centers around the application—or, rather, nonapplication—of UN Security Council Resolution 1325 on Women, Peace, and Security, which sets out guidelines for the involvement of women in negotiations and strategies around postconflict rebuilding (see chapter 3).

Yet even this conversation is not new. I return, again, to Virginia Woolf's assertion in *Three Guineas* ([1938] 1977) that as a woman she "[had] no country" and "want[ed] no country" (125), which has been so inspirational for feminist transnationalism, whatever feminists' individual or collective concerns about Woolf's class attitudes may be. That assertion was made precisely within the context of a discussion of why "the educated man's daughter," an "outsider" from the society created by men to serve men, is indifferent to the question of persuading her brothers to fight for their country:

> "'Our country,'" she will say, "throughout the greater part of its history has treated me as a slave; it has denied me education or any share in its possessions. 'Our' country still ceases to be mine if I marry a foreigner. 'Our' country denies me the means of protecting myself, forces me to pay others a very large sum annually to protect me, and is so little able, even so, to protect me that Air Raid precautions are written on the wall. Therefore if you insist upon fighting to protect me, or 'our' country, let it be understood, soberly and rationally between us, that you are fighting to gratify a sex instinct which I cannot share; to procure benefits which I have not shared and probably will not share; but not to gratify my instincts, or to protect either myself or my country. For," the outsider will say, "in fact, as a woman, I have no country. As a woman I want no country. As a woman my country is the whole world." (125)

Woolf wrote those words as Europe teetered on the edge of World War II. Almost eight decades and innumerable wars later, women, even when dragged into conversations about national sovereignty, are not participants in its creation, nor are they serious participants in conversations about global governance and prevention of war. Because women still do not matter in a masculinist world where guns and money, like so many measures of penis length or bicep thickness, are the "hard currency" (lewd inferences unfortunate but apt) of international governance. It is not simply that possession of guns and money decide *outcomes* of the game (to use another frame popular within realist international relations theory); they *are* the game.

Even international organizations, those entities conceptualized in the wake of the Great War with the failed League of Nations and concretized after World War II with the UN, are conglomerations of nation-states. Their power is limited by the sovereignty of their state members and by the degree to which those members agree or disagree and are prepared to draw their guns or withdraw their money to press home the point. Certainly, those organizations as well as the human rights and supposedly post-Westphalian governance regimes they ushered in were conceptualized not only to ensure a balance of powers, so that the game did not become again as nasty as it did in Shoah-shattered Europe or in the "second front" of East and Southeast Asia (also the "second front" after 9/11), but also to stand as an international "welfare safety net," to offer protections to populations that had become collective subnational or transnational victims when the state could not or would not protect them. Those human rights and governance regimes have been the extranational life raft to which women and some categories of men denied the protection of the national ship have clung to avoid drowning.

In practice, however, even if the UN constitutes a supranational "moral consciousness" where the national one is lacking, there is no international mandate that trumps the national one. In the end, a state—whether constitutive or declarative, whether UN member or observer, whether large and hegemonic or miniscule and practically powerless in geopolitical terms—can still say no to the rights of women living under its laws and can do so with little fear of sanction. This is even the case with the semisupranational entity the EU because all enabling mechanisms that empower the EU to act as the EU are first decided upon by its state members. Nation-state sovereignty still takes paramount importance, as the United Kingdom's frequently isolationist position, the huge variations in asylum procedures from one member state to another, the Syrian refugee crisis, and the Eurozone crisis since 2011 have eloquently demonstrated.

The political power and indeed financial capacity of human rights or development agencies of organizations such as the EU and the UN to counteract or attenuate the impacts of warmongering or global capitalist development or the more everyday "states of emergency" in which women live are thus severely limited. Even these organizations' political will to do so has been criticized, with Argentinean activist and Nobel Peace laureate Adolfo Perez Esquivel suggesting in an interview in 2004 that the UN should be renamed the "Disunited Nations" because it has become completely subjugated to Washington's interests (Esquivel 2004). Similarly, Susan George, writing prior to 9/11, suggested in the satirical *Lugano Report* that the UN exists only to give smaller, less-powerful nations the illusion that they actually have a say in running world affairs (1999, 21). These commentaries about the UN's ineffectualness are ironic in light of the "human rights" (in particular "women's human rights"), "human security," and "responsibility to protect" discourses that have abounded in a post-9/11 context.

I close this chapter on a brief discussion of R2P, which, along with the security talk that I discuss in the next chapter, has had both material and discursive impacts, mobilizing in particular women's rights, security, and dignity as sometimes moral imperatives but more often as a moral veneer to "war talk" (Roy 2003), depending on the context in which they are discussed and by whom. Some see R2P as a human rights imperative (Badescu 2010; Serrano and Weiss 2013; Bellamy 2014), whereas others see it as a new justification for meddling in the affairs of sovereign states (Cunliffe 2012) or otherwise as a counterproductive way to go about humanitarian intervention (Hehir 2012).

The R2P doctrine was elaborated in the Outcomes Document of the UN World Summit in 2005 (A/RES/60/1, UN General Assembly 2005b). That document focused on four areas in which multilateral solutions to ongoing problems were needed: development, peace and collective security, human rights, and the rule of law. The R2P statement is contained in the "Peace and Collective Security" section, under the subhead "Responsibility to Protect Populations from Genocide, War Crimes, Ethnic Cleansing, and Crimes against Humanity." Paragraphs 138 to 140 under that heading contain the seeds of the R2P doctrine. Most importantly for my discussion of international governance, paragraph 139 provides for international intervention authorized by the UN Security Council when a state is "manifestly failing" to protect its citizens from the four crimes and violations specified in the subhead. The R2P doctrine was further formalized and developed in a report of some thirty pages by UN secretary-general Ban Ki-Moon in January 2009 (A/63/677, UN General Assembly 2009). In this report, Ban discussed the "three pillars" of R2P: the state's protection responsibilities; international assistance and capacity building; and timely and decisive response. That same year, eight regional and international NGOs founded the International Coalition for the Responsibility to Protect to "strengthen normative consensus for RtoP, further the understanding of the norm, push for strengthened capacities to prevent and halt genocide, war crimes, ethnic cleansing and crimes against humanity and mobilize NGOs to push for action to save lives in RtoP country-specific situations."[3]

The International Coalition now has close to one hundred members, some of them quasi-institutional, such as regional United Nations Associations and the Kofi Annan International Peacekeeping Training Centre, but many of them national or regional peace or human rights organizations. NGO attitudes to R2P have shown a range of views similar to those expressed in the scholarly literature, with some, such as the International Coalition and its members, being enthusiastic proponents of it, but others, such as UN watchdog Global Policy Forum, being far more skeptical, arguing that the

3. See the coalition website at http://www.responsibilitytoprotect.org/index .php/about-coalition (accessed Nov. 20, 2015).

concept of R2P is "irremediably flawed and provides no real solution to prevent and stop gross human rights violations" (Pingeot and Obenland 2014, 3).

R2P almost did not make it into the Outcomes Document (UN General Assembly 2005b), and, according to a former senior UN official, ensuring that its three paragraphs remained in the document took a great deal of diplomatic effort in which Canada, Australia, and Bangladesh played key roles.[4] The doctrine may, however, remain inapplicable because the five powerful permanent members of the Security Council—the United States, France, the United Kingdom, China, and Russia—play the crucial role in deciding whether interventions should go ahead or not and in what form. Each of these states has the power of veto even when all of the other Security Council members vote for an action, and each has exercised this power more than once. China and Russia, for example, have consistently vetoed resolutions that would have enabled UN intervention in Syria in various forms, including sanctions and referral to the International Criminal Court, thus paralyzing the Security Council for many years in the face of the Syrian civil war.

Although UN General Assembly Resolution 377A (1950)—the "Uniting for Peace" Resolution—technically provided a means for states concerned about the maintenance of international peace and security to override the Security Council veto, it has not been invoked in the case of any direct international intervention in Syria, no more than R2P has. As argued by former UN deputy legal counsel Larry Johnson (2014), neither R2P nor Resolution 377A enables override of Article 2(4) of the UN Charter, which states that "all Members shall refrain in their international relations from the threat or use of force against the territorial integrity or political independence of any state, or in any other manner inconsistent with the Purposes of the United

4. Edward Mortimer, reply to a question in the closing plenary of the annual conference of the Academic Council of the UN System, Kadir Has University, Istanbul, June 21, 2014, from notes I took during the plenary session.

Nations."[5] In other words, neither provision legally permits UN-sanctioned intervention that has nothing to do with maintenance of international security or legitimate self-defense. There is no unambiguous legal provision enabling UN member states to intervene in other states solely for the purpose of averting a human rights catastrophe within that state. Since the Daesh attacks of 2014 and particularly of 2015, the "international security" motive presents more clearly. But as a member of the EU diplomatic mission to Syria told me in late 2013, the Syrian catastrophe had already attained such dimensions by then that the future outlook was very, very bleak, with any future intervention probably being of the wrong sort and definitely coming too late.

The other concern with R2P is, conversely and perhaps paradoxically, its potential to undermine national sovereignty, particularly in providing a UN mandate for military intervention, supported by the world's most powerful nations, against other, weaker, poorer nations (Cunliffe 2012). As Omar Dahbour puts it within the context of a discussion on the advancement of human rights, "If human rights are to have legitimacy—in other words, to become positive law within countries—they must be institutionalized by peoples themselves, not imposed by the international community" (2007, 117). Such arguments do, however, lead us into a circular problem, which Dahbour himself acknowledges to some extent. If interventions occur, it is often because human rights activists, inside and outside the site of intervention, regard the state in that site as untrustworthy in that it is unable or unwilling to codify human rights and ensure their application. In the process of humanitarian intervention, however, what may start as "capacity building" often becomes a politicized process in which local needs are subordinated to other power objectives. Which leaves us with a human rights catch-22.

The R2P doctrine has been increasingly discussed in a range of institutional, civil society, and academic fora on conflict, peace, and

5. Charter of the United Nations, at http://www.un.org/en/documents/char ter/chapter1.shtml (accessed Nov. 20, 2015).

human rights, notably in the context of the Arab uprisings, the Gaza crisis, and ongoing instability in Iraq and Syria. These discussions have focused on the many problems associated with R2P as well as on its implications (positive or negative) for the sovereignty of states deemed to be failed or failing, usually as a result of civil conflict. For example, R2P was threaded through plenary discussions at two international conferences on human rights held at Kadir Has University in Istanbul in June 2014. The first was a human rights conference jointly organized by the International Studies Association, the American Political Science Association, and the International Political Science Association, and the second was the annual conference of the Academic Council of the UN System, which also publishes the journal *Global Governance.*

Tellingly, at a practitioner roundtable that ended the first conference, Matthew Preston from the UK Foreign and Commonwealth Office argued that recent changes within the UN were largely cosmetic and that R2P was not a motivator for states in making decisions within the UN. Similarly, at the closing plenary of the second conference, practitioner-turned-academic Edward Mortimer, formerly director of communications in the Executive Office of the Secretary-General at the UN, noted that if sovereignty ideally implies responsibility, in reality states act in their own interest. Those with the power to intervene don't do so, largely because of domestic priorities, and those targeted for intervention resent international meddling in their affairs and thus resist change.[6] Self-interest and the desire to maintain power clearly trump any multilateral or altruistic motivation; in other words, assertion of state sovereignty once against trumps cooperation in global governance.

The inadequacy, tardiness, or even lack of international intervention—or intervention that only serves to worsen the situation—in pre-9/11 crises such as those in Bosnia and Rwanda in the 1990s and the controversy over the NATO intervention in Kosovo in 1999 were

6. From notes I took at the conference plenaries.

major triggers for the development of the R2P doctrine and of the "human security" doctrine that preceded it. It is, however, far from certain that the existence of an R2P doctrine in 1992 or 1994 would have made any difference. Aidan Hehir (2012) has argued that R2P has been elaborated within the existing politics and structures of the UN and that as such it is an ineffectual and indeed counterproductive framework for humanitarian intervention. Yet many others, such as Abiodun Williams, president of the Hague Institute for Global Justice, who also spoke at the conference in Istanbul, assert the importance of R2P as an instrument of conflict prevention and diplomatic intervention to get regimes to change their behavior, in contrast to military intervention used to change the regime.

The question remains how such diplomatic intervention might be effective or even happen, given the issue of veto power, which blocked any UN Security Council nonmilitary initiatives to put pressure on the Assad regime in Syria. The question similarly remains regarding individual states' ability to bring "soft power" to bear in interventions that bypass the Security Council: the failure of Turkey's "soft-power" strategy in the face of the Syrian conflict comes to mind. The most recent interventions that align with the R2P doctrine remain unilaterally decided, as demonstrated by targeted US air strikes in Iraq ordered by President Obama on August 8, 2014, with the aim of both combating Daesh and providing humanitarian and evacuation assistance to trapped Yazidi Christians. Most recently, the logic of R2P has shifted to the logic of war, which the French state has declared on Daesh (see chapter 7).

At this point in time, then, R2P appears to be very much a tango danced solo, if danced at all, and when it is, it is mostly to the music of "security," a question to which I now turn in relation to women.

3

Are We Saved Yet?

Women's Rights and the Discourse of Securitization

The harnessing of women's rights to nationalist or imperialist ends is not new: Third Republic France and Kemalist Turkey are oft-cited examples in the late nineteenth and early twentieth centuries, respectively. Similarly, "women's rights" have been co-opted as a divide-and-conquer strategy in the name of imperialist "civilizing missions" of various sorts. Feminist research has long critiqued the moral panic that is created around the violation of othered women who need to be rescued from othered men, which becomes the morally palatable justification for various forms of muscular "intervention." It has similarly critiqued imposition on "our" women of "the cross-cultural burden of being viewed as the repositories of (male-defined) morality" (Morgan 1989, 195; see also Enloe 1990; Morgan 2001; Winter 2008). No doubt the most famous critique of this masculinist imperial morality is encapsulated in Gayatri Spivak's image of "white men . . . saving brown women from brown men" (1988, 297–98). I put aside here the many subsequent criticisms of Spivak's essay "Can the Subaltern Speak?," in which this phrase appears, such as her almost exclusive referencing of French male poststructuralists (with a particular preference for Derrida) rather than feminists of any epistemological persuasion or national background (with the exception of Elizabeth Fox-Genovese). I share these criticisms, but the image is still nonetheless powerful and has become a metaphor for imperialist co-optation of "women's rights" ever since.

Since 9/11, state rhetoric on women's rights has been indelibly imprinted with security talk. The latter was already present in imperialist or nationalistic rhetoric before 9/11, and the impact of militarization on women's lives and on women's roles within militarization had been discussed, even at some length, in feminist scholarship for some decades (e.g., Enloe 1983; Morgan 1989; R. Grant 1992; Tickner 1992). "Women's security" was even on the international institutional radar prior to 9/11: UN Security Council Resolution 1325 on Women, Peace, and Security, which I discuss further later in this chapter, was adopted in 2000. Yet it was after 9/11 that the amalgamated "womensrightsandsecurity" or sometimes "womensrightssecurityanddignity" was firmly and widely taken up as a discursive tool in masculinist international relations. Post-9/11 polarization has further separated the world's women into the "already saved" and the "needing to be saved."

In fact, nowhere has the opportunism of post-9/11 politics appeared so clearly as in relation to women. Women's rights have been under international scrutiny, it seems, as never before. As never before, they have been harnessed to various nationalist and imperialist causes under the guise of a politics of rescue and a discourse of securitization, where *human security* and *R2P* are the new buzzwords in international governance. The invocation of "women's rights" as a moral justification for the incursion of the world's biggest (or only) superpower and its allies into Muslim countries has appeared as a fistful of crumbs disingenuously scattered in the path of women's and human rights advocates. Women living in the West were told that it was for the good of the women of Afghanistan and Iraq that war was waged on those countries. We were told that the rights Western women ostensibly already enjoyed had now become accessible for women there. We continue to be told that our governments are doing everything they can to work with the women of Afghanistan, Iraq, and elsewhere to ensure that they participate fully, in a climate free from violence, in rebuilding their societies. We are told that we, as women, have cause to be concerned for Afghan and Iraqi women, but at the same time we also have cause to feel safe ourselves because we are being looked after. Women elsewhere have cause to fear, but we do not—at least, not from our own governments. And even elsewhere, we are told, things are on the mend because "we" have intervened. The US DoS told us in 2003,

"As in Afghanistan, the United States Government is prepared to help Iraqis with the priorities and projects that they identify as the best way to achieve their goals. We will continue to meet with Iraqi women and exchange ideas about their path forward." This version of postwar reconstruction for Iraqi women was at variance with that advanced by Human Rights Watch: "The failure of the occupying power to protect women and girls from violence, and redress it when it occurs, has both immediate and long-term negative implications for the safety of women and girls and for their participation in post-war life in Iraq" (2003, 1).

In fact, when we are confronted with the evidence of women's experience, the rescue operation would appear to be a version of simulacra à la Jean Baudrillard (1981, 1991): all show and no substance in a post-9/11 list media-ted hyperreality, in which the spectacle of events precedes, shapes, and even replaces the events themselves. The real lack of "security" is not only in the much publicized areas of freedom from violence in the day to day. It also has to do with lack of access to services or shelter, particularly for women who cannot afford to pay the bribes that are now a routine feature of Afghan and Iraqi public life—more so, some recent reports suggest, than prior to the 2001 and 2003 invasions. In the face of such overwhelming evidence to the contrary, it is astounding that the rescue fiction has been so successful. It has been successful both in lulling many Western—and even some non-Western—women into a false sense of, er, security and in recasting women's rights within neocolonial and nationalist frames.

Which is why 9/11 is Everywoman's story. We are living, whether we seek to or not, on one or other side of the "human security" divide.

My primary focus in this chapter, however, is not on augmenting the plethora of documentation on what is wrong with the scenario for women in Afghanistan and Iraq, although I revisit that subject briefly in order to frame the subsequent discussion.[1] My focus is rather

1. See, for example, Hawthorne and Winter 2002; Human Rights Watch 2003; Young 2003; Finlay 2006; Winter 2006b; Eisenstein 2007; Riley, Mohanty, and Pratt 2008; Sökmen 2008; Enloe 2010; Lasky n.d.

to ask—as states and the UN discursively mobilize "womensright-sandsecurity," including via Resolution 1325 and R2P—first, how those rights and security are being defined in nonconflict zones and, second, what other aspects of women's rights and security are being overlooked or even hampered. The obsession with security, global governance, and rescuing (Muslim) women has deflected attention from other serious abuses of women living outside 9/11 hot spots but nonetheless within precarious situations of poverty, migration, civil conflict, widespread male violence, and so on. Their situation, like those of so many women under the post-9/11 spotlight, predates the 9/11 attacks and the "war on terror" but has been exacerbated by a post-9/11 global situation in which the militarization of society has become normalized in both "rogue" or "failed" states and functioning democracies that hold themselves up as the exemplar for others. As Fatima Mernissi put it in 2009, "In Tehran, if you do not wear a chador, a policeman will call you to order. In the West, the terror is more immaterial. . . . Western women believe that their system is good for women. As they have some advantages, they do not see the rest." What, then, are the forms taken by the "immaterial terror" that women face in a post-9/11 world? Are they new? Or are we just experiencing new iterations of the same old story?

The Rhetoric and Reality of Rescue

Rescuing Iraqi and Afghan citizens in general and female citizens in particular was a discourse developed to help make the "war on terror" more palatable. Yet both countries had been war zones or militarized zones for roughly a quarter of a century already, whether through the politics of an internal oppressor or owing to an external invader or interstate conflicts. The US invasions of 2001 and 2003, respectively, thus did not take place in countries already at peace, nor was it the first time that the United States had intervened there, overtly or covertly. Although that lack of peace or lack of democracy had been the moral justification for military intervention, the United States and some of its allies had nonetheless contributed, at least in part, to creating that situation in the first place, either in alliance with or in opposition to local despots.

The "war on terror" coalition that was supposedly going to "save" Afghan women had not been particularly concerned with the plight of the latter under the Taliban prior to the 9/11 attacks, although the Clinton administration had been pursuing antiterrorism initiatives since the first World Trade Center bombing in 1993, and the CIA set up the so-called Bin Laden Issue Station in 1996. The treatment of Afghan women by the Taliban, who had been in power for five years prior to 9/11, has been well documented (e.g., in Moghadam 2002). Alongside the more predictable prohibitions on education, adultery, reproductive rights, or showing any part of their bodies other than their eyes in public, women were forbidden to laugh, make a noise while walking, or gather together for any recreational purpose, including religious, without male chaperones.[2] According to the Revolutionary Association of Women of Afghanistan, many of these measures had already been introduced by the Rabbani–Massoud government, which had emerged victorious from the power struggle that followed the withdrawal of the Soviets in 1989, and the report prepared by the UN special rapporteur on human rights in 1989 does indeed document some of these measures (UN General Assembly 1994).[3]

Even if one takes the professed US concern for Afghan women in 2001 at face value, there is scant evidence that the Western intervention has succeeded in its supposed aim of delivering Afghan women from harm. Indeed, in some respects Afghan women's situation is arguably worse now than it was under Soviet occupation (Delphy 2002; Moghadam 2002; Winter 2002b, 2006b; Khan 2008; Joya 2009). Some measures in favor of women—such as reestablishment of

---

2. The Revolutionary Association of Women of Afghanistan maintains on its website a list of some of the main prohibitions inflicted on women during Taliban rule, at http://www.rawa.org/rules.htm (accessed Aug. 2, 2013).

3. See ibid.

schools, parliamentary quotas, and the establishment of the Afghan Independent Human Rights Commission in June 2002—provided for under the terms of the Bonn Agreement of December 2001 on the reconstruction of the Afghan state—have done nothing to stem various forms of violence against women, which can only be characterized as endemic (Amnesty International 2011; Human Rights Watch 2013).[4] According to Human Rights Watch's submission to the UN Committee on the Elimination of Discrimination against Women in 2013 on the occasion of the Afghan government's combined initial and second reports to this committee, the Afghan government's Law on the Elimination of Violence against Women of 2009 has remained largely an unfulfilled promise because the government has done a very poor job of enforcing it. Enforcement of the law has been hampered not only by a lack of leadership and political will but also by practical problems that the government failed to take adequate measures to address (Human Rights Watch 2013; see also Medica Mondiale 2013).

The violence against the women of Afghanistan in the years following the war was so extreme that it led to self-harm behavior, such as much-publicized self-immolations (Medica Mondiale 2007).

In the tenth anniversary year of 9/11 and the "war on terror," an expert poll conducted by Thomson Reuters' TrustLaw Foundation voted Afghanistan the most dangerous country in the world for women (TrustLaw 2011). The report cited statistics that had changed little over the previous decade: one of the highest rates of maternal mortality in the world; 70–80 percent of girls and young women (half of them minors) being forced into marriage; and women's illiteracy officially remaining at 87 percent (with only some 5 percent finishing high school, according to the UNDP's *Human Development Report*

4. The full name of the Bonn Agreement is "Agreement on Provisional Arrangements in Afghanistan Pending the Re-establishment of Permanent Government Institutions." The full text of the agreement can be found via the UN website at http://peacemaker.un.org/afghanistan-bonnagreement2001 (accessed July 14, 2013).

for 2013). Carol Mann (2010, 2012) argues that the lack of progress is in part attributable to aid agencies' insensitivity to local customs and the situation of women within local cultures, so that well-meaning initiatives are presented in ways that are unlikely to meet with local uptake. Mann echoes a common critique of international aid and empowerment programs: that they are "developed thousands of miles away . . . and are incongruent with the lived experience of [local] women" (2012, 135). She also, however, takes to task local authorities for the lack of resources committed to combating "customary" and other violence against women, which is so entrenched as to make combating it extraordinarily difficult (2012, 136–38).

Less widely discussed are the economic difficulties Afghan women face in their day-to-day lives. In the wake of the war in 2001, women were confronted with multiple challenges, as are women everywhere in postconflict situations. As Cynthia Enloe reminds us, "Wars do not end abruptly. Postwar is an era that can last a very long time" (2010, 124). Enloe makes this statement within the context of a discussion of new understandings that women who have experienced war bring to their postwar behavior as social and political actors, but "postwar" is also a long, hard road paved with the sharp stones of deprivation. As I noted in 2002, Afghan women attending a women's conference held prior to the Loya Jirga in 2002 (a political meeting to appoint a caretaker government) spoke of many needs. Notwithstanding the endemic problem of violence against women, ending that violence was not, at that time, at the top of the women's lists, but rather access to clean water, training to enable them to earn money, safe streets and schools for their children, hospitals for the ill and maimed (Winter 2002a, 464–69). Their needs were material and economic. This is not to say that violence against women was not of concern to them, but in the West's preoccupation with burqas and rapes the socioeconomic violence of the day to day is often forgotten. In that postwar era "that can last a very long time," it is women who are cleaning up the mess and taking primary responsibility for "human security."

At the time of the invasion in 2001, Afghanistan was one of the world's poorest countries and has remained so since then (UNDP

2002, 2015): it sits just below Senegal and three places lower than Djibouti in the UNDP *Human Development Report* for 2015. Wealth distribution is predictably unequal and concentrated among the elites of Kabul. There is also widespread corruption, which the intervention and its aftermath have done nothing to address. If anything, corruption has worsened, with bribery being endemic, according to a report by the UN Office on Drugs and Crime (UNODC) (UNODC and Islamic Republic of Afghanistan High Office of Oversight and Anti-Corruption 2012). In Afghanistan, it extends, unfortunately, to officials' pocketing of aid, a familiar story in the world of "development." One such story was recounted to me in 2010 by one of the people who had worked to ensure payment of aid money. It concerned money donated by the government of a western European country to fund a crèche (day care) project so that Afghan women, many of whom are now the sole breadwinner for their households, could work and study. According to my source, the money ended up lining the pockets of the family of a well-known feminist close to the current regime. Such stories are troubling for feminists, who often work in networks parallel to the state and who are obliged to function on trust when detailed background knowledge is lacking.

The high levels of administrative corruption hit women particularly hard. According to the UNODC, working in partnership with the Afghan High Office of Oversight and Anti-Corruption, corruption is "seen by Afghans as one of the most urgent challenges facing their country," yet at the same time "it seems to be increasingly embedded in social practices" (2012, 5). The report also notes a higher rate (although not a higher amount) of bribe paying by women, who have a greater call on public services such as health, education, and utilities (8).

Regarding Iraq, as Nadie al-Ali writes, the 1980–88 Iran–Iraq War, which commenced shortly after Saddam Hussein's rise to power in 1979 (the same year as the Khomeinist revolution in Iran), involved a "shift in rhetoric and government policies vis-à-vis women and gender relations" (2007, 168). In an oft-repeated scenario in militarized societies, Iraqi women increasingly became constructed as the guardians of national honor, "the producers of loyal Iraqi citizens and future fighters. Their bodies became progressively the site of nationalist policies and battles," with attendant restrictions on personal and reproductive freedoms (al-Ali 2007, 168). The Gulf War in 1991 added devastation to this militarization: estimates of civilian deaths from the war were as high as 200,000, and "the air campaign destroyed almost the entire infrastructure of the country" (al-Ali 2007, 177). Far from improving this situation, the US invasion in 2003 made it worse. The war and subsequent occupation have caused a level of destabilization and social disaggregation that, according to al-Ali, were not experienced at the time of the Gulf War (2007, 178–80). Indeed, she suggested in 2005 that women could well turn out to be the "biggest losers" from the later war (739).

Other studies published before and since al-Ali's have proven her right: women in Iraq have become more, not less, prey to the agitation of conservative Islamists (Human Rights Watch 2003; Enloe 2010; Lasky n.d.). In 2009, a report joint-authored by Oxfam and its Iraqi partner organization al-Amal found that on all measures of safety and security—including violence both inside and outside the home (55 percent of respondents); lack of access to humanitarian aid (33 percent); the availability of shelter, health care, sanitation, and potable water (more than 50 percent); electricity and schooling for their children (40 percent)—women reported that conditions had worsened for them since 2003 and had either not improved or worsened following the 2006–7 period of civil war (Oxfam International 2009, 2–3). A key contributing factor was the "debilitating poverty" into which many women had been driven since 2003. Hundreds of thousands of those women (Oxfam estimates 740,000) had been widowed by the war and so now were heads of household; three-quarters of them were not receiving a pension from the government (Oxfam International 2009, 3–4). The situation was so bad, Oxfam noted, that Nawal al-Samaraie, the women's rights minister, resigned on February 5, 2009, "in protest at a lack of resources to cope with 'an army of widows, unemployed, oppressed and detained women' after years of sectarian warfare" (Reuters 2009a; Oxfam International 2009, 17).

The report further notes the lack of access to basic services "despite billions of US dollars that have been spent in the effort to rehabilitate damaged or destroyed infrastructure" (Oxfam International 2009, 3). Oxfam's implicit suggestion that this aid had not been efficient was explicitly backed up soon thereafter by a report by Stuart Bowen, US special inspector general for Iraq reconstruction, to the US Congress. On March 25, 2009, Bowen told the House of Representatives Armed Services Committee that 15–20 percent of the US$21 billion Iraqi Relief and Reconstruction Fund set up by Congress in 2003 had been wasted on ill-designed or failed projects. Bowen warned of a similar outcome for Afghanistan; in both cases, he blamed the US lack of an "established framework for relief and contingency operations" (qtd. in Reuters 2009b).

Oxfam's and al-Amal's findings contradict a US DoD report from mid-2008 that "the security environment in Iraq continues to improve, with all major violence indicators reduced between 40 to 80% from pre-surge levels" (US DoD 2008, iii). Similarly, the think tank Center for Strategic and International Studies reported in 2009 that "the level of violence in Iraq has dropped sharply since the years of open civil war during 2006–2008" (Cordesman 2009, 1). Neither the DoD's seventy-four-page report in 2008 nor the center's forty-three-page report the following year used the word *women* once. Given that in the cases of both the $42 billion appropriated by Congress for Iraq and the $32 billion for Afghanistan, the bulk of the money has gone to developing local army and police forces, it is perhaps unsurprising that women's security does not register on the "security" radar of governmental, corporate, and affiliated bodies. Even if representatives of Afghan police have stressed their efforts to recruit women police and make policing in general more women-friendly, representatives of women's organizations in Afghanistan suggest that little if anything has changed for women, and women police face other sorts of difficulties: hostility from men in the force, tokenism, and so on.[5] According to Zulaikha Rafiq, director of the Afghan Women Educational Center, even if women have become more aware of their rights through progress in education, this awareness rarely filters through to rural or remote areas, and when women do take on roles such as policing or leadership in education, they "stick out like a sore thumb," becoming a target for violence.[6] Rafiq's view concurs with that of dissident Afghan politician Malalai Joya, who had been outspoken in her criticism of Afghan warlords and as a result subsequently had to leave both Parliament and the country. Joya wrote that "going to school is becoming more and more dangerous for girls, with renewed attacks against teachers and students" (2009, 225). UN special rapporteur on violence against women Rashida Manjoo similarly reported in late 2014 that violence against Afghan women and girls was "widespread and systemic" (United Nations Radio 2014). In the written report tabled at the twenty-ninth session of the UN Human Rights Council in 2015, Manjoo concluded that commitments made by the Afghan state at a number of international conferences (the most recent of which, at the time of writing, was in London in 2014) "have not translated into concrete improvements in the lives of the majority of women, who remain marginalized, discriminated against and at high risk of being subjected to violence" (Manjoo 2015, 18, para. 70). All of which begs the question of the spending priorities of the Afghan army and police in receipt of these billions of dollars of foreign aid.

The story of corruption also extends to Iraq. As in Afghanistan, bribery is endemic there, and, according to another UNODC report, authored in partnership with the UNDP and three Iraqi agencies, "corruption is one of the principal challenges facing the authorities

5. From my notes on talks and responses to questions by Najibullah Samsour, chief of District 10 of the Afghan National Police, and Zulaikha Rafiq, director of the Afghan Women Educational Center, Lowy Institute, Sydney, May 15, 2014.
6. Ibid.

as they attempt to lay the foundations of the new democratic system in Iraq" (UNODC et al. 2012, 5). As suggested by the Oxfam report cited earlier, "The great majority of Iraqis still do not have access to decent and reliable public services" (UNODC et al. 2012, 12), "despite good standards of education, almost a decade of reconstruction efforts . . . and a vast potential source of income through oil exports" (UNODC et al. 2012, 12). Unsurprisingly, such a situation favors the development of corruption, which is widespread in the public service, with lack of formal procedures for the appointment of civil servants and lack of transparency in public offices (UNODC et al. 2012, 11). Also unsurprisingly, those who engage most in bribery are the better educated and more highly paid, and bribery is more highly concentrated in Baghdad than elsewhere. Women bribe less than men but are more likely to bribe police and local government officers. It is probable that this situation has worsened considerably with the rise of Daesh, which has further destabilized the country.

Women's rights and security are not, it would seem, a top priority because of a combination of lack of targeted funding, mismanagement or misappropriation of funding, and lack of political will from either aid donors or aid recipients. Women in both Iraq and Afghanistan constitutionally have access to equal political rights and education, and both countries have quota systems for political representation of women. Yet as this overview suggests, and as women worldwide can attest, formal constitutional equality does not automatically translate into actual equality. Moreover, both countries' constitutions stipulate that no laws will be contrary to the principles of Islam. These principles, as we know, are open to interpretation and, given that conservative Islamic jurists formally participate in the courts of both countries, are generally not applied in women's interest.

Although the "freedom, democracy, and rule of law" rhetoric of Western nations that hold themselves up as the model to follow is frequently nauseating, it would nonetheless be absurd to suggest that there are no qualitative differences between the treatment of women in different parts of the world. Countries where there is a legal and political apparatus that outlaws sex discrimination and violence against women and that enables women's participation in public and private life on their own terms—through such things as access to contraception and abortion, health care, education, paid work, and the vote— and where there is some form of separation of religion and state, either explicit or tacit, are demonstrably easier places for women to live than countries where no such political and legal protections exist. In stating this, I do not ignore the evident flaws and inadequacies in such legal apparatuses, which include not only other forms of discrimination, such as gendered racism, but also, and most particularly, the insufficient application of laws owing to the continued overwhelming presence of masculinist ideology in culture, politics, and the economy. Women worldwide, from those living in relatively functional democracies to those living under fundamentalist or totalitarian regimes or in "failed" states, have fought and continue to fight for those legal protections from a state with which, as we saw in the previous chapter, they have at best an ambiguous relationship.

The question is thus not whether the women about whom official concern is expressed—in Afghanistan and in Iraq—are suffering very damaging forms of oppression; they clearly are and often at a far more debilitating level, other things such as class and ranking in the ethnic dominance scale being more or less equal, than suffered by the supposedly already-saved women living in the West. It is far more dangerous to be a woman today in Iraq or Afghanistan than it is to be a woman in, say, France or Australia, notwithstanding recent horrifying statistics about violence against women in both countries (more on this point presently). Moreover, the dangers are present in multiple forms as part of day-to-day life.

The question is not even how well intentioned or otherwise those attempting to help are, even if the "help" is not as effective as one might wish. Many current initiatives, whatever their imperfections, have come into being because of feminists' transnational solidarity and because of collaborative endeavors between international and local feminists both on the ground and at the level of lobbying international institutions. This is so whether the outcomes have been produced at the highest level of international politics, such as Resolution

1325, or at a local practical level, such as any one of the large numbers of NGO-based aid and empowerment programs operating on the ground. Sometimes the initiatives are misguided and badly implemented in the ways Carol Mann suggests and can end up "maternalistically" mirroring the paternalism of imperial masters. They can also go pear shaped as money or goods are siphoned off for purposes not intended by the donors. It would, however, be at best misleading and at worst disingenuous to tar "Western feminism" with the same brush as, for example, various US administrations and their spokeswomen.

I return to feminist actions, their motivations, and their successes or otherwise a little later in this book. In the next section, I look at the way in which, the reasons for which, and sometimes the moment at which governments and other political institutions confront and discuss the problems women experience—or do not confront and discuss them. It is also a question of which women or which oppressions are the subject of global or national concern and which are not and why. I examine these questions in a post-9/11 context to consider, on one hand, the simultaneous and self-contradictory instrumentalization of "womensrightsandsecurity" in the service of masculinist politics and, on the other hand, the exposure of women to greater threats to their rights and security—including the "immaterial terrors" of which Mernissi speaks.

Human Security and Women's Security

Security talk has characterized international relations for a long time. The UN Security Council came into existence as chief among the six main organs of the UN system set out in the UN Charter of 1945. (The other five were the General Assembly, the Economic and Social Council, the Trusteeship Council, the International Court of Justice, and the Secretariat.) The Security Council's purpose was to adopt binding measures to enable the UN to fulfill one of its major aims of keeping peace in the world. It may adopt measures that range from appointing mediators and sending special diplomatic missions and observers to establishing arms and trade embargos and intervening militarily. Its permanent membership reflects the new world power balance as it was perceived at the end of World War II: the United States, the United Kingdom, France, China, and the Soviet Union or, now, the Russian Federation.

If "security talk" was in the postwar years largely synonymous with "Cold War talk," following the disintegration of the Soviet bloc in the 1990s its content shifted to other perceived threats, notably nonstate terrorism, "acts of terror" being formerly associated largely with state actors (Saul 2006). The shift in focus to terrorism was concurrent with another shift to a new "Us and Them" in international relations: the West and the Muslim world. Interestingly, there is no formal definition of terrorism in international law and even less a definition of the "terror" that is apparently so great as to push a democratically elected president to declare war on it. There are, however—and have been for some decades—a number of regional and national legal instruments that contain some form of definition, including attempts to define what it is not. The European Convention on the Suppression of Terrorism of 1977, for example, distinguishes, for the purposes of extradition, between terrorist acts and political offences.

The legal and political chatter around terrorism has been amplified since 9/11, with individual states adopting a number of post-9/11 "antiterror" laws and the EU establishing the European Council Framework Decision of June 13, 2002, on combating terrorism.[7] Many of the national laws containing some form of definition of terrorism, such as those in Australia, Canada, and Morocco, are calqued (copied virtually word for word) on the absurdly named USA PATRIOT Act of 2001 (Uniting and Strengthening America by Providing Appropriate Tools Required to Intercept and Obstruct Terrorism, Public Law 107-56) (Salime 2007; Winter 2007).[8] It has been noted, however, that it is often very difficult to distinguish between "'terrorist

7. The full text of the European Council Framework Decision is available at http://eur-lex.europa.eu/LexUriServ/LexUriServ.do?uri=CELEX:32002F0475:EN:NOT (accessed Aug. 5, 2013).

8. The full text of the USA PATRIOT Act is available at http://www.gpo.gov/fdsys/pkg/PLAW-107publ56/pdf/PLAW-107publ56.pdf (accessed Aug. 5, 2013).

acts' and other politically motivated actions which can include violent crimes" (Borelli 2004, 334). In his contribution to one of the wake-of-9/11 anthologies, Tony Coady observed that there are more than one hundred definitions of terrorism in scholarly literature, and so he proposed his own: "the organised use of violence to target non-combatants ('innocents' in a special sense) for political purposes" (2002, 9). Five years later Jean Bethke Elshtain suggested that the words

> "terrorist" and "terrorism" entered ordinary language to designate a specific phenomenon: killing directed against all ideological enemies indiscriminately and often outside the context of a legal war between combatants fighting under the legitimate authority of a state. According to the logic of terrorism, those designated enemies—as Osama Bin Laden calls all "Americans, Jews and infidels," for example—can legitimately be killed no matter what they are doing, where they are, whether they are young or old, male or female, healthy or infirm. (2007, 120)

Although such definitions correspond by and large to general understandings of what terrorism is, they still remain extremely broad to the point of possible meaninglessness and are thus subject to manipulation.

One could, for example, argue that much male violence against women corresponds to Coady's definition of terrorism and in part to Elshtain's—although Elshtain does not appear to consider femaleness a targetable social or political identity grouping. Indeed, more than two decades ago Robin Morgan famously made links between violence against women, woman hatred, and terrorism in her work *The Demon Lover: On the Sexuality of Terrorism* (1989), and Jane Caputi and Diane Russell (1992) defined women killing, which they named "femicide," as "sexist terrorism against women." Can one, then, classify Marc Lépine, who killed fourteen women and injured ten in Montreal Polytechnic on December 6, 1989, a terrorist because he explicitly targeted women he did not know in his wish to rid the world of feminists? I am not sure that it would be helpful to do so because it disrupts the continuum of male violence against women, classifying some who perpetrate such violence as madmen or "terrorists" and others as "normal." Colette Guillaumin, in her essay on the Montreal massacre, "Folie et norme sociale" (Madness and Social Norms [(1990) 1992a]), argued against such a separation, for Lépine's actions were simply an extreme manifestation of a woman hatred that is integral to social norms. Robin Morgan did not specifically characterize male violence against women as "terrorism," either. To do so would be unlikely to contribute significantly to ending either violence against women or terrorism, however the latter is defined. At the same time, it is dangerous to posit terrorism as somehow the worst violence there is and to separate it out from other forms of violence that are legitimized through "just war," especially because we know that members of the military also engage in actions—even routinely so—that would fit Elshtain's (2003) definition of terrorism.

Another well-known scholar on "just wars," Michael Walzer, writing in the wake of 9/11, suggested that terrorism is "worse than rape or murder commonly are, for in the latter cases the victim has been chosen for a purpose . . . and the attack has some reason, however twisted or ugly it may be. The victims of terrorist attacks are third parties, innocent bystanders" (2004, 51; see also Walzer [1997] 2000). I have two problems with this argument. First, I do not find it useful to hierarchize acts of violence, claiming that "innocent bystander" death is somehow worse than targeted death. Apart from anything else, such hierarchization contains a worrying implication, even if unintended, that those who are not "innocent bystanders" at some level deserve the violence directed against them or that the violence is justifiable in some way. (I return to this point in chapter 7.) Second, as the Lépine example shows—although there are many others, such as the murders of some four hundred women, mostly maquiladora workers, in the Mexican border city Ciudad Juárez between 1993 and 2005 (according to official statistics cited in Otero 2008)—men *do* kill and rape women indiscriminately, simply because they hate women. Such attacks on groups of anonymous women are arguably far more frequent than acts that most people would agree constitute terrorism. The difference is that femicide does not usually involve bombs or machine guns.

Be all that as it may, as Ben Saul notes in his appeal for a workable international definition of terrorism, the concept of terrorism has certainly been to date "ideologically and politically loaded" and "erratically deployed" to cover a range of disparate acts of individual and collective violence (2006, 3). He suggests that "in the absence of a definition of terrorism, the struggle over the representation of a violent act is a struggle over its legitimacy. The more confused a concept, the more it lends itself to opportunistic appropriation" (3).

One could say similar things about the deployment of the idea of security, which has no clear definition in international law, either, notwithstanding the existence of a core UN body to ensure its operation. The term *security* as defined by the *Macquarie Dictionary* (Australia) is at once synonymous with and broader than *safety*, incorporating that which makes safe, the perception of being safe, and the assurance that one is safe. Security, within such a definition, implies both affect and agency. And like terrorism, that thing to which security is an automatic response in a post-9/11 world, security has been "erratically deployed" both historically and since 9/11 to justify not only all sorts of economic and military policies but also all sorts of curtailments of civil rights. If terrorism is the nebulous enemy that threatens states and their citizens, then security is the Hobbesian protector. The primary function of security talk—security chatter—in a post-9/11 world would appear to be to infantilize us, to create a need for protection—in short, to make us feel insecure, a phenomenon Ghassan Hage (2003b) describes as "anthrax culture" (see also Oliver 2007, chap. 3). Combined with a ghoulish fascination with horror that has pervaded the post-9/11 media machine (Martin and Petro 2006; Oliver 2007), security chatter places us in a vicarious state of living dangerously.

Anecdote: While I was crossing the United States on a domestic flight from San Francisco to New York in early March 2005—three and a half years after 9/11—the plane hit some turbulence. The captain came on to the public-announcement system to reassure us: "Do not worry, this is just a little turbulence. Believe me, I take all of your safety just as seriously as I take my own and that of my family, so you will be just fine." He repeated several times how seriously he took our safety and cooed at us and reassured us for what seemed to me like several minutes but may in fact have been less than one. I am not frightened of flying, but by the time the captain had finished reassuring me, I wanted to hide under a blanket with a teddy bear. Arriving in Manhattan, I was struck by what I nicknamed "dob-in-a-terrorist" advertising (in Australian vernacular, the phrase *dob in* means "to denounce"). Posters everywhere, created as part of the US Department of Homeland Security's "If you see something, say something" campaign, displayed a special security hotline to call if one had any information about suspicious behavior, possible terrorism activity, and so on.[9] Some days later, as I was catching the air shuttle to Washington, DC, the hand searches took so long I ended up missing my plane. In front of me in the line was an elderly woman in a wheelchair, also being searched. She was accompanied by a clean-shaven young man "of Middle Eastern appearance," presumably a grandson.

There are many such experiences, and those reading my words will surely be reminded of their own. In isolation, they are banal, trivial. But considered in their multiplicity, they form a discursive pattern, keeping us locked into "paranoid nationalism" and its individual avatars (Hage 2003a). That this climate of fear remained palpable even three years down the track—and indeed remains some fifteen years down the track in various parts of the world, as scattered terrorist threats and attacks as well as "lone wolf" attacks strike Western sites—is remarkable. The intensity of the "security" arsenal, far from dampening the fear (its ostensible purpose), has only served to fuel it (which is perhaps its real design).

I had previously experienced the "security" fallout from terrorist attacks: at European airports after the Lockerbie bombing of 1992 and in Paris following a series of bombings from February 1985 to September 1986, the latter authored mostly by front organizations for Hezbollah. After the last bombing in this series—the most damaging—in

9. For this campaign, see the US Department of Homeland Security website at http://www.dhs.gov/see-something-say-something (accessed Nov. 20, 2015).

a department store on rue de Rennes killed seven people and injured fifty-five, normally authority-bucking Parisians began to submit quietly to having their bags searched at entrances to department stores and other public buildings. I was one of them. Our own mortality, our vulnerability in front of an invisible "terror" whose actions we had no way of anticipating or understanding, shepherded us into meek submission to a "security" regime. Even if we later came to despise such regimes, as we saw them targeting immigrants, including asylum seekers and anyone deemed to be "Arab," the fear and what motivated it were powerful. Bombs did explode, and people did die. As they have again in 2015 and 2016. Contrary to most of the attacks in 2015 and 2016, however, in these earlier attacks there was no single, clearly identifiable author at whom one could point one's finger.

So I understand the New York paranoia, even if its endurance and pervasiveness beyond the immediate impact of 9/11 reek of a melodrama and hyperbole that those of us outside the United States see as quintessentially and even rather quaintly United Statian. But the most fear-inspiring aspect of this post-9/11 behavior was the ease with which security chatter, already in crescendo prior to 9/11 through the activities of an increasingly autonomous and secretive "deep state" described by Peter Dale Scott (2007), reached deafening proportions after 9/11. Security suddenly seemed to inform everything Western governments—as well as quite a few non-Western ones and, indeed, some of their civil society interlocutors—did. Moreover, much post-9/11 analysis, whether in the media or in the burgeoning "security studies" area of university scholarship, lent credence to the security imperative and even at times advocated the benefits of its privatization, as chapter 4 explores. The "deep state" and its business connections do have considerable moral support in our intellectual institutions.

Another aspect of the close relationship between "security" and a number of other international relations arenas had also been developing well before 9/11. Since at least the 1990s, security talk had begun to mesh with the language of rights and socioeconomic equality to create a "political framework [that] has increasingly been utilized for prioritizing unconventional security issues" (N. Hudson 2010, 22).

So we have human security, food security, financial security, environmental security, and so on. Human security is the one I am concerned with here because it has informed much post-9/11 institutional discourse on women as well as on postconflict rebuilding. It has even been picked up in feminist and peace activism and literature. Mary Kaldor (2007a, 2007b), for example, proposes human security as an essential framework for military intervention and for the construction of a "just peace," a concept she prefers to "just war." Cynthia Enloe (2002) notes that masculinist interpretations of national security invariably have to do with military security, whereas it is human security that should matter. In a post-9/11 context, human security has become the vehicle through which a discourse of intervention that prioritizes human welfare rather than profits or political power can be articulated. Yet even this concept is not without its problems.

Human security, championed by Canada and Norway, among other states, was first articulated at the international level in the UNDP's *Human Development Report 1994* (see also MacFarlane and Khong 2006). The introduction to this report, produced during a decade that looked set to become the Decade of Genocides (Bosnia, Rwanda, and so on), to some extent reflects the so-called international community's experience of those genocides and other civil wars (such as that in Algeria):

> The world can never be at peace unless people have security in their daily lives. Future conflicts may often be within nations rather than between them—with their origins buried deep in growing socio-economic deprivation and disparities. The search for security in such a milieu lies in development, not in arms.
>
> More generally, it will not be possible for the community of nations to achieve any of its major goals—not peace, not environmental protection, not human rights or democratization, not fertility reduction, not social integration—except in the context of sustainable development that leads to human security. (UNDP 1994, 1)

I note in passing the articulation of "fertility reduction" as one of the major goals of the international "community of nations" at a time when "baby bonuses" were starting to become commonplace in Western nations as a way to encourage white women to increase rather than decrease their "fertility." What is more interesting, however, for what concerns us here is the cause-and-effect linking of human security to sustainable development, the latter a concept that was developed in 1987 in a report by the UN World Commission on Environment and Development, better known as the Brundtland Commission after its chair. The UN General Assembly set up the Brundtland Commission in 1983 to look into the problem of deterioration of the human environment and natural resources. Although the report addressed challenges for both the so-called developed and developing worlds, it nonetheless explicitly linked the control of population size and growth ("fertility reduction") to the achievement of sustainable development, a comment clearly aimed at countries with higher birth rates, most of which happen not to be in the so-called developed world. The nervousness around sustainable development today is also focused largely on the ecological disasters that could occur as emerging economic powers (e.g., the BRIC, discussed in chapter 1) acquire as much wealth and as many environmentally damaging goods as wealthier nations.

There is no logical or inevitable link between sustainable development and security for women. Women in the United States, notwithstanding the continued presence of various forms of violence against them—physical, sexual, psychological, economic—and the relative lack of political will of state institutions to eradicate such violence, demonstrably benefit from considerably greater security than women in Afghanistan. Yet development in the United States is unsustainable or would be if it were generalized in its current form to the rest of the world. In other words, women's "human security" depends on many, many factors, and it does not logically follow that unsustainable development will harm it more, for example, than the absence of high-quality hospitals or safe public transport. This may seem like hair splitting, but the "sustainable development improves human security" mantra implicitly positions the nondeveloped world as the problem and evacuates the point that the major cause of nondevelopment is, in fact, overdevelopment elsewhere. Or to put it more bluntly, "the cause of poverty is wealth" (Denise Thompson, personal communication many years ago). Initiatives that focus on controlling what happens in the poor world (by reducing its fertility, for example) obscure this point.

Human security was more comprehensively articulated in the report produced in 2003 by the UN Commission on Human Security, set up at the beginning of 2001 in the wake of the UN Millennium Summit held in 2000, which established the Millennium Development Goals. These eight goals were to be achieved by 2015. They are, in the order listed by the UN: eradicating extreme poverty and hunger; achieving universal primary education; promoting gender equality and empowering women; reducing child mortality rates; improving maternal health; combating HIV/AIDS, malaria, and other diseases; ensuring environmental sustainability; and developing a global partnership for development.[10] The Commission on Human Security began its work several months before 9/11 and days after the first-term inauguration of George W. Bush as president. Its report, however, was produced over the period that included 9/11 and the "war on terror" in Afghanistan. Titled *Human Security Now* (UN Commission on Human Security 2003), the report articulated a development–rights–security nexus, which in some ways was positive in that it desiloed the issues of poverty, human rights, and security, three issues that in traditional international relations have not been considered interdependent. At another level, however, the development of the ideas of "human security" and "women's security," as articulated in Resolution 1325, has led to security overtaking rights and economic equality as the issue to focus on. Moreover, the report posited human security, which has to do with the security of individuals and social groups, as distinct from yet complementary to—and interdependent with—state security. As Natalie Hudson notes, "The

10. As listed on the UN Millennium Goals website at http://www.un.org /millenniumgoals/ (accessed Aug. 21, 2013).

report largely fails to address situations where human security and state security might be contradictory, and more importantly how the international community ought to handle such contradictions and trade-offs when it comes to prioritizing resources" (2010, 27).

Indeed, 9/11 demonstrably provided an impetus in many countries of the world, including Western countries, to reprioritize regime security over human security in a series of both national and international measures that limit and even curtail civil liberties and individual rights, including the right to privacy (Hendrickson and Karkoszka 2005, 31–32). Even if security globalization is not new, the legal and technological arsenal deployed in the wake of 9/11 was impressive, with the adoption of a panopticon-like plethora of national and international security measures (Lyon 2003, chap. 1; Mattelart 2008; Dijstelbloem and Meijer 2011). Sometimes this arsenal is compatible with human security as set out in the UN Commission on Human Security report in 2003, but mostly it is not, lending resonance to Hudson's commentary. Moreover, a number of commentators have observed that for regime security and human security to be interdependent and complementary, as the UN report suggests they are or should be, there need to exist the political will, the political capacity, and the skills to ensure such compatibility (Schnabel and Ehrhart 2005). All three are lacking in Afghanistan and Iraq at the time of writing, and one or more of them is either lacking or insufficient practically everywhere else, especially as women are concerned. What is lacking most of all is the political will among national and international elites, who are thus invariably to be found at the source of the human insecurity that various peacekeeping, security, development, gender mainstreaming, and other policies and operations are designed to address. For all the good intentions and genuine commitment of those people employed—by states, international institutions, and NGOs—to implement these "human security" measures, the structural factors involved in the constitution of elites and their power to continue to generate *insecurity* are largely left intact (Mazurana 2005; Raven-Roberts 2005).

Resolution 1325

The UN Commission on Human Security report of 2003 was preceded by a significant document relating to women's security. UN Security Council Resolution 1325 on Women, Peace, and Security, adopted in 2000, is commonly referred to, including within feminist scholarship, as a "landmark" (see, for example, Cohn 2008). Feminist legal scholar Judith Gardam notes that the resolution and the UN study that it launched (published in 2002) are "of particular significance as an indication that the issue of women and armed conflict is perceived as relevant to the maintenance of international peace and security and is consequently being addressed at the highest levels" (2005, 110; see also UN 2002). The result of concerted lobbying by feminist NGOs working in consultation with the UN, notably within the framework of the UN World Conferences on Women and the NGO Working Group on Women and International Peace and Security, Resolution 1325 was the first time the UN Security Council formally paid attention to women as a distinct transnational social group (Porter 2007; Cohn 2008). The oft-cited preamble to Resolution 1325 acknowledges the heavy burden borne by women and children as a result of armed conflict, "reaffirms" (although it had never before been affirmed in the UN context) "the important role of women in the prevention and resolution of conflicts and in peace-building," and stresses "the importance of their equal participation and full involvement in all efforts for the maintenance and promotion of peace and security" (UN Security Council 2000). Resolution 1325 succeeded in articulating concern with the welfare of women in a language that is comprehensible as important within the masculinist "security" framework that drives so much of international relations. In "using security talk as a political framework for action," Resolution 1325 has elevated the status of issues of concern to women (N. Hudson 2010, 31).

At a discursive level at least, the securitization strategy would appear to have worked: the involvement, even equal participation, of women has been taken seriously as important rather than dismissed as marginal or even as irrelevant, as had previously been the case (Tickner 1992; Enloe 1993; Charlesworth and Chinkin 2000, chap. 6). Ten years later, in 2010, the creation of UN Women, the UN's "global champion for gender equality" and the "empowerment of women,"[11] further reinforced the idea that women's rights and security were now firmly on the agenda: not at the end under "any other business" or devolved to underfunded agencies such as the former UN Development Fund for Women, itself dependent on the also underfunded UNDP, but integral to the UN's workings. UN Women has a higher status within the UN system and greater resources than the four agencies devoted to women's issues that it merged and replaced, and, when set up, it promised great things for the world's women.

Yet as Gardam (2005) notes, the UN and other international actors have by and large not addressed inadequacies in existing international humanitarian law, perceiving the problem as more one of enforcement. Existing provisions, dating back to the four Geneva Conventions of 1949, refer to women's need for "special respect" or "consideration" according to the following criteria: weakness; "honor" and "modesty" (to do with rape, forced prostitution, and so on); and pregnancy and childbirth. Apart from the now rather archaic biologism informing this conceptualization of women's needs, what is particularly worrying for Gardam is that "the major underlying cause of the particular vulnerability of women in armed conflict—namely the endemic discrimination that exists against women in all societies—is consistently overlooked in any discussion of IHL [international humanitarian law] and is not addressed in its provisions. The key to moving ahead is not only the acknowledgement of this factor but ensuring that its impact on the existing legal regime is investigated" (2005, 118).

The push to include women in postconflict peacebuilding without a serious examination of the terms and provisions of existing legal frameworks thus results in Resolution 1325 serving largely to

11. As stated in "About Us" at the UN Women website at http://www.un women.org/en/about-us (accessed Oct. 10, 2016).

reinforce biologically or culturally deterministic institutional framings. According to such framings, women are held to be of a more peaceful inclination and should thus participate in peace talks because they are ontologically better placed to get the job done. As Marysia Zalewski puts it, "Though the idea that women carry a metaphorical gene for peace is consistently denounced by feminist scholars, it lingers very strongly" (2013, 87). She sees "the UN's drive to include more women in post-conflict peace talks" as "heavily suggestive of undiminished faith in the equation of women with peace" and quotes a comment made in 2010 by the first head of UN Women, Michelle Bachelet: "'We all know that women count for peace'" (87).

Even putting aside these ontological concerns, the rhetoric within and about Resolution 1325 concerning mechanisms to involve women in peacebuilding has not necessarily been matched in practice. Both institutional and NGO studies conducted from 2002 on show that women "remain disturbingly absent or marginalized from negotiating tables, political decision making opportunities and senior policy and judicial advisory positions" (Porter 2007, 190). In 2002, Elisabeth Rehn and Ellen Johnson Sirleaf, who were commissioned by the UN Development Fund for Women to prepare, in response to the adoption of 1325, a study on the impact of armed conflict on women, concluded that "the standards of protection for women affected by conflict are glaring in their inadequacy, as is the international response" (2002, viii). Although they noted that women were already seizing on 1325 as a vehicle for organizing and for lobbying local authorities, they also argued that violence would "not abate while weapons are easier to acquire than a bag of maize. Weapons in the community translate into violence against women in the home and on the street. For women, more guns do not mean more security" (4). Whether we are talking the Big Guns of military "intervention" or the small arms now routinely bought and sold within and across borders as whole societies become increasingly militarized, the militarization of societies both after wars and outside them has devastating impacts for women (Farr, Myrttinen, and Schnabel 2009). Rehn and Sirleaf further noted that in situations of conflict and postconflict women suffer a range of discriminatory practices that also make them less likely to have equal access to humanitarian assistance (2002, 4–5).

A decade down the track, little had changed. In 2013, a civil society monitoring report on the application of Resolution 1325 showed a depressing lack of progress (Global Network of Women Peacebuilders 2013). The research was conducted on a cross-section of fifteen countries, providing detailed analysis of each country's performance on a range of indicators in relation to implementation of 1325. UN Security Council Resolution 1820 on sexual violence as a weapon of war (UN S/RES/1820 [2008], UN Security Council 2008) was also referenced in the study. The fifteen countries studied in 2013 were, in alphabetical order, Armenia, Canada, Colombia, Democratic Republic of Congo, Fiji, Liberia, Nepal, Netherlands, Philippines, Serbia, Sierra Leone, South Sudan, Sri Lanka, Sweden, and Uganda. Reports for the years 2010 to 2012 had included Afghanistan, Burundi, and Spain but not Armenia or Serbia; Rwanda was studied in 2010 and 2012, and Sri Lanka in 2012 and 2013. The indicators used were:

• Women's participation in governance, justice, peace negotiations, security, and peacekeeping missions

• Participation in constitutional or legislative review commissions

• Level of civil society participation in task forces or committees on Resolutions 1325 and 1820

• "Gender-responsive" laws and practices

• Attention to women's rights in transitional justice processes

• Economic aid to women in conflict resolution and reconstruction processes

• Funding for women, peace, and security programs

• Training for military and police that incorporated 1325 and 1820

• International human rights law and instruments

• Incorporation of gender and peace education in school curricula (an "optional indicator")

Notwithstanding the adoption of National Action Plans on 1325 by thirteen out of the total of nineteen states studied between 2010 and 2013, largely in response to international pressure, progress on all of the indicators was patchy, with mostly either slight progress or no progress and backsliding in some areas, notably by Fiji and Canada. The report noted that the research was hampered by the difficulty in obtaining information either because governments withheld it or were otherwise lacking in transparency or because of inadequacy of government data-collection processes, notably as concerns violence against women (called "sexual and gender-based violence" in the report) (Global Network of Women Peacebuilders 2013, 13). Even though the report's authors qualify the adoption of Resolutions 1325 and 1820 as a "paradigm shift" that has "strengthened the normative standards for the protection of women and girls' rights during and after conflict," implementation has been slow, and the resolutions are "not well known outside of the UN and [the] international development circle" (51). Moreover, governments and even the UN often do little more than pay lip service to 1325 and 1820, and women remain marginalized in institutional processes (Porter 2007, 189–92; Cockburn 2012, 126–30).

Even if governments were to become more open to women's participation, such measures may be met with significant distrust from many feminists who do not have any faith in the institutions that invite their presence or the politics of the men in them. As Palestinian feminist activist Khulud Khamis commented in 2010, there is no lack of women in Israel and Palestine who are experienced in transnational peace activism, but because such women are also opponents of the Israeli occupation of Palestine, it is difficult or even impossible for them to envisage any form of cooperation with the Israeli state (cited in Winter 2012a, 30). So even when feminists are very active in peace movements and in lobbying governments, including as concerns the application of Resolution 1325, they may themselves hesitate to become the handmaidens of a state they see as oppressive. Again, we return to the uneasy and paradoxical relationship women in general and feminists in particular have with the state.

Yet when feminists are both invited in the first place and do end up accepting the invitation, they are more often than not caught up in a pattern that has become typical of so-called gender-mainstreamed or gender-sensitive initiatives in international relations and state practices. This pattern involves one or more of the following:

1. *Lost in the margins.* Initiatives adopted for women still largely remain in the margins of the "main action" of UN missions and national parliaments and committees. Some sort of "gender unit" with limited institutional power or financial resources interacts with local women's organizations, while the policy, structural, and resources decisions with the most important and lasting impacts for women are made elsewhere (Whitworth 2004; N. Hudson 2010). The sorts of changes that occur for women often end up being tokenistic, short term, or superficial, and the tokenism can be exacerbated by lack of commitment to training. Women interviewed by Natalie Hudson in relation to the operationalization of Resolution 1325 commented that "the UN simply does not have the skills, experience, and expertise needed to effectively participate in the security arena from a gender-sensitive perspective." Hudson also suggests that "it is not clear whether the security framework works towards building capacity, or blinds us to its absence" (2010, 59).

2. *Not joining the dots.* Notwithstanding the links supposedly made in the *Human Security Now* report (UN Commission on Human Security 2003), discussed earlier, women's security is addressed as a separate issue from women's rights or women's economic survival. Rather than drawing on existing provisions of the Committee on the Elimination of Discrimination against Women, one of the UN's major treaties, and its protocol (1999), implementation of Resolution 1325 appears to operate in a women's rights vacuum (Cohn 2008; N. Hudson 2010). The approach thus ends up being piecemeal and often driven by short-term objectives rather than holistic and geared toward the longer term.

3. *Add women but definitely do not stir.* Even if attaching a "security" label suggests a higher priority given to women's needs, and is thus likely to achieve greater commitment of resources, it is still based in the language and conceptual/political structures of authority-based models (N. Hudson 2010, 31–33). "Security talk" incorporates a "gender perspective"—a phrase that has now largely become a euphemism

for what are presumed to be women's perspectives—into the main game of international relations without necessarily changing the rules of the game. In other words, "political analyses of the causes of war, militarism, and armed violence are off the table," and the rules and practices of international peace and security institutions are not seriously contested, if they are contested at all (Cohn 2008, 197). Steve Smith's (1998) contribution to Marysia Zalewski and Jane Parpart's (1998) important anthology on masculinity in international relations suggests that, in fact, a liberal incorporation of "gender concerns" into the so-called realist world of international relations can be more damaging to a feminist international relations agenda than outright hostility. Indeed, we have long known that the best tactics available to a liberal masculinist power structure to neutralize the impact of feminism are to ignore it and to co-opt it.

So it frequently is with women's actual participation. As with many other "women's participation" initiatives, such as parliamentary quotas, women are involved in peace talks or peacekeeping missions or an array of other measures designed to address "women's security" and women's role in peacebuilding, but in a performative (descriptive) sense rather than in a transformative (substantive) sense (to draw on Hanna Pitkin's [1967] famous model of political representation). In other words, women are added to existing structures rather than the structures themselves being changed to become more responsive to either women's needs in particular or a peaceful society's needs in general. It is assumed that it is enough simply to achieve a "critical mass" of women (x percent of the total numbers, y positions on the committee, and so on) in order to effect meaningful change. This liberal participation model has some currency among feminists, and it is certain that the presence of a large number of women participating in an institution is more likely to effect changes that are to women's advantage than is the presence of a tokenistic few. When mere participation is itself still such a battle, it is difficult, in practical terms, to develop a more sophisticated strategy that will counteract the tried-and-true masculinist practice of destroying or attempting to destroy any women who have access to power. I write these words from Australia, where the first female prime minister, Julia Gillard (2010–13), despite being disappointing to many from a feminist perspective, was torn down by the most appalling sexism in both the political class and the media (Trenoweth 2013; Walsh 2013). Had there been a larger mass of women occupying key roles in Australian political parties, Parliament, and parliamentary senior civil service, perhaps the playing field on which Gillard entered the game would have been a little less bumpy and potholed.

On the road to attaining the so-called critical mass of women, however, what tends to happen is one of three things: women start to behave more like men rather than demanding that men change their behavior (assimilation); they start to accept and benefit from the system, thus losing their desire to change it (co-optation); or they continue to challenge the system. In the latter case, they may effect change—and, here, the "critical mass" may or may not help, depending on other factors, such as pressure from local and transnational feminists working outside the institutions and, indeed, the women's own politics—or they may not survive within the institution. Or, indeed, they may end up doing both: managing to push through some changes but at heavy personal cost.

4. *Focus on the women but disappear the men.* If women are oppressed, then someone is oppressing them, and someone benefits from that oppression. Just as "development" programs do not address the fundamental truth that the basic cause of poverty is the accumulation of wealth and its concentration in the hands of the few to the exclusion of the many, "gender" programs do not address the fundamental truth that most of the harm done to the world's women is done by the world's men as well as by ideologies and structures that are set up by men and that work to their advantage. "Gender" programs also run the risk of tacitly reproducing essentializing mythologies about women in that they position them as beings with certain ontological properties—a tendency to be oppressed, a natural antiviolence, and so on—rather than as actors that are both materially and epistemologically positioned in certain ways within a political relationship.

Programs to address oppression that focus solely on the oppressed disappear the agency of the oppressor and thus the latter's role in perpetuating the oppression. Violence against women is structural and systemic. It is as much part of peacetime as it is part of wartime. It happens as much during "postconflict" periods as during conflict periods, demonstrated clearly in research on Afghanistan and Iraq. If women are to be empowered, what *disempowers* them must first be understood and addressed.

5. *Disappear the women by calling them "gender."* Much of the language used—in the UN; in development, rights, and security programs; by national governments; and, indeed, in a great deal of scholarship—now refers to "gender" rather than to women and men. The term *gender* has thus become a euphemism variously for women, women and men, or, often, men too! As such, it is rendered meaningless as a tool of equalization. Similarly, the idea of "gender equality" contains or is often interpreted to contain a tacit presumption that "inequality" can work equally to the detriment of women and men, and some sex equality legislation has been interpreted to this effect. This presumption is not borne out by the facts and disappears or at least obscures the real power imbalances that are at the source of "gendering" in the first place. In UN fora as well as in a great deal of scholarship, men's violence against women is now referred to as "gender-based violence," as if men and women were equally violent to each other.

Similarly, initiatives to examine the impact of policies on women have been translated as "gender mainstreaming." Adopted at the Fourth UN Conference on Women in Beijing in 1995 (although it was first mooted in 1985 at the third conference in Nairobi), gender mainstreaming was defined in a UN Economic and Social Council report as follows: "Mainstreaming a gender perspective is the process of assessing the implications for women and men of any planned action, including legislation, policies or programmes, in all areas and at all levels" (1997). An equivalence is thus presumed between "women's concerns" and "men's concerns" even though the issue for women has perennially been and frequently remains that "men's concerns" are already the default position.

"Security chatter" has thus dovetailed with "gender chatter" simultaneously and paradoxically to hypervisibilize (some) women as beings in danger and thus in need of the exercise of someone else's R2P muscle and to disappear the fact that all women are socially, bio-politically, culturally, and economically marked as inferior and unimportant such that they/we remain, in effect, beings in constant danger. The categories "women" and "gender" in international post-9/11 (human) security politics are primarily symbolic, and actual women's actual safety is far from being a priority in either discursive or spending terms. "Women's rights" continue to lag behind the many post-9/11 "security" concerns that states and the UN system prioritize.

On another level, the preoccupation with the multiple disastrous impacts of war on women and the rhetoric of rescue often deployed in relation thereto—genuinely or disingenuously—creates a disturbing disjuncture between the "emergencies" of wars and the banality of violence against women in the every day. Resolution 1820 (UN Security Council 2008) on the use of sexual violence as a weapon of war against civilians—"including women and girls," as paragraph 3 rather oddly puts it, as if women and girls are not the main target—is an important development for which feminists working transnationally had been lobbying for years. It notably reinforces the inclusion of rape and other forms of sexual violence in the Rome Statute of the International Criminal Court as "a war crime, a crime against humanity, or a constitutive act with respect to genocide," and it "stresses the need" for exclusion of such crimes from any amnesty provisions set up in the process of conflict resolution (para. 4). It also explicitly "demands" that troops be properly vetted on recruitment as concerns histories of sexual violence and be trained on the issue, including "debunking myths that fuel sexual violence," and that women of local communities be heard during any conflict-resolution discussions (para. 3). This is indeed a paradigm shift. At the same time, the increased post-9/11 focus on sexual violence against women in conflict situations, as in

Resolution 1820 and elsewhere, reframes the issue of violence against women in two worrying ways.

First, Resolution 1820 posits sexual violence against women and girls as primarily an instrument of war, "to humiliate, dominate, instil fear in, disperse and/or forcibly relocate civilian members of a community or ethnic group" (UN Security Council 2008, preamble). Even if the resolution does not suggest these motives are the only reasons for sexual violence against women and girls, the fact that they are foregrounded contains the tacit message that sexual violence against women in times of war "counts" mainly—or counts more than in peacetime—because it is used as a means of getting at men as well. The group is humiliated, its male members emasculated, because the group's women are raped by the armed enemy. Feminists have long pointed out that rape is routinely used as a metaphor for racial domination and colonization; the communities (men) to which the raped women "belong" are raped symbolically, by proxy, individually and collectively.

Second, as I have pointed out elsewhere (Winter 2012a), the focus on sexual violence in conflict situations sets up a hierarchy between violence that is committed against women in such situations and violence that is committed against women in peacetime. The violence committed during wartime is an atrocity because it is linked to the atrocity of war: it is public, it is collective, it is accompanied by the use or threat of armed violence, and it is intended and/or perceived as a means, as noted earlier, of subjugating specific groups. Violence against women committed in peacetime is anonymous and mostly individual (outside situations of gang rape) and may or may not involve the use of small arms. And most of it occurs within the family or within family-like relationships.

Still the Same Old Story

Catharine MacKinnon, citing US Federal Bureau of Investigation statistics, observed in 2002 that "the number of women who die at the hands of men every year in the United States alone is almost the same as the number of people who died on September 11" (426). This observation led her to ask the question: "When is a war? . . . Nothing in law imagines a war in which one side is trained and armed, the other side taught to cry and not to wield kitchen knives" (427, 428). If the scale of international problems and the urgency of attending to them were measured by the number of people affected; the consistency with which they are affected; the damage done—psychologically, physically, and economically—to individuals suffering the effects of the problems and to those for whom they have caring responsibility; and the costs to society more generally in terms of financial resources deployed (or wealth generation lost), workforce, knowledge base, and social cohesion, then eliminating violence against women by men would receive top priority everywhere at all times. But, of course, if that political choice were made and made widely enough and for long enough, then the problem itself would disappear because the things that cause it would be eradicated. One could make a similar argument concerning poverty and wealth.

Widely cited statistics indicate that more than one-third of women have been or will be in their lifetime subjected to physical and sexual violence by an intimate partner or former intimate partner or sexual violence by a nonpartner, with this figure estimated to be as high as 70 percent in some countries. Although men are globally four times more likely than women to be victims of homicide, women are far more likely to be killed within the family or by intimate partners (UNODC 2014). In fact, of all women killed in any year, half are killed by intimate partners or family members.

These are the official statistics, gathered by international agencies such as the World Health Organization (2013), UNODC (2014), UNICEF (2014), and the EU Agency for Fundamental Rights (2014). These statistics rely more and more on sources other than government data, which are frequently incomplete or skewed by underreporting. For example, the World Health Organization study in 2013 drew on a range of sources, including surveys, interviews, and medical and social sciences scholarly literature, which it analyzed using a variety of quantitative and qualitative methods. This triangulation of different methods helps to some extent to counteract the problem of underreporting or the potentially misleading effects of increases in reporting, which are sometimes interpreted as increases in the prevalence of men's violence against women rather than primarily as increases in reporting.

That said, although some statistical increases may on occasion be owing to increases in reporting, there are also indications that domestic violence is on the increase and that it is increasingly severe. In March 2014, the New South Wales Bureau of Crime Statistics and Research in Australia reported a 2.5 percent increase in domestic violence, based not on increased reporting but on increased numbers of women presenting at emergency wards with serious injuries.

Yet all of these shocking statistics, which are not new and not news for anyone who takes even a mild interest in the subject, are not necessarily translating into changed perceptions in society at large. For example, results of an Australian national survey of 17,500 people conducted in 2013 indicated that domestic violence was the leading cause of death among women younger than forty-five (VicHealth 2014), a finding that rapidly dispels the myth that violence against women is mainly a non-Western (or working-class or ethnic minority) problem—although the Australian survey did find differences in attitudes to men's violence against women according to class, age, and ethnic group. Most disturbingly, the Australian study found that since the first study of this type conducted by VicHealth in 1995 (a second was done in 2009), survey respondents had become less, not more, likely to believe that

• Violence is committed mainly by men (30 percent instead of 50 percent in 1995);

• Women are the majority of those suffering physical harm and fear of harm (86 percent, down from 89 percent);

• Violence against women is common—predictably, fewer men (59 percent) than women (79 percent) believed this to be the case; and

• Most women suffer violence at the hands of someone they know (64 percent, down from 76 percent in 1995). (VicHealth 2014, 2)

Conversely, there was an increase in the percentage of respondents who believed certain myths about why violence against women occurs:

• The main cause of men's violence is men not being able to control their anger (two-thirds of respondents in 2013).

• The main cause of sexual violence perpetrated by men is men's inability to control their need for sex (around 40 percent, an increase from 2009, with the greatest increase, depressingly, among women).

• Victims share responsibility for the violence if they are drunk or drug affected (19 percent). (VicHealth 2014, 2)

Figures for 2009 also showed these trends in perception (VicHealth 2014, 2), all of which run counter to the overwhelming evidence, but the figures for 2013 are worse again. The worrying message that these survey results send is that over a period of roughly twenty years public sensitization to the issue has decreased, not increased, which means that various campaigns by feminists, health professionals, government agencies, and international institutions are not working. Or if they are working, they are serving only to create a perception that because something is "being done," things are improving. But the things "being done" are often cosmetic and hide more sinister realities.

In 2007, for example, I wrote of the Howard government's post-9/11 diversion of funds earmarked for funding initiatives against domestic violence to a nationwide advertising campaign about the "war on terror" in 2003, which carried the slogan "Be alert, but not alarmed" (Winter 2007). A decade later, the women's services sector in Australia continues to be defunded at both federal and state levels, with Australia's very first women's refuge, Elsie, founded by feminists in Sydney in 1974 (and receiving government funding from 1975), facing closure in the year of its fortieth birthday, 2014. A huge feminist campaign, with considerable media support, was not able to stop the ongoing process of Christianization of women's services, with the St. Vincent de Paul Society taking over Elsie in October 2014. Several services for the homeless, among whom women having suffered domestic violence are a significant population, have also had to close or have been tendered out to Christian organizations.

Although the social conservatism combined with an aggressively neoliberal economic stance that are behind these moves are not directly or wholly the effect of 9/11, they are an integral part of the "war on terror" rhetoric that continues to inform both foreign and domestic policy in Western (but not only Western) nations. Along with the resurgence of religion in both domestic and world politics, which is also closely related to post-9/11ist politics, this pugilistic rhetoric has had a decided impact in many countries. Fighting the enemy matters; looking after those at home does not. As governments proclaim a concern for women's rights and dignity, they cynically engage in both foreign and domestic policies and practices that make women's lives more difficult. Women's rights, security, and dignity appear to be more important symbolically to most political leaders than they are important materially.

This revalorization of macho masculinist culture has also brought with it a new spate of victim blaming and perpetrator excusing. The last item in the VicHealth survey conducted in 2013 (VicHealth 2014), showing that roughly one-fifth of respondents believe that a victim is responsible for rape and abuse if she is drunk or drugged, is particularly chilling, especially given that the survey was done after the international scandal of the Steubenville rape. One might have expected, if nothing else, that the horrors of the Steubenville story might have caused sufficient outrage to change public perceptions about victim blaming. But, in fact, no, it did not because the media fully participated in the victim-blaming exercise.

On August 11, 2012, a drunk sixteen-year high school girl was repeatedly assaulted by two high school footballers at a party in the town of Steubenville, Ohio. The abused teenager was drunk to the point of vomiting and passing out on the night in question and recalls little to nothing of events. Her attackers, local football heroes, carted her around from party to party. They not only repeatedly raped her, vaginally and orally, but also urinated on her and photographed her, after which the photographs were circulated by the rapists and their friends on social media, with accompanying denigrating comments about the young woman. On March 17, 2013, Mal'ik Richmond and Trent Mays were convicted of rape and sentenced to short terms in the state juvenile detention system; Richmond was released in January 2014. Following considerable public pressure, in 2013 a grand jury investigated the role of adults in the case (failure to report, cover-ups, tampering with evidence); one teacher was indicted. The case also generated litigation against members of KnightSec (an offshoot of the "hacktivist" group Anonymous) who published allegations against some people they believed to have been involved. The press coverage of the case was full of victim-blaming narratives, with CNN reporter Poppy Harlow (depressingly, a woman) coming in for some particularly trenchant criticism for this reason. In a report on March 17, after the guilty verdict was handed down, Harlow stated: "It was incredibly emotional—incredibly difficult even for an outsider like me to watch what happened as these two young men that had such promising futures, star football players, very good students, literally watched as they believe their life fell apart" (CNN 2013).

Although discussions of men's victimhood may make men feel better and make women feel inclusive and compassionate, they are not helpful in a world where both hatred of women (or simply indifference to the problems women face) and men's tendency to blame anyone or anything but themselves for their behavior are on the rise. Even the stories of young men, including white Anglos and Europeans, who convert to Islamist extremism and take off to Syria or Iraq to join Daesh are now being scripted by the Western media as narratives of young men suffering various existential crises, combined (albeit not always) with social exclusion. From perpetrators they are transformed into victims, for whom tailored programs to help address their problems are needed. Even as their violence is condemned, we are led to pity them; this pity quickly becomes a metaphor for attitudes to male violence more generally.

Men become victims who "act out," so their violence must be understood, and we must feel compassion for them. When women "act out," however, it is more often than not against themselves. Some months before the release in March 2014 of the New South Wales statistics on the increase in domestic violence causing severe injury, the Australian Institute of Health and Welfare released the findings of its study on trends in hospitalization for injury between 1999 and 2011 (Pointer 2013). The study found that more women were hospitalized than men for self-harm in 2010–11 in every age group, with the figure becoming three times higher among fifteen- to nineteen-year-olds. Among Indigenous Australians, however, almost as many men as women self-harmed, and slightly more in the twenty-five to thirty-five age group, which does indicate that socioeconomic marginalization on the grounds of race is a factor in self-harm behaviors.

Unfortunately, the reconfiguration of perpetrators as victims has begun to develop wide currency and has even been legitimized within feminist scholarship. Jacqui True, for example, argues in her political economy analysis of violence against women that men who are denied opportunities to fulfill the expectation of cosmopolitan, economically successful masculinity are resorting to violence against women as a way of acting out their frustration (2012, chap. 3). Although True writes of the need to involve men in campaigns against violence against women, in which they provide alternative images of a caring masculinity (she cites the White Ribbon campaign and the South African campaign "Brothers against Violence"), she adopts, uncritically it seems, the argument that men's violence against women is a response to socioeconomic disempowerment and that empowerment of these men will help to reduce violence. There are of course several reasons why socioeconomic marginalization of any individual or group should end, but to suggest that it is a way to end violence against women is to misunderstand why violence against women happens. Although reliable statistics are difficult to come by, for every socioeconomically marginalized man there are likely to be anywhere from two to six women who are even more marginalized.

True does point out that socioeconomic disparities between men and women are a huge part of the problem and that within the UN there has been resistance—structural, political, or intellectual—to making connections between violence against women and gender inequality more generally. Carol Cohn (2008) made precisely this point in relation to the application of Resolution 1325. True's arguments about disempowered masculinities, however, imply that it is acceptable to "blame" these extrinsic factors for men's violence against women. They also feed the myth that violence against women is always more likely to occur among the poor (or among angry blacks or Muslims), which is essentializing. If there is a need to consider the cases of the poor and the racialized differently, it is more at the level of women's experience and needs that this consideration should start. Poor women have fewer options for escaping abusive men, and racialized women encounter stereotyping from law enforcement, legal and service agencies, or assimilation of their experience to that of white women (Crenshaw 1991; Sokoloff and Dupont 2005).

Analyses of the Ciudad Juárez femicides draw clear links between neoliberal globalization and violence against women. The women who have been murdered in Ciudad Juárez are poor and largely regional immigrants to this factory town, around which are located more than three hundred maquiladoras, those notorious factories operated in the free-trade zone on the Mexico–US border. The links between neoliberal globalization and violence against women are also at the core of True's political economy argument, but where the analyses of the Juárez femicides differ from True's is that poverty and exclusion are named not as causes of violence against women (i.e., because men are marginalized) but as contexts in which it is extremely difficult for women to have access to protection measures (Otero 2008, 47). Jules Falquet (2014) also places analysis of the femicides within the context of neoliberalism, but in its combination with militarism. According to Falquet, Mexico is the "good pupil" of militarized neoliberalism, in which "men in arms" and "women in service" are the gendered expressions (see also Falquet 2008). Drawing on the work of Paola Tabet (2004) and some of the analyses in the anthology *Terrorizing Women: Feminicide in the Américas* (Fregoso and Bejarano 2010), Falquet looks at the Juárez femicides and disappearances as part of a continuum in which women's roles within the patriarchal family are extended to the workplace: the maquiladora women are hypersexualized, decitizened, and available to service men at all moments. They are also, like other women "terrorized" in the Americas, located in a context where the legacy of both domestic political and military violence and capitalist exploitation from the North create conditions in which the woman hatred (or men's fear of women) that is the basis of male domination of women becomes at once monetarized and militarized.

The Juárez femicides began well before 9/11 and are independent of them, and men's violence against women in a world where only men count as fully human and women are there to serve men's "sense of entitlement," as Caputi and Russell put it (1992, 18), is one of the depressing constants of world history. As chapter 4 shows, however, 9/11 provided new opportunities to develop the connections between guns and money, on the one hand, and "men in arms and women in service," on the other, that have characterized neoliberal masculinist globalization, already well in train.

Muscular masculinist politics are being revalorized everywhere, and the "war on terror" internationally thus becomes, through these various discourses and representations, a war on women locally. Notwithstanding the genuine commitment of some in national parliaments and international institutional structures to try to make women's lives less difficult, women largely continue to play a symbolic role in international relations, while the material conditions of their lives worsen.

4

What Does Hurricane Katrina Have to Do with the Subic Rape Case?

Hurricane Katrina devastated a section of the southern coast of the United States in late August 2005, with the destruction of large parts of New Orleans being its most severe impact. A couple of months later, at the beginning of November, Nicole (not her real name), a young woman from Zamboanga, at the southern tip of the island of Mindanao, itself at the southern extremity of the Philippine archipelago, made a complaint to the Subic Bay police that she had been raped by a group of US marines who were in the area on military-training exercises. The marines were tried in a Philippine court the following year, and one of them was found guilty. This was the first time in history that a member of the US military had been sentenced in a Philippine court for raping a Philippine woman (Winter 2011a; Lacsamana 2012, chap. 5).

These two events, both momentous in their own way, nonetheless happened literally continents apart and appear on the face of it to be separate and disparate phenomena. There is no immediately obvious or direct link between the impact of a hurricane in the United States and the impact of a rape case in the Philippines, nationally significant though both may be. Nor does the connection of either of them with 9/11 appear to be more than tenuous at best. Yet when one starts to examine the reasons behind the impacts of these events—who suffered, why they suffered, what was done or not done about it, and how that suffering could have been avoided—a series of parallel problems starts to emerge. As post-Katrina analyses started appearing in scholarly and alternative media, and as the aftermath of the Subic case unfolded, involving a broad grassroots protest movement linking US imperialism, militarism, national sovereignty, and violence against women, along with judicial and parliamentary lobbying to repeal the US–Philippine Visiting Forces Agreement (VFA), those parallels came into sharper focus. They highlight the often indirect and trans-nationalized impacts of 9/11 for women (especially poor and racialized women) and the interaction between militarism, imperialism, and globalization in producing those impacts.

It is arguable, of course, that we are dealing here with *cum hoc, ergo propter hoc*, a variation on the *post hoc* fallacy that places the accent on simultaneity rather than consecutiveness: it is technically possible to trace such lines between any number of global events occurring after 9/11. Blindfolded, one could stick pins in two different locations in a timeline and discover many comparable scenarios in which the lives of women are linked transnationally by guns, money, race, and various national interests as interpreted and articulated by states. But this is precisely my point: notwithstanding the partial (in both senses) understanding of the "world" that was "shaken" by 9/11, as discussed in chapter 1, women's lives across the globe are more closely linked than we at first may believe, just as men's are. This fact is usually obscured by the dark shadows cast by masculinist constructions of the national (and local) interest. Such a huge and labyrinthine architec-ture is constructed over and around the sites in which women's lives are lived—so many walls, facades, secret chambers, and hidden pas-sages—that feminists are, in our transnational analysis and activism, forced to become excavators to bring the links to light.

Moreover, Hurricane Katrina and the Subic rape case are not sim-ply two events that happened to occur in different places within a few months of each other. They occurred in two countries that had long been linked through colonial, neoimperial, and military relationships and within the context of the further development of that relation-ship through the "war on terror." Both the wider war and the spe-cific events discussed here have had material and political impacts for women in both places; the connections between those impacts start to emerge as one starts to consider the broader political and economic agendas behind the war. At the same time, post-9/11ism clearly did not cause Hurricane Katrina (or raced and gendered poverty in Louisiana), and the US military and related development of prostitution were a presence in the Philippines long before 2001 and thus long before the Subic rape case. Their particular impacts, however, and the ways feminists engaged with them are inescapably part of a post-9/11 scenario. The investment of US money in the war rather than in local infrastructure and the deployment of the Louisiana Guard to Iraq rather than in Louisiana—one of the poorest states in the country with a high African American concentration—where they were needed more have been clearly identified as major contributory factors to the devastation wreaked by Hurricane Katrina. Similarly, the investment of US money in the Asian "second front" of the "war on terror" and the subsequent deployment of large numbers of US troops in regular "training" exercises in the Philippines have been clearly identified as contributory factors to the Subic rape case.

In some ways, these two events are even emblematic of the impacts of 9/11 in that most of these impacts have been indirect rather than direct, interacting with existing situations to exacerbate them or alter both their discursive and their material effects. They are also emblematic of the ways in which the interconnectedness of militarism and global capitalism (or, put more simply, guns and money) and their impacts on women's lives have come to the fore on a transnational scale in a post-9/11 world, however that world may be defined.

Before looking more specifically at these two events, I begin by setting the scene, starting with a brief overview of the background to the US–Philippine guns-and-money relationship and moving on to an overview of the development of US military spending after and, indeed, slightly before 9/11.

History of a Relationship

US military presence in the Asia-Pacific region has long been linked to US strategic interests there, which include countering terrorism, preventing the emergence of a "regional coalition or hegemon," keeping air and sea lines of communication open, and "ensuring uninhibited access to key markets, energy supplies and strategic resources" (Cohen 1997). The military and economic relationship between the United States and the Philippines began, in fact, more than a century before 9/11 happened. The Philippines was among the spoils gained by the United States at the end of the Spanish-American War in 1898, and although there was strong resistance to a new occupier, leading to the Philippine-American War (1899–1901), the United States continued to occupy the Philippines until 1946. The postcolonial Philippines remained heavily dependent on the United States, and the Military Bases Agreement reached in 1947, which ensured a continued and significant US military presence, was a key instrument in that dependence. The VFA of 1999 took over where the Bases Agreement left off after the closure of Clark Air Force Base in 1991 and of Subic Naval Base in 1992, following a volcanic eruption in 1991 that destroyed Clark Base. The Philippine Senate then voted in 1992 not to renew the leases on these military bases. US troops continue, however, to arrive in the Philippines for regular military exercises under the VFA.

The VFA, far from giving the United States less access to the Philippines, in fact gives it more and at a fraction of the cost: the United States now has access to twenty-two ports on Luzon and Mindanao and in the Visayas, whereas it previously had access to only four. The nature of US military activities in the Philippines included in the VFA is ill defined, and US forces benefit from unparalleled diplomatic immunity. The treaty also ushered in a new era of US defense strategy that was further developed under Operation Enduring Freedom starting in 2002, involving Cooperative Security Locations (CSLs, local host facilities with no permanent US military presence) and Forward Operating Sites (FOSs, local host facilities with a permanent US military presence of rotating forces). Or in "Claytons" terms, CSLs and FOSs are the US bases you have when you're not having US bases. (Claytons tonic was marketed in the 1970s and 1980s in Australia and New Zealand as a nonalcoholic alternative to whisky at a time of national concern about alcohol-related road deaths. The advertising slogan "The drink you have when you're not having a drink" led to the "Claytons" metaphor becoming an enduring part of Australian vernacular in a variety of contexts.)

These "nonbases" have become ubiquitous in a post-9/11 context, wherein the Philippines became part of the "second front" in the "war on terror" and were folded into the Operation Enduring Freedom activities, of which Djibouti, discussed in chapter 1, was the primary site. Activities in the Philippines increased further following publication of the US DoD's *Global Posture Review* in 2004. The DoD document recommended the creation of "a network of traditional and new facilities, combined with improved flexibility in our legal arrangements," in order to "permit the rapid use of our forward forces" and thus "continue to provide the US with an unmatched ability to assure our allies, deter our enemies, and conduct military missions worldwide" (US DoD 2004, 10). The new facilities, CSLs and FOSs, along with the more traditional Main Operating Bases, formed "the baseline" for the "future global posture" of the United States (US DoD 2004, 10). In particular, the DoD stated its intention to "establish a network of FOSs and CSLs to support the Global War on Terrorism and to provide multiple avenues of access for contingency operations. Such facilities also will serve to expand US and hostnation [*sic*] training opportunities, helping our partners build their own capacity in areas such as counter-terrorism" (12).

The FOS at Camp Navarro in the Philippine "riviera" city Zamboanga, at the southwestern tip of the island of Mindanao and a short boat trip from Basilan, the stronghold of the terrorist organization Abu Sayyaf, is the site of an important US military presence in the Philippines and a key location in this discussion of the Subic case. It was also the base at which former Philippine military officer Nancy Gadian was stationed from late 2006. Gadian reported that following the 2001–2 Balikatan training exercises conducted under the VFA, which she had to study in order to take charge of the operations in 2007, "the US troops stayed and established a permanent and continuous presence in Southern Mindanao" (Gadian 2009). In an affidavit presented before the Philippine Legislative Oversight Committee on the VFA in 2009, Gadian stated that "the Americans decide where their troops can go and we are only informed about it." She "witnessed how officers and enlisted personnel of the US military pick up women prostitutes and how women prostitutes go to their hotel rooms," and she "received reports of many 'sexual activities' of US troops in all sorts of places during their 'R & R'" (Gadian 2009).

US troops also continue to carry out regular military exercises in Subic Bay, and the Subic Freeport Zone (another site centrally linked to our story here), with its foreign- and increasingly Japanese- and Korean-owned nightclubs, has become a favored site for US military personnel's "rest and relaxation." Subic, along with Clark and surrounding areas, has also become a major commercial and export zone, offering advantageous financial incentives, including cheap labor, for foreign investors (Winter 2012b).

The Philippines' continued dependence on the United States is both economic and military because the United States is a major provider of both military and nonmilitary aid. The former includes a donation of US$93.2 million worth of weapons by the Bush II administration in late 2002, "which has been seen as a sweetener to enable relatively unfettered continuation and indeed expansion of US military presence" in the Philippines for both military and economic reasons (Winter 2012b, 83). As noted in chapter 1, a similar offer made subsequently to Turkey was unsuccessful, but the Philippines is poorer and more dependent on the United States economically, militarily, and culturally. US government figures show that spending on aid in East and Southeast Asia increased considerably following 2001, owing primarily to Operation Enduring Freedom counterterrorism activities in Indonesia and the Philippines, with these two countries being by far the greatest recipients of nonfood aid in the region.

In the thirteen years following 9/11, the US state spent an estimated total of US$1.6 trillion on the "war on terror," which was divided among the following three operations:

• Operation Enduring Freedom, covering primarily Afghanistan and other so-called global war on terror operations ranging from the Philippines to Djibouti, beginning immediately after 9/11 and continuing: $US 686 billion or 43 percent

- Operation Noble Eagle, providing enhanced security for US military bases and other homeland security, launched after 9/11 and continuing at a modest level: US$27 billion or 2 percent
- Operation Iraqi Freedom, beginning in late 2002 in preparation for the invasion of Iraq in March 2003, with subsequent substantial military presence in Iraq over close to nine years; rebadged Operation New Dawn in 2010 as the military operations began to be wound back: US $815 billion or 51 percent (figures from Belasco 2014, unnumbered summary page)

Some 5 percent, or US$81 billion, was "for war-designated funding not considered directly related to the Afghanistan or Iraq wars" (Belasco 2014, unnumbered summary page). The total annual cost peaked at $195 billion in fiscal year 2008, dropping to $95 billion in 2014. During the post-9/11 decade, the monthly spending by the United States on its Afghan war effort alone (US$4.7 billion per month in 2009, to a peak of US$8.9 billion per month in 2011 [Belasco 2014, 14]), was several times the entire annual military budget of many countries of the world (Stockholm International Peace Research Institute [SIPRI] 2015a). For example, the Philippines' military spending for 2003, its highest in the post-9/11 decade, was slightly higher than US$2.6 billion (SIPRI 2015a), which was around 15 percent of the United States spending on Afghanistan for the same year (Belasco 2014, 14). But military aid provided to the Philippines by the United States must also be factored in here.

In 2007, the Philippines received US$120 million in nonfood aid, and Indonesia received US$147 million (Lum 2008, 23). Translated into per capita spending, however, the level of nonfood aid to the Philippines in 2007 was approximately double that of Indonesia, at roughly US$1.30 per capita, although these figures changed in subsequent years as aid to Indonesia increased by roughly 25 percent, but aid to the Philippines slightly declined (Lum 2008, 23). Indonesia also emerged more clearly over the years following 9/11, according to some security-studies commentators, as a site in which local Islamist terrorism appeared both to be better organized and to have clearer transnational links to Jamayah al-Islamiyyah (Islamic Congregation) and al Qaeda than did the armed Islamist group Abu Sayyaf in the Philippines (Chalk 2005). The International Military Education and Training Program funded by the United States in the Philippines nonetheless remains the largest of such programs in the region and one of the largest in the world (US DoS 2010b; Winter 2012b).

Islamist terrorism by Abu Sayyaf and other forms of armed Islamic resistance in the Philippines existed well before 9/11. Mindanao, the Sulu Archipelago, and Sabah (subsequently part of Malaysia) had been colonized through Islamic expansion in the region many centuries before the arrival of the Spanish in the sixteenth century. There had been various moments of Muslim (Moro) resistance to the Spanish and US colonizing powers since that time (Rodell 2005), but modern organized armed Islamic resistance in Mindanao and Sulu really developed during the period of martial law under Ferdinand Marcos (1972–86). Abu Sayyaf was formed in 1989 and quickly developed transnational links with Saudi Islamic extremists. The Saudi Arabia–based Muslim World League, which is active in pulling Muslim minorities in non-Muslim countries to the Islamic right through various forms of aid and community programs, has had a presence in Mindanao at least since the 1990s. Under the leadership of the Saudi king's brother-in-law Jamal al-Khalifa (subsequently arrested) in the Philippines, the Muslim World League contributed to providing logistical support for Islamic terrorism in the Philippines, as did Jamayah al-Islamiyyah through a Malaysia-based dummy company (Rodell 2005).

The existence of these networks provided the moral justification for the massive increase in US military presence in the Philippines, notably Mindanao and Sulu, even if under Philippine law foreign troops cannot run bases or be directly involved in armed combat. US troops stationed in the Philippines since 2002 as part of the Balikatan training exercises, however, have been involved in covert operations against Abu Sayyaf (Winter 2011a, 2012b). The ramping up of the US military presence in the Philippines, with the willing cooperation of the Philippine state under then president Gloria Macapagal Arroyo (nicknamed "GMA" in the Philippines) has been perceived by peace and feminist groups in the Philippines and particularly in Mindanao and Sulu as a massive overreaction, with US military presence from 2002 far exceeding that of the bases era.

Indeed, the US military presence would not be possible without the enabling actions of the Philippine state, which continues in an attitude of economic and military dependence on the United States. The Philippine state, its police, and its military are also weakened by the corruption that, according to one commentator, has become "a defining feature of much of everyday life in the [Southeast Asian] region" (Wright-Neville 2004, 54). David Wright-Neville describes the escape in July 2003 of convicted Jamayah al-Islamiyyah bomber Fathur Rohman al-Ghozi from the Philippine police national head-quarters, an escape widely believed to have been facilitated by corrupt police officers, as one of the "most dramatic examples of the problems posed by corruption" (for counterterrorism in this instance) (2004, 54). Bribes are a common way of doing all sorts of political busi-ness from the very top down, as we have already seen in the cases of Iraq and Afghanistan. Arroyo herself was charged with electoral fraud and misuse of state lottery funds, resulting in a failed impeachment attempt in 2004 and arrest in 2011 under the new government led by President Benigno Aquino III, who had vowed to stamp out corrup-tion among the Philippine political elite (as reported by the Associ-ated Press the day of his inauguration on July 1, 2010; see *Guardian* 2010). Aquino, however, has since been tarred with the same corrup-tion brush, the liberal press dubbing him "the worst president ever" because of suspected "pork barreling" in the administration, compa-rable to that of the Arroyo years, and appointment of personal allies to senior positions in the judiciary, thus compromising the latter's inde-pendence (Tiglao 2015). The trial of Arroyo is ongoing at the time of writing but was suspended for a month by the Philippine Supreme Court in late October 2015 because of Arroyo's poor health owing to degenerative bone disease (Canlas 2015). Corruption also allegedly affected the Subic rape trial and its aftermath (Winter 2011a).

The Philippines' continued dependence on the United States is most evident in the economic arena: the United States remains among the Philippines' top three trading partners. Until very recently and certainly during the period discussed here, it was the Philippines' top trading partner, with 17.1 percent of all Philippine trade in 2007 (compared with 80 percent at the time of Philippine independence following World War II), but Japan had outstripped the United States by 2013, with 14.5 percent of all Philippine trade in that year. With 12.9 percent in that year, the United States narrowly beat China, at 12.7 percent. Singapore came in fourth place with 7 percent (Philippine Statistics Authority 2007, 2013). South Korea is also a major player, with the Philippines being a preferred Korean tourist destination and Hanjin Shipyard, located in Subic Bay, being one of the world's largest shipyards. The main export *and* import from all major partners, however, is electronic products: they include the products of offshored component industries, such as semiconductor parts and computer peripherals in the case of exports and finished products or raw and semiprocessed materials for making electronic products in the case of imports. The biggest US trading partner is Canada, followed by the EU. Philippine trade accounts for an infinitesimally small part of total US trade: for many years, it has not moved from its midthirties ranking on the list of US trading partners (US Census Bureau 2014; US International Trade Commission 2015). Moreover, for twenty years, until April 2014, the Philippines was on a US "Special 301" intellectual-property watchlist, which would have acted as a brake to US business investment in the Philippines out of fear of piracy. In a report in 2015, however, the US trade representative noted that "administrative enforcement reforms" in the Philippines had numerous positive impacts, "including increased seizures of pirated and counterfeit goods," so the Philippines was removed from the 301 watchlist (Froman 2015, 6).

The Philippines nonetheless remains Southeast Asia's fastest-growing economy, a position it has occupied for several years, and in 2015 Bloomberg rated it second behind China among the world's fastest-growing economies, with a growth rate of slightly more than 6 percent (*Bloomberg Business* 2015). On the human development scale, however, the Philippines is slipping, indicating that the economic success story is built on the backs of the poor. In 2000, the Philippines ranked 70th in the UN Human Development Index; twelve years later it had slipped to 114th (UNDP 2001, 2013). In the first half of 2015, according to a Philippine Statistics Authority (2016) report, 26.3 percent of Filipinos, or almost 27 million people, were living below the official poverty line. The Autonomous Region of Muslim Mindanao, home of the Philippines' approximately 5 million Moros, forms roughly 10 percent of the entire landmass of the Philippines and is the poorest region in the country: 46.9 percent of people live below the poverty line and have poor access to infrastructure and services. Yet it is also among the country's most fertile and mineral-rich areas, although most intensive agricultural production has been carried out in the eastern (Christian) part of the island.

Poverty is one of the main drivers providing the labor force for one of the Philippines' thriving "export industries": sex tourism, which is another way of saying transnationalized prostitution. Because prostitution and trafficking are technically illegal in the Philippines, it is difficult to know exactly how many women are working in the sex trade, but it may be as many as one million. Many more work as "entertainers" in Southeast and North Asia. I return presently to the question of prostitution, its broader cultural impacts, and its close ties to the history of US military presence in the Philippines.

Guns and Money in the United States after 9/11

Harvard economist Ed Glaeser, among other commentators, has observed that "given the enormous amount of destruction caused by armed conflict, it is remarkable that countries enthusiastically enter into wars when negotiated settlement is presumably always an option" (2009, 33). Wars are indeed costly in terms of both money and lives lost and can also be costly politically, although (often right-wing) governments have invariably used them to shore up their popularity—as was demonstrated, for example, by the contribution of the success of the Falklands War to cementing Margaret Thatcher's popularity in the United Kingdom in 1982. Twenty years later, 9/11 gave Tony Blair's "New Labour" a fillip, turned around a difficult electoral situation for

Prime Minister John Howard in Australia, and provided rich political material for two successive Bush II administrations. In all three cases, the wars and associated domestic security measures cost a great deal of public money and in wag-the-dog style diverted attention and funds from other pressing and arguably more important domestic matters such as health, education, and welfare as well as from other serious international problems, many of the latter also concerning health, education, and welfare. At the same time, war has been good for business on other levels. The United States, as "the largest and most technologically powerful economy in the world, with total GDP of US$16.8 trillion [in 2014]" (CIA n.d.), is, unsurprisingly, both the main big spender and the main big beneficiary from war business, and much has been written about the US military-industrial complex and the post-9/11 militarization of society in the United States (see, e.g., Enloe 2007, 2010; Klein 2007; Hartley 2011).

Data compiled by SIPRI shows that world military spending for the year 2012 was "$1756 billion, representing 2.5 per cent of global gross domestic product (GDP) or $249 for each person in the world" (2013, 6). Even though this figure represents the first slight drop (0.4 percent) since 1998, the overall total for 2012 remained higher than in any year between World War II and 2010. By 2014, the spending total was up to $1,776 billion, but as a percentage of GDP it had dropped again slightly to 2.3 percent or $245 per person. "Total expenditure was [thus] about 0.4 percent lower in real terms than in 2013" (SIPRI 2015c, 14).

SIPRI statistics show evidence that the pattern of increases in military spending after 2010 shifted away from the United States, where spending has fallen since 2010 (largely attributable to cutbacks following the global financial crisis and withdrawal of US troops from Iraq), and toward Asia, where increases have continued, albeit more slowly, as well as toward the Middle East and North Africa, where increases have accelerated, no doubt in part connected to civil unrest in many parts of this region. High-income countries account for roughly 80 percent of world military spending but only 16 percent of world population. The military-industrial complex is also one of the world's major employers of labor. Many of the highly skilled members of defense industry workforces are easily employable in the civil sector, leading one economist to ask "whether defence spending 'crowds-out' valuable civil investment and diverts scientific manpower [*sic*] from civil research projects" (Hartley 2011, 7).

In 2005, the year in which Hurricane Katrina and the Subic rape case occurred, world defense spending was US$1,118 billion, a 34 percent increase in real terms over the previous decade (with the bulk of that increase being in the 2001–3 period). The United States and Asia (China in particular) were responsible for the most significant increases, according to Global Issues (Shah 2013). In that year, the Philippines had a budget deficit of 146.5 billion pesos (roughly US$2.7 billion at December 2005 exchange rates) (Philippine Statistics Authority n.d.c). Philippine military spending in 2004, at US$800 million, was a fraction of that deficit—so small, in fact, as to not even register as a significant fraction of one percent of world military spending. The same year US military defense spending was $495.3 billion, or, put another way, the US spent *per minute* on defense that year roughly what the Philippines spent for the entire year (USGovernmentSpending.com n.d.). Even when one factors in the difference in population to arrive at a per capita figure (there are roughly three times more people living in the United States), the difference between US and Philippine defense spending is still substantial. Although a relatively small percentage of GDP (roughly 4 percent in 2005, which would climb to 6 percent by 2010), defense spending has been consistently a little more than one-fifth of the total US budget since 9/11 and has represented more than half of federal discretionary spending, a significant increase from pre-9/11 levels. The US military is also the most technologically advanced in the world.

US military spending accounts for roughly one-third of the world's spending in dollar terms (SIPRI 2015a), although if expressed as a percentage of GDP its spending is lower than that of Arabian Gulf states, such as the United Arab Emirates, Oman, and Saudi Arabia, which are among the most heavily militarized societies in the world. Saudi Arabia is one of the world's top-ten military spenders in purely dollar terms (SIPRI 2015a). The United States is the main military supplier to the eight states bordering the Gulf (with the exception of Iran, which buys its arms from Russia and China), followed by the United Kingdom (for Bahrain and Saudi Arabia) and France (for the United Arab Emirates and Oman) (Solmirano and Wezeman 2010). US military spending as percentage of GDP is significantly lower than that of Israel, but the United States is also the main military supplier to Israel, which is the largest cumulative recipient of US foreign aid since World War II, almost all of which is military (Sharp 2011). An assessment of defense spending outside the world's major military-industrial centers thus also needs to take in military aid and arms imports as part of the picture.

US military spending climbed sharply in the decade after 9/11, with the greatest increases occurring between 2001 and 2004 and then again between 2007 and 2009 (annual increases of roughly US$50 billion per year during both periods) (SIPRI 2015a). Although the significant increases in 2002, 2003, and 2004 can be attributed to the operations in Afghanistan and Iraq, some commentary suggests that they are not *solely* attributable to these operations. Moreover, the surge in US military spending commenced three years *before* 9/11, which is another indicator that 9/11 simply accelerated a process that was already in train.

A significant proportion of that surge in US military spending has gone toward operations and maintenance (O&M) and accounts for 85 percent of the US DoD's civilian payroll, which, again, is a large increase over the pre-1998 period (Conetta 2010). Apart from payroll, O&M spending goes to the purchase of goods and services. In other words, O&M is at the heart of the DoD's relationship with private contractors. "Since 1989, the 'goods and services' portion has grown significantly. . . . Today, it claims around 80% of the O&M budget. And, within this trend, the portion that is contractor services has grown" (Conetta 2010, 6). Carl Conetta attributes the significant increase in O&M spending, particularly through outsourcing to contractor services, to the fact that after 9/11 existing defense forces and equipment were ill equipped to take on two major wars, not to mention the secondary "security" operations into which Bush launched the United States. "Modernization spending," which includes both procurement and research and development also increased significantly, and both modernization and O&M increased relative to spending on personnel overall. As Conetta (2010) notes, much of the personnel costs has been shifted away from DoD military or civilian personnel to outsourced contract labor, and it is not clear that this outsourcing has always been competitively handled, with sometimes only one company tendering for the contract.

Attention was also drawn in the wake of 9/11 to the number of senior Bush II administration appointments with financial links to the arms and energy industries. An anniversary article, "9/11 in Numbers," published in the *Guardian* in 2002, put these figures at thirty-two and twenty-one, respectively (Templeton and Lumley 2002). Conetta (2010), citing a study by Paul C. Light of the Brookings Institution, further notes that the increase of contract labor is greater than the decrease of DoD labor. Overall, he considers that the US state lacked discipline in its approach to military modernization and spending reform prior to 9/11, and the presence of outsourcing had already laid the groundwork for what followed after 9/11.

A number of post-9/11 analyses are supportive of privatization of a number of military and associated operations within conflict and postconflict situations. In 2002, for example, Allan Gerson and Nat Colletta (the founding manager of the World Bank's postconflict unit) argued that public–private sector partnering had several advantages. They suggested that the two sectors shared "a common interest in eliminating key obstacles to peace"—for example, "a secure and predictable environment in which to work, cost-effective means of achieving results, and satisfied clients" (32). Other reasons advanced include: private companies are sometimes trusted where unstable or corrupt local governments are not; they function pragmatically rather than politically; and they are efficiency driven, maximizing results from minimal resources. Gerson and Colletta thus suggested that the private sector be centrally involved in all levels of UN and multilateral peace processes, including investment in building the postconflict economy. At the same time, they expressed reservations about the use of private security firms, especially as concerns transparency and regulation of their operations, with human rights issues of particular concern (2002, chap. 7).

The rosy picture Gerson and Colletta paint, however, is rarely borne out by the facts. A look at the history of multinational companies' involvement in national politics shows numerous examples of these companies supporting national political parties and political movements of all kinds, including extreme-right movements. More generally, their relationships with the political class are far from transparent, evidenced by any one of a number of political scandals that erupt every year, including in the West. Incidentally, Transparency International ranks the Philippines 85th on its Corruption Perceptions Index for 2014, alongside a number of other countries, including India and Thailand; this position is an improvement from 2013, when it was 94th; in 2005, it was ranked 117th along with such countries as Afghanistan, Bolivia, and Uganda. The United States came in at 17th in 2005 but slipped to 19th by 2014. This makes it less corrupt than, say, France, in 26th position in 2014, but quite a way behind the squeaky-clean Scandinavian countries, Switzerland, and New Zealand (Transparency International 2005, 2014). Transparency International has been criticized for the inadequacy of the research on which its figures are based, notably its narrow focus on national elites' perceptions (Cobham 2013). Its data are nonetheless indicative of trends, and its findings are borne out by other indicators of corruption, such as those briefly mentioned earlier in relation to the Philippines.

The political interests of private enterprise are, of course, invariably linked to financial interest. "War on terror [is] good for defense firms in [the] US," proclaimed the *Taipei Times* on August 21, 2005, a few days before Katrina wreaked its havoc on US states around the Gulf of Mexico. The article cited Lockheed Martin, Boeing, Northrop Grumman, Raytheon, General Dynamics, Honeywell, and United Technologies as benefiting from significant amounts set aside in the US defense budget for procurement and for research and development. According to SIPRI (2015b), in 2013 the United States had thirty-eight of the world's top one hundred arms- and military-service-producing companies, excluding China, and five of the top six, which are the same five as half a decade earlier: Lockheed Martin, Boeing, General Dynamics, Raytheon, and Northrop Grumman. The British company BAE Systems is the other member of the top six, in third position behind Lockheed Martin and Boeing (SIPRI 2015b). The United States had well more than half of the arms- and military-service-market share in 2013, with the United Kingdom and France combined taking roughly another 20 percent (SIPRI 2015b).

US firms with a significant interest in US overseas operations experienced a slight decline in revenue between 2011 and 2013 as the United States wound back its overseas operations. In 2004, however, the picture was quite different. Boeing celebrated a huge jump in its sales figures, turning around a loss of the previous year into a US$607 million profit, driven by military sales (*BBC News* 2004). It was even planning to take on another 3,000 workers, although admittedly this addition did not make much of a dent in the 42,000 it had laid off earlier owing to falls in nonmilitary sales after 9/11. By the end of June 2005, however, business had picked up even more: according to an article posted on the Corporate Watch website, Boeing then had military orders of US$85.7 billion (Bauer 2005). By the end of the third quarter of that year, its profits had jumped 7 percent from 2004 figures, the increase being largely owing to its sales in integrated defense systems (Boeing 2005). Rival firm Lockheed Martin was also sitting pretty. Lockheed Martin is principal supplier of the US government and top seller of secure computer systems (and number one in SIPRI's top one hundred for 2011, 2012, 2013, and 2014—Boeing occupied that position in 2010). Its net profit jumped 41 percent to US$830 million in the first six months of 2005.

These figures are without factoring in the firms that supply infrastructure, such as energy firm Halliburton or technology firm Computer Services Corporation, which took over Dyncorp and gathered up numerous contracts for "rebuilding" work in Iraq and Afghanistan, involving everything from providing transport to training lawyers. These firms became key partners in the military-financial operations of the "deep state." Like Conetta and Light, Peter Scott argued in 2007 that the US response to 9/11 was in the making long before 9/11 occurred, and in some respects 9/11 was an "opportunity" (a term that both Bush and Rumsfeld used) to "refashion the world" (qtd. in Scott 2007, 2). Scott traced the development of the "deep state" (or "security state") over the past several decades, a development characterized by covert actions occurring in a sphere that is immune to public opinion but subservient to big capital (Scott foregrounded the CIA in particular). These actions are concurrent with the weakening of the public state—that is, the state that is responsive to civil society—and the fracturing of civil society. The "deep state," according to Scott, "has tended increasingly toward global dominance at any price, without regard to consequences" (2007, 4). Former vice president Dick Cheney's "one percent doctrine," which institutionalized paranoia and overreaction to any suggestion of a threat, however slight, became, writes Scott, the basis for (deep) state policy and action. Cheney's doctrine was that the United States needed to respond if there was even a one percent threat of terrorists getting hold of a weapon of mass destruction (Suskind 2006). Noam Chomsky similarly describes the "Bush doctrine" as one of "pre-emptive strike" against suspected threats and notes that such politics are not entirely new in the United States. For example, he says, Ronald Reagan justified the US bombing of Libya in 1986 as "self-defense against future attack," and Clinton also used the idea of "pre-emptive response" (2011, 151–52).

According to Naomi Klein, "Halliburton's role," under the leadership of future vice president Dick Cheney while Clinton served as president, "was to expand so dramatically that it would transform the nature of modern war" (2007, 291–92). The Cheney–Halliburton relationship would lead to the company being able "to stretch and expand the meaning of the term 'logistical support' until Halliburton was responsible for creating the entire infrastructure of a US military operation overseas" (Klein 2007, 192). Although the role of Halliburton has been most frequently denounced in relation to Iraq, the model had already been tried out in the Balkans in the 1990s, again under a Clinton-led operation. In Halliburton's case, too, 9/11 provided an "opportunity" to further expand and deploy a military-industrial arsenal that was already well developed.

This arsenal makes the United States the biggest military exporter to the nonindustrialized world, with sales topping US$150 billion in 2004, the year before Katrina and the Subic rape case. It is the main military supplier to the Philippines, but the latter also buys conventional weapons from Canada and small arms from Japan. The next section examines the "service industries" that accompany this military expansion.

Serving the Military

In the United States, 9/11 had an immediate impact on jobs in hospitality and tourism, but this impact was relatively short-lived; the global financial crisis seven years later demonstrably had a much more severe effect on US unemployment figures, which doubled from the middle of the decade to 2011. Militarization and information technology accounted for a great deal of the jobs recovery, but women's employment, as Department of Labor statistics showed for 2014, remained concentrated largely in the usual areas: low-status office and financial work; cleaning and housekeeping; waiting tables; elementary school teaching and related work; care giving; and health care (mostly as nurses and nurses' aides) and social services. Roughly half of all women in the civilian workforce are employed in either education or health services or wholesale and retail, which is double the number of men working in these sectors. This is notwithstanding the fact that some 60 percent of women in the workforce have college degrees or some college education, which is a slightly higher proportion than for men. In every single occupation, whether blue collar, pink collar, white collar, or managerial, women earned between 65 percent and 90 percent of men's earnings, with the national averages for all ethnic groups around 80 percent (US Department of Labor n.d.). Interestingly, many of these low-status feminized service occupations, notably in the areas of care, retail, low-level administration, and food preparation and serving, are where much of the projected growth in jobs to 2022 is supposed to be coming from (US Department of Labor 2016). Women's labor-force participation remains relatively low, at 57 percent of all women, and African American and Hispanic women's unemployment rates are close to double those of white women, with higher rates for African American women, although the projected job-growth figures are for areas in which there are higher concentrations of minority and immigrant women, such as personal care, home health services, and nursing.

In terms of women's work, then, 9/11 would seem to have had little demonstrable impact in the United States: it is more a case of *plus ça change*. It is arguable that offshored call-center and manufacturing work has deleteriously affected the employment rates of low-status white-collar and blue-collar workers in the United States, but 9/11 per se is unrelated to these developments. At the same time, if women's employment remains concentrated in low-status, low-paid traditional areas, and jobs growth is currently in many of those areas, then the post-9/11 climate of militarized masculinity—of "men in arms" and "women in service" (Falquet 2008, chap. 2)—combined with the ongoing post-financial-crisis labor-market downturn and increase in precarious work, will not help improve things for women.

In the Philippines, there are similar stories to tell, except that a high proportion of offshored Western jobs are now done by Philippine women in manufacturing and call centers located in Philippine cities and industrial zones. In addition, anywhere between 2 and 10 million Philippine people have emigrated to work outside the Philippines and have become readily identifiable by the acronym OFW: overseas Filipino workers. The Philippine Statistics Authority (n.d.d) estimates that some 2.3 million Philippine citizens, or roughly 2.25 percent of the entire Philippine population, are OFWs. The US DoS puts this figure much higher, at 10 million (2015). Roughly one-third of OFWs are unskilled, but this proportion rises to 54 percent for women. Slightly more than half of OFWs are young, and there is a much higher concentration of women than men in the younger-than-thirty age group. Remittances from all OFWs were estimated in September 2014 at some 173.2 billion pesos, which is approximately 10 percent of Philippine GDP (Philippines Statistics Authority n.d.a). Of the female OFWs, most work as nurses, domestic workers, or "entertainers," the last often associated with prostitution as well. Most of the "entertainers" overseas are working in Japan.

Although trafficking and prostitution are illegal in the Philippines, the country is identified as a significant source country for trafficking in women for domestic and sex labor, and fraudulent recruiters in these industries operate via social media and websites and sometimes from physical premises in Philippine cities (US DoS 2015). Attempts by the Philippine state to crack down on these unscrupulous recruiters have to date had insufficient results. Filipinas are certainly among the largest numbers of "mobile" Asian labor, to the point where it could be argued that they are the Philippines' most highly exportable and lucrative commodity (Parreñas 2003; Lacsamana 2012). As the wildly varying estimates of OFWs show, however, it is difficult to obtain accurate statistics on their numbers, all the more because many are working overseas illegally. In the mid-1990s, according to statistics cited by Aida Santos, 95 percent of Filipina migrant workers—mostly domestic workers—in Singapore were working without permits (2002, unnumbered page). Philippine women, as offshored call-center and factory workers, as exportable labor, and as members of a growing "precariat" (Standing 2011), are one of the most highly transnationalized workforces in the world and in terms of their socioeconomic status globally have much in common with African American and Hispanic women in the United States.

I prefer the term *prostitution* to *sex work* because, although I agree that "sex work" is indeed work, meaning labor performed in a relationship of economic exchange in an unequal relationship of provider and consumer, I reject the individualist and valorizing connotations that the term *sex work* has taken on in English. Rather, I place "sex work" in a continuum of domestic, reproductive, and sexual labor performed by women and appropriated by men in a relationship that Colette Guillaumin ([1978] 1992b) has called *sexage*, a term that provides a conceptual framework for considering sex(ual work) as comparable to slavery (*esclavage*) and serfdom (*servage*). This appropriation is specific to the embodied and sexualized work that is performed by women (or sometimes by feminized men) for the benefit of men and that, as such, is specifically and profoundly alienating in ways that other "work" cannot be. Whatever one's position concerning the degree to which or circumstances in which prostitution is forced or chosen or concerning the legal measures to be taken to abolish, liberalize, regulate, or otherwise deal with it, prostitution is *not* a job like any other. In the Philippines, it is historically embedded within a raced, gendered, militarized, and globalized political economy, such that Philippine women become constructed as somehow inherently prostitutable (Winter 2011a, 384). To speak of "choice" in such a context is at best naïve and at worst disingenuous; as Nicole-Claude Mathieu put it many years ago, "yielding is not consenting" (1991; see also Baker 2008; Lacsamana 2012).

Accurate numbers of women and children working in prostitution *within* the Philippines are, like accurate statistics on OFWs, notoriously difficult to obtain. I have seen estimates that range from 300,000 women and 75,000 children to 800,000 women and 100,000 children, but none of these estimates is completely reliable, all the less because prostitution is illegal and thus mostly conducted covertly. Whatever the numbers, practically all commentators link prostitution in the Philippines not only to the US military presence but also to poverty. According to official statistics, unemployment in the Philippines was running at approximately 8 percent in 2005; half of the unemployed were younger than twenty-five (Philippine Statistics Authority 2005). The Philippine Statistics Authority (2004) also published data for 2004 that showed that 20 percent of the Philippine population did not have access to safe drinking water, and the Asian Development Bank (2009) estimated poverty levels at a little less than 27 percent in 2006, although "self-reported" poverty levels were double that figure. Roughly one-third of the Philippine population was also younger than fifteen at that time, which is perhaps not unusual in the so-called Global South, particularly when the population is (mostly) Catholic (Philippine Statistics Authority n.d.b).

Following the closure of Clark Air Force Base and Subic Naval Base in 1991 and 1992, both the Clark Zone, adjacent to the city of Angeles in the province of Pampanga in central Luzon, and the Subic

Freeport Zone, adjacent to Olongapo City in the province of Zambales in central Luzon, were redeveloped as "special economic zones" that attract both (sex) tourism and offshored manufacturing. This development is managed by semigovernment, semiprivate organizations set up by the Ramos administration in 1993. Construction of a mega shopping mall in the Clark Zone—the seventh in the area—had begun there the year Hurricane Katrina and the Subic rape case occurred.

International resorts, nightclubs, sex bars, and theme parks (including military-theme resorts along the lines of "jungle warfare") became part of the development blueprint for Clark and Subic. The former Clark airstrip was converted to an international airport, dubbed "Diosdado Macapagal International Airport" after a former president (father of Gloria Macapagal Arroyo), and a growing number of Asian airlines offer discounted direct flights to Angeles (Clark) from places such as Singapore, Kuala Lumpur, Seoul, and Hong Kong. Thai Airlines, for example, commenced direct flights from Bangkok to Angeles in September 2007, notwithstanding the fact that Clark is strong competition for Thailand's own sex tourism industry. Tens of thousands of foreigners visit Clark and Subic every year, many, even most, of them for sex tourism. Even if such tourism declined a little following 9/11 and then again following the global financial crisis, these were but small hiccups: Diosdado Macapagal Airport logged record numbers of international business and tourist passenger traffic in the first five months of 2009 (Winter 2012b). A new ninety-four-kilometer expressway opened in 2008, the SCTEX, linking Clark, Subic, and Manila. It has facilitated road travel between Luzon's main business and (sex) tourism sites. Angeles's approximately one million residents live mainly off tourism, notably sex tourism in connection with Clark, and both the Angeles city tourism website and an Angeles sex tourism website proclaim it is the "entertainment capital of the Philippines."[1]

1. For these websites, see http://www.angelescity.net/ and http://www.sex holidayasia.com/destination/philippines-guide/angeles-city-sex-guide/ (both accessed Nov. 21, 2015).

During US–Philippine military-training exercises, members of the military mingle with the tourists in the sex bars and resorts, which are owned mostly by foreigners. The bigger resorts are increasingly owned by Japanese and Koreans, with many of the smaller bars in both areas owned by Western men from various European countries, the United States, and Australia. The tourists also come from the West and increasingly from Northeast Asia. Along the Clark "entertainment" strip and in some of the sex bars in Subic, Olongapo City, and neighboring Barrio Barretto, which is in the Subic area but outside the Freeport Zone, women must be accompanied by men to gain entry. My informants in these areas also confirmed that pay rates for the staff differ: the dancers earn more than the bar staff and more again if a customer buys them a drink. The rate increases significantly if a customer takes one of the dancers for the night. This "overnight" money is paid to the workers out of the "bar fines" paid by customers: this is the way bars get around Philippine antiprostitution laws (Winter 2012b, 88). It is not difficult to understand why some of the dancers, who are living in poverty, decide to earn significantly more money in this way—assuming they are given a choice in the matter.

My informants also told me how surprised they often were at the choices made by the customers, who tended to pick the "ugliest" girls, by which they meant the most "Filipino" looking: small, dark, full lips, broad turned-up noses, hair not always sleek. By Filipino standards, white is beautiful: Princess Diana remained in the mid-2000s the impossible ideal to aspire to. According to Filipinos, the Philippine mestizo class is the beautiful class, the tall and desirable class of long straight noses, pale skin, and smooth hair; it is also generally the class that holds political power and economic privilege. So my informants had difficulty understanding that for the Western customers the more "exotic" a woman looked, the greater her value as a sex commodity.

Despite pressure to close down the sex industry following adoption of a Philippine antitrafficking law in 2003, the sex bars show no sign of closing. Moreover, many of the women working as "entertainers" in sex tourism or militarized areas in the Philippines are, according to some of my informants, younger than eighteen and are thus working illegally. Along with Manila, the resort island Boracay, and the Cebuano town Camagayan, Clark and Subic are prime sex-work sites to which women and children are trafficked or to which they travel from within Luzon, from the Visayas (where Cebu and Boracay are located), and from Mindanao in search of work.

Increases in the incidence of trafficking and violence against women during US military operations in the Philippines have been well documented (Enloe 2004; Ralston and Keeble 2009; Lacsamana 2012; Winter 2011a, 2012b). The US military is ostensibly there only for "training exercises" because it is no longer legal for it to engage in direct combat in Philippine territory, but local research suggests that US troops engage indirectly through covert operations. In 2002, for example, during the height of "war on terror" exercises, 2,265 US troops were deployed in the region of western Mindanao and the Sulu Archipelago in the six-month Balikatan Operation Enduring Freedom exercise. In 2003, Jean Enriquez from the Coalition against Trafficking in Women in the Asia-Pacific noted that

> in January 2002 alone, during the height of the US troops' "Balikatan" exercises, 35 cases of trafficking in women and children from Davao [in eastern Mindanao] to Zamboanga [in western Mindanao] were recorded. . . . Their ages range from 15 years old to early 20s. According to the victims, the recruiters went to the places where they (children and street freelancers) could usually be found, telling them that there were customers awaiting them in Zamboanga and that they would be paid in dollars.

It was within this context that the Subic rape happened. It was to become a Philippine cause célèbre, linking US military and economic imperialism and violence against women. On November 1, 2005, during a Visiting Forces operation, a young woman who has become known by the pseudonym "Nicole" was gang-raped by five US marines in the Subic Freeport Zone. The marines were initially deemed immune from local prosecution under the terms of the VFA. This immunity, along with an alleged offer of a US$80 million aid package, put the Philippine government under considerable pressure not to prosecute. Prosecution did, however, eventually go ahead, with four of the five marines being charged: an historic event because it was the first time a Philippine court had tried any member of the US military for rape. When the trial began in June 2006, defense lawyers predictably attempted to sully Nicole's reputation and render her somehow responsible for the assault. The trial was plagued by mishaps, including claims of tampering with evidence, the downgrading of charges against three of the marines, and the bowing out by lawyers whom the government had originally selected to represent Nicole. They were replaced (pro bono) by Evalyn Ursua, one of the architects of the Philippines' law against rape adopted in 1997.

In a landmark verdict handed down on December 4, 2006, the court convicted one of the four marines, but he was handed back to US custody under the VFA's terms. In January 2007, a coalition of the Left, including senior civil servants and politicians, petitioned the Philippines Supreme Court to declare the VFA unconstitutional under Philippine law in that it created two classes of criminal. Then in 2009 the nongovernmental movement Stop VFA! was launched: a coalition with feminist groups at its core. Within this coalition, the rights of women and the need for demilitarization were closely linked with claims of national sovereignty against US neoimperialism. The strongly nationalistic thread in these campaigns highlights again the difficulty of nation(alism) for women, as discussed in chapter 2. The state is clearly the enemy for having signed the VFA in the first place and more generally for being elitist and corrupt. The Philippine Left more broadly and feminists in particular have lived a long history of combating both authoritarian (Marcos) and corrupt post-Marcos neoliberal regimes. At the same time, the Philippines has continued to live under the yoke of US military and economic imperialism and now increasingly of East Asian economic imperialism. Like many feminists in the so-called Global South, Philippine feminists live more acutely than their northern counterparts the contradictory relationship all women have to the nation-state. The Stop VFA! movement was a movement for national sovereignty but against the national state.

Since the Subic case, parliamentary inquiries have been made into the VFA, but it has not been repealed, and the business of military operations continues as usual. It even continues more than usually following the Obama administration's refocusing of US defense strategy in 2012 away from Europe and the Middle East and toward Asia—a shift subsequently known as the "pivot to the Pacific"—as part of a general cutback at that time (Winter 2011b; US DoD 2012; Manyin et al. 2012). The "pivot" was no doubt also an acknowledgment of the failure of former secretary of state Condoleezza Rice's doctrine of "transformational diplomacy" in the Middle East, although the bureau set up to pursue that doctrine remains in effect under a new name (since 2011), the "Bureau of Conflict and Stabilization Operations."[2]

So what does all this have to do with Hurricane Katrina?

The Cost of "Security"

By the time Hurricane Katrina had finished with the southern US coastline, it left 80 percent of New Orleans under water. Both mainstream and alternative international media coverage featured indictment of a government that could mobilize troops to invade Afghanistan and Iraq with apparent ease but could not mobilize resources to (*a*) lessen the extent of the Katrina disaster through preventive infrastructure, such as bigger and stronger levees, when federal funding for the Southeastern Louisiana Flood Control Project slowed to a trickle in 2003, or (*b*) assist and evacuate the devastated population in a timely fashion—one reason being that 35 percent of the Louisiana National Guard and 40 percent of the National Guard from neighboring Katrina-affected Mississippi were in Iraq at the time. On September 8, 2005, a few hundred evacuees, most of whom were reportedly women, marched

2. See the Bureau of Conflict and Stabilization Operations website at http://www.state.gov/j/cso/ (accessed Nov. 21, 2015). For more on the Subic rape case, see Winter 2011b and Lacsamana 2012. For more on transformational diplomacy, see Rice 2006 and Vaïsse 2007.

on the White House to demand a more appropriate response to the crisis, while other individuals and groups seized newfound opportunities to make money out of the disaster or to instrumentalize it to make a political point. The Christian fundamentalist website Repent America, for example, claimed the hurricane to be God's punishment for the gay debauchery of New Orleans, and a site called Café Press was advertising for sale a range of "I survived Hurricane Katrina" T-shirts.[3] The latter site came up sixth in a Google search I conducted on the day of the women's march on Washington in 2005, using the keyword *Hurricane Katrina women*.

The devastation left by Hurricane Katrina was compounded by the "failure at all levels of government that significantly undermined and detracted from the heroic efforts of first responders," as the report of a Senate Bipartisan Committee set up to investigate government preparation and response put it in 2006 (Davis et al. 2006, 1). That double devastation highlighted in particular the plight of the US poor, whose numbers were higher than ever according to a report for 2004 released by the US Census Bureau on August 30, 2005, the day after Katrina hit the US coastline. This report showed the number of United Statians officially living in poverty to be 37 million, or 12.7 percent of the population, up 1.1 million from 2003 and the fourth straight increase (DeNavas-Witt, Proctor, and Lee 2005, 9). The number of people without health insurance in 2004 also increased by 800,000 to 45.8 million people but remained stable at 15.7 percent. In a country where a five-day prescription for antibiotics at that time could cost more than US$100 (I know from personal experience), this figure was worrying, even if the number of people *with* health insurance also increased by 2 million in 2004. African Americans remained the poorest ethnic group in the United States, and the South the poorest region, but in percentage terms the rate of poverty among whites had increased

---

3. For these attempts to make money from and to politicize Hurricane Katrina, see http://www.cafepress.com/katrinatshirts and http://www.repentamerica.com /pr_hurricanekatrina.html, respectively (both accessed Sept. 8, 2005).

slightly, from 8.2 percent to 8.6 percent. One-third of the US poor were—and still are—children. The same year, 2004, women's real median income declined 0.6 percent, and their income expressed as a proportion of every dollar earned by men was 77 cents, a figure that had changed little in the previous five years (DeNavas-Witt, Proctor, and Lee 2005, 7). (Twelve years later, the proportion has struggled to reach 80 cents [Proctor, Semega, and Kollar 2016].) The number of female-headed households living in poverty had increased by 1.5 percent. Poverty levels in the United States had in fact become higher in 2005 than in the 1970s as well as being higher than in most of the industrialized world (US Census Bureau 2005).

Analyses of Hurricane Katrina's impact have demonstrated how it threw into sharp relief the race–class–gender links of poverty in the United States. Paul Frymer, Dara Strolovitch, and Dorian Warren noted at the time that 67 percent of New Orleans residents were African American and that the city was "dominated by a low-wage, service, and tourist economy in which 28% of residents live below the poverty line" (2006, 44). That population statistic has changed since then; subsequent research shows that not all African Americans and not all the poor have had the material means to move back to the city since reconstruction. A report published in October 2014 by the New Orleans Data Center (Shrinath, Mack, and Plyer 2014) showed that the population of New Orleans remained lower in 2013 by some 100,000 people than in 2000, notwithstanding a 4 percent increase since 2010. The race demographic of the population had also changed. Although African Americans remained the majority, they were now a smaller majority: 59.1 percent in 2013 compared to 66.7 percent in 2000. The white population had increased over the same period from 26.6 percent to 31 percent, and the Hispanic population had almost doubled from 3.1 percent to 5.5 percent. The share of adults with less than a high school degree had also dropped dramatically during this period, from 22 to 25 percent, depending on the parish, to just 15 percent, which is nonetheless still 2 percent higher than the national average. The poverty rate declined from 1999 to 2007 but rose again subsequently so that in 2013 it was statistically unchanged, at 27 percent, compared to the national average of 16 percent, which was up from 12 percent twelve years earlier.

The level of poverty in New Orleans and surrounding parishes directly affected needs following the hurricane and highlighted the federal government's combined unwillingness and inability to meet those needs (Frymer, Strolovitch, and Warren 2006; see also Davis et al. 2006). Race further affected *perceptions* of whether New Orleans residents "mattered" to the US state. In a poll taken a few days after the hurricane, 66 percent of African Americans surveyed believed the government response would have been markedly better if the majority of victims had been white (Frymer, Strolovitch, and Warren 2006, 42).

With respect to the gendered impact, a report published one year after Hurricane Katrina by the Institute for Women's Policy Research noted that the three states affected by Katrina—Louisiana, Mississippi, and Texas—"rank in the bottom ten among all states in the nation on many indicators of women's economic status calculated by the Institute. . . . Women in the affected metropolitan areas of New Orleans, Biloxi–Gulfport–Pascagoula, and Beaumont–Port Arthur are more likely than men to live in poverty, to raise children on their own, and to hold low-paying jobs" (Williams et al. 2006, 1).

"What does safety mean in a post-disaster world?" asked Pamela Jenkins and Brenda Phillips in 2008. Their answer: "While the patterns of violence may not have changed, the social context has" (2008, 68). So it is with "everyday" violence against women. Post-Katrina studies have indicated exacerbation of domestic violence as well as its mental and physical health impacts on women following the hurricane, in particular poor and African American women and women with very young children (Bergin 2008; Murakami-Ramalho and Durodoye 2008; Harville et al. 2010; Paxson et al. 2012). Many women suffered post-traumatic stress disorder, and the situation of the poorest women was in almost every respect comparable to that of internally displaced persons in far less wealthy countries (Murakami-Ramalho and Durodoye 2008). Kathleen Bergin, in discussing impacts on African American women in terms of sexual violence, argues that "to deny that black women faced a disproportionate risk of sexual violence during Hurricane Katrina naively overlooks what is, at bottom, an unexceptional female life experience," given the high rates of sexual violence against women under normal circumstances (2008, 178). Bergin suggests that the material conditions following Katrina and the lack of any confidence in representatives of law and order that the most disadvantaged of the displaced population felt at that time led to widespread underreporting of violence.

Making the Connections

In the Philippines, women continue to service the soldiers in Angeles, Olongapo City, and Zamboanga and to tell customers in McDonald's to "have a nice day" as they serve them Filipino McBreakfasts. In the hurricane-ravaged South of the United States, some may have thrown out the "I survived Hurricane Katrina" T-shirts they bought online and wore once, maybe twice, while others continue to contemplate the wreck of New Orleans and their lives there. Yet others ask their government why it could find billions to wage war on Iraq but not a few hundred million to shore up levees in the heart of an ethnically and culturally unique part of the country's poor South. Meanwhile, executives of firms such as Boeing, Halliburton, and, indeed, McDonald's are perhaps drinking to their handsome profits in a sleek bar where they are entertained by equally sleek "hostesses," often with exotic names and all with unfaltering smiles. Some of those "hostesses" may even come from the Philippines.

That Hurricane Katrina and the Subic rape case happened within a few short months of each other is coincidental. Yet the two nations in which they occurred are linked by a network of military, political, and economic exchanges and influence in a world where guns and money and those who own and control them matter, but everybody else does not. It is a world where it is possible to make a buck out of practically anything, from vulnerable young women to the devastation wreaked by a hurricane, and where those responsible for this commodification are rarely if ever held to account. When one applies a transnational feminist lens to these scenarios and starts to pay attention to how the lives of the world's women are linked through global capitalist militarization, one begins to see what Hurricane Katrina might have to do with the Subic rape case and to understand better how gender does indeed "make the world go round" (Enloe 1990, 1). One better understands that "what is at work is a powerful alignment of elite interests toward the needs of a gendered, global capitalist economy" (Robinson 2009, 116) that is no more concerned with the oppression of women, with poverty, or with human suffering in the United States than anywhere else.

What happens, then, when feminists try to address these questions transnationally, as they have been since well before 9/11 and more so since then? Given the enormity of the forces of money or lack thereof, race, nation, and other accidents of birth or effects of context that have shaped us and driven wedges between us, how can we not only make feminist sense of these post-9/11ist politics but act constructively and effectively to challenge them? Much has been written about the challenges of this activism and of the courage and achievements of the women who have engaged in it (see, e.g., Moghadam 2005; Cockburn 2007, 2012). In the next chapter, I turn to a somewhat underexamined and particularly vexed aspect of this always challenging transnational feminist conversation: that of lesbian visibility and voice in the face of nationalist and ethnoreligious manipulations of feminist (and in some cases, LGBT) rights claims and allegiances.

5

"Whose Side Are You On?"

Shifting Alliances and Strategic Silencings

Analysis of heterosexuality and lesbian politics may seem to be an odd topic for a book on post-9/11ism and women. In response, I turn first to African American feminism and statements such as Sojourner Truth's oft-cited "Ain't I a woman?" In speaking to a women's convention in Akron, Ohio, in 1851 in the context of a debate on racial equality, Truth argued for equality between women and men: "If the first woman God ever made was strong enough to turn the world upside down all alone, these women together ought to be able to turn it back, and get it right side up again! And now they is asking to do it, the men better let them" (Truth 1851).

Some 130 years later, Barbara Smith (almost as) famously wrote in the much-celebrated anthology *But Some of Us Are Brave* (1982) that feminism is "a political theory and practice to free all women," not just the privileged few, and that "anything less is not feminism, but merely female self-aggrandizement" (49). By such arguments alone, lesbians must be part of the feminist conversation about an end to male domination in whatever form.

Yet, one may respond, such arguments could be made for explicit inclusion of all sorts of groups of women. This discussion is not, however, only about "inclusivity" or even "intersectionality" (Crenshaw 1989, 1991). It is about, first, analysis of heterosexuality as a core mechanism of male domination, including in its militarized aspects. Second, it is about the ongoing and surprising marginalization of lesbian voices within so much of transnational feminism when lesbians have been so centrally present in national and transnational feminist peace activism and when there has been a decades-long conversation about heterosexism in the feminist movement.

Indeed, it remains striking—and depressing—that in transnational feminist conversations about international solidarity in a post-9/11 world (and most particularly about solidarity across the "West/Muslim world" divide) one topic above all others has often remained taboo: lesbianism. This taboo can appear strange within the context of a global "alphabet-soup" movement for LGBT and sometimes LGBTI or even LGBTIQ (the Q designating sometimes *queer*, sometimes *questioning*) rights that has made inroads into the UN since the World Health Organization removed homosexuality from its list of mental illnesses in 1990 and Australian Nicholas Toonen took a civil and political rights case to the then UN Human Rights Committee in 1991.[1] The transnationalization and international institutionalization of LGBTI human rights has proceeded apace since the first international civil society conference specifically on LGBTI human rights took place in Montreal in 2006. Even here, however, concern has been expressed about the marginalization of lesbians in an international conversation that remains primarily about men (Sheill 2009; Otto 2014; Winter 2015, forthcoming b).

One might, however, have thought that heterosexism in the feminist movement, at least in the West and some other industrialized countries, was on the wane after decades and decades of debates and divisions as well as after the production of extraordinary analyses (Rich 1980; Wittig 1992; Jackson 1999). These well-known analyses demonstrate that heterosexuality and homosexuality are not simply matters of personal sexual orientation but are deeply political: they are not partitioned off from the rest of women's lives under male domination but are fundamental to the latter's operation. "Compulsory

---

1. UN Doc CCPR/C/50/D/488/1992 (1994), available at the University of Minnesota Human Rights Library at https://www1.umn.edu/humanrts/undocs /html/vws488.htm (accessed Sept. 14, 2014).

heterosexuality" keeps women subservient, and lesbianism is a form of resistance, a refusal to "become woman" within the system of heterosexuality (Beauvoir 1949; Rich 1980; Wittig 1992; Jackson 1999).

Feminists writing on war and nationalism have extended this analysis of male appropriation of women's bodies and sexuality. Serbian feminist peace activists Lepa Mladenović and Divna Matijasević (1996), in discussing the Serbian state's war on Bosnia and brutal repression of feminist, gay, and peace activism at home in the 1990s, point to the links between the logic of war and the logic of male violence against and control of women and their sexuality. At the same time, as Mladenović argues in a later article, "for a feminist lesbian who is politically responsible, the war is a situation that splits her into several pieces" when human rights groups privilege some rights above others because "war urges a hierarchy of . . . needs" (2001, 386–87, 384). The activism of lesbians in the Serbian peace movement was silenced, yet on the streets and in lesbian meeting places of Belgrade, both private citizens and members of the Serbian police were harassing and beating up lesbians, especially those who were involved in peace activism. Mladenović discusses at length the slow process of realization that Serbian heterosexism was part of a process of othering where even if "each hatred has its own particular form[,] . . . underneath there is a common patriarchal code of hatred of the Other" (2001, 389).

The invisibility of lesbian voices and lesbian activism within the peace movement, even as lesbians suffer daily intimidation and often horrendous violence, leads to a particularly painful form of fragmentation. The war is the emergency; lesbian rights are not. They can be dealt with later. How often have women been told this within anticolonial struggles, only to be betrayed following "liberation"? When lesbian feminist activists, including Mladenović, participated in the movement that brought down the Milošević regime in 2000, they looked toward a future that just might be a little less difficult for them. Yet fascist (masculinist, heterosexist) nationalism continues in Serbia, leading to cancellation of some gay pride marches for fear of violence and to violent attacks when marches have been held, as in 2010, despite 5,000-strong police protection that year (CNN 2010).

In the context of post-9/11 politics, a new sort of "war emergency" once again marginalized lesbian voices and privileged heterosexism in the feminist movement. I explained at the start of this book that post-9/11ism has involved a renewed imbrication of religion and politics. This imbrication holds at both state and civil society levels. Following 9/11 and widespread feminist denunciation of the "war on terror," a new respect for religion (Islam in particular) reintroduced cultural relativism into transnational feminist politics or, rather, gave it greater religious justification because it had not really gone away (Howard 1995; Okin et al. 1999; Benhabib 2002). The enormity of 9/11 created a new political urgency for transnational feminist solidarity, a new need for the certainties of monolithic collective identities accompanied by default priorities for feminist solidarity. A new female "politics of piety" (to borrow the title of a controversial book on the subject [Mahmood 2005]) became, at least in relation to the Muslim world, claimed by both Islamic women and Western women as a—if not *the*—post-9/11 Muslim feminist position. Among other impacts of this new (Western) reluctance to criticize anything Islamic, lesbianism once again became relegated to the status of side issue. Again, this development can appear paradoxical in the context of the emergence in recent years of globally visible and vocal activism and a new body of scholarship on the situation, experience, and analyses of LGBTI individuals and groups in the Muslim world (for example, Babayan and Najmabadi 2008; Habib 2010; Kugle 2013) and of a parallel growth of global movements for the right to asylum for homosexuals and lesbians and for gay rights within the Muslim world. (Parvez Sharma's documentary film *A Jihad for Love* [2007] is one of the iconic representations of this trend; see also Habib 2010 and Jansen and Spijkerboer 2011.) Yet in sections of the transnational feminist movement, the articulation of distinct transnational lesbian voices with serious things to say about race, imperialism, capitalism, militarism, and male domination is still often dismissed as a Westerncentric distractor from the main issues.

In the polarized post-9/11 context of "wars on terror" and antiWestern reactions to them, the question "Whose side are you on?"

became more than usually fraught. Or, rather, the challenge became "You must take a side, and here is the script," surprisingly reminiscent of the heyday of extreme leftism. Accepting the challenge meant accepting the script: no ad-libs or other improvisations allowed. Refusing it meant banishment to the uncomfortable limbo of those who had been found defective in their antiempire politics. I admit to caricaturing a little, but only a little.

This chapter is built around my experience and witnessing of the denial—in a feminist context—of lesbian voice and even lesbian existence in 2005, some four years after 9/11—even as Western or Western-aligned states began to brandish "LGBT rights" as evidence of their supposed progressiveness. This witnessing happened on three occasions, on three different continents, in three different transnational feminist contexts and over a period of three months. One might counter that there have been any number of transnational feminist gatherings in any given year, so three out of this large number is not many. This is true, but I have two reasons for considering these cases emblematic. The first is that the three events to which I refer were distinctive in their context, very well attended by women from diverse national and ethnic backgrounds, and extremely high profile in feminist activist or academic circles or both. I thus consider the conferences and incidents I describe here to be relatively representative as a means of assessing the activist and academic transnational feminist mood of the time. The second reason is that in the many transnational feminist and human rights conferences I attend every year, lesbian issues are rarely presented *outside* the LGBTI alphabet, where male and transgender voices dominate, and when they *are* presented, they are rarely framed within the context of transnational activism and solidarity about something other than persecution of LGBTI populations and the right to asylum. In other words, transnational and particularly non-Western lesbian *activism* around issues not only of lesbian rights and voices in their local context but also of those rights and voices transnationally and in relation to peace, democracy, and anticapitalism is rarely foregrounded, with some notable exceptions (such as Lachheb 2015).

The experiences I discuss in this chapter, which were so pointedly framed within a post-9/11 discussion, led me to ponder the difficulties of transnational feminist activism in a post-9/11ist context. They led me to ask myself how it is possible to navigate past those jagged rocks that threaten at any moment to appear, seemingly out of nowhere, to scuttle our fragile solidarities. They led me to ask how that difficult yet essential trust among feminists working in such different, unequal, and often unstable contexts was to be achieved. Finally, they led me to ask how we, as a transnational feminist movement, can conduct those painful conversations that are clearly still necessary—given our different levels of (willing or unwilling) participation in the ideologies and structures of domination—but without being irretrievably wounded by them.

My first encounter with this problem was at the Women's Worlds triennial International Interdisciplinary Conference on Women in Seoul, South Korea, in June 2005. The second was two months later in Jerusalem at an international conference of the antioccupation network Women in Black (WIB). The third was at a major feminist conference with some international participation held in the ethnically diverse inner–western Sydney suburb Bankstown. The first and second incidents had largely to do with the politics of Western guilt, resulting in both self-silencing and attempts to police others (which resulted, paradoxically, in racialized lesbians being silenced as well). The third was an expression of lesbophobia from within a minority: a well-known Indigenous Australian woman speaking at a plenary session at the Bankstown conference denied the existence of lesbians in Indigenous communities, stating that it was culturally foreign to them. The remark outraged many, not the least Indigenous lesbians. The first two events, however, especially the WIB conference, are my focus here.

In discussing these events here, along with the somewhat related debate around the holding of World Pride (an international LGBTI Pride festival), in Jerusalem (mooted for 2005, it ended up taking place in 2006), I am concerned with the complex and risky nature of acts of speaking in the polarized post-9/11 context. I am concerned with the naming and compartmentalizing of identity or identities, the fragility of alliances, and the internal contradictions with which feminists working transnationally are confronted. I am concerned with the ways in which lesbian feminist politics are either silenced or instrumentalized (sometimes both) in the name of transnational solidarity. I am, finally, concerned with the paradoxical impacts of silencing, including self-silencing, in a context where the primary objective is ostensibly the breaking of silence.

Plagues from the West

"Plague from the West" is the expression sometimes used to translate the title of Jalal Al-e Ahmad's essay *Gharbzadegi* (1982, 1983, 1984), mentioned in passing in chapter 1 with relation to R. W. Connell's (2005) framing of "southern theory" and discussed further in chapter 6. I use the expression here because secular feminism, with its emphasis on women's sexual, reproductive, and marital rights, is frequently held up as a primary manifestation of Western decadence from which re-Islamicization will save Muslim society. Because the political and cultural association of lesbianism with "whitewesternness" and thus some sort of suspect imperialism is central to the discussion here (and because homosexuality is illegal in most albeit not all Muslim-majority countries), it is useful to recall the historical and political roots of this view within the context of the "West/Islam" opposition.

The tension between so-called Enlightenment universalism and so-called cultural particularism in MENA in particular has existed for at least the past century and can be traced in some countries, notably Egypt, to the rise of Enlightenment-influenced modernism in the late nineteenth century and later to the rise of Arab-world socialism. Like modernism elsewhere, Arab and Middle Eastern modernism was characterized by, among other things, secularization and advocacy of some degree of women's emancipation, the latter often harnessed to nationalist projects—Kemalist Turkey being an oft-cited example, as is Tunisia. These moves were met from the outset with trenchant resistance from conservatives, a resistance that has invariably involved a return to religious values, cultural identity politics, and the subjection of women, in the private sphere at least. Women's participation in public life is usually tolerated and in some cases encouraged in order to secure women's support for the conservative politics in question. In the colonial or neoimperial context in which these politics evolved in MENA, the conservative push back has come to be described as "Islamism." The latter is firmly part of the modern polity and its democratic processes and has historically combined an anticolonial and anticapitalist stance as well as a preoccupation with socioeconomic welfare, on the one hand, with a populist return to Islamic identity politics and a dogged antifeminism, on the other. Islamists see feminism, more than any other aspect of Western philosophy, as decadent, imperialist, and antithetical to the development of independent Islamic polities.

Yet just as women participate in many right-wing movements that are demonstrably antifeminist and indeed antiwomen (Dworkin 1983; B. Campbell 1987; Bacchetta and Power 2002), they are also visibly present in modern Islamic and Islamist movements. For this discussion, I use the term *Islamic* to refer to (usually conservative) revivalist movements and the term *Islamist* to refer to integrist movements, for which the goal is political domination. The distinction is often moot because Islamic revivalist movements are frequently also political movements or linked to them, but it is nonetheless worth making because some Islamic movements, such as most Sufi movements, are not interested in political power. In the anti-imperial context in which Islamist movements developed in the twentieth century and in which they have thrived anew in a supposedly "postsecularist" post-9/11 framework, religious conservatism has combined powerfully with antiracism, anti-imperialism, and antiauthoritarianism in places such as Egypt, Turkey, and Tunisia. As I discuss further in chapter 6 and to some extent in chapter 7, Islamist movements have positioned themselves as privileged mouthpieces for the resentment and anger of populations that have been socioeconomically marginalized, racially vilified, and caricatured both globally and locally. They have become the champions of democracy, anti-imperialism, and—even though most of them are very comfortable with capitalism—antiglobalization.

They have also succeeded in re-Islamicizing large sections of what had previously been a more secular Left in both Muslim-majority countries and the Muslim diaspora. Even feminists who are not themselves particularly wedded to the idea of "Islamic feminism" as such now ask whether women of Muslim culture who object to veiling or defend secular values have not become too "Westernized" (as discussed, for example, in Winter 2008, chap. 9), or see more progressive elements developing in some Islamic women's activism (e.g., Ahmed 2011).

I discuss the broader political positioning of Islamist movements in the following chapter, but as concerns us here, the tense polarization of post-9/11ism has made it very difficult indeed for feminists in MENA who are combating either enduring Western imperialism or authoritarian regimes in their countries or the rise of Islamist movements—or, often, combating two or all three of them simultaneously. It is equally difficult for the white-and-Western to take a critical stance in relation to Islamist anti-Westernism without immediately being considered some sort of puppet of US (or French or British) imperialism and being labeled "Islamophobic." Post-9/11ism has thus made it particularly difficult once again for feminists to construct a meaningful transnational solidarity in the face of *all* aspects of male domination. The white and Western among us, plagued with our guilt as oppressors and ashamed of the actions of our governments, which do not speak in our names, worry about the extent to which we can impose "our" views, identities, and priorities. But are they truly only "ours"?

Women in Black and the Conference Context, 2005

In August 2005, lesbians participating in the thirteenth WIB international conference visibly occupied public spaces and places in East and West Jerusalem in ways that, although not previously unheard of, were unusual in their intensity, form, magnitude, and political motivation and impacts. The very act of publicly naming lesbianism and lesbian peace activism and in particular the (semi)public naming of the existence of *Palestinian* lesbians could be seen as a somewhat revolutionary breaking of a silence. Although such processes are potentially salutary, the political reality of Palestine and Israel in August 2005 was unfavorable to such emancipatory communication on the eve of the Israeli evacuation of Gaza and in the lead-up to the Palestinian elections in January 2006, which Hamas was poised to win. There was also at that time a debate on holding World Pride in Jerusalem (originally planned for 2005, it finally occurred in 2006 amid protest from both right and left, as we will see presently).

WIB vigils began in February 1988 after the first Palestinian intifada of 1987. WIB was then and remains "a unique phenomenon in the history and politics of Israeli society. Demonstrating against the politics of the government on issues of war and peace has been a relatively new experience for Israelis in general and for women in particular" (Safran 2005, 193), especially considering the national siege mentality that informed the creation of Israel and continues to inform its internal and external politics. The sole rallying point for the women involved in WIB was at the outset and remains, opposition to the occupation; it had and has no common analysis of the situation or a political or social agenda for a solution. As such, WIB is an internally diverse organization in terms of its feminist politics, although it is relatively homogenous in race, being made up primarily of Ashkenazi women: the white women of Israel. The Ashkenazim constitute the political, military, professional, cultural, and business elite in Israel, even though numerically they are a minority: close to 20 percent of the Israeli population are Arab (that is, without counting Gaza and the West Bank), and slightly more than half are Mizrahim, or Middle Eastern and North African Jews. According to reports produced by the Adva Center (Swirski and Konor-Attias 2004; Swirski, Konor-Attias, and Ophir 2013), an independent social justice research group, Ashkenazis are socioeconomically advantaged in relation to the other two groups. On average in 2003, Ashkenazi employees earned 1.26 times the salary of Mizrahi employees and 1.6 that of Arab employees. This gap widened over the decade to 2012, as did the gap between the top percentile of employees and the lowest, although Israel's economic performance increased overall. In 2012, 30 percent of all employees in Israel earned the minimum wage or less, and salary increases of the highest-income earners had been significantly greater in percentage terms. Unemployment rates show similar gaps: they are higher for residents of the Occupied Territories and higher again in the Bedouin towns in southern Israel. Literacy and education levels among the three groups follow similar patterns. Women are more disadvantaged educationally and economically than men in all ethnic groups: for example, women earned 62.2 percent of salaries paid to men in 2003; in 2012, this figure had risen only to 66.1 percent.

Ashkenazi women in Israel are thus women of the elite, even if they are less elite than Ashkenazi men. They are members of the class that benefits the most from the occupation. That WIB is made up of Ashkenazi women is thus both logical and revolutionary. As one of the founder members, Su Schachter, said to me in 2005, "Women in Black is about us: we don't want to be occupiers. Not in our name" (personal communication, June 2005). This point, for Su, is fundamental: it *has* to be "about us" as much as "about them." Otherwise, one is removing oneself and one's own responsibility from the picture. The force behind the creation of WIB is thus a matter of access both to cultural capital and to a political voice as well as of feminist political responsibility to use that access to challenge one's own class and ethnic privilege in resisting the actions of the Israeli state. I note in passing, however—as evidenced by numerous conversations I had in Israel during two visits in 2005—that some Mizrahi women and some Ashkenazi women who work closely with them have criticized members of WIB for forgetting their racialized Jewish sisters in Israel.

At the same time, WIB's unitary rallying call and general inclusivity meant that internal differences could be invisibilized. For lesbians, this was a mixed experience: for some, it meant, especially in the early years, that they could participate actively, even prominently, "without endangering [their] closeted identities" (Schachter 2005, 176). For others, "the overwhelming participation of lesbians in the peace movement helped solidify lesbian identity" (Schachter 2005, 180)—if not necessarily lesbians' visibility. At a workshop on homophobia at a feminist conference in 1991, for example, a founding WIB activist, herself heterosexual, expressed surprise at learning that so many of her coactivists were lesbian. "She realized that she had ignored a whole group of women, thus collaborating in the oppression of lesbians, and understood that lesbians were her allies in the struggle against women's oppression" (Safran 2005, 204). Would that more women had responded like her from the outset.

The thirteenth international WIB conference took place August 12–16, 2005, in East Jerusalem. It was co-organized by WIB and Palestinian women from the East Jerusalem Center for Women and from the Occupied Territories on the request of the previous WIB conference in Italy in 2003. This task was daunting for several reasons. As one of the Israeli organizers put it, "These international women [i.e., WIB activists from outside Israel/Palestine] assume there is a straightforward and unproblematic solidarity and ongoing working relationship between Jewish Israeli women and Palestinian women from East Jerusalem and the Occupied Territories, but this is simply not the case. We had to create that relationship" (personal communication, Aug. 2005).

The nonstraightforwardness of the relationship has three main causes. The first is common to all attempts by members of a dominant colonizing group to work constructively with those who are being oppressed by this same group. However sincere and profound one's political engagement, one remains a member of the oppressor class and benefits from the privilege bestowed on members of that class. This is an objective and incontrovertible fact. It does not mean that actions of subversion and solidarity are not possible, but, as Su Schachter said, "It's about us." The struggle of (mostly Ashkenazi) Jewish Israeli women is clearly not the same struggle as that of Palestinian women. The two groups have different agendas, and even if their goals—an end to the occupation and the establishment of peaceful coexistence—is the same, their means of achieving it and the populations toward which their actions are focused are necessarily different.

The second cause is also arguably common to colonizer-colonized situations. Feminists of a colonized population are necessarily bound up in a nationalist struggle, with all its problems of contradictory allegiances for women, as we saw with relation to Philippine women in the previous chapter. As Marième Hélie-Lucas wrote in 1987 in relation to women in the Algerian struggle for independence and the ongoing postcolonial struggle against imperialism, for women who "belong to a nation that does not have to prove its existence . . . the concept of the nation can be transcended and criticized. . . . For us it is much more difficult to criticize" ([1987] 1990, 108). Feminists of a colonizing population can not only more straightforwardly and coherently criticize the nationalism of their own already-existing state but also more easily resist male-supremacist agendas within their country more generally. Even if feminists are accused of "betraying" the nation (an early and ongoing accusation leveled against WIB), their colonizing nation is, by feminist definition, there to be betrayed, and one can take feminist pride, as did the founders of WIB, in being a "traitor." As another founder member put it, "When they started calling us traitors, I knew we were having an impact" (personal communication, July 2005). It is so much harder, however, to be a "traitor" to the anticolonial nationalist struggle: this is the political blackmail to which colonized women are always subjected.

Third, in the specific situation in Israel and the Occupied Territories, there is a simple material problem: women from Israel and Palestine have great difficulty in meeting to organize conferences. Passages from one side of the Green Line to the other and through the multiple checkpoints that have been created by the construction of the Separation Fence on the Palestinian side are subject to strict military control. As a result, it is difficult for both Israelis and Palestinians, especially Palestinians, to circulate. Many Palestinian women were not able, for this and financial reasons, even to attend the WIB conference, let alone preparatory meetings for it.

The specific political and practical problems in Israel/Palestine were exacerbated by the context in which the conference happened. It was held just prior to the evacuation of Gaza, amidst demonstrations by the antievacuation Jewish Right in Israel, who sported orange ribbons and T-shirts signifying their opposition to settler evacuation. In response, many participants at the WIB conference took to donning blue ribbons signifying support for evacuation, even though it was obvious to many of us that the evacuation from Gaza was a useful ploy for the Sharon government to deflect attention from the building of the Separation Fence, settlement expansion, and escalation of repressive activities in the West Bank. Subsequent events in Gaza have also shown that the settler evacuation did not stop Israeli military intervention there. Many Israeli participants in the conference did not support the wearing of blue ribbons for this reason: it indicated support for the Israeli state. And in pre-electoral Palestine, center and left-wing political parties were gearing up for a fight against the Islamist push led by Hamas. The climate generally was one of political tension. Even though one might ask, "When is it *not* politically tense in Jerusalem?" it was even more than usually the case at that time.

Given these many political tensions and material problems, the success of the conference is a testament to the goodwill and hard work of all the women involved. Attendance far exceeded expectations, with 750 participants from around the world, but there were far fewer women from occupied Palestine than had been hoped (most Palestinian women present were resident in Israel). This lower attendance was owing in part to logistical and financial issues, as mentioned earlier, and in part to hostility to the conference in some sections of the Palestinian political class, notably from Fatah, the largest but also most centrist faction of the Palestinian Liberation Organization, which was anxious to hold on to its majority in the Palestinian Parliament in the face of a serious electoral challenge from Hamas. Women from some other countries, notably in Africa, had difficulty obtaining visas or were refused entry at the airport.

But even more conspicuous by their absence were feminists from other Muslim countries. Some of the Palestinian members apparently vetoed the participation of feminists from Egypt and Pakistan, whose travel fares had been donated by English WIB members. The official reason for the veto was that the Palestinian women imposing it did not wish to support normalization of relations between Muslim countries and Israel, and many Palestinian women support this position. The rumor circulated, however, that the men from Palestinian political parties with which some of the Palestinian women were working did not wish "their" women to come into contact with feminists from other established Muslim countries with equally established feminist movements. The political climate in Palestine at the time, with a demobilized and demoralized Left attempting to prevent Hamas's rise to power in a climate of increased religious and political conservatism, did not lend itself to open support for transnational Muslim-world feminism within Fatah. Although the existence of the veto and the reasons for it remain the subject of speculation, the absence of women from other Arabo-Muslim countries in MENA was, as the saying goes, conspicuous.

In terms of venues and logistics, the organizers, along with the managers and staff of a number of Palestinian-run hotels where the conference was held and where international participants were lodged, worked wonders, which was all the more evident because the higher than anticipated numbers created some logistical problems in organizing last-minute accommodation in the Old City and sufficient workshop space at the main conference venue, the Seven Arches Hotel in Palestinian East Jerusalem. The hotel, which is located on the Mount of Olives side, overlooks the Kidron Valley and Temple Mount on one side and the Occupied Territories and part of the East Jerusalem wall on the other side. The plenaries happened under a large marquee on the grounds of the hotel. Workshops happened in guest bedrooms that had been cleared for the purpose. There were evident space problems, with many workshops being far too crowded, especially for the August heat, but no single venue in East Jerusalem had adequate facilities with sufficiently large rooms. Interpreters volunteered their services, and simultaneous translation was provided for all plenaries in English, Hebrew, Arabic, Spanish, French, and Italian (Italian and Spanish members of WIB are particularly active, and approximately 120 Italian and 60 Spanish delegates attended the conference). Accommodation and evening activities were in three inexpensive Palestinian-run hotels in the Christian quarter of the Old City (*intramuros*): the New Imperial, the Gloria, and the Knight's Palace. I stayed in the New Imperial, reputedly Jerusalem's oldest hotel.

The conference was organized over five days, with activities in the hotels in the evenings, ranging from dances to film nights to performances. On the first day, participants held a vigil in Paris Square in West Jerusalem, the usual Friday vigil spot for WIB Jerusalem. WIB members have nicknamed the site "Hagar Square" in memory of Hagar Roublev, one of the founding members, as well as in reference to the biblical character Hagar, the Egyptian servant whom the barren Sarah offered to her husband, Abraham, to bear him a son. According to the Old Testament story, narrated in Genesis 16, Hagar gave birth to Ishmael, the legendary ancestor of the Arabs. Some years later Sarah conceived and gave birth to Isaac, the legendary ancestor of the Jews. Following conflict with Sarah, Hagar was freed from service by Abraham and banished to the desert with her son. In banishing them, Abraham followed the advice of Yahweh (God), who told him that Isaac would carry on his line but that Ishmael would also found a great nation. In recent decades, the name "Hagar" has apparently been given to daughters of Israeli Jewish families who lean to the left (personal communications by WIB members, various dates).

That first evening there was a welcome dinner and performance. The second and third days, at the Seven Arches Hotel, were made up of plenary sessions in the morning and workshops in the afternoon (as many as nineteen workshops ran simultaneously). The second day focused on Israel–Palestinian conflict, with each workshop being jointly run by an Israeli and Palestinian woman. The third day was devoted to international issues. On the fourth day, international visitors visited Ramallah, and Israeli women went to East Jerusalem, and the fifth day featured a vigil in Qalandia (East Jerusalem) near a checkpoint and the Separation Fence, followed by a closing plenary at the Seven Arches, which included an open-microphone segment.

The presence of so many feminists (including many "out" lesbians) from around the world together in East and West Jerusalem and *intramuros* was a major event. On another level, however, it was not at all odd: Jerusalem is a highly multicultural city—which can seem surprising to those who have not spent any time there—and is frequently visited by people from around the world. It is the meeting ground for a number of variants of the three monotheistic religions, overlaid with different ethnic and national origins, which coexist at once peacefully and violently depending on the day, the area, the political climate, and which sections of which populations are involved. Jerusalem lives at a level of intensity that does not let you forget for one minute where you are or even that you are alive. Such an intensity is rare outside conflict zones. Yet, although heavily militarized, with a visible army presence on the street, at entrances to department stores, at bus stations, and so on, Jerusalem is not technically a conflict or postconflict zone. West Jerusalem is also very gay-friendly, and Israel has played on the gay rights theme, one of the credentials of liberal modernity, to show how egalitarian it is (more on this tactic presently).

At the same time, the massive and visible presence of so many feminists—and lesbians—was unusual. We stayed in hotels run by Palestinian Christian men (whose courtesy and support were visible in all sorts of large and small ways), where in the evenings packed rooms of women cheered lesbian feminist drag kings who satirized Jewish machismo and the antievacuation conservatives or danced arm in arm to retro rock. In the streets outside, Serbian, English, Australian, French, Israeli, Swiss, and Palestinian lesbians frequented the local cafés and listened to popular singers such as the Algerian Souad Massi. The voice of resistance at this time was female, and it was joyful. From our hotels, we also watched the processions of orange-clad antievacuationists as they converged on the Wailing Wall in the Old City, threatening in their tightly packed numbers and ideology yet strangely detached from the rest of the city.

Yet at the WIB conference itself lesbians were invisibilized and silenced. This silencing paradoxically led to the debate over lesbianism taking up far more space at the conference than it otherwise would have but, as things turned out, every bit as much space as it needed to.

The Debate over Lesbian Visibility

What sparked the polemic was the organizing committee's cancellation of a workshop on lesbians and the peace movement, planned for the third day (devoted to international issues). On the evening of

August 11, just prior to the conference, many of the Israeli lesbians and some Palestinian and international lesbians had met to discuss responses to this decision. At the usual WIB weekly peace vigil on Friday, August 12, which formed the first event of the conference, a number of women were wearing pink ribbons and T-shirts with "Women in Black Jerusalem, August 2005" written in pink English letters on the back and "Lesbians for a Free Palestine" written just as pinkly on the front, but in Arabic. Dalit Baum, who cofounded Kvisa Shchora (Black Laundry), an Israeli lesbian and gay antioccupation group, had had the T-shirts printed for the occasion. (Black Laundry is also known as "Dirty Laundry" in English, no doubt an attempt to provide an English rendering of the Hebrew play on the words *kvisa shchora* [black laundry] and *kivsa shchora* [black sheep], although "Dirty Laundry" loses the original play on words and introduces another figurative reference not present in the original.) That Friday afternoon there was a well-attended meeting over the lesbian issue at Kol Ha'Isha, the West Jerusalem women's center. Some of the lesbians present had cofounded or worked at this center. Some Israeli, Serbian, and Palestinian heterosexual women attended in support.

At that meeting, Yvonne Deutsch, WIB activist and member of the conference organizing committee, explained the complex negotiations with the Palestinian co-organizers concerning the workshop. In her comments on my first draft of this chapter in 2007, she clarified that negotiation process as follows:

> When we introduced the lesbian workshop to the Palestinian representatives of the themes committee, it was suggested by them to name it as sexual politics and peace activism. The Israeli group [initially] opposed this suggestion. After much debate and consultation the Israeli group agreed [because as members of the colonizing society holding a conference in the occupied part of East Jerusalem, they felt they should respect the wishes of the Palestinian women]. But then we were told that it is too late because there is an opposition to hold at all this workshop. (As far as I know the information went out to the parties.) At that stage, it seems to me that

> understanding that for us the workshop is crucial, it was suggested
> [by the Palestinian women] that we move the lesbian workshop to
> West Jerusalem. That was unaccepted by us, so the workshop was
> cancelled. (email communication, May 3, 2007)

Deutsch, like a number of the other members of the Israeli committee, many of whom were themselves lesbian or bisexual, was visibly
upset at the difficulties and distress that these negotiations and the
final decision had created. It had, however, been deemed inappropriate to have the bulk of the conference take place at the Seven Arches
in East Jerusalem and then stigmatize and exclude one workshop.
The change in the Palestinian women's position during the negotiations—suggesting the title "Sexual Politics and Peace Activism" for
the workshop but then withdrawing that compromise suggestion—is
indicative of political-party influence on their position. At a conference workshop later, one of the Palestinian women confirmed that
a number of the Palestinian women associated with the conference
organizing group had no difficulty with the lesbian workshop and
thus had dissented from the formal "Palestinian" position taken.

The reasons advanced for the Palestinian members' objections centered on not alienating their male and some female coactivists, which
would potentially have the effect, as Deutsch put it, of "damag[ing]
their own fragile position in the Palestinian society" (email, May 3,
2007). Some Palestinian women feared that a visible lesbian presence
would undermine an already uncertain working relationship between
Palestinian and Israeli women. As I pointed out earlier, the links of
activism and solidarity between Palestinian and Israeli feminist and
peace activists are patchy and tenuous. As one heterosexual Palestinian woman present at the August 12 meeting explained, both the link
and the tensions were to a great extent an artifact of the brief given at
the conference in Italy in 2003 to co-organize the Jerusalem conference in 2005 when in fact there was no preexisting Israeli–Palestinian feminist structure that would enable such co-organization in any
straightforward way. This is not to say that there were no interactions
or alliances at all—there were many, both individual and collective.

At the same time, however, there was no established "Israeli–Palestinian feminist movement" with the structural capacity to embark immediately on the organization of the conference to be held in 2005. The structures had to be built. Most of the Palestinian women who objected to the lesbian workshop, even when "lesbian" was rebadged "sexuality," were activists within or associated with Palestinian political parties, either Fatah or more left-wing parties in an (albeit uneasy) coalition with Fatah. They feared undermining their political struggle against Israeli colonization as well as within Palestine, notably against Hamas (a struggle they have now lost for the moment in any case). As one Israeli activist from Binyamina, Diana Dolev, put it to me over breakfast one day, "The Palestinian women who are bullying the conference organizers over this are themselves being bullied by Palestinian men" (Aug. 13, 2005).

Whether the conference organizers felt bullied or not is a matter for conjecture, but they certainly felt the weight of colonial guilt in a situation that was fragile and fragilizing for all. As Deutsch put it, "As the oppressors we found it difficult to impose our views, identities, priorities on the occupied society" (email, May 3, 2007). Yet for many of the Ashkenazi Israeli peace activists, a number of whom do work closely with Palestinian women (as well as, in some cases, with Mizrahi women, some of whom have also participated in WIB), their lesbian political analysis informs their work as feminist and peace activists. It was thus unacceptable for them to be expected to compartmentalize their person and their politics by being erased as lesbians. At the August 12 meeting, Gila Svirsky, coordinator of the nine-group Coalition of Women for Peace (which includes WIB) and author of a history of WIB from its founding until 1996 (Svirsky 1996), estimated that at least 40 percent of Israeli peace activists are lesbians. Svirsky herself is an out lesbian. Hannah Safran, another long-term WIB activist, estimated in an article published in 2005 that lesbians formed up to 30 percent of those present at WIB vigils in Jerusalem (199). Others present at the August 12 meeting argued that the feminist movement *is* the peace movement in Israel or certainly its backbone, and the lesbian contingent within it may in fact be the majority (some said as high as

70 percent). Yet others argued that much of the feminist movement in Israel does not concern itself with the antioccupation movement and that, conversely, many women in the antioccupation movement do not identify as feminist. They thus suggested that the figures put forward concerning the percentage of lesbians may be exaggerated. Whatever the actual figures, the strong lesbian presence in the women's peace movement, in Israel as internationally, is undeniable.

In an email addressed to the nonlesbian members of the Israeli side of the organizing committee during the preconference debate among the conference organizers, some days prior to the vigil and meeting on Friday, August 12, Dalit Baum reiterated a frequently stated concern by lesbians in women's movements the world over: "I am . . . tired of spending our energies in organizing the lesbians. It is high time for the heteros to organize in solidarity with us. We should be able to do other things already. But we do not seem to have any choice" (early August 2005).

Indeed, international activists from many countries present at that Friday afternoon meeting, which I also attended, spoke of our experience of heterosexism in the women's movement. In doing so, we pointed out that this particular debate is not just about Palestinian sensitivity around the issue: it is a form of political blackmail used the world over first by men to demonize, discredit, and silence feminists and then by heterosexual feminists to silence lesbians. (See Rothschild 2000 for a telling account of how "accusations" of lesbianism have been used to discredit feminists in national and international politics.) The decision by the conference organizers to cancel the lesbian workshop meant that they were effectively silencing themselves as lesbians or as bisexual women. The organizers came up against the same arguments that lesbians have faced the world over: that lesbianism is a personal issue, a side issue, a less crucial matter for women's liberation, something not to be brought out into the light of day because it might stigmatize feminists and, most important, transnational feminist activism and thus undermine the women's liberation movement's political goals. These arguments are—not, I believe, coincidentally—similar to those consistently used by men against feminist voices within the context of national liberation struggles both in and out of the Muslim world. Such arguments reproduce the ideology of the oppressor, as evidenced by the testimony of Serbian women—both straight and lesbian and including Lepa Mlađenović—at the August 12 meeting. Not only did lesbians in Serbia face persecution, but the label *lesbian* was routinely used to denigrate WIB (and feminism more generally) and to discredit its activists. Contrary, however, to what has often happened elsewhere, straight Serbian women told of their solidarity with lesbians by taking on the label themselves and wearing it with pride. (It is noteworthy that ten years later the European Feminist Caravan, organized by the World March of Women in the first half of 2015, included as part of its calendar of events four days of "lesbian spring" in Belgrade, from April 16 to 19, in solidarity with Serbian lesbian activists.)

The most telling reaction to the decision to cancel the lesbian workshop was from the Palestinian lesbians and the straight Palestinian women who were there in support of them. Rauda Morcos, cofounder and then president of Aswat (Voices): Palestinian Gay Women (now called Palestinian Lesbian Women in English), told of feeling caught between two positions: she was being asked to separate out different parts of herself: Palestinian one minute, lesbian the next, but never the two together. The women of Aswat, which is based at Isha L'Isha (Woman to Woman), the Women's Center in Haifa, use the descriptor "Palestinian Gay (Lesbian) Women" advisedly. These three aspects of their identity and their politics are inseparable: they are women, they are homosexual, and they are Palestinian. Morcos and other Palestinian lesbians present at the August 12 meeting spoke of a huge feeling of betrayal by those they called "sister." As one lesbian, Samira, put it during the meeting, "It's bad enough having to go back into the closet inside our families and local communities without having to do it in the feminist movement as well."

To move forward, the organizers decided that a delegation from the August 12 meeting—made up of two Palestinian women, two Israeli women, and three international activists—would meet with the Palestinian objectors and attempt to talk through the issues. I later heard from some of the women that the meeting had been difficult but had broken some silences—including the silence surrounding the nonparticipation of women from other Muslim countries. One of the Palestinian women from our delegation told me following the meeting, "This was the first time we'd ever really sat down and talked about feminism together." In other words, the lesbian issue started a conversation that was significantly more far-reaching than the issue of lesbian visibility and vocality, and some saw this development as highly salutary. Another Palestinian woman subsequently told one of the Jewish members of our delegation that in Palestinian women's networks, including email, they were starting to raise the issue of differences among themselves that needed airing and discussion. Others, however, felt less positive and optimistic about the outcomes, that little real progress had been made.

The great irony of the decision to cancel the lesbian workshop was thus that lesbians ended up becoming in protest more visible and vocal and lesbian politics more the object of focus and debate than otherwise might have been the case. Throughout the following two days, the "lesbian issue" and broader lesbian feminist peace politics were discussed at plenaries, in workshops, and at the open microphone, and lesbians were joyously and loudly visible at the evening events in the Old City hotels. The "lesbian issue" also pervaded subsequent reports on the conference, international email discussions, and so on.

The "lesbian issue" thus became one of the most discussed at a conference from which it was supposed to be absent. The discussion, painful and often angry as it was, also threw up many difficult questions relating more generally to the politics of naming and silencing. For some at least, it opened the way to breaking other silences, such as that surrounding differences among women *within* the same ethnic or religious community. Most importantly, it raised the question of the extent, limits, and nature of feminist solidarity within transnational and colonial contexts.

The attempt to silence lesbians at the WIB conference in 2005 was justified as being necessitated by a strategic alliance in difficult circumstances as well as by the desire to maintain some sort of "credibility" for WIB with certain Palestinian organizations. This explanation, however, begs the question of how credible WIB then becomes for Palestinian feminists in general and Palestinian lesbians in particular and of how the latter's "strategic" interests are furthered by invisibilizing them. Even though, subsequent to the lesbian caucus and ensuing meetings, concessions were eventually proposed, with Rauda Morcos, then president of Aswat, being offered a place on the podium in the closing plenary, the offer was received as tokenistic at worst and far too little, far too late at best. Morcos refused the offer.

The debate also highlighted some fraught aspects of the process of establishing and developing partnerships in transnational activism. Two Israeli members of the organizing committee stated in a letter to the WIB email discussion list that they felt that the main problem of the conference was that its outcomes did not include formulation of a "global women's strategy"—although it was perhaps a hard task for one conference to deal with such a difficult and divisive issue. The two lay the blame for some of the problems entirely at the door of the Israeli organizers, noting that it was their choice to work with women members of Palestinian political organizations rather than with Palestinian feminists working in the field. Indeed, one of the Palestinian women in the liaison group, Amneh, commented to the Israeli organizers, "You chose us as partners. You could have chosen other Palestinian groups." She had been opposed both to the lesbian workshop and to the participation of feminists from Egypt and Pakistan.

Yet Amneh and her colleagues were a minority of Palestinian feminist voices, as noted by Huda, Palestinian feminist activist and cofacilitator, with Yvonne Deutsch, of a workshop titled "Challenges and Obstacles to Working Together." According to Huda, most Palestinian women did *not* concur with Amneh's objections, which led a workshop participant from El Salvador to ask why the workshop was canceled if the majority did not in fact oppose it. Deutsch replied that the Israeli women, coming from a position of power, felt obliged to accept most of the conditions imposed by some of the Palestinian women. Huda's response, however, was to point out that privilege is a more complex matter than "Israeli versus Palestinian." She offered herself as an example: a middle-class Palestinian living in West Jerusalem and carrying a French passport. She considered herself to be demonstrably better off, on many levels, than many Mizrahi women in Israel. Her comments, like those of the two authors who wrote the letter to the organizing committee, raise the questions of representativeness and rights to speak or silence and what agendas are being served by self-silencing, regardless of whether the original motivations are well meaning.

In May 2006, Rauda Morcos, then president of Aswat, traveled to the United States to accept the International Gay and Lesbian Human Rights Commission (IGLHRC, now OutRight Action International) Felipa de Souza Award for 2006, created in 1994 to recognize grassroots leaders working for lesbian and gay human rights. Felipa de Souza, a Portuguese-born woman who lived most of her life in Brazil in the sixteenth century, was condemned in early 1592 to whipping, a hefty fine, and exile by the Catholic Inquisition because of her intimate relationships with women, an activity framed by the Inquisition as "the nefarious crime of sodomy."[2] On March 28, 2007, Aswat held a highly successful conference in Haifa, "Home and Exile in Queer Experience," to celebrate its fifth anniversary and to launch the first-ever publication of Palestinian lesbian writing in Arabic. An Aswat press release described the book as "a collection of articles, the first of its kind in Arabic, presenting the issue of lesbianism from the feminist point of view. The book was produced in order to raise awareness in Arab society both with respect to freedom of choice concerning sexual preference and the existence of lesbians in Palestinian Arab society."[3]

The conference, which attracted many threats from religious groups and a small demonstration by the religious Right on the day it was held, was attended by more than three hundred women, a greater

2. From the IGLHRC website at http://iglhrc.org/content/celebration-courage -who-was-felipa-de-souza (accessed Apr. 12, 2015).

3. From the Aswat website at http://www.aswatgroup.org/en/article/press -release-aswats-conference-28307 (accessed May 13, 2013).

number than originally expected. Many others, unable to attend the conference, sent donations and messages of solidarity. In an email to Aswat supporters, the organizers wrote: "Your support and belief in Aswat's work has granted us confidence and courage to keep on with our struggle. And the success achieved is yours too."[4]

This was also, perhaps, the biggest success of the WIB conference in 2005. International solidarity with the Palestinian struggle against the occupation and for independence was the conference's raison d'être, but the most important act of international solidarity was perhaps not the one most expected.

A silence was broken in 2002 when Aswat was founded by three Palestinian lesbians living in Haifa. Attempts to reimpose that silence in Jerusalem in 2005 were collectively and successfully combated. For lesbians, whether Ashkenazi, Mizrahi, or Palestinian—or, indeed, outsider to the region—to speak out in the very name of peace at a Jerusalem women's peace conference was to further contest an already-contested and already-contesting space. But as Morcos put it emphatically at the conference, "We are not going to be in the closet again." For one short week, lesbian voices—against the occupation, against male domination, *and* against heterosexism—rocked the Holy City, opening small cracks in its millennial walls of silence.

"Lesbian Is Good" (or Not): Culture, Religion, and Transnational Feminist Solidarity

The ongoing tensions concerning lesbian visibility and voices within transnational feminist activism had already become painfully evident to me less than two months before the WIB conference in a quite different context, where I personally became one of the targets of the controversy. The ninth Women's Worlds triennial International Interdisciplinary Congress on Women (WW05) took place June 19–24, 2005, in Seoul, Korea, at Ewha Women's University. Women's Worlds

4. From a page on the Aswat website (ibid.) that is no longer available (accessed Dec. 3, 2007).

conferences—of which the first, interestingly, took place in Haifa, Israel, in 1981—are the largest women's studies gatherings in the world and, as such, highly significant events. WW05 was the first held in Asia and one of its largest, "gathering 3,000 participants, feminist scholars, activists and policy makers from all over the world."[5] Unlike the WIB conference, lesbian visibility within the conference program was not in itself an issue because there were specific workshops and papers whose titles had the words *lesbian, queer, same-sex,* and so on in them. Young lesbians participated actively and visibly in the conference theme "promoting young feminists in Asia," not only through the parallel sessions but also in the conference's exhibitions. The Asian lesbian panels and contributions to the exhibition were also featured in the conference's daily newsletter.

Yet in one of the parallel sessions, on the feminist movement and lesbian rights in South Korea, the speakers raised problems that were remarkably similar to those discussed in Jerusalem a couple of months later: invisibilizing and silencing lesbians within the feminist movement, heterosexism, and so on. The young speakers raised the problem of how they might continue to work within the feminist movement while addressing their marginalization as lesbians and challenging straight feminists to examine the ideology of heterosexism. A number of Australian and other international women present at the workshop expressed their solidarity: these problems were all too familiar in the history of the feminist movements in our own countries.

One of the workshop presenters later gave us badges the group had made, featuring the somewhat "Koreanglish" slogan "Lesbian is good," and we continued to discuss how we might be able to express our solidarity publicly at that conference and beyond. Concurrently but unrelatedly, the conference organizers invited conference attendees to submit their proposals for participation in a segment of the conference's Farewell Celebration performance evening, scheduled for

---

5. From the WW05 website at http://aaws07.org/english3/ (accessed July 16, 2013).

June 23: a song or poem, for example. Another Australian woman, Susan Hawthorne (coeditor with me of the first international feminist anthology on 9/11 [Hawthorne and Winter 2002]) and I decided that we would propose poems. Our proposal was accepted, and as it turned out, we were the only conference participants who ended up performing in that impromptu segment of the show. It is my understanding that no other proposals had been forthcoming. Susan performed a poem that she had previously written, "Oil and Water" (in Hawthorne 2005, 220), in which she referred, among other things, to lesbians in Iraq and to the bombings of Iraq, and I composed a humorous poem about heterosexism and the silencing of lesbians, dedicating it to the Korean lesbians. I titled it "Lesbian Is Good," picking up the slogan on the badges we had been given (see Winter 2006a).

Susan's poem included the lines "Like oil and water / lesbianlife and patriotism don't mix." Her poetic account of the invisibilization of lesbians in the Middle East within the context of war was chillingly reinforced by a Human Rights Watch report published four years later. Titled *"They Want Us Exterminated": Murder, Torture, Sexual Orientation, and Gender in Iraq*, the report gave an account of the persecution of gay men and any women showing deviation from traditional heterosexual/family norms, carried out in the name of national stability and public order. Within such a context, author Scott Long and researcher Rasha Moumneh communicated their difficulty in obtaining testimony by lesbians (or even by women): all forty-six interviewees were men:

> Despite wide acknowledgement that violence against women is a serious crisis in Iraq, state authorities have ignored it, and most NGOs have concentrated on "public," political patterns of attacks on men. Amid this neglect, the question of whether and how violence targets women for *non-heterosexual* behaviors has been doubly neglected. In researching this report, Human Rights Watch was unable to locate or interview women in Iraq who have experienced intimate or sexual relationships with other women. The pressures to marry and to conform make those women invisible. Only

anecdotal accounts suggest what they might face. (Human Rights
Watch 2009, 42–43)

"Anecdotal accounts"—such as those given in this chapter—are
often the only source of information about lesbian experience in precarious contexts: in war zones and in countries where homosexuality
is illegal or where all women and gay men are the target of state or
nonstate violence or both. We are forced to string together the threads
of lesbian experience across the gulfs of silence that continue to prevent us even *naming* the oppression.

During my performance, I explained the title of my own poem
and its raison d'être as an act of solidarity with Korean lesbians. It
included these words:

Do you see those lesbians
in the rape crisis centres
the women's shelters
the health centres
the reproductive rights campaigns
childcare campaigns
antiviolence campaigns
peace campaigns
for women's rights gay rights children's rights
the rights of the racialised colonised dispossessed disempowered
silenced
Suddenly you are seeing
lesbians everywhere (Winter 2006a, 46)

The audience's response to our poems was overwhelmingly positive:
Susan and I were cheered by straight and lesbian, Western and non-
Western participants alike. Later in the evening, many Korean lesbians
present at the conference, including a number of student volunteers,
introduced themselves to me with enthusiastic thanks.

This could have remained a charming anecdote, a lovely moment
of transnational lesbian solidarity to include in my memoirs, were it
not for a postconference protest. Less than a week after the end of the

conference, a US colleague who had been present and had much appreciated the lesbian performance poems forwarded me a draft protest letter that she had been asked to sign but had declined. I am unable to name the colleague or the author of the protest letter, both of whom are well-known US-based feminist scholars, because I was never supposed to see the letter in question. I am, however, going to cite it here because I believe the prejudices it expresses need to be exposed and examined.

The letter had been drafted following a conversation at the conference between its United Statian author—let us call her "Brenda" for the purpose of this discussion—and an Iranian woman also present at the conference. Brenda praised the organizers of the conference (it was indeed exceptionally well organized) but raised concerns about two aspects of the Farewell Celebration performances on June 23. One was a "fashion show" segment, which had attracted many objections from the audience at the time, and the other was our lesbian poetry segment, which had, contrary to the fashion show, attracted an enthusiastic response from the same audience. Notwithstanding the author's appreciation of the conference organizers' support for "young feminists of Asia," which was for her a highlight of the conference, she was far less appreciative of our expression of support for young *lesbians* of Asia. She objected to Susan's (whose surname she got wrong) "poem speaking for a lesbian woman in Iraq" and to my poem "asserting that lesbianism, as opposed to heterosexuality, was 'good'" (she clearly had not understood the humor or paid attention to my onstage explanation of the origin of the poem's title). Or, rather, she objected to their inclusion in a performance program that was "a wonderful opportunity to celebrate all the richness of feminism."

Although Brenda claimed to respect us as poets and "honor [our] right to express [our] poetry in an appropriate venue," she asserted that "the closing celebration was not that venue," for "both poems could have been interpreted as insensitive to the diverse religious values of our sisters." Writing on behalf of the signatories, Brenda stated that

> the poetry reading privileged one kind of difference as articulated
> by those not self-reflective about the appropriateness of taking the

limelight for their politics, and away from other politics during a moment of potential solidarity. Looking at the program, we guess that a last minute change made this possible, but the seizing of this scheduling opportunity for one perspective of such a controversial political issue required a bit more reflection. As we have discussed the program and the poetry, we have thought of other issues that we would have liked to see highlighted rather than Western middle class lesbian politics and its imagined relationship to war.

Brenda had apparently not understood that participation in this segment was voluntary and that in fact any participant could have proposed a performance piece addressing any feminist theme of her choice.

I do not know what the follow-up was to this letter: whether it was sent to the conference organizers and whether the latter responded. I certainly was not officially informed of the complaint or given any opportunity to respond to it.

The complaint is worrying—including for the transnational feminist solidarity that Brenda claimed to defend—for four reasons. The first is the suggestion that some feminist venues are appropriate for lesbian expression and others are not. I cannot imagine a statement ever being made, in the name of feminism, that some venues are appropriate for us to discuss classism or racism or food sovereignty or disability discrimination, but other venues are not. According to Brenda, however, to discuss lesbianism within the context of an international feminist conference is not "appropriate." I am reminded of a celebrated performance poem by African American lesbian feminist poet Pat Parker, titled "For the straight folks who don't mind gays but wish they weren't so blatant," in which she writes: "Fact is, blatant heterosexuals are all over the place. Supermarkets, movies, at work, in church, in books, on television, every day and night, every place—even in gay bars. And they want gay men and women to go hide in the closets" (1984).

The second problem is Brenda's concern over offence to the "diverse religious values" of "our sisters." Brenda did not make explicit who the "us" and who the "sisters" are, but given the letter was the result of a conversation between Brenda and an Iranian woman, it is likely that the religious sensibilities in question were those of Muslim women, implicitly othered as "our sisters," while the "us" were Western women, implicitly placed at the center of the tableau in the position of subject. Feminists in general and lesbians in particular have fought long and hard and continue to fight—including *within* religious traditions—against the oppressions inflicted upon women in the name of religion and for the right to speak out about these oppressions. The view that an expression of lesbian solidarity should be silenced because it would be offensive to "religious values" thus appears bizarre as a statement of transnational feminist solidarity. It also positions some groups of "sisters" as defined by religion and as a consequence restricted in what they are able to discuss or even think about, whereas others (Westerners, presumably) are apparently unfettered by such concerns. The claim is reductionist, essentializing, even patronizing: it constructs othered women as somehow too politically fragile because of their identity-defining religion to discuss the politically controversial, difficult as such discussions may be, so they must be protected by "us" from exposure to some subjects.

The third problem, related to the second, is the assumption that lesbianism is only about the "Western middle class" and that discussion of it is thus inappropriate in a transnational context. This comment is particularly odd in the light of the fact that the raison d'être of the performance was transnational solidarity, and one of the poems was written expressly for Korean lesbians who felt marginalized within their own feminist movement. Lesbians are not solely white, Western, and middle class. Lesbians are, as the slogan goes, everywhere. Including in Korea. Including in Iraq.

Which brings me to the fourth problem: lesbianism's "imagined relationship to war." I do not think bombs or drones or those dropping or guiding them ask about the sexuality of those they kill, but I do know that lesbians worldwide, including in some parts of some Western countries, are tortured both physically and psychologically; cut off from family (including their own children), employment, and many other aspects of social interaction; and, yes, killed by men— more often than not by men known to them, in keeping with the overall pattern of violence against women—because they are lesbians. "The emphasis on silence [thus] cannot be overstated," writes Susan Hawthorne:

> Lesbians have long been subjected to silence, to denial, to being ignored within the dominant heterosexual discourse. Lesbians who are tortured face multiple layers of silence. First, there is the silence surrounding lesbian existence. Second, in quite a few jurisdictions there is legal silence: punishment is not meted out formally, but occurs instead on an informal basis, inflicted sometimes by the state and sometimes by members of the woman's family or the community. When this occurs it is often difficult to have the punishment recognized as a violation of the lesbian's human rights and as an instance of torture. In such circumstances the torturer can continue with impunity. (2006, 36)

As I have pointed out elsewhere (Winter 2015), in my work with lesbian asylum seekers I have found that although gay men also suffer violence, often extreme, such violence is perpetrated almost systematically against lesbians, such that it almost always fits the definition of torture as set out in Article 1, paragraph 1, of the UN Convention against Torture and Other Cruel, Inhuman, or Degrading Treatment or Punishment of 1984, which reads:

> For the purposes of this Convention, the term "torture" means any act by which severe pain or suffering, whether physical or mental, is intentionally inflicted on a person for such purposes as obtaining from him [*sic*] or a third person information or a confession, punishing him for an act he [*sic*] or a third person has committed or is suspected of having committed, or intimidating or coercing him or a third person, or for any reason based on discrimination of any kind, when such pain or suffering is inflicted by or at the instigation of or with the consent or acquiescence of a public official or other person acting in an official capacity. It does not include pain or suffering arising only from, inherent in or incidental to lawful sanctions. (UN 1984)

The last sentence is potentially problematic for homosexuals in general and lesbians in particular, given that homosexuality remains illegal in some seventy-eight countries and in subnational regions of a handful of others, with the death penalty applied in five countries; moreover, a number of governments are moving backward rather than forward in this area. Governments can and do interpret the last sentence of Article 1.1 as carte blanche to act with impunity against homosexuals, although the counterinterpretation is that such laws and the torture of or discrimination against homosexuals committed under such legal protection constitute discrimination against a social group, which is sanctioned by, among others, the Refugee Convention of 1951. The growing asylum case law for LGBT populations supports such an interpretation.

Chapters 3 and 4 of this book show that violence against women is endemic, and in postconflict or postdisaster situations such violence is likely to increase, but the rate of reporting such violence is likely to decrease. Iraq—the subject of the poem Hawthorne recited at the WW05 event—is no exception. Wars do not just happen and then end, with everything returning to normal. War's main casualties are now civilian, and those casualties continue long after the occupying troops have departed. We know that the situation for women in Iraq since 2003 has become disastrous.

As concerns lesbians more specifically, the post-2003 Iraqi Constitution has no article explicitly prohibiting homosexuality, but a number of other articles referring to morals and national security can be and indeed have been used to persecute homosexuals, as the Human Rights Watch (2009) report quoted earlier points out. Or homosexuals are simply persecuted without any reference to a legal framework, and their persecutors go unpunished. There is some evidence that persecution of homosexuals has even increased following the US withdrawal from Iraq.[6] Even during the US occupation, however,

---

6. A number of reports on the situation for homosexuals in Iraq can be found at the International Gay, Lesbian, Bisexual, Trans, and Intersex Organization website at http://ilga.org/, and typing in the search term 'Iraq' (accessed July 16, 2013).

IGLHRC noted the high levels of antigay violence. In 2006, less than one year after WW05, IGLHRC's executive director Paula Ettelbrick stated that "IGLHRC is alarmed by the documented escalation of violence against gay people in Iraq. . . . The acts of [antigay] violence within the Iraqi community are part of a larger pattern of violence that has arisen out of the current war and sectarian tensions" (IGL-HRC 2006). War increases the vulnerability of the already vulnerable. And in Iraq lesbians are among the very vulnerable, indeed.

I do not know what Brenda's motivations were in writing the protest letter to the Seoul organizing committee. Perhaps, like the Ashkenazi women in Jerusalem, she, as a United Statian, the white citizen of an imperialist nation, was acting out of guilt toward the racialized Muslim other. But the terms in which she expressed her objections are disturbing. They are evidence of an ongoing taboo on transnational articulations of lesbian feminist politics, a taboo that is justified *in the very name of transnational feminist solidarity*. They are also evidence of the post-9/11ist reintervention of religion in politics, which I discuss more fully in chapters 6 and 7.

As Dalit Baum wrote in the email to nonlesbian members of the organizing committee for the WIB conference in 2005, it is irritating and not a little depressing for lesbians to still be forced to raise the same issues of voice and visibility after so many decades of these debates. "We should be doing other things already." Indeed we should. The question of whether we *can*, a decade or so after the incidents I relate here, remains open. But in addition to marginalization of lesbian voices and analyses within the transnational feminist movement, lesbian feminists now face another dilemma: that of co-optation by states as lesbian politics become inserted into a "civil rights doctrine" and radical lesbian critique of heterosexist militarist states becomes neutralized (Shadmi 2005, 257–59). It is to that problem that I now turn, in relation to Israel in particular.

The Politics of Manufactured Consensus

The imbrication of different oppressions does not always fall neatly into the "intersectional" layered structures of the sort described by

Kimberlé Crenshaw (1989). Crenshaw imagined that those standing near the top of an underfloor stack, who have only one oppression to deal with and are standing on the shoulders of those with
more oppressions, can more easily scramble out of the hole than those
near the bottom. At the same time, with respect to the way transnational politics play out, there would indeed appear to be a hierarchy
of oppressions, with some taking precedence over others, even in the
area of gay rights. Those oppressions that also affect men always come
first, then those affecting middle-class heterosexual women second,
and finally those affecting lesbians and working-class women strag-
gling far behind. Race and nation are positioned differently on this
hierarchy depending on the context, but nation usually plays a determining role. In Israel and Palestine, the primary questions of place
and space and of oppression/liberation for Left and Right alike are
those of the status of Palestine and the status of Jerusalem, a symbolic
site for the world's three monotheisms.

Connected to these questions are inevitably wider geopolitical ones, the US state's bankrolling of the occupation of Palestine
being a major part of that scenario. According to a US Congressional
Research Service report prepared in April 2005, the United States
provided for fiscal year 2005 an estimated "$360 million in economic,
$2.22 billion in military, and $50 million in migration resettlement
assistance" to the Israeli state (Mark 2005a, unnumbered summary
page). According to another report prepared by the same service at
roughly the same time, US aid provided to Palestine was $20 million
directly to the Palestinian National Authority, with another US$200
million requested by the president for fiscal year 2005. "About 80% of
US aid to the Palestinians is channeled through contractors and 20%
is channeled through private voluntary organizations, both groups
selected and monitored by USAID" (Mark 2005b, unnumbered summary page).

The magnitude of the "situation" in Israel/Palestine and the
sense of urgency that is felt by antioccupation movements across the
world in attempting to resolve it thus take up, if not all the space,
then a great deal of it, most particularly in Jerusalem. As such, the

issues of Palestinian and Israeli nationhood, however understood and defended, stand on the shoulders of all other issues, to borrow Crenshaw's imagery. In addressing that "situation," then, in a global context of political polarization, high emotion, as well as significant propaganda and disinformation (on both sides), Israeli and Palestinian antioccupation feminist movements are faced with difficult choices. Marginalized within their countries as well as internally divided on many issues, the women in the women's peace movement are hard pressed to find common ground beyond saying that the Israeli occupation of Palestine and international (in particular US) support for it must stop. How does one, in such a heavily charged political and symbolic space, in what is arguably the world's most hotly contested geographical place, provide a relatively safe forum in which internal disagreements can be aired and discussed?

In 2005 and 2006, Israeli antioccupation lesbian feminist politics came up against yet another transnational challenge: the organization of World Pride in Jerusalem, originally planned for 2005 but postponed to 2006. This time the silencing did not concern lesbianism but the occupation. Antioccupation lesbian, gay, and feminist activists, including Black Laundry, Aswat, and some WIB members, called for a boycott of World Pride because the conference did not focus centrally on the occupation of Palestine and the international LGBT movement's responsibility to speak out against it. In a rare but predictable display of monotheistic solidarity, Jewish, Christian, and Muslim religious leaders also joined forces to oppose the event, but of course for reasons quite different from those motivating the antioccupation activists. During a joint press conference held in Jerusalem on March 30, 2005, these leaders characterized World Pride as "ugly" and "dirty" and as constituting a "new provocation" that would further inflame existing tensions in Israel, particularly at that time (as reported in Goodstein and Myre 2005 and Greenberg 2005). These religious oppositions were supported internationally, particularly by conservative Christians in the United States. For example, the conservative Catholic publication the *Remnant* characterized World Pride as "sodomizing Jerusalem" (Alessio n.d.).

The organizers of Jerusalem World Pride did not take a collective position on the occupation, nor did they include any information on it in the proposed conference materials. An alternative conference, Queeruption, was thus organized in Tel Aviv at roughly the same time. This alternative conference presented other problems, however, notably as concerned its promotion of sexual and cultural practices such as sadomasochism and bondage and domination. I was as disturbed by the Queeruption organizers' inability to make connections between the ideology of sadomasochism and bondage and the ideology of the occupation as I was by World Pride's silence. In the end, a number of organizations, Aswat among them, boycotted both conferences for a range of reasons.

One of them was that Tel Aviv, the "gay capital" of the Middle East, was emblematic of the sort of "homonationalism" criticized in the now-famous book by Jasbir Puar (2007). Building on Lisa Duggan's (2002) analysis of "homonormativity," a process by which homosexuals are assimilated to heterosexist structures within liberal capitalist societies (the nuclear family, the market, and so on), Puar suggests that "gay rights" in Western societies privilege certain kinds of people (white) while enabling the reinforcement of other exclusions (notably of Arabs and other racialized Muslims). More recently, Cricket Keating criticized "homoprotectionism," whereby Western governments use measures protecting LGBTI rights to engineer allegiance and consent, "obscuring the ways that the state helped to generate sexual hierarchies and its own stake (sometimes submerged) in their continuation" (2013, 248).

In Israel, the term *pinkwashing* is used to describe these state tactics. In a paper given in the United States in 2004, Dalit Baum pointed out that

it was exactly the extreme nationalism, militarism and racism of Israeli society that have made it possible for some gays and lesbians to belong and gain the rights of "insiders." It is a society that invests a lot in ethnic and religious separations; in guarding the borders of the national collective. In such a society, it is more acceptable for me, as a Jewish woman, to bring home another Jewish woman than it is for me to bring home an Arab man. For example, new residency sub-laws allow my non-Israeli partner to receive resident's status in Israel, isn't it all so very liberal! But it can only work if she is not a Palestinian. That is the only exception. (2006, 572)

In another paper published in 2007, Tallie Ben Daniel echoed Baum's words, arguing that "gay rights activism is mobilized [within Israel] as a barometer of human rights . . . using discourses of modernity and civilization to describe the Israeli gay-rights movement" and, in doing so, making it "complicit with the occupation of Palestine" (1). Ben Daniel describes a "rhetoric of impossibility" (6) that allows Palestinian gayness only within a rhetoric of rescue, whereby modern and civilized Israel can save gay Palestinians who become citizens of Israel, thus politically relinquishing opposition to the occupation. Yet the proposed silencing of lesbian voices at the WIB conference in 2005 because of a desire to preserve a fragile alliance—in short, not to be too "provocative" at a time of extreme tension prior to the Gaza evacuation and the Palestinian election of 2006 (a sentiment that is chillingly close to one of the comments made in the press conference by monotheistic religious leaders on March 30, 2005)—ironically trapped Palestinian lesbians in this same "rhetoric of impossibility." There is no space in which gay—and especially lesbian—Palestinians can exist.

Erella Shadmi suggests that Israeli lesbians who embrace the "civil rights doctrine" (such as marriage and parenting recognition) are complicit with the heterosexist and racist ideology of the Israeli state: "The civil rights doctrine made the lesbian community no more than a minority group fighting for its interests and to be included in society. Such a position adopts the assumption that heterosexual women are the norm, a model for emulation, a goal to pursue" (2005, 259). She argues that this "civil rights doctrine" has been singularly depoliticizing of lesbian existence and has neutralized, along with gay rights and heterofeminist discourses more generally, "the revolutionary and threatening potential" of lesbianism as a challenge to Zionist ideology

(260). One of the "building blocks" of that ideology, writes Shadmi, is the heterosexual woman, notably in her role as idealized mother figure put to the service of "God, masculinity, family and land" (251, 252). By aspiring to enter into the (hetero)sexual contract—to paraphrase Carole Pateman's famous critique of male domination in the postpatriarchal era of "fraternity," *The Sexual Contract* (1988)—lesbians who embrace the "civil rights doctrine" enable the erasure of their own revolutionary potential and tacitly support the Israeli state's "pinkwashing" exercise, whether they intend to or not.

Feminist debates over colonialism and culture and the resulting activist priorities are not new. They have been integral—and fortunately so—to the movement from the outset. Similarly, as noted earlier, debates over lesbian visibility and activism, including as part of racialized minorities, are not new. What is new is, first, the heterosexualization of lesbian lives and politics as a means of co-optation to the agendas of liberal states and, second, the reimbrication of religion in culture, ethnicity, and politics. With respect to this latter point, we are now, it appears, in an age of "postsecularism," where we have begun to develop "an awareness of what is missing" in our secular societies, as Jürgen Habermas famously framed it in a lecture delivered in the wake of 9/11 (Habermas 2001; see also Habermas 2007). Although the term *postsecularism* was already in circulation prior to 9/11, it was Habermas's post-9/11 reframing of the concept that has significantly contributed to the idea that there is something wrong with secularism that needs to be addressed (Winter 2013). It should be noted, however, that Habermas himself was not presenting an argument for the abolition of secularism; others nonetheless took the idea elsewhere, as we are about to see.

6

Religion, Politics, and the Question of Legitimacy

This book would be incomplete without further discussion of feminist and other polemics around the interaction of religion and politics in the post-9/11 context and in particular since the beginning of the so-called Arab spring. The Middle East and Arab-world upheavals of recent years, discussed in this chapter, are not the only manifestation of these political dilemmas. But as debates on "Islamophobia" and "postsecularism" have come to the fore in the West, Islamist parties have positioned themselves as the champions of democracy in a number of countries in MENA.

On one level, these developments can be seen as yet another case of the *post hoc ergo propter hoc* fallacy, for debates over the imbrication of religion and politics and even the association of religious political movements with democratization in MENA predate 9/11. At the same time, desecularization and the rise of religious nationalism have been central to the post-9/11ist conversation in both MENA and the West, including among feminists. The conversation has, moreover, occurred within and around various religious traditions, whether we are talking about the electoral success of the Hindu nationalist Bharatiya Janata Party (BJP, Indian People's Party) in India in 2014; the repeated triumphs of Benjamin Netanyahu (and his extreme-right allies) in Israel; increased political militancy of the Christian Right in the West and eastern Europe; or the ascendancy of Islamist political formations in MENA, from the "moderate" to the "terrorist" ends of that political spectrum. For the BJP and Netanyahu, aggressive nationalism rooted in a politicoreligious identity framed as being under assault by a Muslim other have been key to their success. For right-wing Christian movements, everything from Islam to the secular state to homosexuality to feminism is the enemy. For so-called moderate Islamist movements, discourses of democracy, antiauthoritarianism, and legitimacy have become the apparently self-evident justification for these movements' self-positioning as the privileged interlocutors between the state and Muslim minorities in the West and as the natural inheritors and guardians of "revolutions" in MENA. For militarized and terrorist Islamist movements, everyone is the enemy, and territorial domination accompanied by imposition of their selective and ahistorical interpretations of Islam is the goal.

Western Cognitive Dissonance

From the Left to the liberal Right in the West, there is broad consensus about the Hindu, Zionist, and Christian right-wing movements: they are against women's sexual and reproductive rights, against gay rights, and against racialized Muslim minorities. Such right-wing movements are unfortunately doing well in the post-9/11 atmosphere, which is so heavily charged with the politics of fear. Many Western political leaders, wishing to appear socially progressive, have taken on the religious Right with such measures as the legalization of gay marriage, which is framed by these governments as a barometer of their social justice progressiveness, although the accuracy of this barometric measure is decidedly open to question, as indicated by the discussion on pinkwashing and homonormativity in chapter 5 (see also Duggan 2002; Puar 2007; Keating 2013; Winter 2014b). At the same time, the politics of fear generally involves a socially conservative backlash, whether imposed by right-wing governments that ride to victory on a national identity/security platform accompanied by neoliberal economic policies and god-fearing rhetoric or expressed oppositionally by the extreme-right and religious conservatives against more centrist governments. One telling example of the latter is the rise to prominence of the extreme Right in Sweden, which was until late 2015 the most refugee-friendly country in Europe. In August 2015, the extreme-right party Sverigedemokraterna (Sweden Democrats) polled as the country's most popular party, owing mainly to anti-immigrant sentiment (Reuters 2015a). In France, the vehemence of Catholic opposition since 2012 to the gay marriage law and more generally against the government, a campaign that included racist insults by the Catholic extreme Right against then justice minister Christiane Taubira, caused international outcry and was even vociferously opposed by some French Catholics (Serrette 2012). These protests also increased the "progressive" credentials, at least internationally, of the successive governments serving under President François Hollande. The antigay Christian Right backlash also has international and imperialist dimensions. The proselytizing actions of US antigay groups and individuals have been followed closely by, among others, the Southern Poverty Law Center, based in Montgomery, Alabama, which has identified eighteen such groups (Schlatter 2010). Individuals identified include evangelist Scott Lively, whom a Ugandan gay rights group sued in 2012 for whipping up antigay sentiment in Uganda starting in 2002 and directly contributing to the introduction of more punitive antigay laws there.

At government level, the post-9/11 resurgence of hardline "god talk" in "war on terror" rhetoric and more broadly in US politics under George W. Bush and in other Western governments (as well as a number of eastern European ones) has been amply documented and commented upon (see, e.g., in relation to the United States, Finlay 2006 and Rozell and Whitney 2007). George W. Bush is reputed to have referred to God and Christianity more often than any previous US president—which in the United States is probably saying a great deal. In his first speech after the 9/11 attacks, Bush called on Americans to pray and invoked "a power greater than any of us" through citing Psalm 23 (Bush 2001a). His Australian ally, Prime Minister John Howard, and the latter's government similarly Christianized Australia in both discourse and action, such as tendering out various social services so that they ended up being taken over by Christian groups (Maddox 2005; Winter 2007). Even in the supposed aggressively secularist France, newly elected president Nicolas Sarkozy,

Hollande's predecessor, lamented in 2007 that two years previously France had rejected any mention of Europe's "Christian roots" in the proposed (but defeated) European constitution. In 2011, he reaffirmed his attachment to France's Christian heritage at a speech at Le Puy-en-Velay in France's right-wing Catholic heartland of Auvergne (Sarkozy 2011).

Outside the West, Indian prime minister Narendra Modi was at pains during his election campaign in early 2014 to try to distance himself and the BJP from anti-Muslim sentiment and anti-Muslim violence in India. A year after the BJP's landslide victory, however, tensions between India and both Pakistan and Bangladesh continued, leading media commentators to ask whether current waves of anti-Muslimness in India were independent of the government or fueled by it (see, e.g., Nair 2015; Subramanian 2015; Traub 2015). In Israel, Benjamin Netanyahu and the Likud (Consolidation) Party, ruling in coalition with extreme-right parties, were returned for a fourth term in March 2015 in a surprise election turnabout from his anticipated defeat. Netanyahu is now the longest-serving leader in Israel, a country that is deeply troubled both by the occupation and the militarization of society more generally and by ongoing and even increasing socio-economic inequalities, notwithstanding economic growth well above the OECD average between 2010 and 2013 (although this trend was reversed in 2014) (OECD 2013).

The Western Left overall has no difficulty with identifying any of these movements and governments as right-wing and their appeals to religion as dangerous. It is when we come to discuss the "Muslim world" that there appears to be more difficulty sorting out left from right. Being the (male) underdog has always helped in generating sympathy from the Left, and since 9/11 Muslims have well and truly replaced Jews, at least in the collective political imaginary of the Gentile Left, as universal scapegoat and universal underdog. Moreover, appeals to democracy and legitimacy are persuasive arguments for Western actors and observers, including institutional ones. Many of the latter, anxious not to seem "Islamophobic" in a touchy post-9/11 context, have ever more willingly embraced the idea that we are moving or have already moved into a "postsecularist" era in the West and that the imbrication of religion and politics is a natural reaction to state authoritarianism or, in the West, as a pushback against hostility to Muslim minorities.

Broadly speaking, then, the Western hardline Right has reconnected with its "Christian heritage" in a post-9/11 context, whereas large sections of both the liberal Right and the Left, ill at ease within the post-9/11ist Us-and-Them scenario and its demonstrably racist impacts, have been at pains to distance themselves from hardline Christianity, on one hand, while happily supporting "democratic" Islamist movements in the name of antiracism or anti-"Islamophobia," on the other. Many have written on this problem of apparent cognitive dissonance (see, e.g., with relation to women's rights, Women Living under Muslim Laws 2011). There have even been artistic conversations on the topic, such as British multiethnic physical theater company DV8's courageous silence breaker in 2011, aptly named *Can We Talk About This?* The performance was intended as a criticism of the United Kingdom's multiculturalism gone wrong, where cultural relativist double standards paradoxically ended up having racist effects for Muslim citizens. Company director Lloyd Newsom asked, "Have well intended multicultural policies inadvertently ended up betraying the very minorities and freedoms Britain ought to be protecting?" (Newsome 2011).

Yet the cognitive dissonance remains. It highlights the difficulties and confusions faced by the West and even by international institutions such as the UN, which have had often self-contradictory and idiosyncratic attitudes toward "Islam." On one hand, they have frequently failed to clearly distance themselves from religious extremism or from the imbrication of religion and politics—for example, in their initial support for Islamist opponents to authoritarian states in Tunisia, Egypt, and Libya. Such dubious alliances would and indeed have scandalized many when given Christian expressions.

The politics of religion and revolution in the West and MENA as well as in West–MENA relations, however, existed well before 9/11. The question is thus to understand what, if anything, 9/11 changed, how 9/11 changed it, and why. But first, a wee clarification on terminology.

The term *Arab spring* is not used in the countries to which it refers and is even detested there. It is a term coined in the West (possibly by US political science professor and media commentator Marc Lynch [2011]) in recollection of the European "People's Spring" of 1848 or the "Prague spring" of 1968, perhaps itself named in memory of 1848. In 1848, a revolutionary wave spread throughout many countries in Europe (and parts of South America), but it was quickly quelled by conservative backlash in most of them, and there were few lasting impacts. (There, perhaps, one can indeed see a clear parallel between the "People's Spring" and the "Arab spring.") In the MENA countries where the uprisings have taken place since late 2010, different terms are used. In Tunisia, for example, which is the trigger site for the uprisings, the term *Sidi Bouzid revolution* was used at first because the uprisings followed the self-immolation of a street produce vendor in Sidi Bouzid on December 17, 2010. Twenty-six-year-old Mohamed Bouazizi self-immolated after the Tunisian authorities (via a policewoman, as it happens) confiscated his tools of trade: a cart and a set of scales. Bouazizi, who had been trading without an official permit, no longer had enough money to pay the bribes that had thus far kept him in business. He died from his burns on January 4, 2011. Later, the Tunisian shorthand for the events became "arb'atash janfi / le quatorze janvier"—that is, January 14, the date in 2011 when president Zine El Abidine Ben Ali fled the country—a place marker around which "before" and "after" are now articulated in Tunisian politics.

Before 9/11

There are a few factors to consider here. First, Western support for religious groups in the name of opposition to authoritarianism is not new and not only directed at the Muslim world. Second, oppositional or even revolutionary Islamist movements in MENA and their championing from both inside and outside the countries in question, including sometimes by feminists—despite evidence of these movements' destructive impacts for women—are similarly not recent developments.

Nor, for that matter, is their often violent repression by authoritarian states. Third, the anti-Western discourse within such movements is as old as the movements themselves because it is a core element of their ideological system. Fourth, the imbrication of religion and politics in MENA has not solely been the province of Islamist movements.

Western support for religious groups in the name of opposition to authoritarianism has been most in evidence in relation to the breakdown of the eastern European Communist bloc and nowhere more strikingly so than in relation to Poland. At the beginning of the 1980s, the name of the trade union Solidarność (Solidarity) was the freedom cry on the lips of almost everyone on the western European Left, it seemed, including feminists. This Polish trade union movement came to symbolize for the West all that was good in eastern Europeans' resistance to the Communist state, which was at that time held up to be all that was bad. Yet there were strong Catholic conservative and even anti-Semitic currents in Solidarność, which have survived long past the union's and its related political party's disintegration, and both the union and its leader, Lech Wałęsa, had very traditionalist attitudes toward women (Long 1996; Zubrzycki 2006). Certainly, blame for today's ongoing battles in Poland over social justice, the role of religion and ethnicity in national identity, and women's rights (including the regressive abortion law passed in 1993 and attempts to impose a total ban on abortion in April 2016) can certainly not be placed entirely at the door of Solidarność. Yet the often uncritical support for Solidarność that I observed in the 1980s in Australia, the United Kingdom, and France was cause for concern from a feminist point of view. I am also led to think of international support for the US-backed Afghan anti-Soviet Jehadi in the 1990s, which according to some commentators was one of the keys to the disintegration of the Soviet Union at the end of the 1980s (Reuveny and Prakash 1999)— although this view is not unanimous.

The emergence of modern Islamist movements in MENA can be traced back at least as far as the birth of their granddaddy, al-Ikhwan al-Muslimun, or the Muslim Brotherhood, which was formed as a pan-Islamic movement in Cairo in 1928 (Ahmed 2011). Along with the ideology of Khomeinism, the Brotherhood is the best-known example of Islamist politics in the contemporary history of MENA. Both have been identified with the emancipation of their societies from the yoke of Western imperialism and capitalist exploitation, and both have been fervently opposed to feminism, that "plague from the West." This does not mean that they and their "moderate" Islamist descendants have opposed women's participation in public life. Many have even supported it. Today, for example, women participate, albeit in small numbers, in governments in Palestine, Turkey, and Morocco, where Islamist parties hold the majority. In Tunisia, forty-two of the forty-nine women elected to the Constituent Assembly in October 2013 were members of or aligned with the Islamist party Ennahda (Renaissance), which obtained the greatest number of votes and seats in that election. It is not women's access to education, employment, or public life that is problematic for Islamist organizations: Iranian women, for example, are among the best educated in MENA, and this has been the case for some time (see Chafiq 1991; Roudi-Fahimi and Moghadam 2003; UNDP 2014). Universities are even favored sites to recruit new female activists and male cadres for the movements (Taarji 1990; Rozario 2006; Winter 2008).

It is, rather, in the area of private life—family, religion, and sexuality—that women's behavior is expected to conform to the heterosexist values of Islamic conservatism. Women who have resisted these conservative attitudes have been censured or dismissed as tainted by Western values. We have even seen in pre-9/11 times this framing being reproduced in the West, for example, within the context of the French *hijab* debate waged since 1989. Some women participating in that debate, including those who identify as feminist, have suggested that opposition to wearing the *hijab* or to the renewed imbrication of religion and politics by women of North African background is indicative of their "Westernization" (Winter 2008). This particular criticism has resurfaced in the debate following the attack on the periodical *Charlie Hebdo* in Paris on January 7, 2015, discussed in chapter 7. Such attitudes have profound roots in Islamist thinking. Among the fifty demands established by Muslim Brotherhood cofounder Hassan

al-Banna in 1928, more than one-fifth of them directly concern policing the behavior of women and girls, relations between the sexes, and
the family (al-Banna [1936] 2011). In Algeria in 1975, Islamist Abd
al-Latif Sultani attacked Algerian feminist Fadela Mrabet, one of the
most vocal critics of the Front de libération nationale (FLN, National
Liberation Front) government's treatment of women in the years following Algerian independence, as a "creature of Marxism, in the service of aesthetic pretensions," who supposedly advocated—in addition
to women's free circulation without a male chaperone—rejection of
Islam, "promiscuity," and "diabolical desires" (Sultani 2000, 341; see
also Mrabet 1965, 1967).

Islamist and in particular Brotherhood discourse is also vehemently
anti-Semitic, and the terms *Zionist* and *Jew* are used interchangeably.
Sayyid Qutb, for example, who became the Brotherhood's leading and
most violent ideologue in the 1950s and 1960s (Ahmed 2011; Wickham 2013), clearly advocated Islamic takeover of the world and wrote
of a Jewish aim to pursue "diabolic activities" in the world, which
Jews would conquer through usury, rendering that world "lethargic,
intoxicated and half-alive" (Qutb 2000, 201). The Brotherhood's
anti-Semitism has been reinscribed in many Islamist documents since
then, including the Hamas Charter, which goes beyond demands for
Palestinian independence to advocacy of killing Jews (Winter 2008),
and in many contemporary expressions of "antiracism" in the West, as
I discuss further in chapter 7.

The English translation of Qutb's work that I use here was first
published in Pakistan in the 1980s, which is one indicator of the geographical (and temporal) reach of the Brotherhood's ideas. Another
indicator is the presence of Brotherhood ideas and activists in Europe,
with France being one of its key recent strongholds, as I have discussed elsewhere (Winter 2008), and its capital, Paris, has been a target of Islamist terrorist organizations since the 1980s.

I mentioned in chapters 1 and 5 another ideologue whose work
has inspired anti-Western-decadence thinking: Iranian intellectual
Jalal Al-e Ahmad, chief ideologue of Khomeinism. Son of a Shia religious leader and former Communist activist, Al-e Ahmad had his

essay *Gharbzadegi* published clandestinely in 1962, although the term in the title was first used in Iran in the 1940s (Al-e Ahmad 1982, 1983, 1984). In his pamphlet, Al-e Ahmad compared the Western "affliction" to cholera or to a process by which one is eaten away inside by a foreign parasite. The generalization of the term enabled a reframing of Westernness not only as decadent but as pathological, toxic: a virus or a parasite but in any case an illness that only re-Islamicization can cure. Ironically, however, like many Islamic intellectuals, including women, who advocate a return to Islamic values, Al-e Ahmad had willingly exposed himself to this Western "cholera." He was, for example, invited to Harvard within the framework of a program of intellectual exchanges sponsored by Henry Kissinger (Dabashi 2005, 72–73).

Yet Al-e Ahmad's discourse was modernist as well. *Gharbzadegi* was produced, he explained, by the introduction of machines from the West without a proper cultural context, without historical continuity, and without any structures to facilitate integration. Al-e Ahmad's response—his "cure"—was for Iran to produce its own machines— that is, to become industrialized on its own terms. In fact, Islamist movements have always embraced modern capitalist development, even as they have opposed it ideologically. For example, one of the first Egyptians to advocate anti-Westernism and a return to traditions was Tal'at Harb, founder of the first Egyptian bank, Misr Bank (Ahmed 1992, 163). It is not within modern political or economic systems that the "plague from the West" is principally seen to reside. In fact, modern Islamist political movements have discursively positioned themselves as the champions of a Western political philosophy and system: democracy. The "plague" resides principally within women's bodies, which are and which have been throughout recorded history the battlefield on which men fight their wars over national and cultural identity.

What happens, however, with the Islamist framing of Western feminism is that it is invariably conflated with Western masculinist commodification of women's bodies. "Feminism," according to such framing, is not only about the abandonment of the duties of wife and mother but also about untrammeled sexual exhibitionism (cf. Sultani's attack on Mrabet, mentioned earlier). Most of all, it is about the refusal of "Islamic" values. In this hostility to feminism, Islamism bears noteworthy similarities to Western religious conservatism. The words of notorious US televangelist Pat Robertson in 1992, which have since traveled the Anglo world on a humorous postcard, could have easily (if one removes the reference to destroying capitalism) been pronounced by an Islamist man: "Feminism is not about equal rights for women. It is about a socialist, anti-family political movement that encourages women to leave their husbands, kill their children, practice witchcraft, destroy capitalism and become lesbians" (from the text of an anti–Equal Rights Amendment letter in *Washington Post* 1992).

Yet even feminists—again, well before 9/11—were tantalized by Islamists' anti-Western, social justice message. Egyptian feminist Nawal el Saadawi, for example, who is better known for her opposition to Islamist movements than for her support of them, famously celebrated the Khomeinist revolution in 1979 in the original preface to her renowned book *The Hidden Face of Eve* (1980), claiming that the revolution "is in its essence political and economic. It is a popular explosion which seeks to emancipate the people of Iran, both men and women, and not to send women back to the prison of the veil, the kitchen and the bedroom" (iii).

Anti-imperialism, then as now, was a powerful ideological tool.

Military intervention to displace Islamist oppositional political movements is not new either. More than twenty years before the Egyptian army's coup that ousted the elected government formed by the Muslim Brotherhood in 2012, a similar set of circumstances arose in Algeria. The Front islamique du salut (FIS, Islamic Salvation Front), which until 1997 had an armed wing, had emerged as an oppositional Islamist force during the process of Algerian democratization in the late 1980s. This process was interrupted in December 1991 when it became clear that the FIS was poised to win national legislative elections. These elections had not, it later emerged, been conducted according to entirely democratic principles: there were many reports of voter intimidation by FIS activists, among others, although this was not the reason for the state's intervention. The army-backed FLN government, which had held power since independence and had once been considered a model of Arab revolutionary socialism, intervened and canceled the second round of the elections, due to take place in early January 1992.

A decade-long civil war ensued. It continued past 9/11 as terrorist groups active in the civil war morphed into a new Salafist formation and then into al-Qaïda du Maghreb islamique (al Qaeda in the Islamic Maghreb) in 2006 (Stora 2001; Maghreb-Machrek 2011). In total, the Algerian civil war has cost between 50,000 and 150,000 lives, depending on the source of the estimate. What has been happening in Egypt since 2011 thus appears very déjà vu in the region—except that in terms of political Islamist ideology the Brotherhood preceded the FIS and not the other way around.

The extent of the Brotherhood's influence in MENA can be both overestimated and underestimated. It is neither the sole Islamist influence in the region nor a factor absent from the development of both "moderate" and "extremist" Islamism there. Contemporary Islamist political formations have been around for some decades in their present or earlier forms, such as the Mouvement de la tendance islamique (Movement for the Islamic Trend), founded in Tunisia in 1981, which became Ennahda, or the Parti de la justice et du développement (Justice and Development Party, JDP) in Morocco and the AKP in Turkey—the Moroccan party founded in 1998 with precursors from the 1960s and the Turkish party of the same name founded in 2001 with precursors during the latter half of the 1990s. Many, even most, of these movements have had a period of development in exile, often in the West, and many of them, or sections of them, have at times embraced violent action, then renounced such action, then covertly (or less covertly) readopted it, and then re-renounced it, all the while often undergoing internal splits. When one considers all these factors, it becomes virtually impossible to trace neat lines either through the history of national Islamist movements or between them and the Brotherhood. As Carrie Rosefsky Wickham has pointed out, Islamist organizations "are not monolithic entities whose members think and act in lockstep," nor do they demonstrate "a linear, unidimensional progression towards greater 'moderation'" (2013, 2). Even the Brotherhood has had a number of internal splits and dissents, and ties between it and other Sunni Islamist movements either do not exist or are denied. For example, many of the JDPs—there a number of them with the same or similar name both within and beyond MENA—deny affiliation with the Brotherhood and claim to be nationally based and modernist in their outlook. The latter claim implies that the Brotherhood is definitely *not* modernist, which is as false now as it was in 1928. For example, Moroccan JDP prime minister Abdelilah Benkirane told Washington-based Middle East media site *al Monitor* in February 2013,

> The Islamic movement in Morocco has its own ideology; we have nothing to do with the Muslim Brotherhood as some claim. In general, we are opposed to the idea of interfering in people's private lives. The people are in need of reform and must obtain their rights. Moroccans have known Islam since ancient times, and are characterized by a deep love for the family of the Prophet Muhammad. They were able to build a modern state and maintain stability; and since the beginning have engaged in the logic of the times. (Benkirane 2013)

That said, a number of common threads run through Islamist formations in the region, including the FIS, Hamas, Tunisia's Ennahda, Morocco's JDP, and Turkey's AKP. Two of the commonest threads are claims to democratic legitimacy and attempts to increase men's control of women.

The emergence of the JDP in Morocco, like that of the AKP in Turkey and indeed of Ennahda in Tunisia, has been—in sharp contrast to what has happened in recent years and decades in Palestine, Algeria, Libya, Egypt, Iraq, and Syria—almost completely nonviolent. Although Islamists in Morocco have historically been associated with republicanism, the JDP has worked as a reformist party within the parameters of the constitutional monarchy, notably since the various concessions by the current monarch, Mohamed VI, who in 1999 succeeded his far less liberal father Hassan II. Reforms introduced by Mohamed VI have included a liberalization of the Moudawana, the Personal Status Code, in 2004, granting more rights to women, and a referendum transferring a number of key powers from the monarch to Parliament and the prime minister in 2011, which was seen as a preemptive response to the uprisings elsewhere in MENA. The king has also, however, sought to limit the power of the JDP, which has governed (at the time of writing) in coalition since the election in 2011, by naming more monarch-friendly ministers to prevent the JDP from introducing some unpopular reforms such as the removal of fuel subsidies (El Yaakoubi 2013). (The JDP was returned to power, with a slightly increased majority, in the October 2016 general election.)

In Turkey, the AKP emerged in 2001 as a moderate, reformist party from the remains of the more hardline Fazilet Partisi (Virtue Party), which was formed in 1998 and outlawed in 2001 for violating the constitutional principle of secularism. (Turkey was still the only Muslim-majority country in MENA at the time of writing to have formally encoded secularism in its constitution, although some former Soviet republics outside MENA, also Muslim-majority, have also done so since 1990.) The AKP came to power in a landslide election in 2002 and has remained there ever since, apart from a brief period of hung Parliament between July and November 2015. Although Islamist, the party works within the confines of Turkey's secularist constitutional framework and has been decidedly pro-capitalist, pro-Western, and pro-EU, as discussed in chapter 1. In its fourth term at the time of writing, it has taken successive turns to the right, resulting in a wave of protest against the government in 2013, which I discuss in the next section.

Similarly, as mentioned earlier, Tunisia's Ennahda was a reconfiguration in 1989 of the Mouvement de la tendance islamique, formed in 1981. Contrary to its Turkish and Moroccan counterparts, Ennahda was never legalized by the former regime, and a number of its activists were imprisoned. Its leader, Rachid Ghannouchi, who became influenced by the Brotherhood's ideas after having studied in Cairo, lived in exile in London for twenty years. He returned to Tunisia at the end of

January 2011, claiming Ennahda's place as the natural "leader" of the revolution and the Turkish AKP as the party's inspiration. Some commentators suggested at the time, however, that the comparison was a political tactic to reassure the Tunisian populace and that Ennahda was significantly more conservative than the AKP (Arieff 2011; Bonzon 2011). Yet developments since have suggested that it is hard to pick between the two in terms of conservatism and moderateness.

In any case, the history of the Islamist movements that have become the "democratic" standard bearers for the MENA upheavals goes back well before 9/11. This does not mean, however, that the wake of 9/11 did not affect their fortunes, as we will see presently.

The other pre-9/11 factor that needs to be examined here is that the reimbrication of religion and politics in MENA is not solely the province of Islamist movements. The regressive Algerian Family Code of 1984, which introduced many elements of shari'a law into Arab (but not Kabyle) women's rights in Algeria, was imposed by the non-Islamist FLN, in power since the end of the war of liberation in 1962. Feminists widely denounced the code as marking a significant step backward in a country that had already moved quickly, at the end of the seven-year war of independence, to have women back to toeing a more traditionalist line. Notwithstanding the FLN's strong "Arab socialism" credentials, the Jam'iyat al-'Ulama' al-Muslimin al-Jaza'iriyin (Association of Algerian Muslim Ulamas) remained influential, and the Algerian state's policies toward women became ever more islamicized long before the advent of the FIS. Indeed, in a French play on words, the FIS was often said at the time to be the *fils* (son) of the FLN, both terms having identical pronunciation. The genealogy was proposed either as an argument that authoritarian rule by the FLN had become the fertile terrain in which Islamist oppositional movements could flourish (similar arguments have been made in relation to Tunisia, Turkey, and Egypt) or as an argument that Islamic influence was already present in Algerian politics well before the rise of Islamist movements.

Even the constitutionally secular Turkey under Kemalist rule was not as secular as it seemed—and in fact was far less so than France, with which it is often erroneously compared (Winter 2009–10). Article

24 of the Turkish Constitution, on freedom of conscience, provides for compulsory, state-administered instruction in religion and morals in primary and secondary schools. Moreover, the state, through the Directorate of Religious Affairs, administers the mosques, pays the imams, and prescribes the form of Islam to be practiced. Turkish Alevis (a mystical branch of Islam) have long protested against these prescriptions as discriminatory.

The connections between religion and politics in the Muslim world are thus very far from being a purely Islamist phenomenon, just as constitutionally secular democratic states such as the United States and France are still not free from the strong influence of Christianity, including among the political class. As in most Muslim-majority states today, in the West there was once no concept of separation of religion and state, and much of today's Western positive law, notably that regulating the family, stems from religious law.

After 9/11 I: "Postsecularism"

The "after," then, is not discontinuous from the "before," just as no historical rupture, however violent and revolutionary it may be, can be completely separated from the conditions in which that rupture occurred. That said, three related post-9/11 factors are important in both the way the Arab uprisings have played out and the way they have been received in the West. The first factor, which I discuss in this section, is the idea of postsecularism. The second, which I discuss in the next section, is the claiming of "Islamic" legitimacy in a simultaneous movement of pushback against anti-Arab and anti-Muslim post-9/11 racism, on one hand, and self-positioning as moderate and democratic opposition to authoritarian states, on the other hand. The third, which I discuss in chapter 7, is the development of the concepts of "Islamophobia" and "defamation of religion" within political and intellectual circles and within the UN. To these discursive factors must necessarily be added a material one: just as economic conditions under authoritarian regimes were a significant factor in the emergence of Islamist formations in many MENA countries before 9/11, the global financial crisis affected them significantly after 9/11.

These economic crises were related to the various and often combined impacts of global neoliberalism; fluctuations in oil prices, which have affected Libya and Algeria in particular; debt servicing; and, indeed, the economic consequences of political decisions made in the wake of 9/11.

Although already in circulation prior to 9/11, the term *postsecularism* was originally associated with either Christian "radical orthodoxy" or literary expressions of "new spiritualities." In a post-9/11 context, the idea was popularized largely albeit not exclusively through the work of Jürgen Habermas (2001, 2006, 2007). Speaking in acceptance of a Peace Prize awarded to him by the German Booksellers Association one month after 9/11, Habermas clearly linked the events and impact of 9/11 with the idea of postsecularism. In his speech, titled "Faith and Knowledge," Habermas noted that, "after 11 September, the tension between secular society and religion exploded in an entirely different way" and suggested that "the search for reasons that aspire to general acceptance need not lead to an unfair exclusion of religion from public life, and secular society, for its part, need not cut itself off from the important resources of spiritual explanations, if only the secular side were to retain a feeling for the articulative power of religious discourse" (2001).

Habermas referred to all three monotheistic religions but focused in particular on the forces that created the conditions for Islamic fundamentalism and terrorism, which he saw as the reflection of "an imbalance that has emerged in the perpetrators' home countries between culture and society in the wake of an accelerated and radical modernization," such that "the prospect of spiritual freedom, which finds its political expression in the separation of church and state, has been impeded there [presumably meaning 'in the Muslim world'] by feelings of humiliation" (2001). He is not alone in this observation, nor is it restricted to a post-9/11 conversation (see, e.g., Shayegan 1989), but, unlike other basically secular(ist) commentators, Habermas saw in this state of affairs the need for a reinjection of religious morals into public life, notably in the face of "a globalization that consists of a market without boundaries" (2001).

Habermas joins so-called moderate Islamist thinkers such as Tariq Ramadan, maternal grandson of Hassan Al Banna, cofounder of the Muslim Brotherhood, and son of Saïd Ramadan, who, exiled in Saudi Arabia, became one of the founders of al-Rabita al-Alam al-Islami, or Muslim World League, in 1962. The league's main objective is to combat Arabo-Islamic socialism and other progressive movements through proselytism of conservative Islam (Winter 2008; Ahmed 2011). Not long after 9/11, Tariq Ramadan, in a book addressed to Western Muslims, wrote of a "lack" in Western industrialized societies, where even "spirituality" had become a superficial object of consumption (2003, 202–5, my translation in all instances). As the solution, he advocated the daily practice of and struggle (jihad) for Islamic faith, which "is demanding and, through the virtues of Islamic teaching, touches all dimensions of life" (210). Throughout the book (as indeed in all of his writing), Ramadan asserts a Muslim identity that is fundamentally different from both Christianity and Western secularity in that it combines "faith, practice, and spirituality" and asserts that "respecting Muslim identity means recognizing this primary and fundamental dimension of faith and, by extension, allowing Muslims to accomplish all the religious practices that model their spiritual life" (141). In a similar albeit not the same vein, Habermas does not see this reengagement with "the articulative power of religious discourse" (2001) as undermining secularism but as moving society from a positivist, capitalist model where moral responsibility for others has been diminished to a more just and connected world.

One of the problems with Habermas's argument is that it is based on an assumption that secularism has been fully achieved in the West so that a move to postsecularism is conceptualizable. I have argued at length elsewhere that this is far from being the case (Winter 2008, 2013). Christianity still pervades public life and culture in most Western countries, and this continued imbrication of religion and politics has only, as we have seen, been exacerbated since 9/11, whether we consider the US motto "In God We Trust" and the still heavily Christian symbolic trappings of the US presidency; various other forms of Christian influence on politics in the areas of women's or gay rights; often considerable state subsidies to Christian schools (including in supposedly ultrasecularist France); the fact that personal-status laws such as marriage and the regulation of family relations are based on Christian tradition; or even that most public holidays in Western countries are Christian in origin or were recast as such early in our era. (Most of the remainder of public holidays are associated with nation forming or wars.)

The second problem with Habermas's argument for a postsecular society is that the immorality of global capitalism and the human and societal destruction wreaked in its name are tacitly attributed, at least in part, to secularism "going too far" (which is also tacitly Ramadan's argument). The privileging of knowledge over faith, to use Habermas's frame, and faith's supposed marginalization from public life (which is also Ramadan's frame) have apparently brought us to a point of disconnectedness and immoral disregard for the lives and beliefs of others, even as we smart at the injustices perpetrated in our names. There is not, however, any necessary connection between the belief in a transcendent power (be it "God," "the gods," or some other form of spiritual transcendence) and the ability to develop a sophisticated moral awareness and deep connectedness with others. "What is missing," to cite a later work by Habermas (2007) on the subject, is not spirituality but *solidarity*. The former is not a precondition for the latter and indeed has frequently worked against it, especially where women are concerned.

One could argue that in his speech Habermas was not advocating a reimbrication of religion and politics of the sort we have seen in both pre-9/11 and post-9/11 MENA but an increased accommodation of religion in public life by Western secular societies without abandoning the principle of state neutrality with respect to religion. In practice, however, it is hard to see how such an arrangement would work without bringing about further attacks on that very neutrality, as we have seen from both Christian and Islamic movements in a number of Western countries and as has been so painfully brought home once again by the attacks in Paris in 2015 (and indeed elsewhere, including Turkey and Tunisia), notably those that occurred in January, discussed in the next chapter. The goal of the religious Right is not simply to be given space but to take over: to reintroduce blasphemy laws, to reduce women's economic and reproductive rights, to outlaw homosexuality, and so on. As for the religious Left, it has mostly accommodated secularism without difficulty, although, as we have seen in the case of Solidarność and its offshoots, sorting out the "right" from the "left" as far as women are concerned is not a straightforward exercise, for those concepts are usually defined in masculinist terms. Even the Muslim Brotherhood started out with social justice credentials and continued to position itself in that way during the uprisings in Egypt. This political cognitive dissonance has continued to dog conversations about Islam, the state, and society, and 9/11's impact has been to increase the confusion rather than to dispel it.

After 9/11 II: Democracy and Legitimacy

We have seen that *democracy, women's rights,* and *freedom* were the catchphrases of the United States and its allies in waging the "war on terror." We have seen that the results of such "liberation" and "democratization" are less than brilliant. Even if we accept that democratization is a slow and often painful process anywhere—as history has shown us time and again—the process of democratization in the Arab world has been more painful than most, and in most of that world the goal of democracy has moved farther out of reach, not closer.

Libya, for example, has been the site of sectarian violence since the much-criticized NATO-backed overthrow of Muammar Qaddafi in 2011 (Roberts 2011). In 2013, Islamic law was introduced; in 2014, the Islamist transitional government refused to recognize the electoral victory of secularists, and the country returned to a state of anarchy, of which Daesh has been quick to take advantage. In February 2015, analysts characterized oil-rich Libya as "a magnet for Jihadists" and a "gateway to Europe" for Daesh (cited in Chothia 2015). In March 2015, Daesh also attacked the Bardo Museum in Tunis (or claimed responsibility for the attack) and a Shia mosque in Sanaa in Yemen, where the main Islamist presence had previously been al Qaeda in the Arab Peninsula. The following year, on March 7, 2016, Daesh launched an attack from Libya on the Tunisian border town Ben Guerdane, killing some forty-five people.

In Egypt, the Muslim Brotherhood government elected in 2011 was replaced in a coup d'état, and internal strife continues. Syria is a human disaster site, and the Middle Eastern refugee crisis is seriously overburdening other Middle Eastern countries (Turkey, Jordan, and Lebanon in particular), while the EU is facing a far-right anti-immigrant backlash in most of its member states. The UN has characterized the refugee crisis in Lebanon as a "national calamity," with roughly one-third of Lebanon's population now being refugees (UN News Centre n.d.).

Democracy is not, in fact, having a very good time in MENA. Yet appeals to "democratic legitimacy" have been strongly made both by Islamist parties in the region and by Western governments that have largely enabled or assisted these parties' rise to power. These appeals are reminiscent of the use of the term *legitimacy* by the United States and its allies to justify their own military incursions into Afghanistan, Iraq, and Libya as opposition to despotic regimes and support for democratization. In Syria, however, they stayed well away for some years, when perhaps early intervention of the right kind *may* have been of some use.

In this last section, then, I interrogate the use of the idea of democratic legitimacy as a tool by Islamist parties and by Western states that tacitly or overly supported them. I focus in particular on Tunisia, which a US Congressional Research Service report in 2012 identified as a "test case" for the region owing to its "unique attributes" in the MENA context: "a relatively small territory, a sizable and well educated middle class, and a long history of encouraging women's socioeconomic freedoms" (Arieff 2011, unnumbered summary page). Yet Tunisia's low geopolitical importance relative to larger and more influential states such as Egypt and Syria means that whatever happens there is seen as less momentous than what happens in these other states. Tunisia is nonetheless the only place that can be thought of as anything approaching a "success story" of the "Arab spring" at the time of writing, and even there the success is mitigated.

In Tunisia, 9/11 did have a perceptible impact. According to Olfa Lamloum, writing in the wake of the 9/11 attacks and the declaration of war on Afghanistan but before the war on Iraq in 2003, authoritarian Arab regimes (her reference being Tunisia in particular) found in the combat against Islamism a new way to assert their power and strengthen their relationship with the West, all the more because "Afghanistan is not Iraq" (2001, 175). Lamloum was referring to the 1990–91 Gulf War, which was very unpopular in North Africa. Indeed, Tunisia, among other MENA states ruled by authoritarian governments, received significant military and other aid from both France and the United States prior to the uprisings in 2011, aid from which those regimes benefited. Those states were also propped up by political alliances. In 2008, for example, then French president Nicolas Sarkozy (but now out of the running for a return in 2017) presided over the establishment of the Union for the Mediterranean, which arose phoenixlike out of the ashes of previous trans-Mediterranean initiatives. At the first summit held in Paris in July 2008, a beaming Sarkozy was photographed shaking hands with Hosni Moubarak and Zine El Abidine Ben Ali, the Egyptian and Tunisian leaders ousted in 2011. Sarkozy's government was further wrong-footed in relation to North Africa by a major diplomatic scandal in 2011. In January of that year, two days before Ben Ali fled Tunisia, French foreign minister Michèle Alliot-Marie offered him security assistance to keep things in order there. It was subsequently revealed that Alliot-Marie had a close personal relationship with Ben Ali and his entourage. As a result, she had to resign, and the French state quickly had to refashion itself as Ennahda's new best friend, a position that once again wrong-footed France during the Tunisian political crisis of 2013 and most recently in 2015 following the terrorist attacks in Bardo and Sousse (the latter, which killed thirty-eight people and injured another thirty-nine, mainly British tourists, occurred on June 26). One of the gunmen in the Bardo attack was a member of Ennahda, which gave rise to (unconfirmed) suspicions that Ennahda might be involved. France's support for the Ennahda regime, for the Muslim Brotherhood, and for Qatar, now a major investor in North and West Africa, has been described as complicit to the extent that some commentators believe France has to take some responsibility for the Bardo attack, in which four French tourists died (Beau 2015).

At the same time, Islamist movements were able to find a new form of political legitimation through outrage against the "war on terror," which according to Lamloum was undermining the "Arab order" established from the late 1970s (2001, 177). Indeed, in Tunisia Ennahda emerged as the initial victor after the departure of Ben Ali. Its leader, Rachid Ghannouchi, wasted no time in returning to Tunisia on January 30, 2011, and in positioning himself as the leader of the new democratic movement and his party as democratic and in favor of preserving women's rights. He added to this progressive spin by pointing to the ruling Turkish AKP as a successful model of Islamic democracy to which Ennahda now aspired. Very quickly after the revolution, Ennahda, like the Brotherhood in Egypt, thus emerged as the revolution's champion, even though the popular protests in both countries involved a broad and diverse cross-section of people, including many secularists, and were not "led" as such by any Islamist party or parties.

Economic conditions in many countries in MENA, however, created the fertile terrain in which Islamist movements were able to emerge as champions of the underclass, as they had in Egypt from the late 1920s and as they had in Algeria in the late 1980s. Opinions on the impact of the global financial crisis on the Arab world are varied, with some seeing it as highly significant (Aoudé 2013), but others believing it had less effect in MENA than elsewhere (Brach and Loewe 2010), with the impact on Tunisia being relatively low. Certainly, the crisis affected different countries in the region quite differently, and many of the socioeconomic conditions that fueled the uprisings were part of a precrisis (and indeed pre-9/11) scenario. That said, in the case of Tunisia the financial crisis did exacerbate preexisting problems, such as government corruption and corresponding economic marginalization, notably of young people. Since the departure of Ben Ali, however, things have not looked up. In fact, on socioeconomic indicators, Tunisia regressed significantly between 2011 and 2013. In February 2013, the National Association of Tunisian

Economists published a communiqué in which it attributed Tunisia's socioeconomic malaise to the political malaise, drawing attention to the absence or perceived absence of the rule of law and incompetent management of public services, dwindling investment, sharply rising cost of living, and increasing insecurity and violence (Haddar 2013). This development, however, is not out of keeping with periods of significant political upheaval and is certainly in line with a prediction made in 2011 by OECD senior economist for MENA investment Ania Thiemann. In a February 28, 2011, interview in English with the France 24 TV news network, Thiemann suggested that it could take fifteen to twenty years for "Arab spring" countries to turn around the difficult economic situation in which the uprisings occurred and that things could well get worse during the unstable transitional period before they get better (*Business Interview* 2011). Terrorist attacks such as those at Bardo and Sousse have also deleteriously impacted on the economic outlook because they have seriously affected the tourism industry. The Tunisian minister for Tourism, Salma Lummi, told the media in September 2015 that tourism was down by 25 percent compared to 2014 (*Middle East Monitor* 2015).

Tunisia is, however, definitely still in the "getting worse" period. International and Tunisian sources show that unemployment in Tunisia was running at a little higher than 15 percent in 2014 and 2015, which is lower than the 16.7 percent in 2012 but worse than before the revolution, approximately 13 percent in 2010 (UNDP 2013, 2014, 2015; Tunisian National Institute of Statistics n.d.). When disaggregated by sex or age, the statistics are even more alarming. In 2013, the unemployment rate was more than 23 percent for women, compared to some 14 percent for men; it had only slightly decreased to 22.2 percent by mid-2015 (which was nonetheless worse than the first quarter of the year, when it had dropped below 22 percent). Men's unemployment in mid-2015 had dropped to 12.4 percent. Even though women make up only around one-quarter of the Tunisian labor force, their unemployment rate is one of the highest in the world, compared to a world average of around 6.5 percent. Youth unemployment is around 30 percent and is most severe among graduates; the rate for young women is double that for young men. Youth unemployment was one of the social driving forces of the 2010–11 uprisings, but, again, no significant progress has been made despite the "success" of those uprisings. Unemployment statistics in other countries in the region, Egypt, Morocco, and Algeria—the first two of which rank below Tunisia on both human development and GDP indexes—show that although the overall unemployment rate has increased over the same period, it has remained some three or four percentage points lower than in Tunisia. Statistics on youth and female unemployment, however, are comparable, which indicates that the improved score in the comparator countries is coming from larger numbers of men older than twenty-five in paid employment. Yet Tunisia is supposedly ahead of all three of these countries in terms of long-standing formal recognition of women's rights. In terms of labor-force participation and unemployment, however, it is not much ahead at all. Labor-force participation of women is actually slightly higher in Morocco, according to the UN Human Development Report for 2013 (UNDP 2013).

One might have thought that in terms of basic gender-equality indicators, Tunisia might do a little better. After all, it has the Muslim world's most progressive personal-status law, introduced in 1957 by Habib Bourguiba, leader of the newly decolonized nation, and reinforced by amendments in 1983, and an established feminist movement has been very proactive in the region. As concerns political participation, with 49 seats (23 percent of the total) being held by women after the Constituent Assembly election in 2011, Tunisia did appear on the face of it to be doing better than comparator countries, except for Algeria, where around 36 percent of lower-house members of Parliament were women at that time. In Morocco, this figure falls to 17 percent, although it was even worse in Turkey (the model that Ghannouchi wished to emulate), only 14 percent, and in Egypt following the election in 2012 only 2 percent of seats were held by women. Yet in fact Tunisia had slid backward in relation to its previous election in 2009, when women won 59 of 214 seats, or around 28 percent.

A small secular-left party, the Pôle démocratique et moderniste (Democratic and Modernist Pole), was the only party in 2011 to completely respect the principle of electoral list gender parity to which all lists were supposed to conform and which is now encoded in the Tunisian Constitution. Of the thirty-three lists this party presented, sixteen were headed by women, although because the party received less than 3 percent of the vote, the impact on the numbers of women in Parliament was minimal. As mentioned earlier, the majority of the forty-nine women elected in 2011 belonged to Ennahda. These women were predictably very conservative in their outlook and did little if anything to defend or advance women's rights. On the contrary, they supported repeated attempts by the Ennahda-dominated coalition to encode regressive measures for women in the Constitution and were outspoken in their defense of a return to more traditional values.

When elections were held in October 2014, the neo-Bourguibist party Nidaa Tounes (Call of Tunisia) gained the majority (close to 40 percent of the vote and 85 seats) as well as the presidency (Béji Caïd Essebsi), and Ennahda backslid (although it still gained the second-largest number of votes and 69 seats); there were once again few electoral lists headed by women. Women's electoral score nonetheless increased, with women winning 68 out of 217 seats (31.3 percent), of which 35 went to Nidaa Tounes members and 27 to Ennahda. Yet as we saw with relation to female members of Ennahda, this "descriptive" participation by women (as in representing a constituency by virtue of sharing sociodemographic characteristics with it) is minimalist. Although welcome, it does not in itself mean that women's interests will be represented substantively in terms of greater social and economic gender equality, increased protections against violence, and so on.

A number of Tunisian feminists with whom I spoke in September 2013 talked of an overwhelming disappointment with the supposedly democratic revolution: as one feminist lawyer put it, "Arab spring? Arab hell more like!" The social anomie was visible. I had not visited Tunis for some years, but I remembered a vibrant city where women circulated freely and where there was some impression of functionality, even though everyone I spoke with during that previous visit also expressed concern about the lack of freedom of expression and of the press under Ben Ali. Five years later it was rare to see women walking on their own at night; men—even small boys—seemed to have become more aggressive toward women; and basic infrastructure was falling apart. For example, garbage remained piled up in the streets, and it had become extraordinarily difficult to get around town due to paralyzing traffic congestion. Those I spoke with talked of cronyism within the Ennahda-led government, as incompetent and inexperienced people were appointed to senior public-service roles, with resulting dysfunctionality.

Leyla Dakhli, writing in February 2013, titled her commentary "Une révolution trahie?" (A Revolution Betrayed?). Recalling Trotsky's famous indictment of the Stalinist Russian state (Trotsky [1936] 1937), she wrote, "The revolution of young people enamored of freedom and justice seems to have given birth to an Islamist monster, conservative and destructive of freedoms. The free postrevolutionary elections appear to have given power to the enemies of democracy and freedom" (my translation).

The question mark in Dakhli's title concerns who the actors of the revolution were and who betrayed whom. She pointed out that rural uprisings by an impoverished peasant class had been going on for some years and that this class distrusted urban elites, including the large trade union organization Union générale des travailleurs tunisiens (General Union of Tunisian Workers). Following the departure of Ben Ali, almost daily demonstrations occurred, with tensions emerging between the coastal urban elites and the inland peasant and laborer classes. Those demonstrations continued well into 2012: "The vote and the establishment of a new government have not allayed the fears of blue-collar workers, day-laborers, the unemployed, who in no case are raising the issues in terms of religion, freedoms or even the Constitution. They are speaking of justice, of rights, of equality" (Dakhli 2013, my translation). Ennahda had completely failed to address these issues.

According to some feminists with whom I spoke in 2013, some of the opposition at the time was not addressing them either. For example, one women's rights group I spoke to, which also has male members, worked almost exclusively in the field with poor rural women. Its goal was to make feminist ideas intelligible to such women and rebuild the feminist movement from the ground up: "When you want to be involved in politics, you need to understand your people" (personal communication, Sept. 27, 2013). The clear implication was that the women did not believe that the mainstream opposition parties really "understood their people." At the same time, the group had no intention of making the slightest concession to Ennahda, which it saw as simply a new dictatorship dressed in the clothing of democracy.

There is little sign that the new, largely technocratic government formed in early 2015 after approval of the new constitution and the election in 2014 has done any better than Ennahda. In January 2016, roughly a year after the government was sworn in, Prime Minister Habib Essid launched a significant ministerial reshuffle, including replacement of core ministers, to try to deal with widespread public dissatisfaction (Bobin 2016).

Talibanization and "Laboratories of Resistance"

The election in October 2014 that resulted in the defeat of Ennahda followed a mid-2013 parliamentary walkout and sit-in by some sixty deputies in the Constituent Assembly. After lengthy negotiations, including some pressure on Ennahda from US secretary of state John Kerry, Ennahda agreed to a transition to a caretaker government, followed by final adoption of a new constitution and the organization of elections in late 2014. The walkout and sit-in, which began in July 2013 in Bardo Square near the museum that would be attacked by two gunmen on March 18, 2015, were the Left's frustrated response to the ongoing blockage of the constitutional process, but the trigger was a second political assassination in the space of six months. On February 6, 2013, Chokri Belaïd, general secretary of the secular-left Parti unifié des patriotes démocrates (Unified Democratic Patriots Party), part of the twelve-party coalition the Front populaire (Popular Front), was killed by a gunman outside his home. In the second killing, on July 25, Mohamed Brahmi was also shot outside his home with the same gun as the one that had killed Belaïd. This killing triggered the parliamentary walkout. Brahmi was the leader of the Mouvement du peuple (People's Movement), which was also part of the Popular Front and held two seats in the Constituent Assembly, including his own: he was a representative of Sidi Bouzid, the site of the beginning of the uprisings. Both men had been opposed to Ben Ali but were equally opposed to the three-party coalition led by Ennahda, which held the majority in the Constituent Assembly. The assassinations were part of an increasing wave of Salafist violence believed to be encouraged or at the very least condoned by Ennahda's right flank. (See *Libération* 2015a on a general strike and anti-Ennahda protests following Brahmi's assassination.)

The groundswell of popular opinion against Ennahda built during the sit-in period, which lasted for three months. For example, on August 13, 2013, which is Tunisian Women's Day by virtue of its being the anniversary of Bourguiba's beylical decree in 1956 that became the personal-status law on January 1, 1957, thousands of women took to the streets behind the banners of, among others, Hrayer Tounes (Free Women of Tunisia), a new group that emerged following the Sidi Bouzid revolution to demand justice and protection of women's rights. As the women (and quite a few men) who participated in that march joined the Bardo sit-in, a few hundred female Ennahda members, prayer mats at the ready, enjoined women to support the regime in place and Tunisia's "Muslim identity."

Yet that identity has been denounced as fraudulent and manufactured. Many commentators, including Dakhli, have maintained that Ennahda appropriated a revolution whose origins were clearly socioeconomic and shifted it onto the terrain of Islamic identity politics. A well-known feminist historian saw the Islamist influence in Tunisia as an import, bankrolled by petrodollars (personal communication, Sept. 27, 2013). It should also, however, be noted that the deposed leader, Ben Ali, supposedly secularist, found refuge in Saudi Arabia; the manipulative role of Gulf powers on both sides of "Arab spring" politics thus cannot be underestimated. Latifa Lakhdar, a founding member of one of the oldest contemporary Tunisian feminist organizations, the Association tunisienne des femmes démocrates (Tunisian

Association of Democratic Women)—founded in 1989 and thus to some extent associated with the "old guard"—was appointed minister for culture and for the preservation of heritage in January 2015 but lost that post to singer and music festival director Sonia M'Barek in the ministerial reshuffle of January 2016. As such, Lakhdar was one of the tiny minority of women in the Tunisian government in 2015 (only eight out of forty-two). In her work on the history of Tunisian women and Islam from the twelfth to the twentieth centuries, Lakhdar found that "Islamic orthodoxy has not evolved" (personal communication, Sept. 27, 2013; Lakhdar 2007). Although she is part of the Tunisian left-wing establishment, she was also a strong supporter of the uprisings in 2010–11, which she says were co-opted by Ennahda after the fact. Numerous women of various political backgrounds who worked in different areas—in politics, in the field with poor women, in universities, in literature and culture—repeated this observation to me. They also spoke of Ennahda's "highly ambiguous" attitude, as one interviewee, a writer, put it in relation to increasing Salafist violence in Tunisia.

Manouba University, in the northeastern suburb of Tunis, was one of the targets for Salafist violence because of its liberal secular reputation. The events at Manouba started on November 29, 2011, with a sit-in by some thirty students, who were demanding a prayer room and the right for women to attend classes wearing a *niqab* (face veil). The university had forbidden the *niqab* on the grounds that education is a communicative process and face covering blocks this communication. A number of staff, defending the decision, rallied outside the office of the dean of arts, Hamid Kazdaghli. The situation quickly worsened; classes were suspended, and Salafist demonstrations occurred during which, among other things, the Tunisian flag flying at the university was removed and a black Salafist flag hoisted. Kazdaghli removed the black flag and was accused of hitting two of the *niqab*-wearing young women, who subsequently trashed his office. He was acquitted of all charges, and the women who had destroyed his office were given a suspended sentence. Kazdaghli told me that the women in question had turned up to court surrounded by male Salafists.

When I spoke with him in September 2013, Kazdaghli was under twenty-four-hour police protection and had virtually been confined to his home for some time because of death threats against him. One Manouba University academic observed at the time that Ennahda combined democratic processes with violent methods and believed that Manouba University had become a "laboratory of resistance" in a context where the Left had become dispersed and ineffectual or too bound up in ideology to develop a functioning political and institutional program. It thus seemed in 2013 that democracy in Tunisia—although it had appeared effervescent to the point of unmanageability at the time of the elections in 2011, with 11,686 candidates representing a total of 1,517 lists—remained weak. It was very easy for a well-organized and cashed-up Islamist movement to walk in and fill the void of democracy and legitimacy left after Ben Ali's departure. Rebuilding the Left and the feminist movement from the ground up, whether in the universities or the countryside, seemed urgent.

A great part of the Islamist violence came from the Ligue de la protection de la révolution (League for the Protection of the Revolution), a militia loosely associated with Ennahda and dedicated to the eradication of any hint of Bourguibism in Tunisian politics and society: its primary target was thus the party Nidaa Tounes. In January 2013, Ghannouchi was cited in the French daily *Le Monde* as saying that the league was "the conscience of the revolution," although a spokesperson for Ennahda's political bureau denied any organizational link, notwithstanding a number of Ennahda members' and supporters' membership in the league (Auffray 2013). The Manouba academic I talked to described the league as being "like the SS" in its ideology and operation (personal communication, Sept. 28, 2013). In his book *Chroniques du Manoubistan*, which documents the events that unfolded at Manouba from late 2011 to August 2012, Habib Mellakh refers to one of Ghannouchi's Friday sermons, delivered on August 10, 2012, and published on Facebook, in which he stated that the enemies of his party were the enemies of Islam (2013, 315). Mellakh argues that even if one did not see Salafist agitators and Ennahda as two sides of the same coin, what was clear—especially by the beginning of 2013—was that both desired the Islamicization of Tunisian society and politics, the main difference between them being that Salafists wished to Talibanize them (hence the title of Mellakh's book).

At the time of writing, some at least of the political enemies appear to have patched it up in order to move forward. In February 2015, President Béji Caïd Essebsi appointed a "unity government" of twenty-seven ministers and seventeen undersecretaries led by independent prime minister Habib Essid. Yet the unity is somewhat unbalanced and bears no particular relation to the proportion of the legislative vote won by the various parties. Many see it as cosmetic or tokenistic and, in particular, as an attempt to appease Ennahda, which has accepted the compromise, it is believed, in order to maintain a power base within the government. The coalition government appointed at the beginning of 2015 included twenty-one independents (of which thirteen are ministers, including the prime minister, or deputy ministers) and five parties: Nidaa Tounes (86 seats, six ministers, two deputy ministers, and two undersecretaries), Ennahda (69 seats but only one minister and three undersecretaries), the Union patriotique libre (Free Patriotic Union, modernist neoliberal, 16 seats, three ministers), the centrist liberal party Afek Tounes (Tunisian Horizons, 8 seats but three ministers), and the Front national du salut (National Salvation Front, rebadged the Mouvement national tunisien [National Tunisian Movement]), a broad left-leaning coalition (one seat, one deputy minister). The Popular Front, the party of the assassinated politicians Belaïd and Brahmi and the fourth-largest group in Parliament with 15 seats, refused to join any coalition involving Islamist parties and is thus not a member of the government.

Even before the attack that killed twenty-one people in the Bardo National Museum on March 18, 2015, "security" was identified as a top priority for the new government, which on other levels has not proposed any particularly radical measures to revitalize Tunisian society and economy. The attack on the Bardo happened so easily because the museum and the grounds were not well guarded, yet the Bardo not only is Tunisia's most prestigious museum but also adjoins the national Parliament. On March 24, the Tunisian prime minister sacked the chiefs of police of Tunis and the Bardo and arrested one of the Bardo security guards for reasons not disclosed at the time of writing. After three years during which Salafist violence and indeed intimidation of women (including by the police) continued relatively unchecked, belying the image of the so-called Jasmine revolution, where the change of regime supposedly happened very peacefully in comparison to changes in other countries in the region, the new Tunisian government is anxious to appear strong on security.

Yet, once again, those most in need of "security" in Tunisia, both before and after the Sidi Bouzid revolution, are women. Up to half of Tunisian women are subjected to violence at some stage in their lives, a proportion much higher than the international average of one-third, and this was the case under Ben Ali as well (Office National de la Famille et de la Population and Agencia Española de Cooperación Internacional para el Desarrollo 2010; see also Winter 2016). Discussion on a framework law against violence against women, launched following a report and recommendation by the UN Population Fund, remains stalled at the time of writing (UN Population Fund 2014). Combined with Tunisia's lackluster performance in terms of women's political and workforce participation, the Tunisian "success story" is mitigated, indeed, notwithstanding its relatively strong women's rights framework, encoded in Article 46 of the Constitution of 2013.

The new government also appears anxious to rehabilitate the image of the ousted Ben Ali regime. In September 2015, its proposed "economic reconciliation law," a presidential initiative that would grant amnesty to those involved in corruption during the Ben Ali regime if they agreed to reimburse the embezzled monies, met with vocal opposition. This proposal runs at variance with the Instance vérité et dignité (Truth and Dignity Authority), set up under the terms of the Law on Transitional Justice adopted on December 14, 2013, to investigate human rights abuses in Tunisia since 1955 and to compensate victims. The authority, presided by Sihem Ben Sedrine, has been embattled virtually since its creation, with accusations that the authority in general and Ben Sedrine in particular have been too indulgent toward Islamist groups, even including violent groups such as Daesh (RFI 2015a). Indeed, Ennahda leader Rachid Ghannouchi, to whose party Ben Sedrine is reputedly close, has himself called for moves to repatriate Tunisian extremists who have been engaged in terrorist activity in Syria and Iraq, "for whom the doors of repentance must remain open" (qtd. in *Tunisie Numérique* 2015; see also Ghorbal 2015). Ben Sedrine has also allegedly engaged in her own acts of corruption at the head of the authority (Dahmani 2015). As for the "economic reconciliation law" proposed by the new president, various commentators of different political persuasions cited by *Le Monde* on September 12, 2015, speak of "whitewashing" and "betrayal of the revolution" (Bobin 2015). Representatives of Nidaa Tounes, however, beg to differ. Among them is human rights expert Mohsen Marzouk, former extreme-left resistant arrested (along with fellow activist Chokri Belaïd) during the final months of Bourguiba's rule in 1987 and now general secretary of Nidaa Tounes (Ghorbal 2015). Tunisia would thus seem, once again, to be engaged in a fight between its two main political clans: the neo-Bourguibists and their allies on one side, incorporating at least some of those who also suffered under Bourguiba and Ben Ali, and Ennahda and its allies on the other.

The first government of the new regime, like that of the Constituent Assembly of 2011, has claimed democratic legitimacy and national unity as its justifying principles. But as in any democracy anywhere, if institutions and civil society remain weak, if power is largely the result of political and financial deals made between male political actors both nationally and internationally, and if politics are subjected to the demands of religious lobbies and political clans, then the regime's legitimacy, particularly for women, is open to question. Tunisia thus still seems in need of "laboratories of resistance" and certainly not of the Islamist kind.

7

Being Charlie, Being Paris

On January 7, 8, and 9, 2015, three self-declared Islamists, two of them associated with al Qaeda and one associated with Daesh, assassinated seventeen people in three separate attacks in Paris. The January 7 attack was on the offices of satirical paper *Charlie Hebdo*, long the subject of polemic because of its caricatures of religions and religious leaders, among other things, and the January 9 attack was on a kosher supermarket. All three attackers were subsequently found and killed by police, and further suspects believed to be plotters of the attacks were tracked down and killed in Belgium. On November 13 of the same year, a number of attacks occurred in central Paris—at a restaurant, a bar, the well-known Bataclan music performance venue, and a sports stadium in the inner northern suburb of Saint-Denis, where the president, among thousands of others, was watching a friendly soccer match between France and Germany. In total, 131 people were killed, and 351 were injured. The November attackers were suicide bombers, most of whom detonated their explosives to kill themselves prior to arrest. Others were arrested and killed by police, and one of the presumed masterminds, Salah Abdeslam, was arrested in Brussels on March 18, 2016. Four days after Abdeslam's arrest, on March 22, two further suicide bombings took place at the Zaventem Airport and Maalbeek metro station in Brussels. The attacks killed 32 people plus three suicide bombers and injured more than 300. It is possible but unconfirmed at the time of writing in early April 2016 whether the attacks on March 22 were directly linked to Abdeslam's arrest.

On November 14, 2015, Daesh claimed responsibility for the Paris attacks of the previous day, in a communiqué in Arabic and French.

The communiqué named France as primary target, which "carried the banner of the cross in Europe," and Paris as "the capital of abominations and perversions." The communiqué further stated that "this attack is only the beginning of the storm" and is a "warning" to others (the full text is given in Boudet 2015, my translation here). French president François Hollande immediately declared a state of emergency and organized bombing raids on Daesh stronghold Raqqa in Syria. The events following the killings in Paris and Brussels are still unfolding at the time of writing, as the double problem of refugee influx and terrorist attacks has led many EU states to close their borders or declare states of emergency or both.

The assassinations in January 2015 happened as I was attempting to finish the first full manuscript of this book, which has taken years longer to put together than I intended. Part of the difficulty was that 9/11 does not end. The events in Paris and Brussels and the ensuing inter- and transnational debates have thrown into painful relief the impossibility of finding a turning point, a moment where one can say, "It's over now; we have moved on." The November and March attacks, which occurred as I was completing revisions and updates to the manuscript, drove that point home chillingly as I dealt with both personal and collective grieving for Paris, a place I have long considered my other home.

Certainly, these attacks are not the only post-9/11 events to occur as I was deciding that this book had to have an end, even if what the book is about does not end. One might cite the suspicious death, some ten days after the January Paris attacks, of Argentinian prosecutor Alberto Nisman, discussed in chapter 1, or the bombing at an Ankara train station in August 2015 or the bombing in a poor neighborhood in Beirut the day before the November attacks in Paris or the attacks in Mali and Cameroon and then in Tunisia a week to ten days later. One might discuss the states of emergency declared in these African countries and in Belgium and their implications for civil liberties and for the development—or blockage—of transnational negotiations over war against Daesh, all of which is still unfolding as I write these words. Or one might cite the attack on the Canadian national

Parliament in Ottawa by a Western convert to Islamist extremism in October 2014 or the increasing number of young male converts of various backgrounds who hop on a plane to Syria or Iraq from France or Tunisia or Belgium or a number of other countries, finding in Daesh the outlet for their frustrations. Not to mention the victims of warfare and related violence in Iraq and particularly in Syria, who desperately seek refuge in Lebanon, Jordan, Turkey, or EU countries.

Or, more specifically in relation to women, one might discuss the case of some 276 Nigerian schoolgirls who were kidnapped by Boko Haram in April 2014 and who had committed no greater crime than being girls attempting to get an education. I first wrote these words on day 588 of their kidnapping, which also happened to be the International Day against Violence against Women (November 25, 2015). Although the Nigerian army succeeded in releasing several hundred of an overall total of more than 2,000 women and girls kidnapped by Boko Haram, and others have escaped, the whereabouts of many of the kidnapped schoolgirls still remains unknown at the time of writing. Moreover, many of those rescued were pregnant following rapes by their kidnappers. One might consider these kidnappings in the context of modern slavery and trafficking, which are at their highest level in recorded history, according to figures reported by a number of antislavery organizations as well as by the International Labor Organization, summarized in a *Huffington Post* article aimed at a middle-class US readership (Goldberg 2014).

Or one might, like *Wikipedia*, establish a long list of all terrorist attacks that have taken place in 2015 and now 2016, which puts the Paris attacks into a global framework of apparently ever-increasing and ever more random violence. The English-language version of *Wikipedia*, for example, provides details of 298 terrorist attacks between January 1 and November 20, 2015 (*Wikipedia* n.d.). Or one might speak in more general terms of Western and other governments' repeated failures to live up to their promise of protecting the vulnerable, especially women.

There are so many trigger moments that take us ricocheting back, rightly or wrongly, to the Us-and-Them-ness of 9/11. And, both battered and angered, we struggle to continue in our efforts to make feminist sense of the world, which seems to become ever more "stuck in a spiral" of violence and vengeance, as a BBC commentator put it on *The World This Week* program of November 20, 2015.[1]

Among all these escalations of post-9/11ist violence, however, the January and November Paris attacks and their aftermath warrant discussion here for a number of reasons. First, they have triggered huge and multidimensional international reactions, notably albeit not only in the West, which are reminiscent of the reactions to 9/11. Second, the attacks and ensuing debates—in particular the *Charlie Hebdo* debate—return us so pointedly to the cognitive dissonance discussed in chapter 6. Third, both the January and the November attacks and their aftermath highlight the multiple layers of state and nonstate masculinist violence in a post-9/11 world.

The debate, which continues at the time of this writing, also occurs within the context of the development, in both national and international political discourse and notably in UN declarations, of the ideas of "Islamophobia" and "defamation of religion/Islam." These concepts were particularly in the foreground following the *Charlie Hebdo* attack on January 7, 2015. The idea of postsecularism has not really gained a discursive hold in France, which is the bastion of separation of church and state, despite—or perhaps as much because of—having historically "carried the banner of the Cross in Europe." "Islamophobia" and defamation of religion, however, most decidedly have been central to the French conversation, and debate over them has been fierce and polarized, most particularly since 9/11 and the 2002–4 debate over the law banning "conspicuous" religious insignia in schools (Winter 2008). Thus, before discussing the debates following the attacks of January and November 2015, I retrace the "Islamophobia"/defamation of religion debate.

---

1. Rebroadcast by Australian ABC News Radio on November 21, 2015, and downloadable from http://www.bbc.co.uk/programmes/p0299wgd/episodes /downloads (accessed Nov. 22, 2015).

Are Religions Defamable?

The UN General Assembly first issued a declaration on discrimination on the grounds of religion and belief in 1981, but that declaration was framed within the affirmation of a principle of freedom of thought and conscience as well as freedom from coercion. The idea of defamation of religions first appears in a declaration adopted without a vote by the UN Council on Human Rights in 1999, although the first UN Declaration on Religious Intolerance was made almost two decades earlier (UN General Assembly 1981). The Council on Human Rights declaration of 1999 was based on a proposal brought before the council by Pakistan, supported by the Organization of the Islamic Conference. The text introduces the notion of incitement (by media or other means) to "violence, xenophobia, or related intolerance and discrimination towards Islam or any other religion" (UN Office of the High Commissioner for Human Rights 1999, Art. 3). This declaration is the first UN document to conflate flesh-and-blood human beings practicing a religion or identifying culturally with it (in particular Muslims) with religion as a belief system. In doing so, it effectively frames *religions* as having antidiscrimination "rights" (Winter 2013; see also Ghanea 2007). Even though this declaration is not a binding treaty, it set the stage for a number of other UN Commission for Human Rights declarations that followed (every year from 2000 to 2005), culminating in a General Assembly resolution, which I discuss later. "Islamophobia" is first mentioned in the declaration of 2004, alongside Christianophobia and anti-Semitism, although the term first appeared in a UN context in 2001 in the Declaration of the World Conference against Racism, Racial Discrimination, Xenophobia, and Related Intolerance, otherwise known as the Durban Declaration (World Conference 2001; Ghanea 2007). Article 8 of the Durban Declaration, which was published just days before the 9/11 attacks, reads as follows: "We recognize that religion, spirituality and belief play a central role in the lives of millions of women and men, and in the way they live and treat other persons. Religion, spirituality and belief may and can contribute to the promotion of the inherent dignity and worth of the human person and to the eradication of racism, racial discrimination, xenophobia and related intolerance."

The Commission for Human Rights declarations provide a discursive framework for constituting religions as legal persons, with the result that mockery or other denigration of religion is posited as a legally actionable offence, at least in theory. The political impacts of this development have been demonstrated by controversies such as those over the Danish caricatures of the Prophet Mohammed and French reproductions of them; by certain proposed (but defeated) provisions of the UK Racial and Religious Hatred Act (2006); and by European deliberations over whether blasphemy laws are admissible. I discuss these debates later in this chapter. Contemporary political debates over insult to religion have not, of course, been limited only to Islam. There have been related controversies within Christendom, such as religious groups' attempt to have Martin Scorcese's film *The Last Temptation of Christ* (1988) banned. These controversies, however, have not developed within a post-9/11ist frame and have certainly not been imbricated with institutional discussions over racism and "discrimination" or "phobia" against religions.

The introduction of religion as a positive value into UN documents and opposition to religion's "defamation" were thus pre-9/11 phenomena, as was the beginning of the global conversation about "Islamophobia," a term originally coined in 1925 and popularized in the United Kingdom in the 1990s (Richardson 2004; Winter 2008, 288–93). These ideas, however, gained widespread popular and institutional currency in a post-9/11 context, to the point that by the end of 2005 the terms *defamation of religion* and *Islamophobia* had made it into a UN General Assembly resolution (UN General Assembly 2005a). This resolution picks up some of the language of the original Commission for Human Rights declaration of 1999 but adds an explicit post-9/11 frame. Article 3 reads that the General Assembly *"notes with deep concern* the intensification of the campaign of defamation of religions and the ethnic and religious profiling of Muslim minorities in the aftermath of the tragic events of 11 September 2001" (UN General Assembly 2005a, italics in original).

"Defamation of religions" had thus by 2005 become constructed not simply as an act but as a *campaign*. Linking this campaign to denunciation of the demonstrable post-9/11 racial profiling of Muslim people and most especially Arab people is problematic for a number of reasons. First of all, it dehumanizes and consequently trivializes the real post-9/11 racist discrimination and prejudice suffered by a large number of people in the West and indeed elsewhere. Second, it further legitimizes the idea that religions per se have antidiscrimination "rights," an idea that is reinforced in Article 8 of the General Assembly resolution of 2005, which stresses the need to combat defamation of religions in human rights fora. Third, the "religions" under discussion are essentially Islam: Islam is foregrounded in a number of articles of the resolution, leaving no doubt as to which religion is being constructed as a legal person in this document. The resolution was adopted by a clear majority of member states, with 101 voting for it, 53 voting against it, and 20 abstentions. All officially Muslim countries voted for it except Mauritania (which voted against it), as did all Latin American and Caribbean countries. EU member states and the four non-European Western English-speaking countries formed just more than half of those voting against it.

The question of incitement to *religious* rather than *racial* hatred has been much debated in politics and law in the West since 9/11. Some countries, such as France and the United Kingdom, have amended their race-vilification laws to include targeting of religious persons or groups, but not of religions per se. The provisions concerning incitement to religious hatred have, however, proven confusing and unhelpful. As Kay Goodall (2007) argues, race discrimination laws in the United Kingdom already enabled prosecution of most acts of religious vilification because these acts were *also* racial. This provision was also available to both Christians and Muslims, who are less easily identifiable with a particular ethnic group than, say, Jews or Sikhs, because most hate speech against "Muslims" in Britain was *also* hate speech against (primarily) South Asians, regardless of their actual religious belief. In this way, for those expressing racial hate against particular ethnic groups, "Muslim" became a racial marker. The existing Race

Discrimination Act allowed criticism—even vehemently expressed criticism—of Islamic beliefs and practices; such criticism may be hateful, but it is also protected by freedom of speech, as is vehement criticism of any other religion. At the same time, the existing act enabled prosecution of those using "Muslim" as a racial marker. Goodall (2007) further argues that a major contributor to the perceived need for a new legal framework was the extreme Right's attempts to distinguish between race and religion as a form of legal loophole to attempt to avoid prosecution for incitement to racial hatred.

The Racial and Religious Hatred Act of 2006, however, does not necessarily address that need in any unambiguous way, in part, writes Goodall (2007), because there is a significant contextual factor determining whether hate speech is unlawful or not. That is, it is not unlawful to hate things or even people per se. One may hate fast drivers, for example, and express this hatred publicly, but such hatred and its expression do not constitute grounds for legal sanction. If one were to make hateful comments associating driving style with ethnicity, then such comments may qualify as hate speech, but, again, racial and religious categories are established within a context and established discursively. "A 'contextual meaning' approach to incitement cases, judicially developed," argues Goodall, is thus "long overdue" (2007, 99).

Dermot Feenan further argues, in relation to legislation in the Australian states of Victoria and Queensland (he mentions the UK law in passing), that such laws lack a "human rights analysis" (2006, 154). Referring to the International Covenant on Civil and Political Rights as well as to some decisions by the European Court of Human Rights, Feenan argues that "the lack of a human rights infrastructure and jurisprudence in Australia severely hinders adequate balancing of the claimed right to freedom of expression with the rights and responsibilities inherent in the religious vilification laws" (155). He suggests that the Victorian Racial and Religious Tolerance Act of 2001 was "incompatible with the countervailing right to freedom of expression" (157). Without serious attention to socioeconomic disadvantage and other forms of social marginalization, he argues, religious vilification legislation is more likely to result in a "chilling" (156) of expression (a term also used in relation to the UK legislation) rather than addressing the actual sociopolitical problem of discrimination.

It has further been argued that pushes for such legislation can constitute a backdoor return to blasphemy laws, some of which have only recently been removed from the statute books in relation to Christianity (Zimmerman 2013). The UK antiblasphemy law, for example, was not repealed until 2008. Helen Pringle (2011) argues conditional support for a law against incitement to hatred on the basis of a person's religion, whereas Augusto Zimmerman (2013) is opposed to such laws, which he characterizes as blasphemy laws by stealth. Evelyn Aswad (2013), in discussing state decisions not to ban the video *Innocence of Muslims* (2012), criticized as much for its dreadful production qualities as for its offensiveness, has further pointed to the Organization of the Islamic Conference's lobbying at the UN level, mentioned earlier. The controversy over this video was such that both the UN special rapporteur on freedom of expression and the UN special rapporteur on freedom of religion chose to explicitly counter the previous UN trend by issuing statements opposing any bans on speech for the sole reason that it is offensive to religious sensibilities. They stated that religions as either institutions or abstract concepts do not have "rights" that can be violated by such speech (qtd. in Aswad 2013, 1326–27). Similarly, in October 2008 the European Commission for Democracy through Law (the Venice Commission), a body of the Council of Europe (non-EU), issued a report on the relationship between freedom of expression and freedom of religion. The report came down firmly against any reintroduction of blasphemy laws or the use of any existing criminal law to deal with insult to religious feeling. The report emphasized that "it must be possible to criticise religious ideas, even if such criticism may be perceived by some as hurting their religious feeling" (European Commission for Democracy through Law 2008, 16, para. 76). The debate about religious insult and freedom of expression, however, far from having gone away, has taken some violent expressions, as we are about to see.

Not Out of Nowhere

Three months before the UN Resolution on Defamation of Religions was signed in 2005, the September 30 edition of the Danish newspaper *Jyllands-Posten* published twelve cartoons, most of which depicted the Prophet Mohamed. The publication caused a controversy that resounded internationally. On February 8 the following year, French satirical weekly *Charlie Hebdo* reproduced the by now famous (or infamous) Danish caricatures. The Paris Mosque, the Union des organisations islamiques de France (Union of Islamic Organizations of France), and the Muslim World League promptly sued Philippe Val, then editor in chief of *Charlie Hebdo*, for "affront to a group of persons because of their ethnicity, national origin, race or religion" (French Law of 1881, Art. 48). In doing so, they clearly espoused the defamation of religions argument, attempting to construct Islam and its long-deceased founder as "a group of persons" under the terms of the 1881 law.

Val characterized this lawsuit as a "witch hunt," and, undaunted, the cartoonist Cabu (one of those killed on January 7, 2015) produced the front-page cartoon for the February 8, 2006, edition of *Charlie Hebdo*. The cartoon was a drawing of an exasperated Mohamed holding his head in his hands and saying, "It's hard being loved by jerks" ("C'est dur d'être aimé par des cons"), with the additional caption: "Mohamed overwhelmed by fundamentalists" ("Mohamed débordé par les intégristes"). The case was thrown out the following January, when the court found that there had not been affront to French *Muslims*—that is, to actual people. In 2008, a documentary by Daniel Leconte, using as its title words from Cabu's cover, *C'est dur d'être aimé par des cons*, was released in France and subsequently shown internationally. The documentary was re-released following the attacks in January 2015.

The polemic over *Charlie Hebdo*'s reproduction of the *Jyllands-Posten* caricatures and Cabu's comic graphic commentary on the ensuing court action remind us that the debate over *Charlie Hebdo* and caricatures of the Prophet began long before 2015. In the midst of that debate in 2006, Franco-Tunisian feminist and politician Nadia Chaabane, publishing on the feminist commentary website Sisyphe,[2] denounced the hypocrisy of the anticaricature stance, taking the West to task for its complicity with authoritarian regimes in MENA: "Arab prisons are overflowing with prisoners of opinion, writings are continually censured, cut, revised according to the will of the ruler. . . . At the same time, the Arab press is overflowing with caricatures of Jews and Christians, with stereotypical associations and allusions that compete to be in the worst taste, and at each publication of these, to my great surprise, there is silence, a deafening silence" (2006, my translation).

Chaabane refused to self-censor "out of fear that some group or other use [our words] to create hate and build walls. My only preoccupation today is to raise the true question, that of freedom of expression, and beyond that, of freedoms. Freedoms that are today confiscated, hijacked, muzzled" (2006, my translation).

High profile as the Mohamed caricatures controversy was, it is far from the first or only time that *Charlie Hebdo* has been taken to court under the 1881 law. In fact, over the two decades prior to 2015, *Charlie Hebdo* was taken to court once every six months, on average, and the French extreme Right, media and journalists, and Catholic organizations have far outnumbered Muslims or Islamic organizations among the plaintiffs. Most of these cases were thrown out, and of the nine where a verdict was handed down against *Charlie Hebdo*, it was for defamation of a living individual in the public eye (Pope John Paul II among them). Associations did far less well in persuading the courts that there had been defamation or incitement to hatred. Even in the so-called *concordataire* regions of Alsace-Lorraine—where the Napoleonic agreement with the Catholic Church in 1801 is applied rather than the French law on separation of church and state established in

2. The site Sisyphe is named for the mythical character who every day pushes a rock up a hill, only to have to start all over again the next day because the rock has rolled back downhill overnight.

1905 because these provinces were German in 1905—religious associations have failed to obtain a condemnation. In 2013, the Ligue de défense judiciaire des musulmans (League for Legal Defense of Muslims) took *Charlie Hebdo* to court in Strasbourg for breach of the blasphemy law that is still in force there but not applied since 1918, the date at which these provinces were returned to France. Nor was it applied in 2013: the tribunal found against the League for Legal Defense (*Le Monde* 2015a).

Following all of these lawsuits, including the "caricatures of Mohamed" suit defeated in 2007, *Charlie Hebdo* continued its provocative satire, which resulted in threats against it and a firebombing of its premises in the twentieth arrondissement in 2011. The new premises—which were later the site of the attacks in 2015—and a number of staff were then placed under police protection.

On January 7, 2015, the day on which issue 1,777 of *Charlie Hebdo* was to be published, two men burst into the newspaper's office, which was located in a side street roughly halfway between two iconic Paris landmarks: place de la Bastille and place de la République. They killed eleven people and injured several others. Of those killed, nine were employees of or contributors to *Charlie Hebdo*, one was a contract cleaner, and one was a police officer, Franck Brinsolaro, who had been assigned to the editor in chief's protection detail following previous threats and attacks against the newspaper. A particularly high profile was given in subsequent media coverage to the five cartoonists killed, all men and all very well known: Charb (Stéphane Charbonnier, also editor in chief), Cabu (Jean Cabut), (Georges) Wolinski, Honoré, and Tignous (Bernard Verlhac). Cabu and Wolinski, ages seventy-six and eighty, respectively, had worked with *Charlie Hebdo*'s previous incarnation, *Hara Kiri*, and both were described the following day in the French edition of the *Huffington Post* (2015) as "pillars" of *Charlie Hebdo*, as indeed they were of the genre of satirical cartooning in France. Among the others killed were one woman, Elsa Cayat, a psychoanalyst who wrote a column for the paper, and a person of Maghrebian (North African) Muslim background: Mustapha Ourrad, employed by the paper as a proofreader.

As the assassins, brothers Saïd and Chérif Kouachi, fled, they killed police officer Ahmed Merabet from the local district police, taking the death toll to twelve, which now included two people of Muslim background—killed, ironically, in the name of Islam, which was the Kouachi brothers' stated motivation. The assassins openly positioned themselves as representatives of the Yemeni branch of al Qaeda. They had undergone a process of radicalization since 2004, when they were in their early twenties—although for the elder brother, Saïd Kouachi, this process may have begun in 2001 (Cornevin 2015). His younger brother, Chérif, reportedly was incited to fight the United States by the horrors of Abu Ghraib, but he was subsequently arrested and spent time in prison. One of the brothers visited Yemen in 2011, after which both men were placed under French surveillance; Chérif Kouachi also went to Syria in 2014. They were, however, by that time no longer twenty-something amateurs with dreams of vengeance. They had reportedly become trained professionals, keeping such a low profile that the surveillance was called off in 2014, a time at which the French secret service was overwhelmed by the stream of young Muslim would-be jihadist men leaving for Syria. According to French terrorism expert Jean-Charles Brisard, interviewed by the news magazine *Le Nouvel Observateur*, French authorities had been expecting and fearing an attack of this type for some time: one that was carried out by a small group of highly trained individuals against a symbolic site. According to Brisard, such attacks have become almost impossible to foresee and to prevent precisely because of their small-scale nature and the covertness of the networks that the attackers are part of (Brisard 2015).

The day after the attack on *Charlie Hebdo*, an accomplice of the Kouachi brothers, Amedy Coulibaly, a Frenchman of Malian background with a history of armed holdups and drug trafficking, killed a female police officer in Montrouge, an inner suburb to the south of central Paris. The day after that, January 9, he took staff and customers hostage in a Jewish supermarket at the Porte de Vincennes at the eastern boundary of central Paris, killing four of them. The hero of the kosher supermarket hostage incident also turned out to be of

Muslim faith and a Malian immigrant. Lassana Bathily, a supermarket employee, turned off the cool-room refrigeration and hid customers there; they were then able to communicate with the outside by phone. The same day, the Kouachi brothers took a hostage in the outer northeastern suburb of Dammartin-en-Goële but were killed by police, and the hostage was freed unharmed (Cornevin 2015).

Anti-Semitic attacks in France are not a new phenomenon, but prior to 9/11 and the siege of Ramallah in 2002 the main perpetrators were white Gentile men. Increasingly, however, the perpetrators have been male Islamist extremists, and the supermarket attack on January 9, 2015, resonates with many such attacks that had occurred in the previous years and have continued since. Although the attack on *Charlie Hebdo* dominated much of the media coverage, especially international coverage, the anti-Semitic attacks nonetheless received much attention from the French media, sometimes of a somewhat sensationalist nature, as is demonstrated by the headline of the news magazine *L'Express*, on January 11, 2015: "Wave of Anti-Semitism in 2014: Is the Worst Yet to Come?" ("Flambée de l'antisémitisme en 2014: Le pire est-il encore à venir?" [Politi 2015]). The *Express* article reported a 10 percent rise in anti-Semitic attacks in 2014, and Jewish community representatives reported another ninety attacks in the days following the Porte de Vincennes hostage taking. The article referred to Mohamed Merah's attack against a Jewish school in 2012 and a number of other attacks as well as to the comedian Dieudonné's repeated anti-Semitism (discussed later in this chapter), notably Holocaust denial and comparison of Jewish people to Nazis, which led to banning of one of his shows in early 2014. The reasons suggested for the rise in anti-Semitic attacks were this ban as well as an anti-Hollande demonstration, Day of Anger (Jour de colère), on January 26, 2014, which brought together an eclectic but overwhelmingly right-wing and extreme-right crowd of people with a grudge against the government. Printemps Français, founded on the wave of opposition to gay marriage in France, was the main organizer. The attacks on the kosher supermarket at Porte de Vincennes thus form part of a context that had been polarized and tense for many years.

The main focus throughout the world was decidedly on the *Charlie Hebdo* attacks and on the "Je suis Charlie" demonstrations held both in France and elsewhere, including a demonstration of some 2 million people in Paris on January 11 in which a number of French and foreign political leaders participated. The foreign political representatives included presidents, ambassadors, and foreign-affairs ministers from practically all European countries, Canada, the United States, and a number of countries in the Middle East and Africa. There were also a number of anti-*Charlie* demonstrations in Europe and elsewhere, of which some of the most strident and indeed violent took place in various parts of Pakistan, featuring, among other things, placards saying "I am Mohamed." Parallel to these demonstrations, international "cartoon solidarity" abounded, with one of the most famous and widely circulated cartoons being the one David Pope posted on Twitter the day of the shootings. His cartoon showed a masked terrorist and the cartoonist he had just killed, with the terrorist looking wide-eyed at someone out of the frame and uttering the play on words, "He drew first."

In addition, the attack almost immediately sparked an international debate in mainstream, alternative, and social media on freedom of speech, the press, and conscience; the rights of religions; Islamism and Islamist terrorism; racism; and even sexism. Political co-optation of the tragedy was also debated: one of the French "solidarity cartoons," for example, circulated on Twitter by Olac on January 10, 2015, showed Cabu in a pictorial echo of his own "It's hard being loved by jerks" cartoon of 2006. Cabu was drawn with his head in his hands in front of Sarkozy, Hollande, Marine Le Pen (leader of the Front national [National Front]), and an archbishop, among others, saying, "It's hard being co-opted by jerks!" ("C'est dur d'être récupéré par des cons").

Remaining *Charlie Hebdo* staff, working out of the offices of the left-wing, large-circulation daily newspaper *Libération*, continued to publish in their well-known provocative style. The front page of the following week's edition (January 14, 2015) showed Mohamed saying, "All is forgiven," and holding up a "Je suis Charlie" placard. This act of defiance further contributed to a particularly polarizing and rather curious aspect of the French and international debate—namely, the merits or otherwise of *Charlie Hebdo* as an ideal victim. To the numerous deployments of "Je suis Charlie" came the response "Je ne suis pas Charlie," with or without *mais* (but) added. As if "siding" or otherwise with *Charlie Hebdo* were the point.

How far, then, does "freedom of speech" extend? Why should Dieudonné's show be banned while *Charlie Hebdo* continues to publish? Is "Je suis Charlie" yet another way of sweeping the extremely serious problem of racism and socioeconomic marginalization in France under the carpet? What feminist commentary can one offer on these issues?

The Debate over Freedom of Speech and Censorship I: "Sexism"

Feminists have long criticized masculinist ideas of freedom of speech that have resulted in abuse of women in text and image being protected in the name of this freedom. In her controversial essay *Only Words* ([1993] 1994), Catharine A. MacKinnon argued that "the law of equality and the law of freedom of speech are on a collision course" and that "free speech protections have developed worldwide without taking seriously the problems of social inequality or the need for substantive legal equality" (51). She made these arguments in support of her opposition to the free-speech protection of pornography because pornography harms women and thus perpetuates inequality. She also made them in a US context. Although MacKinnon's arguments have been as widely criticized—most famously, perhaps, by Judith Butler in her book *Excitable Speech* (1997)—as they have been supported, they do beg the question, as have the *Charlie Hebdo* killings, of how freedom of speech and equality can be taken *off* the "collision course" without undermining either.

The answer to such questions is not straightforward. Is one person's pornography another person's erotica? Would banning all pornography have unwanted effects, such as prohibitions of gay erotica—which some feminists, however, would also consider to be pornographic—and other obscenity trials? Many now acclaimed classic plays and novels were once banned as obscene. In the mid–nineteenth century, for example, Charles Baudelaire's collection of poetry *Les Fleurs du mal* (1861) and Gustave Flaubert's novel *Madame Bovary* (1857) faced obscenity trials, and Oscar Wilde's play *Salomé* (1891) was banned in London for some two decades, from 1892 to 1910. Aristophanes's play *Lysistrata* (411 BCE) was banned in several countries in the nineteenth and twentieth centuries because of its proto-feminist and antiwar message. Several attempts were made in the United States to ban Margaret Atwood's dystopian novel *The Handmaid's Tale* (1985) because it was deemed "pornographic" and "anti-Christian." Radclyffe Hall's lesbian novel *The Well of Loneliness* was banned in the United States when first published in 1928. The work of Hanan al-Shaykh, a leading Lebanese feminist writer, is still banned in many Arab countries. And so on.

Whatever one's opinions of the merits of these works, their banning raises fundamental questions for any feminist: What are the limits to free speech, and how may one avert the "collision course" between freedom of speech and equality MacKinnon describes? Would attempts to censor pornography backfire? The problem is one of determining who and what are being targeted as well as how and by whom "harm" is interpreted. Censorship has invariably been a primary ideological tool of religious conservatives and antifeminists as well as of repressive states both inside and outside the West. I think, for example, of the long list of books banned by the French state during the Algerian War: they include Frantz Fanon's now classic work *Les Damnés de la terre* (*Wretched of the Earth*, 1961). How can censorship be used to ensure equality rather than reinforce inequality, given that the latter has almost always been the case when censorship has been applied?

One of the many "fast books" (so called because of the rapidity of publication after a major event) to have been published in France in the wake of January 7 is a study by legal scholar Emmanuel Pierrat (2015) on censorship and freedom of expression. Pierrat points out that contrary to popular belief there are a number of limitations to freedom of speech in France. Those particularly affecting women and sexuality have to do with pornography, public nudity, and exhibition of any act deemed to be of an offensive sexual nature in public. It was under one of these laws, Article 222-32 of the Penal Code, that a French member (now former member) of Femen was ordered to pay damages and legal costs to the Catholic Church after staging a mock protest abortion in the Madeleine Church in Paris (*Le Figaro* 2014). Right-wing Catholic associations such as the very active Promouvoir are forever on the lookout for artistic productions of various kinds that they deem offensive and are particularly concerned that minors do not see any representation of sex in films. One of Promouvoir's targets was Abdellatif Kechiche's film *La Vie d'Adèle* (Blue Is the Warmest Color, 2013), adapted from Julie Maroh's lesbian graphic novel *Le Bleu est une couleur chaude* (2010). (The film ended up being restricted to viewers age twelve and older.) There has been a great deal of debate in lesbian circles both within and outside France concerning the film's political or artistic merits (see, e.g., Chetcuti 2013). Fortunately, however, for teenage lesbians in France who have little opportunity to see mainstream cinema culture reflect any aspect of their lives, Promouvoir did not succeed in having *La Vie d'Adèle* either banned or restricted to viewers age eighteen and older.

Pierrat makes the distinction between those acts that simply cause *offense* and those that lead to *harm* (2015, 88–91). Mackinnon would argue that pornography incites behavior that causes harm, but to date those works that have been censored or banned in the West are by and large not those most likely to incite violence against women, but those most likely to offend the sensibilities of religious conservatives of various ilks.

Charlie Hebdo's style is provocative and vulgar, and it certainly has frequently gone beyond the limits of what many would call good taste. It is noteworthy, however, that prior to January 7, 2015, *Charlie* did not come under particular fire, even within feminist circles, for its frequent recourse to phallic and hypersexualized imagery. That said, few French feminists read the publication regularly, and the weekly had relatively limited circulation more generally—less than 30,000 per week—before January 7. Even when the message was (more or less) pro-feminist, which has often, in fact, been the case, many feminists found the imagery offensive or irritating.

Since January 7, 2015, feminists in the Western, English-speaking world in particular have taken *Charlie* to task for alleged sexism and racism, the castigation for the latter reflecting a widespread judgment in the Anglo world, to which I return a little later. The criticism has been repeated so often that it has become received wisdom: *Charlie Hebdo* is portrayed as "inarguably" both sexist and racist (Cross 2015). The comments are often, however, based on immediate knee-jerk reactions to the cartoons' vulgar style and often involve misunderstandings of the satirical message within the context of publication.

One cartoon that has come in for some feminist fire from the Anglo world since January 7 is the cover of the October 22, 2014, issue. The cartoon shows four angry-looking, hijab-wearing, black pregnant women, with the caption "The angry sex slaves of Boko Haram" ("Les esclaves sexuelles de Boko Haram en colère") and a speech bubble: "Hands off our [welfare] benefits!" ("Touchez pas à nos allocs!"). Katherine Cross (2015) holds this cartoon up as an example of the supposed racism and sexism of *Charlie Hebdo*, but without any reference to the context in which it was produced. In two decisions handed down in April 2013, France's Cour de cassation (Court of Final Appeal) had ruled that immigrant children from Turkey and Algeria, respectively, of parents residing in France had the right to family benefit payments if they came to join their parents, even illegally, whether the children were born in France or not. The right-wing and extreme right-wing press immediately reacted with scaremongering, claiming that "foreigners" had advantages that "French" people did not. In November 2013, for example, the public-opinion pollster IFOP conducted a survey for the right-wing publication *Valeurs Actuelles* that revealed that 67 percent of the sample of 1,002 people polled believed that the French state did more for immigrants than for the "French." This was a 50 percent increase in relation to 2008 (Lejeune 2013). Comparable surveys conducted since that time have shown this percentage to hold steady.

In terms of actual figures, immigrant women do end up receiving greater amounts of family benefits because, first, there are a higher proportion of mothers of minors among them; second, they have more children than white women; and third, they are much poorer than white women and thus more dependent on welfare (Trouvelot 2015). Yet the higher numbers of children, argues Sandrine Trouvelot (2015), writing in the online financial magazine *Capital*, are good news in the longer term for France, with its ageing population and related potential blowout in the pension budget. She dismisses as nonsense the argument that nonwhite immigrant mothers are better off than white French mothers because the actual rate of family benefit received is not higher for them than for other women in similar circumstances. Moreover, France's current wealth has been built largely thanks to immigrants, as Philippe Eliakim (2015) points out in the following week's edition of the same publication. Citing national demographic statistics, Eliakim points out that the real "cost" of immigration today is largely borne by immigrants themselves and their descendants. Unemployment among the children of African immigrants is the highest in France, at 24 percent, and the rate of poverty among households of immigrants is a little more than three times higher than that of other households. The fact that *Capital*'s report was published in April 2015, two years after the Cour de cassation decisions that aroused the ire of, it appears, two-thirds of the French population and three months after the killings in January 2015, shows that the issue had remained very much in the forefront.

Charlie Hebdo's Boko Haram cartoon came in the middle of this panic mongering about immigrants and at a time when news was filtering through that many of the schoolgirls originally kidnapped in Chibok, Nigeria, in April 2014 were feared to have been married by force and taken to neighboring countries. Although many (myself included) found the cartoon distasteful, it was intended to show up the positions taken by the white Right on immigrant women as ridiculous and hypocritical. Read in context, the cartoon was ironic: it implied that the myth of "abuse" of welfare by immigrants in France appeared to be more important to the average French person than the sexual abuse of schoolgirls in Nigeria. A feminist may well have drawn a quite different cartoon, but the intent of the *Charlie Hebdo* cartoon was, in fact, the opposite of the (sexualized) racism that Cross denounces.

Charlie Hebdo has published a number of other covers featuring women and women's issues, and although one would often be hard-pressed to say unequivocally that these covers always meet high feminist standards, one would be equally hard-pressed to call them completely misogynist—even when they lampoon feminists. For example, covers of some issues published since around 2012 have poked fun at the provocative breast-baring Ukrainian group Femen. Other covers, however, mock the conservatives who oppose Femen. Moreover, Femen is a politically problematic group for many reasons that I do not have the space to go into here but that have been discussed elsewhere (e.g., Murphy 2012; O'Keefe 2014).

Other *Charlie Hebdo* cartoons, however, are more overtly in support of feminist ideas and have been since the heyday of the "second wave" of feminism in the 1970s. Sexist double standards are particular targets for *Charlie*'s brand of satire. In December 2013, for example, as the law penalizing the clients of prostitution (but not the women) was first being debated in Parliament (it was adopted on April 6, 2016), the Miss France beauty contest was being held in Dijon. The cover of *Charlie Hebdo* on December 4, 2013, featured a blond Miss France dressed in a bikini, with the caption: "We no longer have any prostitutes, just as well we still have Miss France" ("On n'a plus de putes; heureusement il nous reste Miss France"). Again, the cartoon pointed to hypocrisy and targeted beauty contests as a manifestation of sexual objectification of women comparable to prostitution.

Other cartoons admittedly contain a less obviously "feminist" message, but it is a far cry from this to comparing *Charlie Hebdo* to *Hustler*, as Deborah Campbell (2015) tacitly did in an article in the online UK radical feminist magazine *Trouble and Strife*. Campbell commenced her article by asking her readers to imagine a scenario in which feminist terrorists stormed into the offices of the pornographic magazine *Hustler* and shot a number of staff. Her argument was that the legitimate condemnation of the assassinations by feminists should not mean that they feel obliged to display placards stating "I am Hustler" and in doing so provide tacit approval of the ideas and images contained in the magazine. As reasonable as that argument may be, Campbell's analogy was not innocent or accidental; it damns *Charlie Hebdo* as pornographic and woman hating by association.

Charlie Hebdo's caricatures are directed at everyone, and the noses of the archbishops, priests, white politicians, and cultural figures are as long as those of the rabbis and the imams and, indeed, the women. (Campbell's [2015] article also took issue with "hook-nosed" caricatures of "Muslims.") One famous cartoon, by Luz, one of the surviving cartoonists, who left the publication in September 2015, was tweeted and retweeted in the week following the January 7, 2015, attack (although it had appeared in a much earlier edition of *Charlie Hebdo*). Combining antifundamentalism with an apparent profeminist stance, the cartoon features an image of a rabbi, an imam, and a priest (all with equally prominent noses) sitting together on a couch, all with their feet on the back of a naked and startled-looking woman (whose nose also happens to be long and pointy) crouched on all fours. The priest looks at the other two religious leaders and says, "In the end, we pretty much agree on the essential points" ("Finalement, sur l'essentiel on est plutôt d'accord"). In addition to such material, the presence of feminist Caroline Fourest on the payroll for many years and before her of Fiammetta Venner did lend the publication some feminist street cred.

The charge of sexism remains, however, and even in France after January 7 one found the occasional comment to this effect. One of them appeared on the website Les Mots sont importants (Words Matter), generally associated with the cultural-relativist side of the "Islamophobia" debate in France. Sisters C. and D. Billard, who also raise the "Islamophobia" issue, discuss *Charlie Hebdo* cartoons that are far more blatantly and unambiguously sexist than those discussed by Anglo-world commentators: "[Cabu, Wolinski, Reiser, Cavanna, Choron] incessantly reminded us who we were: Girls, Women, that is, the second sex, but a sex above all. They taught us very early that a woman is a blow-up doll, an ass, breasts, a cunt." The authors finish their article on this tender note: "So in looking at these drawings, oozing hatred of women, which for forty years have belittled us and while everyone is mourning them [the cartoonists killed on January 7], we ask ourselves: Should we seriously miss these guys and their disgusting humor?" (Billard and Billard 2015, my translation).

The cartoons shown by the Billard sisters are indeed blatantly phallic and (hetero)sexist. They highlight the fact that *Charlie Hebdo* is not by any means a feminist publication, notwithstanding the occasional pro-feminist epiphany, as discussed earlier. In this respect, however, *Charlie Hebdo* is simply part of the wider mainstream/malestream media, which is not generally known for its outspoken radical feminist critique. For example, although the photo-reportage of topics such as Miss France that one can see in the pages of society magazines such as *Paris Match* may not be openly phallic and vulgar, the imagery is just as disturbingly sexist and, as noted earlier, was criticized as such by none other than *Charlie Hebdo*. For French feminists, any vulgar and sexist material published on the front cover of *Charlie Hebdo* becomes lost in a sea of sexist cultural imagery, advertising, products such as "slimming creams" aimed at women, and so on. As the name of a column that was published for several decades in the pages of the journal *Les Temps Modernes* reminds us, *le sexisme ordinaire* (everyday sexism) is still flourishing in French society and culture. But, then, France is not unique in this regard, and *Charlie* is far from the worst offender. As well-known feminist activist Christine Le Doaré put it on January 12, 2015, *Charlie* was, like the rest of the Left, never feminist enough, but its unconditional stance against the sexism of religions makes the publication an "undisputed ally" of feminists in a world where women are being assassinated both by men known to them in their private lives and by totalitarian regimes. For her, "blindly killing designated targets in order to impose one's own point of view is the most perverse culmination of machism."

The Debate over Freedom of Speech and Censorship II: "Islamophobia"

Far more widespread, however, than the charge of sexism against *Charlie Hebdo* is the charge of "Islamophobia" and the related criticisms of

French racism. (The latter also resurfaced after the attacks on November 13, to which I return presently.) It is as if the assassins had some sort of point to make; they just made it inappropriately. Although no one outside the Islamist extreme Right openly applauded the assassinations, the immediate charges of "Islamophobia" against *Charlie Hebdo* have carried a tacit message that *Charlie Hebdo* staff were somehow "asking for it." The term *Islamophobia* has been hotly contested by many participating in the *Charlie Hebdo* debate in France (such as Fourest 2015), but even if one were to accept the term, how guilty is *Charlie* of "Islamophobic" representations?

The extent and vehemence of criticism of *Charlie*'s presumed racism and "Islamophobia" leads one to assume that the magazine's primary focus is mockery of Muslims. Not so. To take only the covers (about which there is infinitely more debate than about the inside content), according to Caroline Fourest only 4 percent of them concern Islam: "Most of the paper remains focused on political satire or mockery of Christian fundamentalists, particularly during the Manif pour Tous" (2015, 100, my translation). (The Manif pour Tous was a coalition formed in late 2013 to protest against the same-sex marriage law or "mariage pour tous" [Winter 2014b, forthcoming a].) As Karim Rissouli pointed out in the January 13, 2015, edition of the *Grand Journal* program on television station CanalPlus, out of the fifty-two covers of the year up to January 7, 2015, thirty-five concerned France's internal politics, with some swipes at President Hollande's apparently lively sex life, at a time when the exact nature of Hollande's relationship with actor Julie Gayet was the subject of much media speculation; ten lampooned the extreme-right party the National Front; two caricatured Catholics, one showed a gleeful baby Jesus in his crib below the caption "Yes to creches in public places"; and one concerned Israel and Palestine (*Charlie Hebdo* has consistently been very critical of Israel), with a cartoon showing Palestine's "two problems": the first being "its enemies over there," with a drawing of an Israeli soldier saying, "Israel will overcome," and the second being "its friends here," with a drawing of a supporter of the soccer team Paris-St-Germain saying, "Death to Jews." The latter was a reference to the revelation that radical anti-Semitic groups, using the Palestinian cause as a cover, were among the supporters of the team. Only one of the fifty-two covers showed the Prophet or Muslims.[3] That cover featured a balaclava-wearing Islamist soldier, presumably from Daesh, holding a knife to the throat of a kneeling Mohamed, whose nose is not hooked or penile or particularly bigger than the nose of any other figure caricatured by *Charlie Hebdo*. The caption accompanying the drawing read, "If Mahomet were to return. . . ." Mohamed's speech bubble contained the words, "I'm the Prophet, you moron!" ("Je suis le Prophète, imbécile!"), and the soldier's speech bubble said, "Shut up, infidel!" ("Ta gueule, infidèle!"). This cartoon is somewhat reminiscent of the "It's hard being loved by jerks" cartoon of 2006.

If one examines who and what *Charlie Hebdo* has lampooned, it is never "Muslims" as such or even the Prophet but rather fundamentalists: the Prophet consistently appears as a figure frustrated, even incensed, by the stupidity of extremists. Jewish and Christian fundamentalists are also frequently mocked, as was novelist Michel Houellebecq in the issue that came out the day of the shooting. Houellebecq's latest novel, *Soumission* (2015), also published the day of the shooting, imagines a France that will have a Muslim president in 2022 and a government that will Islamicize education and public service, forcing employees to convert to Islam and women to veil. The novel has had mixed reactions, but for Laurent Joffrin (2015), editor of *Libération*, it marks the sudden entry, or the return, of the extreme Right into high literature.

The debate over *Charlie Hebdo*, freedom of speech, and "Islamophobia" has taken place in a political climate in which extreme rights of all persuasions, often positioning themselves as champions of the underdog, have involved themselves with debates over Islam, national/republican identity, and the Israeli occupation of Palestine. In the weeks

3. The *Grand Journal* segment can be viewed on the CanalPlus site at http://www.canalplus.fr/c-emissions/c-le-grand-journal/pid7492-karim-rissouli.html?vid=1197087 (accessed July 4, 2015).

and months following the attacks, many, many claims and counter-claims of "Islamophobia" and racism were made about *Charlie Hebdo* in the press and online media, in blogs, on television, and in what amounted already, six months after the killings, to quite a few books.

On the side of those accusing *Charlie* of "Islamophobia," for example, are anthropologist and historian Emmanuel Todd and leading figure of the Parti des Indigènes de la République (Party of the "Natives" of the Republic), Houria Bouteldja. On the side of those defending *Charlie Hebdo*'s (and indeed everyone else's) "right to blasphemy" are feminists such as Caroline Fourest and Christine Le Doaré (see Bouteldja 2015; Fourest 2015; Le Doaré 2015; Todd 2015).

A key argument used against *Charlie Hebdo*'s caricatures representing the Prophet was that regardless of the image's intent, the very act of figurative representation of the Prophet was offensive, and those of Muslim culture in France felt slighted. For Bouteldja, all those of Muslim culture, whatever their religious practice, are offended by the "insult" to the Prophet by his graphic representation because such representation is supposedly forbidden in Islam (Bouteldja 2015). However, nothing in the Qur'an forbids such representation, and miniatures of the Prophet were common in certain countries and at certain periods of Islamic history. Some hadiths forbid any graphic representation of humans or animals because the artist, in doing so, is placing himself or herself in the place of God. Hadiths, however, form the basis of different Islamic traditions but not the core of Islamic law: only the Qur'an is considered to be the true source of law. Graphic representations of the Prophet are thus not "blasphemous" as such. Moreover, as scholars such as Alain Cabantous (2015) and Jeanne Favret-Saada (1992) have pointed out, "blasphemy" is a political concept that has changed over time and in different places. The concept is far less the product of religious belief than of sociopolitical relations and has frequently been difficult to define unequivocally. For example, from the time of Pope Innocent III in the twelfth century until the end of absolutist monarchy in Catholic Europe, the line between the crimes of blasphemy or heresy and the crime of *lèse-majesté* (insult to the king) was often extremely blurred.

That said, some women of North African background living in France have commented to me that many nonetheless take personally and feel keenly the "insult to the Prophet." US scholar Meaghan Emery has further suggested that there are "elite" and "popular" reactions to the *Charlie Hebdo* caricatures among French people of Muslim culture (personal communication, Sept. 3, 2015). I am not, however, convinced that the differences in understanding and reaction fall so neatly along class lines because I have also heard and read comments from members of the "Muslim elite" in France that are as diametrically opposed as those expressed by a Todd or a Fourest.

Members of racialized minorities in France do have many legitimate grounds for grievances, not only the "Muslims" (usually code for "Arabs") but also Roma and people of sub-Saharan African, South Asian, and sometimes East Asian backgrounds. Regardless of their place of birth and education—which is often, even mostly, France—racialized minorities face the usual socioeconomic discriminations in such areas as access to housing (longer waiting periods for subsidized housing, rejection of tenancy applications, and so on); employment (at hiring, even when more highly qualified than "white" French people, as well as in the type of work assigned once hired—for example, in jobs that have minimal contact with the public); and education (more likely to be oriented toward lower-level qualifications). In addition, people of North African (especially Algerian) and sub-Saharan backgrounds are statistically overrepresented among the poor and the unemployed (Eliakim 2015; see also *Économie et Statistique* 2013). These material discriminations are compounded by the "everyday racism" that the racialized face through stereotyping and othering comments from colleagues, acquaintances, and service providers, many of which are documented on the Racisme Ordinaire website maintained by France-Télévisions.[4] The comments foreground assumptions that the people targeted are stupid, belligerent, dirty, occupy low-status

4. At http://www.francetv.fr/temoignages/racisme-ordinaire/ (last accessed on Apr. 8, 2016).

jobs, "foreign," or all of the above. Some comments make explicit reference to the presumed Muslimness of the targets, who are often *hijab*-wearing women, but the gendered nature of "Islamophobia," as of many of the other forms of racism, was not foregrounded in the *Charlie Hebdo* debates. All these expressions of racism are abhorrent, as is classism regardless of the presumed ethnicity of the socioeconomically marginalized. They point to serious structural and sociocultural problems that should indeed make any feminist angry. These problems, however, were not the central point made in the anti-*Charlie* "Islamophobia" arguments.

After more than a decade of post-9/11 ist propaganda around "terrorism" and random persecutions of anyone looking "Muslim" through spot searches, workplace discrimination, hate speech of various kinds, physical attacks on *hijab*-wearing women, and so on, the increased popularity of the term *Islamophobia* on the left and attempts by states to placate "Muslim communities" are understandable. Unfortunately, the state's primary interlocutors in "Muslim communities" are usually religiously conservative self-proclaimed representatives because they are the ones with a vested interest in organizing politically *as Muslim* and in seeking the state's ear. Concurrently, accusations of "Islamophobia" become the knee-jerk reaction to any criticism of Islamism or indeed of Islam, much as knee-jerk reactions claiming anti-Semitism have been and still are used to attempt to deflect criticism of the Israeli state or the Jewish religious Right. Where, then, do this hypervisibility and hypervocality of the Muslim religious Right and the displacement of the race debate onto a religious terrain leave the majority of Muslims, believers or not, practicing or not, politically active or not? Most especially, where do they leave the many women who do not recognize themselves within religiously conservative definitions of "Muslim-ness" and certainly not within Islamist definitions?

The Debate over Freedom of Speech and Censorship III: Drawing a Line

From Aristophanes and Juvenal onward, satirists have had little regard for political correctness or the effects of offense. Even if the various sociopolitical roles and uses of satire have changed through centuries and cultures, the core elements of irony, double-entendre, and provocation remain. In fact, if satire does not offend *anyone*, then it is probably *not* satire: as Fourest puts it, "a satirical paper is not there to please people" (2015, 84, my translation).

As noted earlier, the attacks on *Charlie Hebdo*, although the most copiously discussed, were not the only ones to occur in that second week of January 2015 in Paris. A kosher supermarket was also targeted, specifically because the people within it were presumed to be Jewish. Like the discussion around "Islamophobia," it is extremely difficult in a post-9/11 context to have a coherent discussion around anti-Semitism in which one's right remains clearly demarcated from one's left. In France, practically any debate around "Muslims" today invariably ends up having some link, however tenuous or far-fetched, to the debate over the Israeli occupation of Palestine. Although this problem and its violent expressions are not limited to France, the terrorist attacks under discussion here took place in France, so it is important to understand the context.

If one were to name the two transnational historical events in the twentieth century that have remained deep wounds in the French collective psyche, they would surely be the Algerian War and the Shoah (Holocaust). Both divided France in two in more senses than one, and both involved state responsibility for persecution, incarceration, torture, and, indeed, genocide. Anti-Semitism runs deeply through French society and politics, and the new twenty-first-century players in its expression, as mentioned earlier, have roots in the Arabo-Muslim world. The Israeli occupation of Palestine has become one of the main battlefields on which the racism wars over "Islamophobia" and "anti-Semitism" are waged (Winter 2008, 2014a). As concerns our discussion here, the question of censorship once again comes fully to the fore.

I mentioned earlier the comedian Dieudonné, who has been fined several times for racial hatred because of his anti-Semitic comments and performances and was given a suspended sentence of two months following the attacks in January 2015 for posting the Facebook message "I feel I am Charlie Coulibaly," which was deemed to present Amedy Coulibaly's attack on Jewish people on January 9 in a positive light. He regularly uses the word *Jews* as a synonym for "Zionism," which he describes as a Satanic project to take over humanity. He has played on long-standing Western anti-Semitic stereotypes to accuse these "Jews" of being the majority of slave owners and slave traders (false), the majority of today's swindlers (false), and so on. He has called Shoah memorialization "memorial pornography." One has difficulty imagining how anyone outside the French extreme Right would use that same term, *memorial pornography*, to describe the yearly commemoration of October 17, 1961, when a demonstration against the Algerian War in Paris resulted in the deaths of a number of demonstrators, presumably at the hands of the police, although there has never been a trial. If anyone did use the term in this context, they would, like Dieudonné, be prosecuted for incitement to racial hatred. Dieudonné has also celebrated the state of Iran and appeared often on Iranian television, where he has blamed "Jews" for slavery, "Islamophobia," and just about everything else. He has appeared beside Shoah deniers at events organized by the French National Front. He has invented a gesture, *la quenelle*, which he has described as an "up yours" gesture to the establishment but which he subsequently used in the poster for his Anti-Zionist Party election campaign in 2009 and which he explicitly described at that time as an "up yours" gesture to Zionism—and presumably, given that for Dieudonné the terms *Zionism* and *Jews* are synonymous, to all Jews. A number of people, Shoah denier Alain Soral and National Front founder Jean-Marie Le Pen among them, have picked up the *quenelle*.

Dieudonné is far from being the only person in France to spread anti-Semitic slurs, but he and his supporters claim "comedy" as a defense. His frequent association of "Jews" and indeed of Gentiles who accuse him of anti-Semitism with responsibility for the slave trade provides an "antiracist" veneer that is also invariably mobilized by Islamists—and by a number of Gentile supporters in the French Left—who make anti-Semitic statements in the name of the defense of Palestine. In these statements, the terms *Jewish* and *Zionist* are also used interchangeably, and both groups are characterized as oppressive of others by definition.

Even within *Charlie Hebdo*, the question of anti-Semitism has arisen. On July 2, 2008, the cartoonist and humorist Siné published a text in which he associated Jean Sarkozy (son of former president Nicolas Sarkozy), Jewishness, and wealth and insinuated that Jean Sarkozy's intention to convert to Judaism in order to marry a Jewish heiress would get him places in life. The Ligue internationale contre le racisme et l'antisémitisme (International League against Racism and Anti-Semitism) took Siné to court for incitement to racial hatred. The administrative tribunal of Lyons, where the action was taken, found for the defendant, citing his *right to use satire*. Following some internal debate in *Charlie Hebdo*, then editor in chief Philippe Val fired Siné. The action was not unanimously supported by the staff, and Siné was subsequently awarded 40,000 euros in damages for unfair dismissal, augmented to 90,000 euros on appeal, to be paid to Siné by les Editions Rotatives, the company that publishes *Charlie Hebdo*. Olivier Cyran (2013) cited this affair in his trenchant online criticism of *Charlie Hebdo*, claiming that a double standard was being used. Certainly, the Lyons and Paris courts appeared to agree that this was the case. Siné himself claimed that his comment had more to do with the Sarkozy family's avarice than with any stereotypical association of Jews with such avarice.

I am among those who find Siné's comment borderline, but on the face of it his dismissal over this action alone seems unwarranted, especially given that *Charlie Hebdo* published the piece in the first place. Whatever one thinks of the Siné case, however, it is far more difficult to dismiss Dieudonné's anti-Semitism as being justified in the name of the right to satire. Whereas *Charlie Hebdo* criticizes *religious conservatism and political Islam*, not all Muslims, and whereas Siné's comment was a one-off and, for some at least, ambiguous, Dieudonné regularly charges Jews with being responsible for all the wrongs of the world, using historical disinformation of the sort familiar to anyone who has studied anti-Semitic stereotyping. If Muslims are demonstrably the new scapegoat of many in the West, notably its Christian

Right and extreme Right—as well as sections of the Zionist extreme Right, which is also active in France—then Jews have been the universal scapegoat throughout the Middle East and the West for many centuries. This scapegoating continues today in the name of "antiracism" or "anti-Islamophobia." Indeed, anti-Semitism on the French left has a long history and represents as much of a paradox as does the apparent lack of critical distance of sections of the Western Left today concerning Islamism (Dreyfus 2014).

More recently and more chillingly, Hani Ramadan (brother of Tariq Ramadan), in a series of "reflections" on the attacks of November 13, 2015, claimed that there remain "persistent grey areas" over the responsibility for the attacks and suggested that the first step would be to place Mossad (the Israeli intelligence agency) under surveillance, thus implying Israel's direct or indirect responsibility for what happened on November 13 (see H. Ramadan 2015).

It is difficult to make a reasoned argument that double standards have applied in the cases of *Charlie Hebdo* and Dieudonné. The former has mostly *not* been found guilty of *offense to religions*, whereas the latter has mostly been found guilty of statements that *incite racial hatred of people*. There is a clear line that can be drawn between the two. If one were to substitute, in Dieudonné's sketches and comments, the word *Muslims* for the word *Jews*, then the racist attacks would be just as actionable.

Even if one does make such an argument, however, there remains the incontrovertible fact that the four people killed on January 9 were targeted for no other reason than that they were shopping while Jewish, and they were targeted in the name of an Islamist terrorist organization.

9/11 and *le treize novembre*: Political Manipulations

The attacks in Paris in January 2015 gutted a population. Even if some were more gutted than others, the immediate collective reaction was one of shock, grief, and fear. Very soon, however, that reaction turned to serious concern, even anger, about actual and potential political manipulation—by the French state, by Western states, by extreme rights of various political and religious persuasions—to various ends.

On November 13, 2015, however, the impact of the January killings was significantly compounded, and to some extent "11/13" (*le treize novembre*) began to resemble a French 9/11. Notwithstanding the significant differences between the two events and their contexts, one can trace some similarities as concerns both civil society and political reactions, nationally and internationally. In both cases, a nation and its people were shocked and engaged in collective mourning that was rapidly co-opted to political ends. In both cases (and contrary to the attacks in January 2015), although Western *symbols* were explicitly targeted, the people who died were indiscriminately massacred. In both cases, there was a marked movement of international and transnational—not only Western—solidarity that was not in evidence to the same extent in reaction to other attacks such as those of Tunis, Ankara, or Beirut or even those that occurred in London in 2005 or Madrid in 2008. Like New York and Washington, Paris—one of the world's most visited cities—is symbolic, even iconic, especially for the West, and the attacks were explicitly framed as an assault on the West as a whole. In both cases, the state's immediate reaction was to declare war and begin bombing raids—against al Qaeda in the case of the United States and against Daesh in the case of France—and to seek a coalition of allies in waging such a war. After 9/11, George W. Bush was successful in marshalling the troops to declare war on al Qaeda in Afghanistan. He was far less successful, however, in relation to Iraq in 2003. France notably declined to participate in the Iraq War. The *treize novembre* attacks took place in a context where the opposite was true: the United States had withdrawn from a planned action against the Assad government in August 2013, and relations between the United States and France concerning Syria had been strained since that time. Hollande thus initially had trouble getting the United States on board to fight Daesh, although within two weeks that difficulty had been resolved as the two states reached agreement on November 24 to ramp up military operations against Daesh. Hopes of a US–EU–Turkey–Russia coalition against Daesh were nonetheless dashed, at least temporarily, by Turkey's shooting down of a Russian warplane near the Turkey–Syria border on November 24, 2015. Finally, after 9/11, feminists and pacifists and the broader Left across the world denounced Bush's "war on terror." After *le treize novembre*, similar denunciations began to be made. Except . . .

Le treize novembre occurred more than fourteen years after 9/11, and "the world" had become a much different place. The ravages of war in the Middle East in 2015 and their impacts in France were in great part a consequence of 9/11 and subsequent ill-advised and ill-managed Western interventions or a lack thereof in places and in ways where they might have done some good. And France is not the United States. What Bush did in 2001 in the name of freedom, democracy, justice, and God (Bush 2001b), Hollande did in late 2015 in the name of freedom, democracy, *la République*, and *la laïcité* (secularism) (Hollande 2015a). Where the US state shut down its refugee-resettlement program in 2001 (Schoenholtz 2005), the French state reaffirmed its commitment to the right of asylum for refugees from Syria and Iraq and Europe's duty to assist the frontline countries—Lebanon, Turkey, and Jordan—that are the most affected by the refugee influx (Hollande 2015a). The EU and member states have since 2011 paid or committed more than 5 billion euros of extra aid to Syria and the frontline countries, in part with the aim of stemming the tide of asylum seekers into Europe (European Commission 2016). Yet Hollande's reaffirmation in November 2015 of the French commitment to take in 30,000 Syrian refugees has at the time of writing, in April 2016, not translated into rapid action. Similarly, the EU–Turkey Agreement reached on March 18, 2016, to return refugees from Greece to Turkey in exchange for EU commitments to match return numbers with resettlements in Europe, which is widely criticized as violating refugee rights under international and European law, has so far resulted in more refugees being sent back to Turkey than being settled in EU member states (all to date have been settled in Germany).

Yet the mismatch between French rhetoric and reality concerning refugees goes back much further. Even as the French president was reaffirming, in the wake of the November 13 attacks, France's commitment to welcoming refugees from Syria and Iraq, those same refugees were living in what the French Council of State (the highest court in the land) confirmed to be "inhuman and degrading conditions" (qtd. in *Le Monde* 2015b). The NGOs Médecins du monde (Doctors of the World) and Secours catholique (Catholic Aid), along with a number of asylum seekers, had petitioned the administrative tribunal of Lille in late October for protection of the fundamental liberties of some 6,000 asylum seekers, mostly from Afghanistan, Darfur, Syria, Iraq, and Eritrea, camped in a shanty town in Calais, nicknamed "the Calais jungle." The nickname comes from the Persian word for "forest," *jangal,* because the asylum seekers are living in a forest near Calais, but its figurative connotations are apt. Asylum seekers have become marooned there after being blocked from entering the United Kingdom, which is outside the Schengen Area, the area that allows the free circulation of people (that is, without passports) within the EU.

The Calais jungle's origins—and problems—go back to 1999, when the Red Cross set up a center for asylum seekers in a hangar situated near the entrance to the tunnel at the coastal town of Sangatte. The center quickly became overcrowded and was closed down in 2002, with asylum seekers moving to a nearby forest (the "jungle"). Their numbers have increased, however, since 9/11 and most rapidly since 2014, with some dying as they have attempted to cross the English Channel in containers or on the top of trains (Athwal 2015).

French authorities have periodically "cleaned up" the jungle following outbreaks of intergroup violence or health epidemics (such as scabies or influenza) and have placed asylum seekers in detention centers or other temporary housing while their asylum claims are being considered. These government measures, however, have been piecemeal and woefully inadequate. In a few short weeks in the autumn of 2015, the Calais jungle's population doubled, creating the crisis situation that pushed the NGOs Médecins du monde and Secours catholique to act (Morice 2015).

On November 2, 2015, the Lille Administrative Tribunal, ruling on the NGO case, ordered the French state to determine the numbers of unaccompanied minors (the most vulnerable among the Calais jungle's population), to ensure the provision of fresh running water and toilets, to look after cleaning the settlement and removing rubbish, and to ensure access roads for emergency vehicles. Both Minister for the Interior Bernard Cazeneuve and the City of Calais appealed the judgment to the Council of State, which on November 23 confirmed the original Lille judgment (Benabent 2015). Law academic Henri Labayle, commenting on this decision, considered that there had definitely been a violation of fundamental liberties and suggested that Cazeneuve, in appealing the judgment (even though the government had in fact begun measures to action it), feared that it would set a precedent for other refugee camps and indeed Roma camps (interview in Benabent 2015). Labayle stressed that under European law member states now have "positive obligations." It is not enough simply to refrain from preventing the exercise of liberties (negative liberty): EU states are also obliged to ensure the conditions in which liberties can be exercised (positive liberty). The French state has an obligation to protect all those in its territory, whether they are there legally or not.

This conception of rights, liberties, and protections is consistent with the French ideal of *la République*. As a friend commented to me in an email discussing the Calais situation, it is "such a pity that we are obliged to take action against the state, which should be the guarantor of hospitality, a rampart against fascists" (personal communication, Nov. 25, 2015). At the time of writing, the French state is proceeding with the dismantling of "the jungle," but many of its residents are now resisting and refusing alternative housing.

The French state's hypocrisy in response to terrorist attacks, however, has not only been in the area of refugee resettlement and has been as roundly criticized as was the US state's hypocrisy in 2001. The co-optation of the *Charlie Hebdo* assassinations was expressed at multiple levels, from the parade of political dignitaries at the demonstration in Paris on January 11 to the much-publicized celebration by the socialist mayor of Paris, Anne Hidalgo, of the marriage on September 26 of a *Charlie* staffer seriously injured in the attacks. The survivor in question, *Charlie*'s webmaster and social media manager

Simon Fieschi, was shot in the spine and at the time of writing is still undergoing intensive physical therapy and cannot walk unaided. His marriage received publicity in Australia because his bride was Australian (Koziol 2015). In France, he was characterized as the "forgotten one" of the *Charlie Hebdo* assassinations. Among the mourning for the dead, the living continue to pay the costs.

This personal anecdote, one of what are now more than 350 as the survivors of the massacre of November 13 are on their own road to recovery, highlights the difficulty of the political class in the face of these attacks. Even as we know that the political class—whether represented by Bush, Obama, Hollande, Cameron (UK), Erdoğan (Turkey), Cabbesi (Tunisia), or indeed Hidalgo—will inevitably co-opt such tragedies to its own ends, the same political class can never be a winner in such circumstances. Had the French political class not marched on January 11, had it not been represented at Simon Fieschi's wedding, it would have been seen as uncaring in the face of the violence that French citizens had suffered because they dared exercise their right to freedom of speech and conscience. Yet in participating in the "Je suis Charlie" demonstrations of solidarity, the political class also left itself open to criticism for its hypocrisy in the face of the systemic and ongoing racism operating in the République of Equality. Either way, the political class remains the political class and suspect in the eyes of a pluralist civil society Left, including feminists, which, whatever its views on *Charlie Hebdo* and "Islamophobia," is deeply distrustful of a state that has betrayed the disenfranchised and marginalized more often than it has served them.

President Hollande has also invoked the French ideal of *la République* since November 13 in the name of the *raison d'État* (although he did not use that term): that is, violation of some rights to serve a higher purpose (usually a war). The declaration of states of emergency in both France and Belgium, although perfectly legal, involved a curtailment of many civil liberties in the name of national defense, such as the right to demonstrate peacefully. Such measures have not met with a warm response from many French citizens. On November 29, 2015, Parisians found a creative answer to the prohibition of demonstrations by placing pairs of shoes on the place de la République in lieu of demonstrators as the world summit on climate change commenced (see, e.g., *BBC News* 2015). Similarly, in Belgium over the previous two weeks, dozens of photographs and videos of "cat terrorists" and "cat soldiers"—even "cat drones"—were posted to a government Twitter account in protest at the lockdown there in response to the Paris attacks and the hunt for the perpetrators.

In his speech at the commemoration ceremony on November 27, 2015, for the 130 people who were killed on November 13, Hollande stressed the values contained in the republican motto: liberty, equality, fraternity, along with the rule of law, democracy, and of course *laïcité*. Governments have placed the latter at the heart of republican values since the law on separation of church and state of 1905 and most particularly since the first *hijab* debate in 1989 (Winter 2008). Hollande, however, also subtly introduced the logic of war alongside these lofty ideals. Even as he stated that "freedom does not ask to be avenged but to be served," he characterized the 130 dead as "martyrs," "fallen" in an "act of war organized from afar and coldly executed," and emphasized the importance of the military abroad and the police at home in combatting the enemy, which he named "hatred" (Hollande 2015b, my translation). Even though the speech, which Hollande himself unusually authored, was a model of sobriety compared to what one may have imagined from his presidential predecessor Nicolas Sarkozy, it nonetheless made implicitly clear that the *raison d'État* was necessary to defend the values of *la République* in the longer term. The holding of the ceremony in the cour des Invalides, normally associated with war commemorations, cemented the image of the 130 dead as "martyrs" in a "war."

My friend who lamented the betrayal of the republic by the government's treatment of asylum seekers in Calais, commented, in tacit reference to the French state's immediate military reaction to the November 13 attacks, that she and others feared the development of a "third world war." Alarmist? Perhaps. We are, however, by now primed for such reactions. Terrorist attacks are becoming more frequent and more destructive, and Daesh has identified France as the epicenter of what it sees as Western decadence and thus as a prime target. Both France and Belgium have been transformed overnight into police states. Despite attempts to dampen the hysteria through humor—such as the defiant cover of *Charlie Hebdo* on November 18, 2015, "They have the arms; screw them, we have the champagne!" ("Ils ont les armes; on les emmerde, on a le champagne"), or the Photoshopping of photographs of members of Daesh to make them appear to be rubber ducks—France and by extension the rest of Europe are jittery.

Another similarity with 9/11: France has become, since November 13, 2015, seized by a wave of nationalism and militarization. This may seem surprising among a populace that, notwithstanding its staunch defense of the ideals of *la République*, does not appear, perhaps, as belligerently nationalist as the United States. Yet the very word *nationalism* was invented during the French revolutionary decade in the late eighteenth century and was routinely used in the United Kingdom during the following century to describe France. Moreover, France is sixth in the world in terms of military strength and second in Europe, according to the Global Firepower Index.[5] (The top ten are, in order of ranking, the United States, Russia, China, India, the United Kingdom, France, South Korea, Germany, Japan, and Turkey.) Following November 13, both the French army and flag makers were deluged with increased demand. Enquiries to join the army went from 500 per day to 1,500 per day in the week after the attacks, and following a presidential invitation to the French to display the flag on November 27, the day of the commemoration ceremony, flag manufacturers had trouble keeping up with the demand (Guibert 2015; Vulser 2015). Unlike the United States, where the national flag is frequently displayed in front of private homes—to the best of my knowledge the case even before 9/11—it is very unusual indeed to see such private flag displaying in France. The sudden frenzy of flag waving is

---

5. The index is available at http://www.globalfirepower.com/countries-listing .asp (accessed Nov. 28, 2015). The site also provides an overview of criteria used to determine the listing.

thus noteworthy. President Hollande has also, following his January decision to reverse the reduction of army jobs in 2013–14, made a commitment to increase recruitment in 2016, with some 16,000 new posts planned (Guibert 2015). Increases in personnel are also planned for the police, customs (France reintroduced controls on its borders with other Schengen countries, as have a number of countries in the Schengen Area between November 2015 and March 2016), and the Justice Department, notably prison administration. The cost of all this means that France will not be able to respect its European commitment to keep its budget deficit under control, and the cost of heightened security in France and elsewhere may have further implications for Eurozone stability.

A number of media outlets have documented Hollande's remarkable transformation from a president who seemed limp, even nondescript, to a "war leader." A Reuters/Radio France International report on November 20, 2015, even hyperbolically dubbed him the "most bellicose president in [French] history," which is debatable, but it indicates the impact of Hollande's new stance. The report also suggested that the imperative of "national unity" behind a war president had to some extent pulled the rug out from under the right-wing opposition on the eve of French regional elections and a year and a half out from the presidential election of 2017 (RFI 2015b). War is not only good for business but also usually good for politicians as well in that the nationalism of a nation constructed, rightly or wrongly, as being under siege trumps just about anything else.

A *Western* nation constructed in this way also trumps, at an international level, whatever grief we—as in "we the West"—may feel for a non-Western nation. Following the November 13 attacks, there was much discussion—in the press, in social media, in conversations—of why France benefited from such immediate transnational sentiment of solidarity, complete with "Je suis Paris" messages echoing the "Je suis Charlie" of January and city landmarks being lit up in the blue, white, and red stripes of the French flag, whereas Lebanon, which had been targeted just the previous day, did not. There are many explanations. For some, the discrepancy was yet another example of Western bias.

For others, it was owing to the connection many felt to Paris, having been there, that they did not feel to Beirut, never having been there. For yet others, it was because the attacks were different in nature: even if innocent people died in both cities, the Beirut attack was seen, rightly or wrongly, as fratricide, with a Sunni terrorist group targeting the perceived stronghold of a perceived Shia rival (Hezbollah). The Paris attacks, in contrast, were seen as an attack on values, on a way of life (again, the comparison with 9/11 beckons). In Australia, the lack of public solidarity with Lebanon was felt keenly in a country that has historically been a major destination for Lebanese emigration: some drew the conclusion that "white lives matter more" (Hamad 2015). On one level, this comment seems unwittingly ironic: the area targeted on November 13 was one of the most multicultural of central Paris, and many who died that night were not in fact white. The point, however, was that deaths occurring in Western cities matter more than those occurring outside them.

As in the weeks and months following 9/11, there remained little to feel optimistic about in the wake of *le treize novembre*. As Australian commentator Waleed Aly put it in the *Sydney Morning Herald*, the combat against Daesh is likely to be

> the fight that goes around in circles. . . . In the visceral urge to smash things after Paris, you can overlook the fact that whenever we've tried to use our armies to smash terrorism we've generally scattered it all over the world. Remember when US president George W. Bush said that we were fighting terrorists in Baghdad so we wouldn't have to fight them in Boston? . . . The idea that we can gather terrorism in one place and then destroy it is now surely one of the most demonstrably wrong-headed of our age. (2015)

Just as wrongheaded have been the long-standing Western complicity with authoritarian regimes in MENA and subsequent callousness in the face of the disarray of political institutions and socioeconomic disintegration once (some) regimes have broken down or been overthrown (with or without Western intervention).

Finally, as was the case in the United States after 9/11, feminists in France have responded to the events of *le treize novembre* and their aftermath by refusing the logic of war. A petition circulated via email on November 28, 2015, opposed the declaration of a state of emergency and "the militarization of France," calling for an immediate halt to the bombings in Syria and Iraq and for reallocation of government funds from the military to concrete solutions to the problems of racism, sexism, and class within French society. At the time of writing, the origin of the petition is unclear, but it is indicative of feminist hostility to the French state's use of the November 13 tragedy as a pretext for escalating militarization. Similarly, Elaine Audet, creator and manager of the feminist website Sisyphe, published on November 24, 2015, a long "diary of a somber week" ("journal d'une semaine de plomb"). She denounced both radical Islamism and the actions of a government that has always "so little reflected our [feminist] aspirations." She noted that the French state proceeded without any public debate to impose "the law of bombs, whose inefficiency has been repeatedly proven by all those humanitarian catastrophes to which it has repeatedly and unceasingly given rise" (my translation). Like a number of other commentators, Audet pointed out that the truly "heroic" work against Daesh is being done on the ground by the Kurdish forces and the Free Syrian Army. The aptness of the adjective *heroic* is open to debate, but it is true that Western nations have not to date either deployed ground troops or developed a coherent military strategy—let alone a coherent political one—in relation to Syria. Amid such incoherence and lack of agreement, the French bombings, which actually began on a much smaller scale in September 2015, do indeed seem to correspond to a state-level "visceral urge to smash things" (Aly 2015). Finally, like the authors of the unattributed petition, Audet also urged the French government to pay greater attention to the "social inclusion" of stigmatized and ghettoized Muslim minorities. At the same time, she firmly distanced herself from any position that might tacitly seek to excuse the perpetrators of the attacks as victims of racism.

Terrorism, Masculinity, and Victim Blaming

There has understandably been much discussion of racism in France since the attacks in January and November 2015. Since November 13, the French media have reported a sharp rise in attacks against Muslims (which they now routinely describe as "Islamophobic," in a marked shift in media terminology, which is relatively recent). Three days after the November attacks, the newspaper *Libération* reported that, as happened in January, mosques in various parts of France were desecrated, kebab houses vandalized, and individuals insulted, attacked, and harassed via social media (*Libération* 2015b). According to the Conseil français du culte musulman (French Council of the Muslim Faith), there had been at least twenty-five separate attacks during that three-day period, including assaults on women in headscarves (as reported in FranceTVInfo 2015). Such attacks, as well as the polarized debate that reprises many elements of the one that followed the January attacks, play directly into Daesh's hands. If French society and if the West more broadly become more deeply divided over race and "Islamophobia," then Daesh's work is if not done, then at least well advanced.

The climate of racism in France is not, however, new and is not likely to disappear soon. An estimated 7 to 8 percent of the French population is Muslim, with some estimates going as high as 10 percent. That percentage, however, is nowhere near the overestimation of 15 to 20 million by Jean-Marie Le Pen (founder of the National Front and father of its present leader, Marine Le Pen), which is also routinely the figure imagined in response to periodic surveys (Tribalat 2014). Demographer Michèle Tribalat, in commenting on the responses to a survey on the topic in 2014, dedramatized the results, saying that, first, the public overestimated other demographics relating to perceived social problems, such as the number of teenage pregnancies or the percentage of the population older than sixty-five. She also noted that the French do not overestimate the "Islamic problem" any more than other Western countries do and a great deal less than some. French public opinion multiplies the actual number of Muslims in France by about four, which is around average for perceptions in western European countries and much less than for Australians and Canadians, whose multiplier is a little less than ten. United Statians have the most exaggerated overestimation: they believe there are fifteen times more Muslims in the United States than there actually are (Tribalat 2014).

For others commenting on the same survey as Tribalat, however, the results were an indicator of the rise of racism in France. According to academic Nacira Guénif-Soulimas, for example, the survey demonstrated that "racist ideology is making headway in France" (2014). She is certainly right to suggest that Muslims are scapegoated in France, as the wave of racist reactions to the November 13 terrorist attacks demonstrates. Unfortunately, the well-justified concern over that scapegoating has some aberrant manifestations.

Emmanuel Todd argues that the "grandiose" Paris demonstration of January 11, 2015, was framed around "a *duty* to blaspheme concerning the emblematic character of a *minority* religion, borne by a *disadvantaged* group" (2015, 87, my italics of *duty*, Todd's italics of *minority* and *disadvantaged*). Similarly, Houria Bouteldja, of the Parti des Indigènes de la République (see Winter 2008), portrays the attacks against *Charlie Hebdo*, like those committed by Mohammed Merah against members of the French military and Jewish schoolchildren in Toulouse and Montauban in March 2012, as the consequence of racism. Such attacks, for Bouteldja, were the "time bombs" produced by a racist society that does not respect the "sacred" (2015). Bouteldja echoes the words of Rokhaya Diallo, who wrote in the pages of the French edition of the *Huffington Post* on January 14, 2015, that "through its own denial, France has created its own monsters." Bouteldja has since produced a book titled *Les Blancs, les Juifs et nous: Vers une politique d'amour révolutionnaire* (White People, Jews, and Us: Towards a Politics of Revolutionary Love, 2016), which has been criticized as not only incoherent in its arguments but also anti-Semitic, racist, misogynist, and homophobic (see, e.g., Rieth 2016; Segré 2016; Yves 2016).

Following the November 13 attacks, similar comments were made both in France and around the world concerning the responsibility of French racism—and even secularism, framed as racist almost by definition—for the attacks (see, e.g., Kuzu 2015). Although this time it is impossible to portray the actual victims as somehow asking for what happened to them because the killings were indiscriminate and not targeted, France is perceived as having to bear some burden of responsibility for not having addressed the problem of socioeconomic and cultural exclusion of its Muslim minority. That there is a demonstrable problem of racism in France is without doubt. More dubious, however, is the argument that one can establish a direct relationship of cause and effect between this experience of racism and the attacks on January 7, 8, and 9 and November 13, 2015. The international/ Anglo world discussions of French racism are all the more grating in that those discussions did not occur to the same extent with relation to London in 2005 or Madrid in 2008 or, indeed, Ankara in 2015 or any one of a number of places that one can identify on the world map, inside and outside the West, and that have their own problems of socioeconomic exclusion linked to religion and ethnicity. Alongside the question "Why is Daesh targeting France?" one might also ask the question "Why is the Anglo world targeting France?" And a third: "Why are terrorists being constructed as victims?"

Historian Gérard Noiriel, in his revisiting of the question Ernest Renan asked in 1882, "Qu'est-ce qu'une nation?" (see chapter 2), critiques "the assigning of identities on both sides of the fence. . . . [T]hose who detest all Muslims because they saw assassins slit the throats of innocents in the name of Islam react in the same way as Muslims who consider themselves to be personally offended by all French people when media reproduce negative images of their religion" (2015, 102, my translation). The perverse effect of these negative identity politics, for Noiriel, is to paradoxically lock violent men into the very negative stereotype against which Bouteldja rails: "Those who feel humiliated by public representations of their community can go as far as denying other dimensions of their identity in order to redefine themselves according to the stigma. They end up conforming completely to the negative image that is given of them" (102–3, my translation). In other words, Muslims and in particular Muslim men are left in a political impasse: socioculturally overdetermined by both their religion and their context of racialization, they are constructed as *inexorably* drawn to violence. They end up performing the delinquent "Arab boy" stereotype that Nacira Guénif-Soulimas and Eric Macé discuss in their book *Les Féministes et le garçon arabe* (Feminists and the Arab Boy, 2004)—a stereotype that the authors also accuse feminists of constructing.

Yet if Islamist terrorism is solely a question of the West's chickens coming home to roost, then one wonders why it is not a more generalized phenomenon. One wonders why, for example, the riots in France in 2005 did not develop into a civil war between "othered" Muslims and the French state. The answer is simple: *some* Muslim men are engaging in violent or terrorist acts, not all, not even the majority or even a significant minority. Terrorists do damage that has an impact far beyond their actual numbers, and they are surely indoctrinated, but they are no more automatons than they are victims. They make choices.

The question is also begged of why it is *men* who are engaging in these activities, the increased existence of female suicide bombers notwithstanding. Not only are fewer women engaged in terrorist activities, but their motivations are vastly different (see, e.g., Sjoberg and Gentry 2011; Berko 2012). Although some women may desire to become "martyrs for the cause," this "martyrdom" may combine with social exclusion for gender-specific reasons (to do with women's sexual activity or perceived unmarriageability or barrenness, for example), and women are far more likely than men to be coerced into terrorist activities, often through pressure exerted by boyfriends or family members. Perversely, the increase in female suicide bombers may also be owing to development of a more "egalitarian" attitude in Islamist organizations.

Violence is central to the construction of masculinity, whether that violence is claimed in the name of Allah or democracy. As Cynthia Cockburn put it in 2010,

> The disposition in societies such as those we live in, characterized
> by a patriarchal gender regime, is towards an association of mas-
> culinity with authority, coercion and violence. It is a masculinity
> (and a complementary femininity) that not only serves militarism
> very well indeed, but seeks *and needs militarization and war for its*
> *fulfilment.* . . . . [The violence] produces re-burnished ethnic identi-
> ties, sharpened by memories of wrong and a desire for revenge.
> (152, her italics)

Cockburn places war within a continuum of men's violence—and its
related construction of wounded, heroic, and/or vengeful masculinities and victimized or "momentarily empowered" women.

A corollary to the construction of terrorist acts as an extreme
expression of Arabo-Muslim males' victimhood is the concern
expressed in media and by governments across the Western world
concerning the recruitment of ever-younger jihadists. In cases where
the latter cannot be represented as victims of racism—because they
are not all ethnically Muslim—they are constructed as socially iso-
lated young men who have lost their way. Solutions being attempted
by Western governments include community deradicalization programs; whether such programs will be effective in the longer term
remains to be seen. Canadian antiterrorism expert Mubin Shaikh,
himself a former jihadist, explains that jihadism "resonated with
[him] as a young male with a sense of adventure and a sense of religious fervour" at a time of identity crisis (qtd. in Wroe 2015). For
him, the political grievances came later, and he suggests that recruits
to Islamist terrorist organizations are diverse and have diverse reasons
for joining them, ranging from thugs or petty criminals in search
of a cause to indoctrinated religious converts or those with political grievances of one sort or another. I would suggest that all these
motivations resonate with the "young male with a sense of adventure," that the construction of heroic masculinity necessarily involves
violence against someone constructed as enemy. Until clear connections are made between extremist violence and this construction of
masculinity—and the concurrent devalorization and exploitation of

women—then militarized violence, whether terrorist or coordinated by recognized states, is not going to go away.

I wrote the previous paragraph a few days after the International Day of Action on Violence against Women, November 25. As part of the events marking that day in Australia, the Australian Broadcasting Corporation, a national public-television network, broadcast Sarah Ferguson's documentary *Hitting Home* on domestic violence in Australia, which killed seventy women that year up to November 2015—that is, more than half as many again as died in Paris on November 13 (see Ferguson 2015). In Colorado Springs, Colorado, on November 28, a gunman killed three people and wounded others at a Planned Parenthood clinic. Although the US authorities did not comment on a motive, the CEO of Planned Parenthood of the Rocky Mountains, Vicki Cowart, issued the following written statement: "We share the concerns of many Americans that extremists are creating a poisonous environment that feeds domestic terrorism in this country" (qtd. in Shoichet, Stapleton, and Botelho 2015), and US attorney general Loretta Lynch described the shooting as a "crime against women" (qtd. in Conlon, Botelho, and Brown 2015).

Such events are part of the everyday of women worldwide, not the stuff of national tragedies and of homage paid to "martyrs" at sites of war memorial ceremonies—outside feminist antiwar protests, of course. The white man who shot people in Colorado Springs, however, has much in common with the fifteen-year-old boys who become jihadists: a taste for violence, a sense of victimhood, a need to take revenge or exact punishment, and, most certainly, a hatred of women, in particular those who seek to exercise their autonomy from men's control.

It is particularly of concern for feminist analysis when our ability to denounce an act of violence becomes hampered by the necessity that the victims be the right kind, somehow unimpeachable in every way, and we lose our critical distance in relation to religious extremism. The Paris attacks in 2015 have more than ever shown up how tightly religion and politics have become imbricated in a "post-9/11 world" and how manichean—simplistically black and white—much thinking in the West continues to be. In 2011, an Iranian lesbian living in Paris commented to me concerning the idea of "Islamophobia": "Islamophobic, me? You bet I am!" thus expressing her aversion to the manipulative use of the term to silence criticism of Islam and Islamist extremism. I consider her neither particularly "representative" as a "native informant" nor particularly "alienated" or "Westernized" (although the treatment of lesbians in Iran must indeed be highly alienating). She has made a political choice based on her experience and based on evidence, as we all, whether "white Western" or "Muslim" or otherwise positioned in the "post-9/11 world," are capable of doing. None of us is an automaton. For my part, I make political choices based on evidence, on reading and listening, and through the understanding that the enemy of my enemy is not necessarily my friend. The Islamic Right is no more my ally in any campaign I join against racism than is the French state in any campaign I join against Islamic extremism. That sections of the French and international Left make alliances with the Islamic Right in the name of combating Islamic extremism is a betrayal not only of feminists, including those of Muslim culture, but also of the Left more generally.

Conclusion

Intersections Are Meeting Places

Among the many post-9/11 dilemmas or dilemmas exacerbated by post-9/11ism that confronted me in the preparation of this book was the question of reciprocity. With greater international attention paid by institutions, civil society corporate actors, and researchers to issues faced by women in a post-9/11 context, more complex questions of accountability, of moral and material responsibility, have arisen. How are equal and long-term exchanges negotiated in situations of instability and inequality? Feminists, even those who belong to political and intellectual elites of the West, rarely have access to the sort of political power and economic resources that would truly enable our transnational interactions with grassroots activists to be as beneficial to the latter as might be wished. Yet with interaction comes expectation: a tacit promise to deliver some sort of improvement and a hope that delivery will occur. How do feminist researchers from outside complex and often volatile contexts, which are frequently the object of mis- and disinformation, develop understanding and coherent engagement without creating extra burdens or risk for the human subjects of such research—and, indeed, without perpetuating the mis- and disinformation? I have no straightforward answer to that question, just as I do not have a straightforward answer to the question "Has 9/11 changed the world for women?" But I offer in these concluding pages some reflections on them via a discussion of some of my interactions with feminists in the Philippines.

On July 20, 2004, Gloria Macapagal Arroyo, then Philippine president, signed Proclamation 675, which designated the month of September from then on to be National Peace Consciousness Month in recognition of the UN International Peace Day of September 21 as well as of 9/11. The date September 21 is doubly significant in the Philippines because it is also the anniversary of President Ferdinand Marcos's declaration of martial law in 1972. Every September since 2004, numerous governmental and nongovernmental initiatives have been organized in the Philippines, focusing on the themes of war and peace. These initiatives have had mostly national but sometimes international reach.

I have been to the Philippines a few times since 9/11, to various locations on Luzon, Cebu, Mindanao, and the Sulu Archipelago. My connections there—like my connections with Afghanistan, Pakistan, North Africa, Israel/Palestine, Turkey, Argentina, as well as, indeed, France, the United Kingdom, Canada, and to some extent the United States—developed through feminist and gay networks, mostly activist ones. With the exception of France, Pakistan, parts of North Africa, the United Kingdom, and the United States, all of these networks developed after 9/11 and in most cases because of it. I could say that as a result 9/11 "shook the world" for me. It certainly contributed to making the world bigger and a great deal more daunting. Materially, however, 9/11 had almost zero impact (unless I consider the cost of traveling to these places to be a material impact), and I am not so sure how much it really did shake up the world for most of its women.

In fact, what has depressed me in my post-9/11 travels, both physical and metaphorical, is how much things have stayed exactly the same for women, even if lacquered over with a new veneer—that is, if they have not gotten worse. What has delighted and moved me, however, and even on occasion given me hope is not only women's extraordinary resilience, courage, and determination to keep pushing back in the face of crushing forces lined up against them but also many women's (self-identified as feminist or not) willingness and ability to reach across the seemingly impossible divides that separate us and that militate against our acting in solidarity with each other.

In chapter 5, I briefly discussed Kimberlé Crenshaw's (1989) concept of "intersectionality," which she developed to describe the cumulative impacts of race, sex, and class for African American women pursuing discrimination cases within the US legal system. I would like to reconfigure the feminist meaning of this concept for the purpose of what follows here. If Crenshaw thought of the experience of individuals within a specific system, I am thinking of how individuals interact within vastly different systems. An intersection, in its basic definition, is a place where two or more things come together and is often conceptualized as a meeting of pathways. How do women who are differently located within both national and transnational contexts respond when their paths cross? How do conversations develop or not?

The intersections at which I have found myself in various countries both before and since 9/11 have traversed class, race, religion, nationality, location, sexual orientation, age, (dis)ability, native language—all the categories of oppression that one can conceivably compile in the so-called shopping list of oppressions. I suggested in chapter 5 that Crenshaw's way of framing the concept does not adequately address the problem of this shopping list, where one adds up how many oppressions one has and those who tick the most boxes end up at the bottom of the pile. If oppression worked so neatly, our feminist solidarities would be more straightforward enterprises.

For example, in Afghanistan, Pakistan, and the Philippines I have found myself in situations where in terms of class my hosts have been far more privileged within their context, relative to social status and cost of living, than I am in mine, although in absolute terms I have a higher income and thus more money. For example, in 2005 in Marawi in western (Muslim) Mindanao in the Philippines, I was the guest of a Maranao family that was part of the local traditional feudal elite and the most religiously conservative ethnic group among the Moro population. The nearest thing Australia has to a feudal elite is the historical "squattocracy," those white settlers who claimed large tracts of land and made fortunes from farming and in some cases mining. I, the descendant of assisted-passage, working-class, and lower-middle-class Anglo-Celtic migrants, am nowhere near that stratosphere in my own society. At the same time, even the feudal elite of Marawi is part of a marginalized group within the Philippines more generally.

My Marawi hosts in 2005 were also heavily involved in both the political and the military wings of the Jabhat Tahrir Moro al-'Islamiyyah (Moro Islamic Liberation Front, MILF). In many other contexts, we would have been standing far distant from each other across a political divide, but in 2005 we met at a crossroads of geo-politics and history and feminist activism. The woman who invited me to dinner, a Moro intellectual and activist, daughter of a ruling feudal family, and wife of a MILF commander, also identified as a femi-nist activist. She had been introduced to me by yet another feminist activist: a peace activist from the "North"—that is, Catholic-majority Luzon, the most heavily populated and politically dominant island in the Philippines. I was openly irreligious and made no pretense of being otherwise. Because I am a Westerner, this stance was no doubt more easily accepted than if I had been from Luzon or western Mindanao.

In the space of a few days in Marawi, at a miniconference of women at Mindanao State University, in the streets, in the feudal home, I spoke with women for whom the Muslim World League comprises the good guys. I was shown with pride the mosque the league had built for them and then shown the virtually empty university library. I donated some feminist books but wonder, ten years later, what vol-umes are now on the bookshelves of this relatively poor university where Christian and Muslim students mingle but where the Muslim students have an increasingly militant presence, and I wonder who paid for them. As elsewhere, the Muslim World League has been very active in western Mindanao as well as in Manila, where, among other things, it organizes Arabic classes for Muslim university students from Mindanao. I wonder, writing a little more than a year after the sig-nature of the Comprehensive Agreement on the Bangsamoro, what the Muslim World League's role has been and will be, along with the combined effects of poverty, racialization, and ongoing violence, in pulling Bangsamoro to the Islamist right.

The Bangsamoro Agreement, negotiated between the Philippine state and the MILF, incorporates a number of previous agreements signed since 1997 and provides for the replacement of the Autonomous Region of Muslim Mindanao, previously negotiated between the state and the Moro National Liberation Front in the Tripoli Agreement of 1996. Bangsamoro parliamentary self-rule was scheduled to commence in 2016, under the terms of the proposed Bangsamoro Basic Law (House Bill no. 4994, redrafted in 2015 as House Bill no. 5118). That bill was shelved indefinitely in February 2016, but in August 2016 President Rodrigo Duterte announced a new push to have the bill passed in 2017 as part of a transition from a unitary to a federal system of government in the Philippines from 2019 (Depasupil 2016). It is unclear at the time of writing whether the original plan for Bangsamoro to become a substate, with similar status in relation to the Philippine state as that of Scotland in relation to the United Kingdom, will go ahead, or Bangsamoro will have the same status as other regions under a new federal system. Although technically secular (i.e., not planned as an Islamic substate), Bangsamoro nonetheless provides for the application of shar'ia law in all personal-status and civil matters involving Muslims, and the subject has been highly controversial. The rise of Daesh and the violent clash between special police forces and Islamist militants in Mamasapano in late January 2015 fueled concerns expressed in national media, which contributed to the temporary shelving of the Bangsamoro Basic Law.

In Marawi in 2005, in a side conversation during the miniconference, I asked an older women present, one of the academic and community leaders, whether sexual and domestic violence was a problem, as it had not really been discussed. She told me, "Of course it is, but we don't talk about it much; it's taboo. And we have other priorities right now." As for women in anti-imperialist national struggles everywhere, self-censorship is routinely practiced in the name of national liberation.

The Philippine state, like the Israeli state, both of them backed by the United States with considerable financial and military might, has contributed to the further marginalization, militarization, and Islamicization of a persecuted minority. But counterpowers have also used places such as Palestine, Bangsamoro, Turkey, Egypt, and a number of other countries as laboratories for development of a new Islamist international that claims to defend the rights of the marginalized and invokes democratic legitimacy. In writing these words, I worry, as I have throughout the process of writing this book, in particular since the attacks in Paris on November 13, 2015, about feeding into the Us-and-Them-ness that underpinned the discursive construction of the "just wars" waged by the United States against Afghanistan and Iraq. I worry about fueling the horrendous racist bigotry that became more strident in many places in the West in 2014 and especially 2015. I worry as greatly, however, about the equally Us-and-Them construction of a collective Islamic victim fighting its own "just war" against the Western hegemon. I think not only of Daesh and its ever more sophisticated networks of recruitment but also of the supposedly more moderate Islamic political formations that are using democratic processes to impose their worldview. Neither the "West" nor the "Muslim world" is monolithic. We know this, and yet how easily we still fall into the patterns. The simple truth is that masculinist alliances of guns, money, and religion are dangerous for women everywhere, whatever nation these alliances speak for and however just they claim their wars to be. They are also demonstrably dangerous for a considerable number of men, but my concern is with the women. There are already plenty of people, both men and women, worrying about the men.

During a visit to Australia in 2006 or 2007, one of the Maranao women, knowing my own views on religion, asked me if I thought that religion and feminism were incompatible. I replied that I did but that I did not think it was impossible for religious women to also be feminist. We all live with multiple and often contradictory allegiances, and feminists engage with a range of masculinist institutions in all sorts of ways. In doing so, they often carve out more women-friendly spaces, making the institutions accountable for women's welfare and enabling women's greater social participation as actors and deciders. The presence of some feminists within a religious faith, however, does not make the faith feminist. No more than the presence of feminists within the police force or our national governments, for that matter, makes the police force or the nation-state feminist. Religions, like the nations of which they are always in some way a foundational or historical element, are what we have to work with. We do not stand outside nation and faith but within them, whether we believe in them or not. We never make choices as atomized individuals, and as feminists we know in any case that "choice" is an ideologically loaded concept (Mathieu 1991; Baker 2008).

Many Moro women, including those I spoke with in 2005, 2007, and 2009, are no doubt staunch supporters of the Bangsamoro Agreement. I have not had an opportunity to discuss with any of them their personal position on the shar'ia law provisions, but other research indicates that Maranao women leaders from Lanao del Sur Province, of which Marawi is the capital, consider that it restricts women's autonomy, and they consequently advocate "a much broader program of rights" (Hilsdon 2009, 361). Anne-Marie Hilsdon (2009) argues that women's participation in the peace-negotiation process has been underrecognized and that the framing of violence in the region around war and religious issues has led to invisibilization of other forms of violence to which women are routinely subjected through domestic violence, clan wars, and the lack of social justice more generally.

In any case, the intersections at which I would meet my Maranao interlocutors today would be quite different from those of a decade or even five years ago, and we would also be different. What form would our conversations take now? Would they take place at all?

In my more optimistic moments, I think of intersections as meeting places rather than places one passes through because the traffic lights are in one's favor, oblivious to those who wait. If there is one single thing that 9/11 changed for the world's women, it was perhaps to increase the number of intersections at which we might meet and linger to talk a little rather than just charging on through once again or rather than standing aside, meekly or resentfully, so that others may charge through instead of us.

In 2009, I talked with women involved in the Tri-People's Peace Movement in Mindanao, the "Tri-People" in question being Moros, "immigrants" (Catholics), and Lumad (tribal women). Along with some other women from a number of countries who, like me, had attended an international feminist peace conference held in Manila during Peace Month, I participated in several events set up in and around Cotobato City in western Mindanao, which is to become part of Bangsamoro under the new agreement. Even though these events contained an element of showcasing at which we "international" women were called upon to play particular roles as well as to view particular things (and not others), the experience was nonetheless illuminating. One of the events was a Tri-People women's meeting, which brought together a hugely diverse group of women: Trotskyist students from Marawi; Catholic nuns; Protestant converts active in the relatively liberal United Church of Christ; Muslim women fasting for Ramadan; Lumad peasant farmers and fisherfolk; and a number of other activists. Among the last group, to my astonishment, were some young women who would have looked perfectly at home in the gay areas of Manila or indeed Sydney. They were members of the Initiative and Movement for Gender Liberation against Discrimination, IM GLAD, the first and, to my knowledge at that time, the only Muslim gay group in the Philippines. Lesbian and gay members of Young Activists for Peace and Solidarity had set up the group in 2008.

At a request from me and three others in our "international" contingent, a separate meeting was set up between IM GLAD and us the following day in Cotabato City. The other three "international" women were Israeli activist Ruchama Martón, who in 1988 had cofounded Physicians for Human Rights, an Israeli–Palestinian medical aid association that provides health care in the West Bank and Gaza; Palestinian activist Khulud Khamis, who at that time was the international officer at Isha L'Isha, the Haifa women's center; and Olivera Simic, a Bosnian-born law academic living in Australia.

Of all the extraordinary intersectional meetings I have had the privilege to be involved in since 9/11, this was no doubt the most extraordinary. At that time and no doubt still, Cotabato City was a violent place, and being overtly homosexual made one a target. In July and October 2009, on either end of our visit, armed Islamist groups bombed Catholic churches there, and spasmodic violence, including clan wars, continues. Yet these young lesbians and gay men—all of whom identified as Muslim, with varying degrees of religious practice (for example, some were fasting for Ramadan, whereas others were not), but none of whom wore any form of Islamic dress—were braving the stormy seas of Mindanao politics. They spoke of personal experiences of harassment, violence, and imprisonment in the usual places: family, police (although homosexuality is not illegal in the Philippines), religious authorities. They spoke of their campaign for the right to worship in mosques as openly gay people, a right at that time denied them. They also spoke of socioeconomic marginalization as both gays and Moros. Significantly yet predictably, this marginalization was greater for the women: the men had better education, better English, and better employment or employment prospects, even though they also faced socioeconomic disadvantage owing both to their Muslimness and to their sexual orientation.

Some five years down the track, as reported in an article published in the online Philippine "LGBTQIA" magazine *Outrage* in February 2014, IM GLAD was still very active, although its representatives reported difficulties in maintaining membership over the years because of both religious opposition and individual financial pressures—that is, the need to earn a living. Although the organization is still focused primarily on Muslims, *Outrage* (2014a) reported that it also identified strongly as Tri-People and reached out to Christians and Lumad in the region.

IM GLAD, along with the actions of feminists in Muslim Mindanao, and probably LGBT(I) activism in the Philippines more broadly, has had a decided impact. In April 2014, *Outrage* also reported on Tumba Lata (Knock Down the Can, the name of a Filipino street game), an association set up in Jolo, in the Sulu Archipelago, by Merilyn "Mherz" Jamad to fight for lesbian rights and against violence against women and lesbians (*Outrage* 2014b). This combat includes standing up to local government and police corruption, a problem also foregrounded in my conversation with IM GLAD in 2009. Sulu is not a particularly safe place at the best of times, which makes Jamad's activism all the more inspiring.

One can say with relative certainty that although the "troubles" in Mindanao began well before 9/11, the wake of 9/11 shaped the way in which they were to play out, especially in aggravating the violence. It is less easy, however, to draw a line linking 9/11 with IM GLAD or Tumba Lata. Would these organizations have existed had 9/11 not happened? Hard to tell. IM GLAD grew out of the Mindanao People's Peace Movement (Tri-People's Peace Movement), which was founded in 1999, thus before 9/11. At the same time, the movement and the challenges it faced gathered momentum in the wake of 9/11. *Post hoc ergo propter hoc?*

Over the past couple of decades, particularly in the aftermath of 9/11, much has been made of transnational feminist organizing in the face of the combined forces of globalization, religious fundamentalism, and war (see Mohanty 2003; Moghadam 2005; Ferree and Tripp 2006; Cockburn 2007; Enloe 2007). Yet just as state structures come galloping back to assert themselves in our supposedly post-Westphalian world, even if they are frequently bankrolled and thus to some extent dictated to by other states, feminists' energy is drawn back to the state, back to local contexts, as my Mindanao vignettes illustrate. We can, after all, be in only one place at a time. When we do try to transnationalize our efforts, focusing on issues of common interest, nation-bound tears may often start to appear in our transnational fabric, as Valentine Moghadam observes with relation to the Association of Women of the Mediterranean Region, particularly in the immediate wake of 9/11 (2005, chap. 7). Even if we can often "see the whole picture," identifying the continuum between male domination and violence, war, and globalization (Enloe 2007; Cockburn 2012), it is difficult in an activist context to frame the picture with other than local materials. Our relationships with our local cultures and nations, however problematic, are going to be what primarily inform our responses to the post-9/11 "world."

Amid all the post-9/11 noise, to whom or what should we listen? How do we look beyond the showcases performed for the "internationals" or various agendas being pushed in the name of liberation or democracy or freedom or anti-imperialism or women's rights, security, dignity to understand the local dynamics and how they are being played out for often well-meaning transnational audiences? In the Philippines, for example, left-wing politics, including feminist politics, are traversed by the "RA versus RJ" split. The RAs are the "reaffirmationists" who remained faithful to the Communist Party of the Philippines, so called because of the party's document "Reaffirm our Basic Principles and Carry the Revolution Forward," written in 1991. The RJs are those who reject the politics and practices of the Communist Party leadership, including its alleged widespread extrajudicial killings. GABRIELA, one of the best-known and best-networked feminist groups internationally, is identified with the RA tendency, although local groups or individual members may not identify as such, whereas other groups, often less well known internationally, are RJs. In Mindanao, yet other divides operate as many voices clamor for the Moro microphone, yet it is often the Maranao elites who control the conversation.

Who is "representative," and how do we know? It is impossible to find any particular group or tendency or network that is going to "represent" women or even the much smaller subgroup of feminists. The Western Right's use of "native informants" to comfort its own ideological stances has been roundly criticized, the cases of Ayaan Ali Hirsi and Azar Nafisi being among the best known. Both are ambiguous figures who, although they have had legitimate criticisms of Islamic fundamentalism, have been discredited for some because of their association with the Western political Right. I would suggest, in fact, that the search for "representative" feminists is futile and arguably somewhat disingenuous at times. In particular, it can place an enormous weight on "informants" to embody their whole context, which is never possible.

It is, in the end, impossible to know exactly how 9/11 "shook the world" and what it changed, if anything, for women. It is equally impossible, however, to escape its symbolism. The day September 11, 2001, is perhaps to the twenty-first century what the Great War was to the twentieth: the moment after which nothing could ever be the same again in world politics. One thing, unfortunately, that we can count on is that such moments will always take the form of wars.

Amid the post-9/11ist noise, it takes a most singular feminist effort, at those intersections where we find ourselves, not only to become articulate talkers so as to be heard above the din but also to become very keen and careful listeners. Whatever form transnational feminist accountability should take, it necessarily starts with these basic elements of a meaningful conversation.

References | Index

References

Abbott, Lieutenant Colonel Philip K. 2004. "Terrorist Threat in the Tri-Border Area: Myth or Reality?" *Military Review*, Sept.–Oct., 51–55.

ABC Radio National. 2013. "The *Griffith Review* Turns 10." July 24. At http://www.abc.net.au/radionational/programs/booksandarts/the-griffith-review-turns-10/4839678. Accessed July 25, 2013.

Abramson, Kara. 2012. "Gender, Uyghur Identity, and the Story of Nuzugum." *Journal of Asian Studies* 71, no. 4: 1069–91.

African Commission for Human and People's Rights. 2010. *Factual Summary of Publicly Available Information on the U.S. Government's Extraordinary Rendition, Secret Detention, and Interrogation Program and Djibouti's Role in the Program.* Document forming part of Communication No. 383/2010 in the matter between Mohammed Abdullah Saleh al-Asad and Djibouti before the African Commission for Human & Peoples' Rights Forty-Ninth Ordinary Session, Apr.–May 2011. Available at the Global Justice Clinic and Interights website, http://chrgj.org/clinics/global-justice-clinic/national-security-counter-terrorism-and-human-rights/cia-rendition-secret-detention-and-torture/. Accessed Aug. 11, 2014.

———. 2011. *Communication No. 383/2010, in the Matter between Mohammed Abdullah Saleh Al-Asad and Djibouti: Factual Summary of Publicly Available Information on the U.S. Government's Extraordinary Rendition, Secret Detention, and Interrogation Program and Djibouti's Role in the Program.* At http://www.achpr.org/sessions/49th/. Accessed Jan. 17, 2012.

Al-e Ahmad, Jalal. 1982. *Plagued by the West (Gharbzadegi).* Translated by Paul Sprachman. Delmar, NY: Caravan Books.

———. 1983. *Weststruckness (Gharbzadegi).* Translated by John Green and Ahmad Alizadeh. Costa Mesa, CA: Mazda.

———. 1984. *Occidentosis: A Plague from the West (Gharbzadegi)*. Translated by R. Campbell. Berkeley, CA: Mizan Press.

Ahmed, Leila. 1992. *Women and Gender in Islam: Historical Roots of a Modern Debate*. New Haven, CT: Yale Univ. Press.

———. 2011. *A Quiet Revolution: The Veil's Resurgence, from the Middle East to America*. New Haven, CT: Yale Univ. Press.

AK Parti. 2012. "Political Vision of AK Parti 2023: Politics, Society, and the World." At http://www.akparti.org.tr/english/akparti/2023-political-vision. Accessed Mar. 15, 2015.

Alessio, Mark. n.d. "Sodomizing Jerusalem." *Remnant*. At http://remnant newspaper.com/Archives/sodomizing_jerusalem.htm. Accessed Mar. 20, 2015.

Alexander, Karen, and Mary E. Hawkesworth, eds. 2008. *War & Terror: Feminist Perspectives*. Chicago: Univ. of Chicago Press.

Al-Ali, Nadje. 2005. "Reconstructing Gender: Iraqi Women between Dictatorship, War, Sanctions, and Occupation." *Third World Quarterly* 26, nos. 4–5: 739–58.

———. 2007. *Iraqi Women: Untold Stories from 1948 to the Present*. London: Zed Books.

Ali, Saleem. 2015. "The Case for Japan to Play a Bigger Part in Global Affairs and Security." *The Conversation*, Feb. 18. At https://theconver sation.com/the-case-for-japan-to-play-a-bigger-part-in-global-affairs-and-security-37405. Accessed Mar. 26, 2015.

Altınay, Ayşe Gül, and Amy Holmes. 2009. "Opposition to the US Military Presence in Turkey in the Context of the Iraq War." In *The Bases of Empire: The Global Struggle against U.S. Military Posts*, edited by Catherine A. Lutz, 270–98. New York: New York Univ. Press.

Aly, Waleed. 2015. "The Fight That Goes Around in Circles." *Sydney Morning Herald*, Nov. 27.

Amnesty International. 2006. *USA: Below the Radar: Secret Flights to Torture and "Disappearance."* At https://www.amnesty.org/en/documents /AMR51/051/2006/en/. Accessed Jan. 17, 2015.

———. 2011. *The State of the World's Human Rights: Amnesty International Report 2011*. London: Amnesty International.

———. 2012. *Death Sentences and Executions 2011*. London: Amnesty International.

———. 2014. *Nowhere Safe: Civilians under Attack in South Sudan.* London: Amnesty International.

Anderson, Benedict. 1983. *Imagined Communities: Reflections on the Origin and Spread of Nationalism.* London: Verso.

Aoudé, Ibrahim G. 2013. "Egypt: Revolutionary Process and Global Capitalist Crisis." *Arab Studies Quarterly* 35, no. 3: 241–54.

Arieff, Alexis. 2011. *Political Transition in Tunisia.* Document RS21666. Washington, DC: Congressional Research Service.

Aristophanes. 411 BCE. *Lysistrata.* At https://www.gutenberg.org/files /7700/7700-h/7700-h.htm. Accessed May 28, 2011.

Asian Development Bank. 2009. *Poverty in the Philippines: Causes, Constraints, and Opportunities.* Manila: Asian Development Bank. At http://www .adb.org/sites/default/files/publication/27529/poverty-philippines -causes-constraints-opportunities.pdf. Accessed Nov. 21, 2015.

Aswad, Evelyn M. 2013. "To Ban or Not to Ban Blasphemous Videos." *Georgetown Journal of International Law* 44, no. 4: 1313–28.

Athwal, Harmit. 2015. "Asylum Seeker Death Toll Rising." Institute of Race Relations, July 30. At http://www.irr.org.uk/news/asylum-seeker-death -toll-rising/. Accessed Nov. 28, 2015.

Atwood, Margaret. 1985. *The Handmaid's Tale.* Toronto: McClelland & Stewart.

Audet, Elaine. 2015. "Journal d'une semaine de plomb." Sisyphe, Nov. 24. At http://sisyphe.org/spip.php?article5190. Accessed Nov. 29, 2015.

Auffray, Elodie. 2013. "Ces Ligues qui 'protègent' la révolution tunisienne." *Le Monde,* Jan. 14. At http://www.liberation.fr/monde/2013/01/14 /ces-ligues-qui-protegent-la-revolution-tunisienne_873949. Accessed Mar. 23, 2015.

Australian Red Cross. 2011. "A Lack of Access to Clean Water and Sanitation Is a Worldwide Killer Claiming Millions of Lives." Mar. 22. At http:// www.redcross.org.au/a-lack-of-access-to-clean-water-and-sanitation -is-a-worldwide-killer-claiming-millions-of-lives.aspx. Accessed Feb. 29, 2012.

Aykut, Dilek, and Andrea Goldstein. 2006. *Developing Country Multinationals: South–South Investment Comes of Age.* Development Centre Working Paper no. 257. Paris: Organization for Economic Cooperation and Development.

Babayan, Kathryn, and Afsaneh Najmabadi, eds. 2008. *Islamicate Sexualities: Translations across Temporal Geographies of Desire*. Cambridge, MA: Center for Middle Eastern Studies, Harvard Univ.

Bacchetta, Paola, and Margaret Power, eds. 2002. *Right-Wing Women: From Conservatives to Extremists around the World*. New York: Routledge.

Badescu, Cristina Gabriela. 2010. *Humanitarian Intervention and the Responsibility to Protect*. London: Routledge.

Baer, Madeline. 2008. "The Global Water Crisis, Privatization, and the Bolivian Water War." In *Water, Place, & Equity*, edited by John M. Whiteley, Helen Ingram, and Richard Warren Perry, 195–224. Cambridge, MA: MIT Press.

Baker, Joanne. 2008. "The Ideology of Choice: Overstating Progress and Hiding Injustice in the Lives of Young Women: Findings from a Study in North Queensland, Australia." *Women's Studies International Forum* 31, no. 1: 53–64.

Al-Banna, Hassan. [1936] 2011. "Fifty-Point Manifesto." At http://point debasculecanada.ca/the-50-point-manifesto-of-hassan-al-banna/. Accessed Sept. 26, 2016.

Barlow, Maude, and Tony Clarke. 2002. *Blue Gold: The Fight to Stop the Corporate Theft of the World's Water*. New York: New Press.

Baudelaire, Charles. 1861. *Les Fleurs du mal*. Paris: Auguste Pulet-Malassis. At https://fr.wikisource.org/wiki/Les_Fleurs_du_mal/Texte_entier. Accessed May 28, 2011.

Baudrillard, Jean. 1981. *Simulacres et simulation*. Paris: Galilée.

———. 1991. *La Guerre du Golfe n'a pas eu lieu*. Paris: Galilée.

Bauer, Peter. 2005. "US: Business Booming for U.S. Defense Contractors." Corporate Watch, Aug. 20. At http://www.corpwatch.org/article.php ?id=12661. Accessed Aug. 10, 2013.

Baum, Dalit. 2006. "Women in Black and Men in Pink: Protesting against the Israeli Occupation." *Social Identities* 12, no. 5: 563–74.

Baxter, Jenny, and Malcolm Downing. 2001. *The Day That Shook the World: Understanding September 11th*. Sydney: ABC Books.

BBC News. 2004. "Defence Deals Drive Boeing Profit." July 28. At http:// news.bbc.co.uk/1/hi/business/3934113.stm. Accessed Sept. 8, 2005.

———. 2015. "UN Climate Conference: Empty Shoes Replace Cancelled Paris March." Nov. 29. At http://www.bbc.com/news/science-environ ment-34957032. Accessed Nov. 30, 2015.

Beau, Nicolas. 2015. "Attentat du Bardo: La diplomatie française pro-Ennahdha a-t-elle joué avec le feu?" *Mondafrique*, Mar. 18. At http://mondafrique.com/lire/international/2015/03/18/lextreme-complaisance-de-la-diplomatie-francaise-pour-les-islamistes-dennah. Accessed Mar. 24, 2015.

Beauvoir, Simone de. 1949. *Le Deuxième sexe*. Paris: Gallimard.

Belasco, Amy. 2014. *The Cost of Iraq, Afghanistan, and Other Global War on Terror Operations since 9/11*. Washington, DC: Congressional Research Service.

Bellamy, Alex J. 2014. *The Responsibility to Protect: A Defence*. Oxford: Oxford Univ. Press.

Benabent, Juliette. 2015. "Jungle de Calais: L'état définitivement condamné à aménager le campement." *Télérama*, Nov. 24. At http://www.telerama.fr/monde/jungle-de-calais-l-etat-definitivement-condamne-a-amenager-le-campement,134696.php. Accessed Nov. 28, 2015.

Ben Daniel, Tallie. 2007. "Ani Geh Bisrael: Zionism and the Paradox of Gay Rights." Center for the Study of Women, Univ. of California, Los Angeles. At https://escholarship.org/uc/item/43s5k7nf. Accessed Mar. 20, 2015.

Benhabib, Seyla. 2002. *The Claims of Culture: Equality and Diversity in the Global Era*. Princeton, NJ: Princeton Univ. Press.

Benkirane, Abdelilah. 2013. "Moroccan MP: We Are Not Affiliated with the Muslim Brotherhood." Interview by al-Masry al-Youm. *Al Monitor*, Feb. 28. At http://www.al-monitor.com/pulse/tr/contents/articles/politics/2013/02/interview-morocco-mp-benkirane.html. Accessed Nov. 19, 2013.

Bergin, Kathleen A. 2008. "Witness: The Racialized Gender Implications of Katrina." In *Seeking Higher Ground: The Hurricane Katrina Crisis, Race, and Public Policy Reader*, edited by Manning Marable and Kristen Clarke, 173–90. New York: Palgrave Macmillan.

Berko, Anat. 2012. *The Smarter Bomb: Women and Children as Suicide Bombers*. Lanham, MD: Rowman and Littlefield.

Billard, C., and D. Billard. 2015. "#JeSuisMisogyne. Quelques souvenirs de deux soeurs qui ont du mal à être Charlie." *Les Mots Sont Importants*, Feb. 14. At http://lmsi.net/JeSuisMisogyne. Accessed Apr. 2, 2015.

Blake, Erin C. 1999. "Where Be '*Here Be Dragons*'? Ubi sunt '*Hic sunt dracones*'?" Maphist. At http://www.maphist.nl/extra/herebedragons.html. Accessed Feb. 15, 2010.

Bloomberg Business. 2015. "The 20 Fastest Growing Economies This Year." Feb. 26. At http://www.bloomberg.com/news/articles/2015-02-25 /the-20-fastest-growing-economies-this-year. Accessed Nov. 21, 2015.

Bobin, Fréderic. 2015. "En Tunisie, la contestation monte contre un projet de loi sur la 'réconciliation économique.'" *Le Monde*, Sept. 12. At http:// www.lemonde.fr/afrique/article/2015/09/12/en-tunisie-la-contesta tion-monte-contre-un-projet-de-loi-sur-la-reconciliation-economique _4754778_3212.html. Accessed Nov. 22, 2015.

———. 2016. "Un Gouvernement tunisien remanié pour dissiper le désen-chantement ambiant." *Le Monde*, Jan. 6. At http://www.lemonde.fr /afrique/article/2016/01/06/vaste-remaniement-du-gouvernement -tunisien_4842817_3212.html. Accessed Apr. 9, 2016.

Boeing. 2005. "Third-Quarter Earnings Release." At http://www.boeing .com/boeing/companyoffices/financial/quarterly.page. Accessed Aug. 18, 2014.

Bolton, Patrick, Xavier Freixas, and Joel Shapiro. 2012. "The Credit Ratings Game." *Journal of Finance* 67, no. 1: 85–111.

Bonzon, Ariane. 2011. "Turquie–Tunisie, la filiation de l'AKP." *Slate* (France), Feb. 3. At http://www.slate.fr/story/33527/turquie-tunisie -filiation-akp. Accessed Nov. 19, 2013.

Borelli, Sylvia. 2004. "The Rendition of Terrorist Suspects to the United States: Human Rights and the Limits of International Cooperation." In *Enforcing International Law Norms against Terrorism*, edited by An-drea Bianchi, with Yasmin Naqvi, 331–75. Oxford: Hart.

Boudet, Alexandre. 2015. "Ce que l'on sait des auteurs des attentats de Paris." *Huffington Post* (France), Nov. 14. At http://www.huffingtonpost .fr/2015/11/14/attentats-de-paris-ce-que-sait-auteurs-terroristes_n _8562610.html. Accessed Nov. 23, 2015.

Bourdieu, Pierre. 1980. *Le Sens pratique.* Paris: Editions de Minuit.

Bouteldja, Houria. 2015. "*Charlie Hebdo*: Du sacré des 'Damnés de la terre' et de sa profanation." Parti des Indigènes de la République, Jan. 26. At http://indigenes-republique.fr/charlie-hebdo-du-sacre-des-damnes-de -la-terre-et-de-sa-profanation/. Accessed Apr. 15, 2015.

———. 2016. *Les Blancs, les Juifs et nous: Vers une politique de l'amour révo-lutionnaire.* Paris: La Fabrique.

Bozdémir, Michel. 2007. *Turquie: Entre Islam et l'Europe.* Paris: Ellipses.

Brach, Juliane, and Markus Loewe. 2010. "The Global Financial Crisis and the Arab World: Impact, Reactions, and Consequences." *Mediterranean Politics* 15, no. 1: 45–71.

Brafman Kittner, Cristiana C. 2007. "The Role of Safe Havens in Islamist Terrorism." *Terrorism and Political Violence* 19, no. 3: 307–29.

Brisard, Jacques. 2015. "'Charlie Hebdo' attaqué: 'On s'attendait à un attentat dans un lieu symbolique.'" Interview by Violette Lazard. *Le Nouvel Observateur*, Jan. 7. At http://tempsreel.nouvelobs.com/charlie-hebdo/20150107.OBS9465/charlie-hebdo-attaque-on-s-attendait-a-un-attentat-dans-un-lieu-symbolique.html?xtor=RSS-25. Accessed Mar. 11, 2015.

Bush, George W. 2001a. "Address after the Terrorist Attacks in New York and Washington, September 11." At http://edition.cnn.com/2001/US/09/11/bush.speech.text/. Accessed Nov. 18, 2013.

———. 2001b. "Address to a Joint Session of Congress, September 20." At http://edition.cnn.com/2001/US/09/20/gen.bush.transcript/. Accessed Nov. 27, 2015.

———. 2001c. "Remarks by the President upon Arrival, the South Lawn, September 16." At http://georgewbush-whitehouse.archives.gov/news/releases/2001/09/20010916-2.html. Accessed Apr. 9, 2015.

Business Interview. 2011. "Ania Thiemann, Senior Economist, OECD, MENA Investment Programme." France 24 TV, Feb. 28. At http://www.france24.com/en/20110218-middle-east-north-africa-egypt-tunisia-algeria-economy-revolution-ania-thiemann-oecd/. Accessed Apr. 12, 2015.

Butler, Judith. 1997. *Excitable Speech: A Politics of the Performative*. London: Routledge.

Cabantous, Alain. 2015. *Histoire du blasphème en Occident: XVIᵉ–XIXᵉ siècle*. Paris: Albin Michel.

Campbell, Beatrix. 1987. *Iron Ladies: Why Do Women Vote Tory?* London: Virago.

Campbell, Delilah. 2015. "A Rock and a Hard Place." *Trouble and Strife*, Jan. 9. At http://www.troubleandstrife.org/2015/01/a-rock-and-a-hard-place/. Accessed Jan. 20, 2015.

Canlas, Jomar. 2015. "SC Halts GMA Plunder Trial." *Manila Times*, Oct. 20. At http://www.manilatimes.net/sc-halts-gma-plunder-trial/224823/. Accessed Nov. 21, 2015.

Caputi, Jane, and Diana E. H. Russell. 1992. "Femicide: Sexist Terrorism against Women." In *Femicide: The Politics of Woman Killing*, edited by Jill Radford and Diana E. H. Russell, 13–21. New York: Twayne.

Center for Reproductive Rights. 2000. *The Holy See at the United Nations: An Obstacle to Women's Reproductive Health and Rights*. New York: Center for Reproductive Rights. At http://reproductiverights.org/sites/default/fils/documents/pub_bp_holyseeattheun.pdf. Accessed Jan. 6, 2012.

Central Intelligence Agency (CIA). n.d. "North America: United States." In *The World Factbook*. Washington, DC: CIA. At https://www.cia.gov/library/publications/the-world-factbook/geos/us.html. Accessed Aug. 18, 2014.

Chaabane, Nadia. 2006. "Caricatures de Mahomet: Ça suffit, la complaisance et l'hypocrisie!" Sisyphe, Apr. 4. At http://sisyphe.org/spip.php ?article2288. Accessed Nov. 27, 2014.

Chafiq, Chahla. 1991. *La Femme et le retour de l'Islam: L'experience iranienne*. Paris: Le Félin.

Chalk, Peter. 2005. "Militant Islamic Extremism in Southeast Asia." In *Terrorism and Violence in Southeast Asia: Transnational Challenges to States and Regional Security*, edited by Paul J. Smith, 19–37. New York: M. E. Sharpe.

Channel 4 (United Kingdom). 2013. "Gulnaz: The Woman Forced to Marry Her Rapist." June 20. At http://www.channel4.com/news/gulnaz-afghan-rape-afghanistan-adultery-karzai. Accessed Mar. 21, 2015.

Charlesworth, Hilary, and Christine Chinkin. 2000. *The Boundaries of International Law: A Feminist Analysis*. Manchester, UK: Manchester Univ. Press.

Chetcuti, Natacha. 2013. "*La Vie d'Adèle*: Le lesbianisme à l'épreuve des classes sociales." *Huffington Post* (France), Oct. 17. At http://www.huffingtonpost.fr/natacha-chetcuti/-le-lesbianisme-a-lepreuve-des-classes-sociales_b_4107723.html. Accessed Oct. 23, 2013.

Chinese State Council. 2009. *Development and Progress in Xinjiang*. Government White Paper. Beijing: People's Republic of China. At http://www.gov.cn/english/official/2009-09/21/content_1422566.htm. Accessed Nov. 20, 2015.

Chomsky, Noam. 2011. *9-11: Was There an Alternative?* Crawley: Univ. of Western Australia.

Chothia, Farouk. 2015. "Islamic State Gains Libya Foothold." *BBC News Africa*, Feb. 24. At http://www.bbc.com/news/world-africa-31518698. Accessed Mar. 22, 2015.

CNN. 2010. "Serbia Gay Pride March Attacked with Bombs, Stones." Oct. 10. At http://edition.cnn.com/2010/WORLD/europe/10/10/serbia .gay.violence/. Accessed Sept. 26, 2016.

———. 2011. "Afghan Woman's Choice: 12 Years in Jail or Marry Her Rapist and Risk Death." Nov. 22. At http://edition.cnn.com/2011/11/22 /world/asia/afghanistan-rape/. Accessed Mar. 21, 2015.

———. 2013. "Guilty Verdict in Steubenville Rape Trial." Mar. 17. Transcript at http://edition.cnn.com/TRANSCRIPTS/1303/17/rs.01.html. Accessed Apr. 20, 2013.

Coady, Tony. 2002. "Terrorism, Just War, and Supreme Emergency." In *Terrorism and Justice: Moral Argument in a Threatened World*, edited by Tony Coady and Michael O'Keefe, 8–21. Melbourne: Melbourne Univ. Press.

Cobham, Alex. 2013. "Corrupting Perceptions: Why Transparency International's Flagship Corruption Index Falls Short." *Foreign Policy*, July 22. At http://foreignpolicy.com/2013/07/22/corrupting-perceptions/. Accessed Nov. 19, 2015.

Cockburn, Cynthia. 2007. *From Where We Stand: War, Women's Activism, and Feminist Analysis*. London: Zed Books.

———. 2010. "Gender Relations as Causal in Militarization and War." *International Feminist Journal of Politics* 12, no. 2: 139–57. DOI:10.1080/14616741003665169.

———. 2012. *Anti-militarism: Political and Gender Dynamics of Peace Movements*. Basingstoke, UK: Palgrave Macmillan.

Cohen, William S. 1997. *Report of the Quadrennial Defense Review*. Washington, DC: US Department of Defense. At http://www.dod.mil/pubs /qdr/index.html. Accessed Aug. 18, 2014.

Cohn, Carol. 2008. "Mainstreaming Gender in UN Security Policy: A Path to Political Transformation?" In *Global Governance: Feminist Perspectives*, edited by Shirin M. Rai and Georgina Waylen, 185–206. Basingstoke, UK: Palgrave Macmillan.

Conca, Ken. 2006. *Governing Water: Contentious Transnational Politics and Global Institution Building*. Cambridge, MA: MIT Press.

Conetta, Carl. 2010. *An Undisciplined Defense: Understanding the $2 Trillion Surge in US Defense Spending*. Project on Defense Alternatives Briefing Report no. 20. Cambridge, MA: Commonwealth Institute.

Conlon, Kevin, Greg Botelho, and Pamela Brown. 2015. "Source: Suspect Spoke of 'Baby Parts' after Planned Parenthood Shooting." CNN, Nov. 29. At http://edition.cnn.com/2015/11/28/us/colorado-planned-parenthood-shooting/. Accessed Nov. 29, 2015.

Connell, R. W. 1987. *Gender and Power: Society, the Person, and Sexual Politics*. Cambridge, UK: Polity Press.

———. 2005. *Southern Theory*. Sydney: Allen and Unwin.

Cordesman, Anthony H. 2009. *Iraq: Security Trends*. Washington, DC: Center for Strategic and International Studies. At https://www.csis.org/analysis/iraq-security-trends. Accessed Apr. 3, 2015.

Cornevin, Christophe. 2015. "Attentats de Paris: Le scénario bien préparé des frères Kouachi et d'Amedy Coulibaly." *Le Figaro*, Mar. 1. At http://www.lefigaro.fr/actualite-france/2015/03/01/01016-20150301ART FIG00151-attentats-de-paris-le-scenario-bien-prepare-des-freres-koua chi-et-d-amedy-coulibaly.php. Accessed Nov. 23, 2015.

Crenshaw, Kimberlé. 1989. "Demarginalizing the Intersection of Race and Sex: A Black Feminist Critique of Antidiscrimination Doctrine, Feminist Theory, and Antiracist Politics." *University of Chicago Legal Forum* 1989, art. 8:139–67.

———. 1991. "Mapping the Margins: Intersectionality, Identity Politics, and Violence against Women of Color." *Stanford Law Review* 43:1241–99.

Cross, Katherine. 2015. "Je ne suis pas Charlie: On the Charlie Hebdo Massacre and Duelling Extremisms." *Feministing*, Aug. 1. At http://feministing.com/2015/01/08/je-ne-suis-pas-charlie-on-the-charlie-hebdo-massacre-and-duelling-extremisms/. Accessed July 1, 2015.

Crotty, James. 2009. "Structural Causes of the Global Financial Crisis: A Critical Assessment of the 'New Financial Architecture.'" *Cambridge Journal of Economics* 33:563–80.

Cunliffe, Philip, ed. 2012. *Critical Perspectives on the Responsibility to Protect: Interrogating Theory and Practice*. London: Routledge.

Cyran, Olivier. 2013. "'Charlie Hebdo,' pas raciste? Si vous le dites . . . (Article 11)." Cercle des Volontaires, Dec. 5. At http://www.cercle desvolontaires.fr/2013/12/05/charlie-hebdo-pas-raciste-si-vous-le-dites-article11/. Accessed Mar. 10, 2015.

Dabashi, Hamid. 2005. *Theology of Discontent: The Ideological Foundations of the Islamic Revolution in Iran*. Piscataway, NJ: Transaction.

Dahbour, Omar. 2007. "Hegemony and Rights: On the Liberal Justification for Empire." In *Exceptional State: Contemporary U.S. Culture and the New Imperialism*, 105–30. Durham, NC: Duke Univ. Press.

Dahmani, Frida. 2015. "Tunisie: Sihem Ben Sedrine, femme de discorde." *Jeune Afrique*, Sept. 16. At http://www.jeuneafrique.com/mag/263992/politique/tunisie-sihem-ben-sedrine-femme-de-discorde/. Accessed Nov. 22, 2015.

Dakhli, Leyla. 2013. "Une Révolution trahie? Sur le soulèvement tunisien et la transition démocratique." *La Vie des Idées*, Feb. 19. At http://www.laviedesidees.fr/Une-revolution-trahie.html. Accessed July 30, 2013.

Davis, Tom, Harold Rogers, Christopher Shays, Henry Bonilla, Steve Buyer, Sue Myrick, Mac Thornberry, et al. 2006. *A Failure of Initiative: The Final Report of the Select Bipartisan Committee to Investigate the Preparation for and Response to Hurricane Katrina*. Report no. 109-377. Washington, DC: US Congress. At http://katrina.house.gov/full_katrina_report.htm. Accessed Nov. 21, 2015.

Delphy, Christine. 2002. "A War for Afghan Women?" In *September 11, 2001: Feminist Perspectives*, edited by Susan Hawthorne and Bronwyn Winter, 302–15. Melbourne: Spinifex.

DeNavas-Witt, Carmen, Bernadette D. Proctor, and Cheryl Hill Lee. 2005. *Income, Poverty, and Health Insurance Coverage in the United States: 2004*. Washington, DC: US Census Bureau. At https://www.census.gov/prod/2005pubs/p60-229.pdf. Accessed Mar. 15, 2006.

Department of Peace and Conflict Research, Uppsala University. n.d. "UCDP Datasets." At http://ucdp.uu.se/?id=1. Accessed Sept. 26, 2016.

Depasupil, William. 2016. "Palace Wants Bangsamoro Measure Passed in 2017." *Manila Times*, Aug. 17. At http://www.manilatimes.net/palace-wants-bangsamoro-measure-passed-in-2017/280584/. Accessed Oct. 2, 2016.

Diallo, Rokhaya. 2015. "A force de déni, la France a créé ses propres monstres." *Huffington Post* (France), Jan. 14. At http://www.huffingtonpost.fr/rokhaya-diallo/charlie-hebdo-terrorisme-islam_b_6468790.html. Accessed Mar. 4, 2015.

Dijstelbloem, Huub, and Albert Meijer, eds. 2011. *Migration and the New Technological Borders of Europe*. Basingstoke, UK: Palgrave Macmillan.

Ditmars, Hadani. 2015. "Iraqi Women: 'Things Were so Much Better Before.'" Al Jazeera, Mar. 8. At http://www.aljazeera.com/indepth/opin ion/2015/03/iraqi-women-150308055143624.html. Accessed Apr. 9, 2015.

Dombrowski, Peter. 2005. "The New Security Environment: Policy Implications." In *Guns and Butter: The Political Economy of International Security*, edited by Peter Dombrowski, 231–36. Boulder, CO: Lynne Rienner.

Dreyfus, Michel. 2009. *L'antisémitisme à gauche: Histoire d'un paradoxe*. Paris: Découverte.

Duggan, Lisa. 2002. "The New Homonormativity: The Sexual Politics of Neoliberalism." In *Materializing Democracy: Toward a Revitalized Cultural Politics*, edited by Russ Castronovo and Dana D. Nelson, 175–94. Durham, NC: Duke Univ. Press.

Dworkin, Andrea. 1983. *Right Wing Women*. New York: Perigee Books.

Dwyer, Arienne M. 2005. *The Xinjiang Conflict: Uyghur Identity, Language Policy, and Political Discourse*. Honolulu: East-West Center. At http:// www.eastwestcenter.org/publications/xinjiang-conflict-uyghur-iden tity-language-policy-and-political-discourse. Accessed Nov. 30, 2014.

Eager, Paige Whaley. 2008. *From Freedom Fighters to Terrorists: Women and Political Violence*. Aldershot, UK: Ashgate.

Économie et Statistique (Institut national de la statistique et des études éonomiques). 2013. Nos. 464, 465, 466.

Eisenstein, Zillah. 2007. *Sexual Decoys: Gender, Race, and War in Imperial Democracy*. Melbourne: Spinifex.

Eliakim, Philippe. 2015. "Le Vrai coût de l'immigration en France." *Capital*, Apr. 15. At http://www.capital.fr/enquetes/dossiers/le-vrai-cout -de-l-immigration-en-france-1030475#. Accessed Nov. 23, 2015.

Ellyat, Holly. 2013. "Can Turkey Become the China of Europe?" CNBC, Jan. 18. At http://www.cnbc.com/id/100390252#. Accessed Mar. 15, 2015.

Elmer, Charlotte. 2005. "Spotlight on US Troops in Paraguay." *BBC News*, Sept. 28. At http://news.bbc.co.uk/2/hi/americas/4289224.stm. Accessed Feb. 15, 2012.

El Saadawi, Nawal. 1980. *The Hidden Face of Eve*. London: Zed Books.

Elshtain, Jean Bethke. 2003. *Just War against Terror: The Burden of American Power in a Violent World*. New York: Basic Books.

———. 2007. "Terrorism." In *The Price of Peace: Just War in the Twenty-First Century*, edited by Charles Reed and David Ryall, 118–35. Cambridge: Cambridge Univ. Press.

El Yaakoubi, Aziz. 2013. "Morocco's King Names New Ministers, Islamists Lose Ground." Reuters, Oct. 10. At http://www.reuters.com/article/2013/10/10/us-morocco-politics-idUSBRE99910Z20131010. Accessed Nov. 19, 2013.

Enloe, Cynthia. 1983. *Does Khaki Become You?* Cambridge, MA: South End Press.

———. 1990. *Bananas, Beaches, and Bases: Making Feminist Sense of International Politics*. Berkeley: Univ. of California Press.

———. 1993. *The Morning After: Sexual Politics at the End of the Cold War*. Berkeley: Univ. of California Press.

———. 2000. *Maneuvers: The International Politics of Militarizing Women's Lives*. Berkeley: Univ. of California Press.

———. 2002. "Masculinity as a Foreign Policy Issue." In *September 11, 2001: Feminist Perspectives*, edited by Susan Hawthorne and Bronwyn Winter, 254–49. Melbourne: Spinifex.

———. 2004. *The Curious Feminist: Searching for Women in a New Age of Empire*. Berkeley: Univ. of California Press.

———. 2007. *Globalization and Militarism: Feminists Make the Link*. Lanham, MD: Rowman and Littlefield.

———. 2010. *Nimo's War, Emma's War: Making Feminist Sense of the Iraq War*. Berkeley: Univ. of California Press.

Enriquez, Jean. 2003. *Trafficking of Women and Children: Updates, Trends, and Challenges*. Manila: CATW-AP. At http://www.catw-ap.org/towc.htm. Accessed Aug. 13, 2005.

Esquivel, Adolfo Perez. 2004. "Con sofismas EE.UU: Busca apoderarse del acuífero guaraní en la triple frontera de Brasil, Argentina y Paraguay" (interview). *Rebelión*, Oct. 5. At http://www.rebelion.org/noticia.php?id=5589. Accessed Feb. 15, 2012.

European Commission. 2016. "Fact Sheet: EU Support in Response to the Syrian Crisis." Europa (European Union official website), Feb. 5. At http://europa.eu/rapid/press-release_MEMO-16-222_fr.htm. Accessed Mar. 30, 2016.

European Commission for Democracy through Law (Venice Commission). 2008. *Report on the Relationship between Freedom of Expression and*

Freedom of Religion: The Issue of Regulation and Prosecution of Blasphemy, Religious Insult, and Incitement to Religious Hatred. Document CDL-AD(2008)026. Strasbourg: Council of Europe.

European Union Agency for Fundamental Rights. 2014. *Violence against Women: An EU-wide Survey. Main Results Report.* Europa (European Union official website). At http://fra.europa.eu/en/publication/2014/violence-against-women-eu-wide-survey-main-results-report. Accessed Mar. 15, 2015.

Evans, Gareth. 2004. "The Impact of September 11 on Global Security." In *Regional Security in the Asia-Pacific: 9/11 and After,* edited by Marika Vicziany, David Wright-Neville, and Pete Lentini, 30–39. Cheltenham, UK: Edward Elgar.

Falquet, Jules. 2008. *De gré ou de force: Les femmes dans la mondialisation.* Paris: La Dispute.

———. 2014. "Des assassinats de Ciudad Juárez au phénomène des féminicides: De nouvelles formes de violences contre les femmes?" *Contretemps,* Oct. 1. At http://www.contretemps.eu/interventions/assassinats-ciudad-juárez-phénomène-féminicides-nouvelles-formes-violences-contre-femm. Accessed Mar. 18, 2015.

Fanon, Frantz. 1961. *Les Damnés de la terre.* Paris: Maspero.

Farr, Vanessa, Henri Myrttinen, and Albrecht Schnabel, eds. 2009. *Sexed Pistols: The Gendered Impacts of Small Arms & Light Weapons.* Tokyo: United Nations Univ. Press.

Favret-Saada, Jeanne. 1992. "Rushdie et compagnie: Préalables à une anthropologie du blasphème." *Ethnologie française* 22, no. 3: 251–60.

Feenan, Dermot. 2006. "Religious Vilification Laws: Quelling Fires of Hatred?" *Alternative Law Journal* 31, no. 3: 153–58.

Ferguson, Sarah. 2015. "Hitting Home: The Hard Truth about Australia's Domestic Violence Crime Wave." *ABC News: The Drum,* Nov. 26. At http://www.abc.net.au/news/2015-11-24/ferguson-australia's-domestic-violence-crime-wave/6970460. Accessed Nov. 29, 2015.

Ferree, Myra Marx, and Aili Mari Tripp, eds. 2006. *Global Feminism: Transnational Women's Activism, Organizing, and Human Rights.* New York: New York Univ. Press.

Le Figaro. 2014. "Une Ex-Femen condamnée pour 'exhibition sexuelle.'" Dec. 17. At http://www.lefigaro.fr/actualite-france/2014/12/17/01016

-20141217ARTFIG00257-une-ex-femen-condamnee-pour-exhibition -sexuelle-a-l8216eglise-de-la-madeleine.php. Accessed Nov. 20, 2015.

Finlay, Barbara. 2006. *George W. Bush and the War on Women: Turning Back the Clock on Progress.* London: Zed Books.

Finley, Joanne Smith, and Xiaowei Zang. 2015. *Language, Education, and Uyghur Identity in Urban Xinjiang.* London: Routledge.

Flaubert, Gustave. 1857. *Madame Bovary.* Paris: Michel Lévy Frères. At http://flaubert.univ-rouen.fr/bovary/bovary_6/doc0/roman.html. Accessed Mar. 10, 2012.

Fleishman, Rishona. 2000. "The Battle against Reproductive Rights: The Impact of the Catholic Church on Abortion Law in Both International and Domestic Arenas." *Emory International Law Review* 14:277–314.

Fourest, Caroline. 2015. *Eloge du blasphème.* Paris: Grasset.

FranceTVInfo. 2015. "25 actes islamophobes recensés en France depuis les attentats de Paris, selon le CFCM." Franceinfo, Nov. 17. At http://www.francetvinfo.fr/faits-divers/terrorisme/attaques-du-13-novembre-a-paris/plusieurs-actes-islamophobes-recenses-en-france-depuis-les-attentats-de-paris_1179565.html. Accessed Nov. 28, 2015.

Fraser, Nancy. 2007. "Transnationalising the Public Sphere: On the Legitimacy and Efficacy of Public Opinion in a Post Westphalian World." *Theory, Culture, and Society* 24, no. 4: 7–30.

Fregoso, Rosa-Linda, and Cynthia Bejarano, eds. 2010. *Terrorizing Women: Feminicide in the Americas.* Durham, NC: Duke Univ. Press.

Froman, Michael B. G. 2015. *2015 Special 301 Report.* Washington, DC: Executive Office of the President of the United States. At https://ustr.gov/about-us/policy-offices/press-office/press-releases/2015/april/ustr-releases-annual-special-301. Accessed Nov. 21, 2015.

Froude, James Anthony. [1886] 2010. *Oceana, or England and Her Colonies.* Cambridge: Cambridge Univ. Press.

Frymer, Paul, Dara Z. Strolovitch, and Dorian T. Warren. 2006. "New Orleans Is Not the Exception: Re-politicizing the Study of Racial Inequality." *Du Bois Review* 3, no. 1: 37–57.

Gadian, Mary Nancy P. 2009. "Affidavit, Quezon City, Philippines, Aug. 26. Presented before the Legislative Oversight Committee on the Visiting Forces Agreement, Philippine Senate, Aug. 27, 2009." At https://

fr.scribd.com/document/40149967/Nancy-Gadian-Affidavit. Accessed Sept. 26, 2016.

Gardam, Judith. 2005. "Women and Armed Conflict: The Response of International Humanitarian Law." In *Listening to the Silences: Women and War*, edited by Helen Durham and Tracey Gurd, 109–23. Leiden: Martinus Nijhoff.

George, Susan. 1999. *The Lugano Report: On Preserving Capitalism in the Twenty-First Century*. London: Pluto Press.

Gerson, Allan, and Nat J. Colletta. 2002. *Privatizing Peace: From Conflict to Security*. Ardsley, NY: Transnational.

Ghanea, Nazila. 2007. "'Phobias' and 'Isms': Recognition of Difference or the Slippery Slope of Particularisms?" In *Does God Believe in Human Rights? Essays on Religion and Human Rights*, edited by Nazila Ghanea, Alan Stephens, and Raphael Walden, 211–32. Leiden: Martinus Nijhoff.

Ghorbal, Samy. 2015. "Tunisie—Mohsen Marzouk: 'La crédibilité de l'Instance vérité et dignité est entamée.'" *Jeune Afrique*, Sept. 3. At http://www.jeuneafrique.com/261909/politique/tunisie-mohsen-marzouk-la-credibilite-de-linstance-verite-et-dignite-est-entamee/. Accessed Nov. 22, 2015.

Glaeser, Edward L. 2009. "The Political Economy of Warfare." In *Guns and Butter: The Economic Causes and Consequences of Conflict*, edited by Gregory D. Hess, 33–74. Cambridge, MA: MIT Press.

Global Network of Women Peacebuilders (GNWP). 2013. *Women Count: Security Council Resolution 1325: Civil Society Monitoring Report 2013*. New York: GNWP. At http://www.peacewomen.org/portal_resources_resource.php?id=1986. Accessed Aug. 17, 2014.

Global Security. 2011. "Dr. Luis Maria Argana International Airport, Mariscal Estigarribia, Paraguay." GlobalSecurity.org. At http://www.globalsecurity.org/military/facility/mariscal-estigarribia.htm. Last updated May 7, 2011. Accessed Feb. 23, 2012.

Goldberg, Eleanor. 2014. "10 Things You Didn't Know about Slavery, Human Trafficking (and What You Can Do about It)." *Huffington Post*, Jan. 16. At http://www.huffingtonpost.com.au/2014/01/15/human-trafficking-month_n_4590587.html?ir=Australia. Accessed Nov. 29, 2015.

Goodall, Kay. 2007. "Incitement to Religious Hatred: All Talk and No Substance?" *Modern Law Review* 70, no. 1: 89–113.

Goodstein, Laurie, and Greg Myre. 2005. "Clerics Fighting a Gay Festival for Jerusalem." *New York Times*, Mar. 31. At http://www.nytimes.com/2005/03/31/international/worldspecial/31gay.html. Accessed Mar. 20, 2015.

Grant, Rebecca. 1992. "The Quagmire of Gender and International Security." In *Gendered States: Feminist (Re)Visions of International Relations Theory*, edited by V. Spike Peterson, 83–98. Boulder, CO: Lynne Rienner.

Grant, Thomas. 1999. "Defining Statehood: The Montevideo Convention and Its Discontents." *Columbia Journal of Transnational Law* 37:403–57.

Granta. 2002. "What We Think of America." Special issue, no. 77.

Greenberg, Joel. 2005. "Opposition to Gay Pride Event in Holy City Unites Diverse Faiths." *Chicago Tribune*, Mar. 31. At http://articles.chicagotribune.com/2005-03-31/news/0503310317_1_gay-pride-gay-gathering-jerusalem. Accessed Mar. 20, 2015.

Griffith Review. 2003. "Insecurity in the New World Order." Special issue, no. 1.

———. 2013. "Now We Are Ten." Special issue, no. 41.

Guardian, The. 2010. "Benigno Aquino Vows to End Corruption in the Philippines." Associated Press, July 1. At http://www.theguardian.com/world/2010/jun/30/benigno-aquino-philippines-president1. Accessed Nov. 21, 2015.

Guénif-Soulimas, Nacira. 2014. "Le Nombre de musulmans surévalué par les Français: L'idéologie raciste fait son chemin." *Le Nouvel Observateur* (*L'Obs Plus*), Oct. 30. At http://leplus.nouvelobs.com/contribution/1267442-le-nombre-de-musulmans-surevalue-par-les-francais-l-ideologie-raciste-fait-son-chemin.html. Accessed Nov. 28, 2015.

Guénif-Soulimas, Nacira, and Eric Macé. 2004. *Les Féministes et le garçon arabe*. La Tour d'Aigues, France: Editions de l'Aube.

Guibert, Nathalie. 2015. "Ruée des jeunes Français vers les armées." *Le Monde*, Nov. 19. At http://www.lemonde.fr/attaques-a-paris/article/2015/11/19/ruee-des-jeunes-francais-vers-les-armees_4813438_4809495.html. Accessed Nov. 28, 2015.

Guillaumin, Colette. [1990] 1992a. "Folie et norme sociale: A propos de l'attentat du 6 décembre 1989." In *Sexe, race et pratique du pouvoir: L'idée de nature*, 143–49. Paris: Côté-femmes.

———. [1978] 1992b. "Pratique du pouvoir et idée de Nature." In *Sexe, race et pratique du pouvoir: L'idée de nature*, 15–82. Paris: Côté-femmes.

Gutteridge, Clara. 2012. *Declaration*. Document forming part of Communication No. 383/2010 in the matter between Mohammed Abdullah Saleh Al-Asad and Djibouti before the African Commission for Human & Peoples' Rights, Fifty-Second Ordinary Session. Formerly at the African Commission for Human and People's Rights website at http://achpr.org, but no longer available. Accessed Aug. 11, 2014.

Habermas, Jürgen. 2001. "Faith and Knowledge: An Opening Speech by Jürgen Habermas Accepting the Peace Prize of the German Publishers and Booksellers Association." Paulskirche, Frankfurt, Oct. 14. Translated by Kermit Snelson. *Sueddeutsche Zeitung*, Oct. 15. At http://www.sueddeutsche.de/aktuell/sz/artikel86740.php. Accessed Jan. 15, 2011.

———. 2006. "On the Relations between the Secular Liberal State and Religion." In *Political Theologies: Public Religions in a Post-Secular World*, edited by Hent de Vries and Lawrence E. Sullivan, 251–60. New York: Fordham Univ. Press.

———. 2007. "An Awareness of What Is Missing." Translated by Ciaran Cronin. In Jürgen Habermas et al., *An Awareness of What Is Missing: Faith and Reason in a Post-secular Age*, 15–23. Cambridge, UK: Polity.

Habib, Samar, ed. 2010. *Islam and Homosexuality*. Santa Barbara, CA: Praeger.

Haddar, Mohamed. 2013. *Les Défis de la transition*. Tunis: ASECTU, PS2D, Université Tunis, El Manar, United Nations Development Program. At http://www.asectu.org/Documents/PDF/LES%20DEFIS%20DE%20LA%20TRANSITION.pdf. Accessed May 15, 2014.

Hage, Ghassan. 2003a. *Against Paranoid Nationalism: Searching for Hope in a Shrinking Society*. Melbourne: Pluto Press.

———. 2003b. "'Comes a Time We Are All Enthusiasm': Understanding Palestinian Suicide Bombers in Times of Exighophobia." *Public Culture* 15, no. 1: 65–98.

Hall, Radclyffe. 1928. *The Well of Loneliness*. London: Jonathan Cape. At http://gutenberg.net.au/ebooks06/0609021.txt. Accessed Mar. 3, 2012.

Hamad, Ruby. 2015. "Paris Attacks: Is Solidarity for White Terror Victims Only?" *Sydney Morning Herald*, Nov. 15. At http://www.dailylife.com.au/news-and-views/dl-opinion/paris-attacks-is-solidarity-for-white-terror-victims-only-20151115-gkzci8.html. Accessed Nov. 16, 2015.

Hartley, Keith. 2011. *The Economics of Defence Policy: A New Perspective.* London: Routledge.

Harville, Emily W., Catherine A. Taylor, Helen Tesfai, Xu Xiong, and Pierre Buekens. 2010. "Experience of Hurricane Katrina and Reported Intimate Partner Violence." *Journal of Interpersonal Violence* 26, no. 4: 833–45.

Hawthorne, Susan. 2002. *Wild Politics: Feminism, Globalisation, and Bio/diversity.* Melbourne: Spinifex.

———. 2005. *The Butterfly Effect.* Melbourne: Spinifex.

———. 2006. "Ancient Hatred and Its Contemporary Manifestations: The Torture of Lesbians." *Journal of Hate Studies* 4, no. 1: 33–58.

Hawthorne, Susan, and Bronwyn Winter, eds. 2002. *September 11, 2001: Feminist Perspectives.* Melbourne: Spinifex.

Hearn, Kelly. 2006. "Conspiracists Allege U.S. Seizing Vast S. American Reservoir." *National Geographic News*, Aug. 28. At http://news.national geographic.com/news/2006/08/060828-guarani.html. Accessed Feb. 12, 2012.

Hehir, Aidan. 2012. *The Responsibility to Protect: Rhetoric, Reality, and the Future of Humanitarian Intervention.* Basingstoke, UK: Palgrave Macmillan.

Hélie-Lucas, Marie-Aimée (Marième). [1987] 1990. "Women, Nationalism, and Religion in the Algerian Liberation Struggle." In *Opening the Gates: A Century of Arab Feminist Writing*, edited by Margot Badran and Miriam Cooke, 104–14. London: Virago.

Hendrickson, Dylan, and Andrzej Karkoszka. 2005. "Security Sector Reform and Donor Policies." In *Security Sector Reform and Post-conflict Peacebuilding*, edited by Albrecht Schnabel and Hans-Georg Ehrhart, 19–44. Tokyo: United Nations Univ. Press.

Heng, Yee-Kuang. 2006. *War as Risk Management: Strategy and Conflict in an Age of Globalised Risks.* London: Routledge.

Hilsdon, Anne-Marie. 2009. "Invisible Bodies: Gender, Conflict, and Peace in Mindanao." *Asian Studies Review* 33, no. 3: 349–65.

Hollande, François. 2015a. "Discours du président de la République devant le Parlement réuni en Congrès." Versailles, Nov. 16. At http://www .elysee.fr/declarations/article/discours-du-president-de-la-republique -devant-le-parlement-reuni-en-congres-3/. Accessed Nov. 18, 2015.

———. 2015b. "Hommage aux 130 victimes des attentats du 13 novembre." Cour des Invalides, Paris, Nov. 27. At http://www.slate.fr/story

/110717/hommage-national-texte-discours-francois-hollande. Accessed Nov. 28, 2015.

Houellebecq, Michel. 2015. *Soumission*. Paris: Flammarion.

Howard, Rhoda E. 1995. *Human Rights and the Search for Community*. Boulder, CO: Westview Press.

Hudson, Natalie Florea. 2010. *Gender, Human Security, and the United Nations: Security Language as a Political Framework for Women*. London: Routledge.

Hudson, Rex. 2003. *Terrorist and Organized Crime Groups in the Tri-Border Area (TBA) of South America*. Washington, DC: Federal Research Division, Library of Congress.

Huffington Post (France). 2015. "Victimes de l'attentat à *Charlie Hebdo*: Qui sont les 12 personnes tuées." Jan. 8. At http://www.huffingtonpost .fr/2015/01/08/victimes-charlie-hebdo_n_6434150.html. Accessed Mar. 11, 2015.

Human Rights Watch. 2003. *Climate of Fear: Sexual Violence and Abduction of Women and Girls in Baghdad*. Washington, DC: Human Rights Watch. At http://www.hrw.org/reports/2003/iraq0703/iraq0703.pdf. Accessed July 14, 2013.

———. 2009. *"They Want Us Exterminated": Murder, Torture, Sexual Orientation, and Gender in Iraq*. Aug. 17. At https://www.hrw.org/report /2009/08/17/they-want-us-exterminated/murder-torture-sexual-ori entation-and-gender-iraq. Accessed Nov. 30, 2015.

———. 2013. *Submission on the Combined Initial and Second Periodic Report of Afghanistan to the United Nations Committee on the Elimination of Discrimination against Women*. July 4. At http://www.hrw.org /news/2013/07/04/submission-combined-initial-and-second-periodic -report-afghanistan-united-nations-co. Accessed July 11, 2013.

Huntington, Samuel P. 1993. "The Clash of Civilizations?" *Foreign Affairs* 72, no. 3: 22–49.

———. 1996. *The Clash of Civilizations and the Remaking of World Order*. New York: Simon & Schuster.

Hurriyet Daily News. 2014. "Women Should Not Laugh in Public, Turkish Deputy PM Says." July 29. At http://www.hurriyetdailynews.com /women-should-not-laugh-in-public-turkish-deputy-pm-says-.aspx?page ID=238&nID=69732&NewsCatID=338. Accessed July 29, 2014.

———. 2015a. "Turkey Slams European Parliament's Call to Recognize 'Armenian Genocide.'" Mar. 14. At http://www.hurriyetdailynews.com /turkey-slams-european-parliaments-call-to-recognize-armenian-geno cide.aspx?PageID=238&NID=79678&NewsCatID=510. Accessed Mar. 20, 2015.

———. 2015b. "Turkish President Erdoğan Slams Women Protesting Özgecan's Murder by Dancing." Feb. 16. At http://www.hurriyetdaily news.com/turkish-president-erdogan-slams-women-protesting-ozgecans -murder-by-dancing-.aspx?pageID=238&nID=78423&NewsCatID =338. Accessed Apr. 12, 2015.

International Atomic Energy Agency. n.d. "Transboundary aquifers and River Basins: Guaraní Aquifer System." At http://www-naweb.iaea.org /napc/ih/documents/factsheetsPosters/Guarani%20-%20Transbound ary%20Aquifers%20and%20Rivers%20Basins.pdf. Accessed Feb. 23, 2012.

International Gay and Lesbian Human Rights Commission (IGLHRC). 2006. "Iraq: IGLHRC Calls for Immediate Investigation into Reports of Gay Iraqis Targeted for Violence, Kidnappings, and Murder." Press release, Apr. 20. At http://www.iglhrc.org/content/iraq-iglhrc-calls -immediate-investigation-reports-gay-iraqis-targeted-violence-kidnap pings. Accessed July 16, 2013.

International Peace Bureau. 2002. *The Military's Impact on the Environment: A Neglected Aspect of the Sustainable Development Debate. A Briefing Paper for States and Non-governmental Organisations.* Geneva: International Peace Bureau.

Itani, Faysal. 2014. "We Must Treat ISIS Like a State to Defeat It." *Time*, Aug. 14. At http://time.com/3111276/isis-terror-iraq-treat-it-like-a-state/. Accessed Mar. 14, 2015.

Jackson, Stevi. 1999. *Heterosexuality in Question.* London: Sage.

Jakarta Post. 2015. "Indonesia Jails Uighur over Attempt to Join Militants." July 29. At http://www.thejakartapost.com/news/2015/07/29/indo nesia-jails-uighur-over-attempt-join-militants.html. Accessed Nov. 20, 2015.

Jansen, Sabine, and Thomas Spijkerboer. 2011. *Fleeing Homophobia: Asylum Claims Related to Sexual Orientation and Gender Identity in Europe.* Amsterdam: COC Nederland and Vrije Univ. Amsterdam.

Al Jazeera America. 2015. "Uyghurs Flee Turkey for China in Search of Peace." Feb. 3. At http://america.aljazeera.com/articles/2015/2/3/Uighurs-flee-China-for-Turkey-in-search-of-peace.html. Accessed Nov. 20, 2015.

Jenkins, Pamela, and Brenda Phillips. 2008. "Domestic Violence and Hurricane Katrina." In *Katrina and the Women of New Orleans,* edited by Beth Willinger, 65–69. New Orleans: Newcomb College Center for Research on Women, Tulane Univ.

Joffrin, Laurent. 2015. "'Soumission,' Le Pen au Flore." *Libération,* Jan. 2. At http://www.liberation.fr/livres/2015/01/02/le-pen-au-flore_1173182. Accessed Mar. 12, 2015.

Johnson, Larry D. 2014. "'Uniting for Peace': Does It Still Serve Any Useful Purpose?" *AJIL Unbound* (American Society of International Law), July 15. At https://www.asil.org/blogs/%E2%80%9Cuniting-peace%E2%80%9D-does-it-still-serve-any-useful-purpose. Accessed Nov. 20, 2015.

Jolly, Margaret. 2007. "Imagining Oceania: Indigenous and Foreign Representations of a Sea of Islands." *Contemporary Pacific* 19, no. 2: 508–45.

———. 2008. "The South in *Southern Theory*: Antipodean Reflections on the Pacific." *Australian Humanities Review* 44 (Mar.). At http://www.australianhumanitiesreview.org/archive/Issue-Mar.-2008/jolly.html. Accessed Dec. 20, 2011.

Jones, Kathleen B. 1993. *Compassionate Authority.* London: Routledge.

Joya, Malalai. 2009. *Raising My Voice.* Sydney: Pan Macmillan Australia.

Kadeer, Rebiya. 2011. "Uyghur Women and Human Rights." Speech delivered at the fourth session of the United Nations Forum on Minority Issues, Geneva, Nov. 29–30. At http://www.uyghurcongress.org/en/?p=12588. Accessed Mar. 13, 2015.

Kaldor, Mary. 2003. *Global Civil Society: An Answer to War.* Cambridge, MA: Polity Press.

———. 2007a. "From Just War to Just Peace." In *The Price of Peace: Just War in the Twenty-First Century,* edited by Charles Reed and David Ryall, 255–74. Cambridge: Cambridge Univ. Press.

———. 2007b. *Human Security: Reflections on Globalization and Intervention.* Cambridge, MA: Polity Press.

Keating, Christine (Cricket). 2013. "Conclusion." In *Global Homophobia: States, Movements, and the Politics of Oppression,* edited by Meredith L. Weiss and Michael J. Bosia, 246–54. Champaign: Univ. of Illinois Press.

Khan, Shahnaz. 2008. "Afghan Women: The Limits of Colonial Rescue." In *Feminism and War: Confronting U.S. Imperialism*, edited by Robin L. Riley, Chandra Talpade Mohanty, and Minnie Bruce Pratt, 161–78. London: Zed Books.

Kilinç, Ramazan. 2009. "Turkey and the Alliance of Civilizations: Norm Adoption as a Survival Strategy." *Insight Turkey* 11, no. 3: 57–75.

Klein, Naomi. 2007. *The Shock Doctrine: The Rise of Disaster Capitalism.* London: Allen Lane.

Korol, Claudia. 2004. "La Triple Frontera vive bajo vigilancia de EE.UU." Unión Internacional de Trabajadores de Alimentación, July 7. At http://www.rel-uita.org/internacional/triple-frontera.htm. Accessed Feb. 15, 2012.

Koziol, Michael. 2015. "Charlie Hebdo Survivor Simon Fieschi Marries Australian Girlfriend Maisie Dubosarsky in Paris." *Sydney Morning Herald*, Oct. 3. At http://www.smh.com.au/national/charlie-hebdo-survivor-simon-fieschi-marries-australian-girlfriend-maisie-dubosarsky-in-paris-20151002-gjzrub.html. Accessed Nov. 27, 2015.

Kugle, Scott, and Siraj al-Haqq. 2013. *Living Out Islam: Voices of Gay, Lesbian, and Transgender Muslims.* New York: New York Univ. Press.

Kuzu, Durukan. 2015. "Paris Attacks: Closing Migration Routes into France Won't Stop Terrorism—Resisting Xenophobia Might." *The Conversation*, Nov. 16. At https://theconversation.com/paris-attacks-closing-migration-routes-into-france-wont-stop-terrorism-resisting-xenophobia-might-50725. Accessed Nov. 28, 2015.

Lachheb, Monia. 2015. "'Chouf' ou l'émergence d'une lutte lesbienne en Tunisie." Paper presented at the Congrès international de recherches féministes francophones, Montréal, Aug. 25.

Lacsamana, Anne E. 2012. *Revolutionizing Feminism: The Philippine Women's Movement in the Age of Terror.* Boulder, CO: Paradigm.

Lake, Marilyn, and Henry Reynolds, eds. 2010. *What's Wrong with ANZAC? The Militarisation of Australian History.* Sydney: Univ. of New South Wales Press.

Lakhdar, Latifa. 2007. *Les Femmes au miroir de l'orthodoxie Islamique.* Translated from Arabic by Hichem Abdessamad. La Tour d'Aigues: Editions de l'Aube.

Lallemand, Alain. 2007. "Profiteering on Location: Djibouti's Repressive Regime, Not Its People, Has Prospered since 9/11." Center for Public

Integrity, May 22. At https://www.publicintegrity.org/2007/05/22/5741/profiteering-location. Accessed Jan. 14, 2012.

Lamloum, Olfa. 2001. "La Tunisie après le 11 septembre." *Confluences Méditerranée* 40:171–78.

Lasky, Marjorie P., with Medea Benjamin and Andrea Buffa. n.d. *Iraqi Women under Siege*. Washington, DC: Codepink, Women for Peace.

Le Doaré, Christine. 2015. "Je suis féministe, je suis Charlie." *Irréductiblement Féministe*, blog, Jan. 12. At https://christineld75.wordpress.com/2015/01/12/je-suis-feministe-je-suis-charlie/. Accessed Mar. 13, 2015.

Lejeune, Geoffroy. 2013. "Sondage exclusif: L'immigration n'est pas une chance pour la France." *Valeurs Actuelles*, Nov. 13. At http://www.valeursactuelles.com/politique/sondage-exclusif-limmigration-nest-pas-une-chance-pour-la-france-41964. Accessed July 10, 2015.

Libération. 2015a. "à Tunis, 'il faut éliminer Ennahda!'" July 26. At http://www.liberation.fr/planete/2013/07/26/rues-desertes-a-tunis-en-greve-generale_920972. Accessed Nov. 22, 2015.

———. 2015b. "Une Série d'actes islamophobes après les attentats." *Libération*, Nov. 16. At http://www.liberation.fr/france/2015/11/16/une-serie-d-actes-islamophobes-apres-les-attentats_1413820. Accessed Nov. 28, 2015.

Lindsay-Poland, John. 2009. "U.S. Military Bases in Latin America and the Caribbean." In *The Bases of Empire: The Global Struggle against U.S. Military Posts*, edited by Catherine A. Lutz, 71–95. New York: New York Univ. Press.

Long, Kristi S. 1996. *We All Fought for Freedom: Women in Poland's Solidarity Movement*. Boulder, CO: Westview Press.

Lum, Thomas. 2008. *U.S. Foreign Aid to East and South Asia: Selected Recipients*. Washington, DC: Congressional Research Service.

Lutz, Catherine A., ed. 2009. *The Bases of Empire: The Global Struggle against U.S. Military Posts*. New York: New York Univ. Press.

Lynch, Marc. 2011. "Obama's 'Arab Spring'?" *Foreign Policy*, Jan. 6. At http://foreignpolicy.com/2011/01/06/obamas-arab-spring/. Accessed Mar. 21, 2015.

Lyon, David. 2003. *Surveillance after September 11*. Cambridge, UK: Polity.

MacFarlane, S. Neil, and Yuen Foong Khong. 2006. *Human Security and the UN: A Critical History*. Bloomington: Indiana Univ. Press.

MacKinnon, Catharine A. [1993] 1994. *Only Words*. New York: Harper Collins.

———. 2002. "State of Emergency." In *September 11, 2001: Feminist Perspectives*, edited by Susan Hawthorne and Bronwyn Winter, 426–31. Melbourne: Spinifex.

Maddox, Marion. 2005. *God under Howard: The Rise of the Religious Right in Australian Politics*. Sydney: Allen & Unwin.

Maghreb-Machrek. 2011. "Al-Qaïda au Maghreb islamique: Les suites des révolutions arabes." Special issue, 208 (Summer).

Mahmood, Saba. 2005. *Politics of Piety: The Islamic Revival and the Feminist Subject*. Princeton, NJ: Princeton Univ. Press.

Makinda, Samuel. 2009. "Contesting Sovereignty." In *The Ethics of Global Governance*, edited by Antonio Franceschet, 21–34. Boulder, CO: Lynne Rienner.

Manjoo, Rashida. 2015. *Report of the Special Rapporteur on Violence against Women, Its Causes, and Consequences. Addendum: Mission to Afghanistan*. UN Document A/HRC/29/27/Add.3. Geneva: UN Office of the High Commissioner for Human Rights.

Mann, Carol. 2010. *Femmes afghanes en guerre*. Bellecombe-en-Bauge, France: Editions du Croquant.

———. 2012. "The Afghan State and the Issue of Sexual Violence against Women." In *Conflict-Related Sexual Violence: International Law, Local Responses*, edited by Tonia St. Germain and Susan Dewey, 123–40. Sterling, VA: Kumarian Press.

Manyin, Mark E., Steven Daggett, Ben Dolven, Susan V. Lawrence, Michael E. Martin, Ronald O'Rourke, and Bruce Vaughn. 2012. *Pivot to the Pacific? The Obama Administration's "Rebalancing" toward Asia*. Washington, DC: Congressional Research Service. At https://www.fas.org/sgp/crs/natsec/R42448.pdf. Accessed Nov. 21, 2015.

Mark, Clyde R. 2005a. *Israel: US Foreign Assistance*. Issue Brief. Washington, DC: Congressional Research Service.

———. 2005b. *United States Aid to the Palestinians*. Washington, DC: Congressional Research Service.

Maroh, Julie. 2010. *Le Bleu est une couleur chaude*. Paris: Glénat.

Martin, Andrew, and Patrice Petro, eds. 2006. *Rethinking Global Security: Media, Popular Culture, and the "War on Terror."* New Brunswick, NJ: Rutgers Univ. Press.

Mathieu, Nicole-Claude. 1991. "Quand céder n'est pas consentir." In *L'anatomie politique: Catégorisations et idéologies du sexe*, 131–225. Paris: Côté-femmes.

Mattelart, Armand. 2008. *La Globalisation de la surveillance: Aux origines de l'ordre sécuritaire*. Paris: Découverte.

Maublanc, Séverine. 2016. "Soldats violeurs à Djibouti: Dix Djiboutiennes en grève de la faim à Paris." *TV5Monde*, Mar. 31. At http://information.tv5monde.com/terriennes/soldats-violeurs-djibouti-dix-djiboutiennes-se-soulevent-depuis-la-france-99583. Accessed Apr. 1, 2016.

Mazurana, Dyan. 2005. "Gender and the Causes and Consequences of Armed Conflict." In *Gender, Conflict, and Peacekeeping*, edited by Dyan Mazurana, Angela Raven-Roberts, and Jane Parpart, 29–42. Lanham, MD: Rowman and Littlefield.

Medica Mondiale. 2007. *Dying to Be Heard: Self-Immolation of Women in Afghanistan*. Cologne: Medica Mondiale.

———. 2013. *The EVAW Law in Medica Afghanistan's Legal Aid Practise*. Cologne: Medica Mondiale.

Mellakh, Habib. 2013. *Chroniques du Manoubistan*. Tunis: Cérès Editions.

Mernissi, Fatima. 2009. "Seules les musulmanes persécutées intéressent l'Occident." Interview by Valérie Colin-Simard. *Psychologies*, July. At http://www.psychologies.com/Planete/Societe/Interviews/Seules-les-musulmanes-persecutees-interessent-l-Occident#. Accessed Aug. 2, 2013.

Middle East Monitor. 2015. "Tunisia Tourism Minister Says Country Lost One Million Tourists This Year." Sept. 4. At https://www.middleeastmonitor.com/news/africa/20847-tunisia-tourism-minister-says-country-lost-one-million-tourists-this-year. Accessed Nov. 22, 2015.

Mies, Maria. 1986. *Patriarchy and Accumulation on a World Scale*. London: Zed Press.

Mladenović, Lepa. 2001. "Notes of a Feminist Lesbian during Wartime." *European Journal of Women's Studies* 8, no. 3: 381–91.

Mladenović, Lepa, and Divna Matijasević. 1996. "SOS Belgrade July 1993–1995: Dirty Streets." In *Women in a Violent World: Feminist Analyses and Resistance across Europe*, edited by Chris Corrin, 119–32. Edinburgh: Edinburgh Univ. Press.

Moghadam, Valentine M. 1993. *Modernizing Women: Gender and Social Change in the Middle East*. Boulder, CO: Lynne Rienner.

————, ed. 1994. *Gender and National Identity: Women and Politics in Muslim Societies*. London: Zed Books.

————. 2002. "Women, the Taliban, and the Politics of Public Space in Afghanistan." In *September 11, 2001: Feminist Perspectives*, edited by Susan Hawthorne and Bronwyn Winter, 260–84. Melbourne: Spinifex.

————. 2005. *Globalizing Women: Transnational Feminist Networks*. Baltimore: Johns Hopkins Univ. Press.

Mohanty, Chandra Talpade. 2003. *Feminism without Borders: Decolonizing Theory, Practicing Solidarity*. Durham, NC: Duke Univ. Press.

Le Monde. 2015a. "'Charlie Hebdo,' 22 ans de procès en tous genres." Jan. 8. At http://www.lemonde.fr/societe/article/2015/01/08/charlie-hebdo-22-ans-de-proces-en-tous-genres_4551824_3224.html#. Accessed July 28, 2015.

————. 2015b. "L'état définitivement condamné à aménager la 'jungle' de Calais." Nov. 23. At http://www.lemonde.fr/immigration-et-diversite/article/2015/11/23/l-etat-definitivement-condamne-a-amenager-la-jungle-de-calais_4815806_1654200.html. Accessed Nov. 28, 2015.

Montevideo Convention on the Rights and Duties of States. 1933. At http://www.cfr.org/sovereignty/montevideo-convention-rights-dutes-states/p15897. Accessed Jan. 6, 2012.

Morgan, Robin. 1989. *The Demon Lover: On the Sexuality of Terrorism*. New York: Norton.

————. 2001. *The Demon Lover: The Roots of Terrorism*. London: Piatkus.

Morice, Louis. 2015. "6.000 migrants dans la 'jungle' de Calais: 'Il faut les sortir de ce lieu pourri.'" *Le Nouvel Observateur*, Oct. 21. At http://tempsreel.nouvelobs.com/monde/migrants/20151021.OBS8046/6-000-migrants-dans-la-jungle-de-calais-il-faut-les-sortir-de-ce-lieu-pourri.html. Accessed Nov. 15, 2015.

Mrabet, Fadela. 1965. *La Femme algérienne*. Paris: Maspéro.

————. 1967. *Les Algériennes*. Paris: Maspéro.

Murakami-Ramalho, Elizabeth, and Beth A. Durodoye. 2008. "Looking Back to Move Forward: Katrina's Black Women Survivors Speak." *NWSA Journal* 20, no. 3: 115–37.

Murphy, Megan. 2012. "There Is a Wrong Way to Do Feminism. And Femen Is Doing It Wrong." *Feminist Current*, Oct. 31. At http://www.feministcurrent.com/2012/10/31/there-is-a-wrong-way-to-do-feminism-and-femen-is-doing-it-wrong/. Accessed Nov. 23, 2015.

Nair, Rupam Jain. 2015. "New Recruits to Hindu Cause Hear Anti-Muslim Message." Reuters, Oct. 13. At http://in.reuters.com/article/2015/10/13/india-rss-muslims-idINKCN0S700M20151013. Accessed Nov. 22, 2015.

Newman, Edward. 2007. *A Crisis of Global Institutions? Multilateralism and International Security.* London: Routledge.

Newsome, Lloyd. 2011. Foreword to *Can We Talk about This?* DV8. At https://www.dv8.co.uk/projects/can-we-talk-about-this/foreword-by-lloyd-newson. Accessed Nov. 18, 2013.

New South Wales Bureau of Crime Statistics and Research. 2014. "NSW Recorded Crime Statistics: March 2014 Quarterly." Released June 2. At http://www.bocsar.nsw.gov.au/Pages/bocsar_media_releases/2014/mr_rcs_mar14.aspx. Accessed Mar. 16, 2015.

Noiriel, Gérard. 2015. *Qu'est-ce qu'une nation?* Paris: Bayard.

Obama, Barack. 2015. "Remarks at the National Prayer Breakfast, February 5." At https://www.whitehouse.gov/the-press-office/2015/02/05/remarks-president-national-prayer-breakfast. Accessed Apr. 9, 2015.

Obama, Barack, and Michelle Obama. 2011. "Remarks by the President and First Lady on the End of the War in Iraq, December 14." At https://www.whitehouse.gov/the-press-office/2011/12/14/remarks-president-and-first-lady-end-war-iraq. Accessed Apr. 9, 2015.

Office National de la Famille et de la Population (ONFP) and Agencia Española de Cooperación Internacional para el Desarrollo (AECID). 2010. *Enquête nationale sur la violence à l'égard des femmes en Tunisie: Rapport de l'enquête.* Tunis: ONFP-AECID.

Oguzlu, H. Tarik. 2005–6. "The Changing Turkish Approach towards the European Union after 9/11." *International Journal,* Winter, 83–104.

O'Keefe, Theresa. 2014. "My Body Is My Manifesto! SlutWalk, FEMEN, and Femmenist Protest." *Feminist Review* 107:1–19. DOI:10.1057/fr.2014.4.

Okin, Susan Moller, and others. 1999. *Is Multiculturalism Bad for Women?* Princeton, NJ: Princeton Univ. Press.

Oliver, Kelly. 2007. *Women as Weapons of War: Iraq, Sex, and the Media.* New York: Columbia Univ. Press.

O'Neill, Jim. 2001. *Building Better Global Economic BRICs.* Goldman Sachs Global Economics Paper no. 66. New York: Goldman Sachs. At http://

www2.goldmansachs.com/our-thinking/brics/building-better.html. Accessed June 5, 2011.

———. 2011. "Some BRICs Built but More Still Needed." Dec. At http://www.emergingmarkets.me/2011/12/some-brics-built-but-more-still-needed/. Accessed Dec. 20, 2011.

Organization for Economic Cooperation and Development (OECD). 2007. *OECD Communications Outlook for 2007.* Paris: OECD Directorate for Science, Technology, and Industry.

———. 2015. *Statistical Profiles: Israel.* At http://www.oecd-ilibrary.org/economics/country-statistical-profile-israel_20752288-table-isr. Accessed Nov. 22, 2015.

Otero, María Guadalupe Morfín. 2008. "Violence against the Women of Juárez." *Canadian Woman Studies* 27, no. 1: 45–49.

Otto, Diane. 2014. "Between Pleasure and Danger: Lesbian Human Rights." *European Human Rights Law Review* 6:618–28.

Outrage. 2014a. "IM GLAD: Advocating Equal Rights in Muslim Mindanao." Feb. 24. At http://outragemag.com/im-glad-advocating-equal-rights-muslim-mindanao/. Accessed Mar. 24, 2014.

———. 2014b. "Mherz Jamad: Empowering Bangsamoro Lesbians in Sulu." Apr. 1. At http://outragemag.com/mherz-jamad-empowering-bangsamoro-lesbians-sulu/. Accessed Mar. 24, 2015.

Oxfam International. 2009. *In Her Own Words: Iraqi Women Talk about Their Greatest Concerns and Challenges.* Oxford: Oxfam International. At http://www.oxfam.org/sites/www.oxfam.org/files/oxfam-in-her-own-words-iraqi-women-survey-08mar2009.pdf. Accessed July 14, 2013.

Parker, Pat. 1984. "For the Straight Folks Who Don't Mind Gays but Wish They Weren't so Blatant." At http://lyrics.wikia.com/wiki/Pat_Parker:For_The_Straight_Folks_Who_Don't_Mind_Gays_But_Wish_They_Weren't_So_Blatant. Accessed Nov. 22, 2015.

Parreñas, Rhacel Salazar. 2003. *Servants of Globalization: Women, Migration, and Domestic Work.* Manila: Ateneo de Manila Univ. Press.

Pateman, Carole. 1988. *The Sexual Contract.* Stanford, CA: Stanford Univ. Press.

Paxson, Christina, Elizabeth Fussell, Jean Rhodes, and Mary Waters. 2012. "Five Years Later: Recovery from Post Traumatic Stress and Psychological Distress among Low-Income Mothers Affected by Hurricane Katrina." *Social Science & Medicine* 74:150–57.

Pettman, Jan Jindy. 1996. *Worlding Women: A Feminist International Politics.* St. Leonards, Australia: Allen & Unwin.

Philippine Statistics Authority. 2004. "2004 Annual Poverty Indicators Survey." At https://psa.gov.ph/content/2004-annual-poverty-indicators -survey-apis-preliminary-results. Accessed Nov. 21, 2015.

———. 2005. "Philippine Labor Force Survey July 2005." At https://psa .gov.ph/content/philippine-labor-force-survey-july-2005-preliminary -results. Accessed Aug. 14, 2014.

———. 2007. "Foreign Trade Statistics of the Philippines: 2006." At https://psa.gov.ph/old/data/sectordata/sr07284tx.html. Accessed Dec. 7, 2009.

———. 2013. "Foreign Trade Statistics of the Philippines: First Semester 2013." At http://www.census.gov.ph/content/foreign-trade-statistics -philippines-first-semester-2013. Accessed Aug. 18, 2014.

———. 2016. "Poverty Incidence among Filipinos Registered at 26.3%, as of First Semester of 2015." Document no. 2016-PHDSD-018. At https:// psa.gov.ph/poverty-press-releases. Accessed Sept. 21, 2016.

———. n.d.a. "Economic and Financial Data of the Philippines." At http:// www.nscb.gov.ph/sdds/nsdp_online_all.asp. Accessed Nov. 21, 2015.

———. n.d.b. "Philippines in Figures." At https://psa.gov.ph/content /philippines-figures-0. Accessed Nov. 21, 2015.

———. n.d.c. "Statistics: Public Finance." At http://www.nscb.gov.ph /secstat/d_finance.asp. Accessed Sept. 21, 2016.

———. n.d.d. "Total Number of OFWs." At https://psa.gov.ph/content /total-number-ofws-estimated-23-million-results-2014-survey-overseas -filipinos%C2%B9. Accessed Nov. 21, 2015.

Pierrat, Emmanuel. 2015. *La Liberté sans expression?* Paris: Flammarion.

Pingeot, Lou, and Wolfgang Obenland. 2014. *In Whose Name? A Critical View on the Responsibility to Protect.* Bonn: Global Policy Forum. At https://www.globalpolicy.org/qhumanitarianq-intervention.html. Accessed Nov. 20, 2015.

Pitkin, Hanna. 1967. *The Concept of Representation.* Berkeley: Univ. of California Press.

Pointer, Sophie. 2013. *Trends in hospitalised injury, Australia: 1999–00 to 2010–11.* Canberra: Ausatralian Institute of Health and Welfare. At www.aihw.gov.au/WorkArea/DownloadAsset.aspx?id=60129544396. Accessed Mar. 18, 2015.

Politi, Caroline. 2015. "Flambée de l'antisémitisme en 2014: Le pire est-il encore à venir?" *L'Express*, Jan. 11. At http://www.lexpress.fr/actualite/societe/attentat-de-vincennes-une-flambee-de-l-antisemitisme-est-elle-a-craindre_1639476.html. Accessed Mar. 11, 2015.

Porter, Elisabeth J. 2007. *Peacebuilding: Women in International Perspective*. New York: Routledge.

Pringle, Helen. 2011. "Regulating Offence to the Godly: Blasphemy and the Future of Religious Vilification Laws." *University of New South Wales Law Journal* 34, no. 1: 316–32.

Proctor, Bernadette D., Jessica L. Semega, and Melissa A. Kollar. 2016. *Income and Poverty in the United States: 2015*. Washington, DC: US Census Bureau. At https://www.census.gov/library/publications/2016/demo/p60-256.html. Accessed Sept. 21, 2016.

Puar, Jasbir. 2007. *Terrorist Assemblages: Homonationalism in Queer Times*. Durham, NC: Duke Univ. Press.

Qutb, Sayyid. 2000. "Islam as the Foundation of Knowledge." In *Modernist and Fundamentalist Debates in Islam*, edited by Mansoor Moaddel and Kamran Talattof, 197–206. Basingstoke, UK: Palgrave MacMillan.

Radio Free Asia. 2014. "Detained 'Religious Extremists' Mostly Uyghur Women and Children." Dec. 25. At http://www.rfa.org/english/news/uyghur/extremists-12252014230546.html. Accessed Mar. 26, 2015.

Rai, Shirin M. 2008. "Analyzing Global Governance." In *Global Governance: Feminist Perspectives*, edited by Shirin M. Rai and Georgina Waylen, 19–42. Basingstoke, UK: Palgrave Macmillan.

Rai, Shirin M., and Georgina Waylen, eds. 2008. *Global Governance: Feminist Perspectives*. Basingstoke, UK: Palgrave Macmillan.

Ralston, Meredith, and Edna Keeble. 2009. *Reluctant Bedfellows: Feminism, Activism, and Prostitution in the Philippines*. Sterling, VA: Kumarian Press.

Ramadan, Hani. 2015. "Sur les attentats de Paris (13 novembre 2015): Réflexions." At http://haniramadan.blog.tdg.ch/. Accessed Nov. 27, 2015.

Ramadan, Tariq. 2003. *Les Musulmans d'Occident et l'avenir de l'islam*. Arles, France: Sindbad, Actes Sud.

Raven-Roberts, Angela. 2005. "Gender Mainstreaming in United Nations Peacekeeping Operations: Talking the Talk, Tripping over the Walk." In *Gender, Conflict, and Peacekeeping*, edited by Dyan Mazurana, Angela Raven-Roberts, and Jane Parpart, 43–63. Lanham, MD: Rowman and Littlefield.

Rehn, Elisabeth, and Ellen Sirleaf Johnson. 2002. *Women, War, Peace: The Independent Experts' Assessment on the Impact of Armed Conflict on Women and Women's Role in Peace-Building.* Progress of the World's Women, vol. 1. New York: United Nations. At http://www.unwomen.org/en /digital-library/publications/2002/1/women-war-peace-the-indepen dent-experts-assessment-on-the-impact-of-armed-conflict-on-women -and-women-s-role-in-peace-building-progress-of-the-world-s-women -2002-vol-1. Accessed Aug. 17, 2013.

Renan, Ernest. 1882. "Qu'est-ce qu'une nation?" At http://www.rutebeuf .com/textes/renan01.html. Accessed Feb. 2, 2012.

Reuters. 2009a. "Iraqi Women's Affairs Minister Resigns in Protest." Feb. 5. At http://www.reuters.com/article/us-iraq-women-idUSTRE5146L 720090205. Accessed Aug. 13, 2013.

———. 2009b. "U.S. Watchdog Says Billions of U.S. Aid Wasted in Iraq." Mar. 25. At http://www.reuters.com/article/us-usa-iraq-afghanistan -idUSN2544653120090325. Accessed Aug. 14, 2013.

———. 2015a. "Anti-immigration Sweden Democrats Country's Largest Party—Poll." Aug. 20. At http://uk.reuters.com/article/uk-sweden -politics-poll-idUKKCN0QP0Q120150820. Accessed Jan. 15, 2016.

———. 2015b. "China Shows Unusual Pictures of Its Fight against Terror." Nov. 14. At http://www.reuters.com/article/2015/11/14/us-france -shooting-china-idUSKCN0T30K120151114#IqOYGib2CPhrmo2p.97. Accessed Nov. 20, 2015.

Reuveny, Rafael, and Aseem Prakash. 1999. "The Afghanistan War and the Breakdown of the Soviet Union." *Review of International Studies* 25:693–708.

RFI. 2015a. "La Présidente de l'Instance vérité et dignité visée par une plainte." Aug. 23. At http://www.rfi.fr/afrique/20150823-tunisie -polemique-instance-verite-dignite-presidente-propos-blogueur-aziz -amami-sih. Accessed Nov. 22, 2015.

———. 2015b. "La Semaine où François Hollande est devenu chef de guerre." Nov. 20. At http://www.rfi.fr/france/20151120-semaine-fran cois-hollande-devenu-chef-guerre-attentats-paris-securite-syrie. Accessed Nov. 28, 2015.

Rice, Condoleezza. 2006. "Transformational Diplomacy." Speech at Georgetown Univ., Jan. 18. At http://2001-2009.state.gov/secretary /rm/2006/59306.htm. Accessed Nov. 21, 2015.

Rich, Adrienne. 1980. "Compulsory Heterosexuality and Lesbian Existence." *Signs* 5, no. 4: 631–60.

Richardson, Robin, ed. 2004. *Islamophobia: Issues, Challenges, and Action.* Stoke on Trent, UK: Trentham Books.

Rieth, Bruno. 2016. "Indigènes de la République: Thomas Guénolé démontre le racisme, la misogynie et l'homophobie de Houria Bouteldja." *Marianne*, Mar. 21. At http://www.marianne.net/indigenes-republique -thomas-guenole-demontre-racisme-misogynie-homophobie-houria -bouteldja-100241272. Accessed Apr. 8, 2016.

Riley, Robin L., Chandra Talpade Mohanty, and Minnie Bruce Pratt, eds. 2008. *Feminism and War: Confronting U.S. Imperialism.* London: Zed Books.

Roberts, Hugh. 2011. "Who Said Gaddafi Had to Go?" *London Review of Books* 33, no. 22: 8–18. At http://www.lrb.co.uk/v33/n22/hugh-roberts /who-said-gaddafi-had-to-go. Accessed Nov. 30, 2011.

Robin, Marie-Monique. 2008. *Le Monde selon Monsanto: De la dioxine aux OGM, une multinationale qui vous veut du bien.* Paris: La Découverte.

Robinson, Fiona. 2009. "Feminist Ethics and Global Security Governance." In *The Ethics of Global Governance*, edited by Antonio Franceschet, 103–18. Boulder, CO: Lynne Rienner.

Rodell, Paul A. 2005. "The Philippines and the Challenge of International Terrorism." In *Terrorism and Violence in Southeast Asia: Transnational Challenges to States and Regional Security*, edited by Paul J. Smith, 122–42. New York: M. E. Sharpe.

Rosenau, James. 1992. "Governance, Order, and Change in World Politics." In *Governance without Government: Order and Change in World Politics*, edited by James Rosenau and Ernst-Otto Czempiel, 1–29. New York: Cambridge Univ. Press.

———. 1995. "Governance in the Twenty-First Century." *Global Governance: A Review of Multilateralism and International Organizations* 1, no. 1: 13–43.

Rothschild, Cynthia, with Scott Long, Charlotte Bunch, Susana Fried, and Ali Miller. 2000. *Written Out: How Sexuality Is Used to Attack Women's Organizing.* New York: International Gay and Lesbian Human Rights Commission and Center for Women's Global Leadership.

Roudi-Fahimi, Farzaneh, and Valentine M. Moghadam. 2003. *Empowering Women, Developing Society: Female Education in the Middle East and North Africa*. Washington, DC: Population Reference Bureau. At http://www.prb.org/Publications/Reports/2003/EmpoweringWomen DevelopingSocietyFemaleEducationintheMiddleEastandNorthAfrica .aspx. Accessed Mar. 21, 2015.

Roy, Arundhati. 2002. "The Algebra of Infinite Justice." In *The Algebra of Infinite Justice*, 193–212. London: Flamingo.

———. 2003. *War Talk*. Cambridge, MA: South End Press.

Rozario, Santi. 2006. "The New Burqa in Bangladesh: Empowerment or Violation of Women's Rights?" *Women's Studies International Forum* 29, no. 4: 368–80.

Rozell, Mark J., and Gleaves Whitney, eds. 2007. *Religion and the Bush Presidency*. New York: Palgrave Macmillan.

Rubin, Michael. 2005. "A Comedy of Errors: American Turkish Diplomacy and the Iraq War." *Turkish Policy Quarterly* 4, no. 1. At http://www .turkishpolicy.com/article/456/a-comedy-of-errors-american-turkish -diplomacy-and-the-iraq-war-spring-2005. Accessed Nov. 19, 2015.

Rumsfeld, Donald. 2002. US Department of Defense press briefing on Iraq, Feb. 12. At http://www.defense.gov/transcripts/transcript.aspx ?transcriptid=2636. Accessed Feb. 3, 2012.

Rupp, Leila. 1997. *Worlds of Women: The Making of an International Women's Movement*. Princeton, NJ: Princeton Univ. Press.

Safran, Hannah. 2005. "Alliance and Denial: Lesbian Protest in Women in Black." In *Sappho in the Holy Land: Lesbian Existence and Dilemmas in Contemporary Israel*, edited by Chava Frankfort-Nachmias and Erella Shadmi, 191–209. Albany: State Univ. of New York Press.

Salime, Zakia. 2007. "The War on Terrorism: Appropriation and Subversion of Moroccan Women." *Signs: A Journal of Women, Culture, and Society* 33, no. 1: 1–24.

Santos, Aida F., with Noreen Belarmino and Raquel B. Ignacio. 2002. "The Philippines: Migration and Trafficking in Women." In *A Comparative Study of Women in the International Migration Process: Patterns, Profiles, and Health Consequences of Sexual Exploitation*, edited by Janice G. Raymond, 22–28. Manila: Coalition against Trafficking in Women, Asia-Pacific.

Sarkozy, Nicolas. 2011. "Discours au Puy-en-Velay." Mar. 3. At http:// www.la-croix.com/Actualite/Monde/Discours-de-Nicolas-Sarkozy-au -Puy-en-Velay-_NG_-2011-03-03-564431. Accessed Nov. 18, 2013.

Sassen, Saskia. 2002. "Governance Hotspots: Challenges We Must Confront in the Post–September 11 World." In *Understanding September 11*, edited by Craig Calhoun, Paul Price, and Ashley Timmer, 106–20. New York: Social Science Research Council and New Press.

Saul, Ben. 2006. *Defining Terrorism in International Law*. Oxford: Oxford Univ. Press.

Schachter, Su. 2005. "Lesbians in the Women's Peace Movement." In *Sappho in the Holy Land: Lesbian Existence and Dilemmas in Contemporary Israel*, edited by Chava Frankfort-Nachmias and Erella Shadmi, 175–89. Albany: State Univ. of New York Press.

Schlatter, Evelyn. 2010. "18 Anti-Gay Groups and Their Propaganda." Southern Poverty Law Center, Nov. 4. At https://www.splcenter.org /fighting-hate/intelligence-report/2010/18-anti-gay-groups-and-their -propaganda. Accessed Sept. 26, 2016.

Schnabel, Albrecht, and Hans-Georg Ehrhart, eds. 2005. *Security Sector Reform and Post-Conflict Peacebuilding*. Tokyo: United Nations Univ. Press.

Schoenholtz, Andrew I. 2005. "Refugee Protection in the United States Post–September 11." *Columbia Human Rights Law Review* 36:323–64.

Scott, Peter Dale. 2007. *The Road to 9/11: Wealth, Empire, and the Future of America*. Berkeley: Univ. of California Press.

Segré, Ivan. 2016. "Une Indigène au visage pâle." *Lundimatin*. At https:// lundi.am/Une-indigene-au-visage-pale. Accessed Mar. 25, 2016.

Selek, Pinar. 2015. *Parce qu'ils sont arméniens*. Translated by Ali Terzioglu. Paris: Liana Levi.

Serrano, Monica, and Thomas G. Weiss, eds. 2013. *The International Politics of Human Rights : Rallying to the R2P Cause?* London: Routledge.

Serrette, Florent. 2012. "Elu, catho et en faveur du mariage pour tous." *Libération*, Nov. 22. At http://www.liberation.fr/societe/2012/11/22 /elu-catho-et-en-faveur-du-mariage-pour-tous_862350. Accessed Nov. 18, 2013.

Shadmi, Erella. 2005. "The Construction of Lesbianism as a Nonissue in Israel." In *Sappho in the Holy Land: Lesbian Existence and Dilemmas in Contemporary Israel*, edited by Chava Frankfort-Nachmias and Erella Shadmi, 251–67. Albany: State Univ. of New York Press.

Shah, Anup. 2013. "World Military Spending." *Global Issues*, June 13. At http://www.globalissues.org/Geopolitics/ArmsTrade/Spending.asp. Accessed July 20, 2013.

Sharp, Jeremy. 2011. *U.S. Foreign Aid to Israel.* Washington, DC: Congressional Research Service. At http://www.fas.org/sgp/crs/mideast/RL3 3222.pdf. Accessed Aug. 22, 2013.

Shayegan, Darush. 1989. *Le Regard mutilé. Schizophrénie culturelle: Pays traditionnels face* à *la modernité.* La Tour d'Aigues, France: Editions de l'Aube.

Sheill, Kate. 2009. "Losing Out in the Intersections: Lesbians, Human Rights, Law, and Activism." *Contemporary Politics* 15, no. 1: 55–71.

Shoichet, Catherine E., AnneClaire Stapleton, and Greg Botelho. 2015. "Colorado Planned Parenthood Shooting: 3 Dead, Suspect Captured." Nov. 27. At http://edition.cnn.com/2015/11/27/us/colorado-shooting -probe/. Accessed Nov. 29, 2015.

Shrinath, Nihal, Vicki Mack, and Allison Plyer. 2014. "Who Lives in New Orleans and Metro Parishes Now?" New Orleans Data Center, Oct. 16. At http://www.datacenterresearch.org/data-resources/who-lives-in-new -orleans-now/. Accessed Mar. 19, 2015.

Sjoberg, Laura, and Caron E. Gentry, eds. 2011. *Women, Gender, and Terrorism.* Athens: Univ. of Georgia Press.

Sjørup, Lene. 1999. "Religion and Reproduction: The Vatican as an Actor in the Global Field." *Gender Technology and Development* 3, no. 3: 379–410.

Skidmore, Monique, and Patricia Lawrence, eds. 2007. *Women and the Contested State: Religion, Violence, and Agency in South and Southeast Asia.* Notre Dame, IN: Notre Dame Univ. Press.

Sly, Liz. 2014. "The Islamic State Is Failing at Being a State." *Washington Post,* Dec. 25. At https://www.washingtonpost.com/world/middle_east /the-islamic-state-is-failing-at-being-a-state/2014/12/24/bfbf8962-8 092-11e4-b936-f3afab0155a7_story.html. Accessed Sept. 18, 2016.

Smith, Anthony D. 1991. *The Ethnic Origins of Nationalism.* Oxford: Wiley-Blackwell.

Smith, Barbara. 1982. "Racism and Women's Studies." In *All the Women Are White, All the Blacks Are Men, but Some of Us Are Brave,* edited by Gloria T. Hull, Patricia Bell Scott, and Barbara Smith, 48–51. New York: Feminist Press.

Smith, Steve. 1998. "'Unacceptable Conclusions' and the 'Man' Question: Masculinity, Gender, and International Relations." In *The "Man"*

Question in International Relations, edited by Marysia Zalewski and Jane Parpart, 54–72. Boulder, CO: Westview Press.

Sökmen, Müge Gürsöy, ed. 2008. *World Tribunal on Iraq: Making the Case against War*. Northampton, MA: Olive Branch Press.

Sokoloff, Natalie J., and Ida Dupont. 2005. "Domestic Violence at the Intersections of Race, Class, and Gender: Challenges and Contributions to Understanding Violence against Marginalized Women in Diverse Communities." *Violence against Women* 11, no. 1: 38–64.

Solmirano, Carina, and Pieter D. Wezeman. 2010. "Military Spending and Arms Procurement in the Gulf States." Stockholm International Peace Research Institute Fact Sheet. At http://books.sipri.org/files/FS/SIPRIFS1010.pdfhttp://books.sipri.org/files/FS/SIPRIFS1010.pdf. Accessed Aug. 22, 2013.

Spivak, Gayatri Chakravorty. 1988. "Can the Subaltern Speak?" In *Marxism and the Interpretation of Culture*, edited by Lawrence Grossberg and Cary Nelson, 271–313. Urbana: Univ. of Illinois Press.

Standing, Guy. 2011. *The Precariat: The New Dangerous Class*. London: Bloomsbury.

Starke, J. G. 1967. "The Acquisition of Title to Territory by Newly Emerged States." *British Year Book of International Law* 41:411–16.

Stein, Laura Guzman. 2001. "The Politics of Implementing Women's Rights in Catholic Countries of Latin America." In *Globalization, Gender, and Religion: The Politics of Women Rights in Catholic and Muslim Contexts*, edited by Jane Bayes and Nayereh Tohidi, 127–55. New York: Palgrave.

Stockholm International Peace Research Institute (SIPRI). 2013. *SIPRI Yearbook 2013: Armaments, Disarmament, and International Security: Summary*. Stockholm: SIPRI. At http://www.sipri.org/yearbook/2013/files/SIPRIYB13Summary.pdf. Accessed July 5, 2013.

———. 2015a. *SIPRI Military Expenditure Database*. Stockholm: SIPRI. At http://www.sipri.org/research/armaments/milex/milex_database. Accessed Nov. 21, 2015.

———. 2015b. *The Sipri Top 100 ArmsProducing and Military Services Companies, 2013*. Stockholm: SIPRI. At http://www.sipri.org/research/armaments/production/recent-trends-in-arms-industry. Accessed Nov. 21, 2015.

———. 2015c. *SIPRI Yearbook 2015: Armaments, Disarmaments, and International Security: Summary.* Stockholm: SIPRI. At http://www.sipri.org/yearbook/2015. Accessed Nov. 21, 2015.

Stora, Benjamin. 2001. *La Guerre invisible: Algérie, années 90.* Paris: Presses de Sciences Po.

Subramanian, Kadayam. 2015. "Persistent Anti-Muslim Violence in India (1992–2015): Gainers and Losers." *Asia Times*, Oct. 25. At http://atimes.com/2015/10/persistent-anti-muslim-violence-in-india-1992-2015-gainers-and-losers/. Accessed Nov. 22, 2015.

Sultani, Abd al-Latif. 2000. "Islam and Its Adversaries." In *Modernist and Fundamentalist Debates in Islam*, edited by Mansoor Moaddel and Kamran Talattof, 341–42. New York: Palgrave Macmillan.

Suny, Ronald Grigor. 2015. *"They Can Live in the Desert but Nowhere Else": A History of the Armenian Genocide.* Princeton, NJ: Princeton Univ. Press.

Suskind, Ron. 2006. *The One Percent Doctrine: Deep Inside America's Pursuit of Its Enemies since 9/11.* New York: Simon & Schuster.

Sutton, Barbara, Sandra Morgen, and Julie Novkov, eds. 2008. *Security Disarmed: Critical Perspectives on Gender, Race, and Militarization.* New Brunswick, NJ: Rutgers Univ. Press.

Svirsky, Gila. 1996. *Standing for Peace: A History of Women in Black in Israel.* N.p.: Gila Svirksy. At http://www.gilasvirsky.com/wib_book.html. Accessed Sept. 15, 2013.

Swirski, Shlomo, and Etti Konor-Attias. 2004. *Israel: A Social Report 2004.* Tel Aviv: Adva Center.

Swirski, Shlomo, Etti Konor-Attias, and Ariane Ophir. 2013. *Israel: A Social Report 2013.* Tel Aviv: Adva Center.

Sydney Morning Herald, The. 2011. "China Uses 9/11 to Crack Down on Xinjiang." Agence France Presse, Sept. 11. At http://www.smh.com.au/breaking-news-world/china-uses-911-to-crack-down-on-xinjiang-20110911-1k3tp.html. Accessed Dec. 23, 2013.

Taarji, Hinde. 1990. *Les Voilées de l'Islam.* Paris: Balland.

Tabet, Paola. 2004. *La Grande arnaque: Sexualité des femmes et* échange économico-sexuel. Paris: L'Harmattan.

Taipei Times. 2005. "War on Terror Good for Defense Firms in US." Aug. 21.

Talmon, Stefan A. G. 2004. "The Constitutive versus the Declaratory Doctrine of Recognition: Tertium non datur?" *British Year Book of International Law* 75:101–81.

Templeton, Tom, and Tom Lumley. 2002. "9/11 in Numbers." *Guardian*, Aug. 18. At http://www.theguardian.com/world/2002/aug/18/usa .terrorism. Accessed Aug. 18, 2014.

Theroux, Paul. [1992] 2006. *The Happy Isles of Oceania: Paddling the Pacific*. New York: Mariner Books.

Tickner, J. Ann. 1992. *Gender in International Relations: Feminist Perspectives on Achieving Global Security*. New York: Columbia Univ. Press.

Tiglao, Bobi. 2015. "Aquino the Worst President Ever: He Damaged Our Institutions." *Manila Times*, July 26. At http://www.manilatimes.net /aquino-the-worst-president-ever-he-damaged-our-institutions/2037 70/. Accessed Nov. 21, 2015.

Todd, Emmanuel. 2015. *Qui est Charlie? Sociologie d'une crise religieuse*. Paris: Seuil.

Transparency International. 2005. "Corruption Perceptions Index 2005: Results." At http://www.transparency.org/research/cpi/cpi_2005/0 /#results. Accessed Mar. 19, 2015.

———. 2014. "Corruption Perceptions Index 2014: Results." At https:// www.transparency.org/cpi2014/results#myAnchor1. Accessed Mar. 16, 2015.

Traub, James. 2015. "Is Modi's India Safe for Muslims?" *Foreign Policy*, Aug. 18. At http://foreignpolicy.com/2015/06/26/narendra-modi-india -safe-for-muslims-hindu-nationalism-bjp-rss/. Accessed Nov. 22, 2015.

Trenoweth, Samantha, ed. 2013. *Bewitched and Bedevilled: Women Write the Gillard Years*. Richmond, Australia: Hardie Grant Books.

Tribalat, Michèle. 2014. "Surestimation du nombre de musulmans en France: Le décryptage de Michèle Tribalat." *Le Figaro*, Nov. 3. At http://www .lefigaro.fr/vox/societe/2014/10/31/31003-20141031ARTFIG00311 -surestimation-du-nombre-de-musulmans-en-france-le-decryptage-de -michele-tribalat.php. Accessed Nov. 28, 2015.

Trotsky, Leon. [1936] 1937. *The Revolution Betrayed: What Is the Soviet State and Where Is It Going?* Translated by Max Eastman. Garden City, NY: Doubleday, Doran. At https://www.marxists.org/archive/trotsky /1936/revbet/. Accessed Mar. 23, 2015.

Trouvelot, Sandrine. 2015. "Les Immigrés abusent-ils de notre système?" *Capital*, Apr. 7. At http://www.capital.fr/enquetes/dossiers/les-immi gres-abusent-ils-de-notre-systeme-1028599. Accessed July 3, 2015.

True, Jacqui. 2012. *The Political Economy of Violence against Women.* Oxford: Oxford University Press.

TrustLaw. 2011. "Factsheet: The World's Most Dangerous Countries for Women." At http://www.trust.org/item/?map=factsheet-the-worlds -most-dangerous-countries-for-women. Accessed July 11, 2013.

Truth, Sojourner. 1851. "Ain't I a Woman?" Speech to Women's Convention, Akron, Ohio, Dec. Available in the Fordham University Modern History Archives at http://legacy.fordham.edu/halsall/mod/sojtruth -woman.asp. Accessed Nov. 22, 2015.

Tunisian National Institute of Statistics. n.d. "Emploi." At http://www.ins .tn/fr/themes/emploi#sub-374. Accessed Sept. 26, 2016.

Tunisie Numérique. 2015. "Tunisie—que peuvent nous cacher les élans de cœur de Ghannouchi?" Sept. 5. At http://www.tunisienumerique.com /tunisie-que-peuvent-nous-cacher-les-elans-de-coeur-de-ghannouchi /265575. Accessed Nov. 22, 2015.

United Nations. 1984. *Convention against Torture and Other Cruel, Inhuman or Degrading Treatment or Punishment.* At http://www.ohchr.org/EN /ProfessionalInterest/Pages/CAT.aspx. Accessed Sept. 12, 2015.

———. 2002. *Women, Peace, and Security: Study Submitted by the Secretary-General Pursuant to Security Council Resolution 1325 (2000).* New York: United Nations. At http://www.un.org/womenwatch/daw/public/eWPS .pdf. Accessed Aug. 16, 2013.

United Nations Children's Emergency Fund (UNICEF). 2013. *Female Genital Mutilation/Cutting: A Statistical Overview and Exploration of the Dynamics of Change.* New York: UNICEF. At http://www.unicef.org /esaro/FGCM_Lo_res.pdf. Accessed Aug. 14, 2014.

———. 2014. *Hidden in Plain Sight: A Statistical Analysis of Violence against Children.* New York: UNICEF. At http://www.unicef.org/publications /files/Hidden_in_plain_sight_statistical_analysis_Summary_EN_2 _Sept_2014.pdf#sthash.1LezM9Ry.dpuf. Accessed Feb. 3, 2015.

United Nations Commission on Human Security. 2003. *Human Security Now.* New York: United Nations. At http://www.unocha.org/human security/chs/finalreport/index.html. Accessed Aug. 15, 2014.

United Nations Development Program (UNDP). 1994. *Human Development Report 1994*. New York: UNDP. At http://hdr.undp.org/en/reports/global/hdr1994/chapters/. Accessed Aug. 5, 2013.

———. 2001. *Human Development Report 2001*. New York: UNDP. At http://hdr.undp.org/en/reports/global/hdr2001/. Accessed Aug. 2, 2013.

———. 2002. *Human Development Report 2002*. New York: UNDP. At hdr.undp.org/sites/default/files/reports/263/hdr_2002_en_complete.pdf. Accessed Aug. 3, 2013.

———. 2013. *Human Development Report 2013*. New York: UNDP. At http://hdr.undp.org/en/reports/global/hdr2013/. Accessed Aug. 2, 2013.

———. 2014. *Human Development Report 2014*. New York: UNDP. At http://www.undp.org/content/undp/en/home/librarypage/hdr/2014-human-development-report.html. Accessed Mar. 3, 2015.

———. 2015. *Human Development Report 2015*. New York: UNDP. At http://hdr.undp.org/sites/default/files/hdr15-report-en-1.pdf. Accessed Apr. 9, 2016.

United Nations Economic and Social Council. 1997. *Report of the Economic and Social Council for 1997*. General Assembly, 52nd sess. New York: United Nations. At http://www.un.org/documents/ga/docs/52/plenary/a52-3.htm. Accessed May 15, 2007.

United Nations General Assembly. 1981. *Declaration on the Elimination of All Forms of Intolerance and of Discrimination Based on Religion or Belief*. Document A/RES/36/55. At http://www.un.org/documents/ga/res/36/a36r055.htm. Accessed Nov. 24, 2013.

———. 1994. "Situation of Human Rights in Afghanistan. Note by the Secretary-General." Document A/49/650. At http://daccess-dds-ny.un.org/doc/UNDOC/GEN/N94/438/48/PDF/N9443848.pdf?OpenElement. Accessed Aug. 2, 2013.

———. 2005a. "Combating Defamation of Religions." Document A/RES/60/150, Dec. 16. At http://www.worldlii.org/int/other/UNGARsn/2005/175.pdf. Accessed Nov. 24, 2013.

———. 2005b. *Resolution Adopted by the General Assembly 60/1. 2005 World Summit Outcome*. Document A/RES/60/1, Oct. 24. At http://www.un.org/womenwatch/ods/A-RES-60-1-E.pdf. Accessed Aug. 12, 2014.

———. 2009. *Implementing the Responsibility to Protect: Report of the Secretary-General.* Document A/63/677, Jan. 12. At http://www.un.org /en/ga/search/view_doc.asp?symbol=A/63/677. Accessed Aug. 12, 2014.

United Nations High Commission for Refugees. 2015. Press release, July 9. At http://www.unhcr.org/559d67d46.html. Accessed Nov. 19, 2015.

United Nations Mission in the Republic of South Sudan (UNMISS). 2014. *Conflict in South Sudan: A Human Rights Report.* Juba, South Sudan: UNMISS.

United Nations News Centre. n.d. [c. 2014]. "Lebanon Faces 'National Calamity' as Refugee Crisis Deepens, UN Relief Official Warns." At http://www.un.org/apps/news/story.asp?NewsID=48264#.VQ5LW mY7w7A. Accessed Mar. 22, 2015.

United Nations Office of the High Commissioner for Human Rights. 1999. *Defamation of Religions.* Commission on Human Rights Resolution 1999/82. At http://ap.ohchr.org/Documents/E/CHR/resolutions/E -CN_4-RES-1999-82.doc. Accessed Nov. 24, 2013.

United Nations Office on Drugs and Crime (UNODC). 2014. *Global Study on Homicide 2013: Trends, Contexts, Data.* Vienna: UNODC. At http:// www.unodc.org/gsh/. Accessed Mar. 15, 2015.

United Nations Office on Drugs and Crime (UNODC) and the Islamic Republic of Afghanistan High Office of Oversight and Anti-Corruption. 2012. *Corruption in Afghanistan: Recent Patterns and Trends: Summary Findings.* Vienna: UNODC. At http://www.unodc.org/documents /frontpage/Corruption_in_Afghanistan_FINAL.pdf. Accessed Aug. 2, 2013.

United Nations Office on Drugs and Crime (UNODC), United Nations Development Program Iraq, Central Statistical Office of Iraq, Kurdistan Regional Statistical Office, and the Iraq Commission of Integrity. 2012. *Corruption and Integrity Challenges in the Public Sector of Iraq: An Evidence-Based Study.* Vienna: UNODC. At https://www.unodc .org/documents/publications/2013_Report_on_Corruption_and_In tegrity_Iraq.pdf. Accessed Aug. 2, 2013.

United Nations Population Fund, Secrétariat d'état à la femme et la famille. 2014. *État du droit tunisien sur les violences faites aux femmes et aux filles.* Tunis: United Nations Population Fund.

United Nations Radio. 2013. "UN Committee Urges Djibouti to Curb Violence against Women." Media release and podcast, Oct. 31. At http://www.unmultimedia.org/radio/english/2013/10/un-committee-urges-djibouti-to-curb-violence-against-women/. Accessed Aug. 14, 2014.

———. 2014. "Violence against Afghan Women and Girls Widespread and Systemic." Press release, Nov. 13. At http://www.unmultimedia.org/radio/english/2014/11/violence-against-afghan-women-and-girls-widespread-and-systemic-2/#.VShcPmY7w7A. Accessed Apr. 12, 2015.

United Nations Security Council. 2000. *Resolution 1325. Adopted by the Security Council at Its 4213th Meeting on 31 October 2000.* S/RES/1325. At http://unscr.com/en/resolutions/doc/1325. Accessed Sept. 9, 2016.

———. 2008. *Resolution 1820. Adopted by the Security Council at Its 5916th meeting, on 19 June 2008.* S/RES/1820. At http://unscr.com/en/resolutions/doc/1820. Accessed Sept. 9, 2016.

United Nations Statistics Division. 2013. "Composition of Macro Geographical (Continental) Regions, Geographical Sub-regions, and Selected Economic and Other Groupings." Revised Oct. 13. At http://unstats.un.org/unsd/methods/m49/m49regin.htm. Accessed May 13, 2014.

United Nations World Commission on Environment and Development. 1987. *Our Common Future.* New York: United Nations. At conspect.nl/pdf/Our_Common_Future-Brundtland_Report_1987.pdf. Accessed Aug. 15, 2014.

United States Institute of Peace. 2004. *Terrorism in the Horn of Africa.* Washington, DC: United States Institute of Peace. At https://www.usip.org/sites/default/files/sr113.pdf. Accessed Feb. 23, 2015.

Unrepresented Nations and Peoples Organization (UNPO). 2014. *Alternative Report to the 59th Session of CEDAW.* Brussels: UNPO. At http://unpo.org/article/17645. Accessed Nov. 20, 2014.

US Department of Defense (DoD). 2004. *Global Posture: Report to Congress.* Washington, DC: US DoD. At https://archive.org/details/globalposturerev00unit. Accessed Nov. 23, 2006.

———. 2008. *Measuring Stability and Security in Iraq.* Report to Congress, June. Washington, DC: US DoD. At http://www.defense.gov/pubs/pdfs/Master_16_June_08_%20FINAL_SIGNED%20.pdf. Accessed July 14, 2013.

———. 2012. *Sustaining U.S. Global Leadership: Priorities for 21st Century Defense*. Washington, DC: US DoD. At http://www.defense.gov/news /defense_strategic_guidance.pdf. Accessed Aug. 18, 2014.

———. 2014. *2014 Quadrennial Defense Review*. At archive.defense.gov /pubs/2014_Quadrennial_Defense_Review.pdf. Accessed Mar. 14, 2015.

US Department of Labor. n.d. "Data & Statistics: Women in the Labor Force." At http://www.dol.gov/wb/stats/stats_data.htm. Accessed Nov. 21, 2015.

US Department of Labor, Bureau of Labor Statistics. 2016. "Table 1.4: Occupations with the Most Job Growth, 2014 and Projected 2024." At http://www.bls.gov/emp/ep_table_104.htm. Last updated Apr. 18, 2016. Accessed Aug. 18, 2014.

US Department of State (DoS). 2003. "Office of International Women's Issues Fact Sheet." Mar. 20. At http://www.state.gov/g/wi/rls/18877 .htm. Accessed Nov. 22, 2007.

———. 2010a. *Country Reports on Terrorism 2009*. Washington, DC: US DoS.

———. 2010b. "International Military Education and Training Account Summary." At http://www.state.gov/t/pm/ppa/sat/c14562.htm. Accessed July 5, 2013.

———. 2013. *Djibouti 2013 Human Rights Report*. Washington, DC: US DoS. At http://www.state.gov/documents/organization/220318.pdf. Accessed Aug. 13, 2014.

———. 2014a. *2014 Investment Climate Statement: Turkey*. Washington, DC: US DoS. At http://www.state.gov/e/eb/rls/othr/ics/2014/index .htm. Accessed Mar. 15, 2015.

———. 2014b. *Trafficking in Persons Report 2014*. Washington, DC: US DoS. At http://www.state.gov/j/tip/rls/tiprpt/2014/index.htm. Accessed Aug. 14, 2014.

———. 2015. *Trafficking in Persons Report 2015*. Washington, DC: US DoS. At http://www.state.gov/j/tip/rls/tiprpt/2015/index.htm. Accessed Nov. 21, 2015.

USGovernmentSpending.com. n.d. "Government Spending Details." At http://www.usgovernmentspending.com/year_spending_2005USbn _13bsln_30#usgs302. Accessed Jan. 16, 2012.

US International Trade Commission. 2015. "U.S. Merchandise Trade Balance, by Partner Country 2015 in Descending Order of Trade Turnover (General Imports Plus Total Exports): A Note on U.S. Trade Statistics." At http://dataweb.usitc.gov/scripts/cy_m3_run.asp. Accessed Aug. 18, 2014.

US Senate, Select Intelligence Committee. 2014. *The Senate Intelligence Committee Report on Torture: Committee Study of the Central Intelligence Agency's Detention and Interrogation Program.* New York: Melville House.

Vaïsse, Justin. 2007. *Transformational Diplomacy.* European Union Institute for Security Studies, Chaillot Paper no. 103. Paris: European Union. At http://www.iss.europa.eu/publications/detail/article/transformational-diplomacy/. Accessed Nov. 21, 2015.

VicHealth. 2014. *Findings from the 2013 National Community Attitudes towards Violence against Women Survey (NCAS).* At https://www.vichealth.vic.gov.au/media-and-resources/publications/2013-national-community-attitudes-towards-violence-against-women-survey. Accessed Mar. 15, 2015.

Vicziany, Marika. 2004. "Islamic Terrorism in Xinjiang." In *Regional Security in the Asia-Pacific: 9/11 and After*, edited by Marika Vicziany, David Wright-Neville, and Pete Lentini, 149–69. Cheltenham, UK: Edward Elgar.

Vulser, Nicole. 2015. "Les Fabricants de drapeaux 'débordés' par la demande." *Le Monde*, Nov. 26. At http://www.lemonde.fr/economie/article/2015/11/26/les-fabricants-de-drapeaux-debordes-par-la-demande_4818172_3234.html. Accessed Nov. 29, 2015.

Wallerstein, Immanuel. 1974. *The Modern World-System I: Capitalist Agriculture and the Origins of the European World-Economy in the Sixteenth Century.* New York: Academic Press.

———. 2002. "America and the World: The Twin Towers as Metaphor." In *Understanding September 11*, edited by Craig Calhoun, Paul Price, and Ashley Timmer, 345–60. New York: Social Science Research Council and New Press.

Walsh, Kerry-Anne. 2013. *The Stalking of Julia Gillard: How the Media and Team Rudd Brought Down the Prime Minister.* Sydney: Allen & Unwin.

Walt, Stephen M. 1991. "The Renaissance of Security Studies." *International Studies Quarterly* 35, no. 2: 211–39.

Walzer, Michael. [1997] 2000. *Just and Unjust Wars*. 3rd ed. New York: Basic Books.

———. 2004. *Arguing about War*. New Haven, CT: Yale Univ. Press.

Washington Post. 1992. "Equal Rights Initiative in Iowa Attacked." August 23.

Weber, Cynthia. 2014. "Encountering Violence: Terrorism and Horrorism in War and Citizenship." *International Political Sociology* 8, no. 3: 237–55.

Weiss, Thomas, and Rorden Wilkinson. 2007. Foreword to Edward Newman, *A Crisis of Global Institutions? Multilateralism and International Security*, viii–xi. London: Routledge.

White, Lawrence J. 2010. "Markets: The Credit Rating Agencies." *Journal of Economic Perspectives* 24, no. 2: 211–26.

Whitworth, Sandra. 2004. *Men, Militarism, and UN Peacekeeping: A Gendered Analysis*. Boulder, CO: Lynne Rienner.

Wickham, Carrie Rosefsky. 2013. *The Muslim Brotherhood: Evolution of an Islamist Movement*. Princeton, NJ: Princeton Univ. Press.

Wikipedia. n.d. "List of Terrorist Incidents, 2015." At https://en.wikipedia.org/wiki/List_of_terrorist_incidents_2015. Last modified Aug. 15, 2016. Accessed Nov. 23, 2015.

Wilde, Oscar. 1891. *Salomé*. At http://www.atramenta.net/lire/salome/14716/1#oeuvre_page. Accessed Mar. 3, 2013.

Williams, Erica, Olga Sorokina, Avis Jones-DeWeever, and Heidi Hartmann. 2006. *The Women of New Orleans and the Gulf Coast: Multiple Disadvantages and Key Assets for Recovery*. Washington, DC: Institute for Women's Policy Research.

Wilson, Dominic, and Roopa Purushothaman. 2003. *Dreaming with BRICs: The Path to 2050*. Goldman Sachs Global Economics Paper no. 99. New York: Goldman Sachs. At http://www2.goldmansachs.com/our-thinking/brics/brics-dream.html. Accessed Dec. 20, 2011.

Winter, Bronwyn. 2002a. "If Women Really Mattered. . . ." In *September 11, 2001: Feminist Perspectives*, edited by Susan Hawthorne and Bronwyn Winter, 450–80. Melbourne: Spinifex.

———. 2002b. "Women's Rights, Globalisation, and the Nation-State: Are Human Rights and Democracy Enough?" *Australian Feminist Law Journal* 17 (Dec.): 1–16.

———. 2006a. "Lesbian Is Good." In *Perverse Verse: Celebrating Readings Held at NSW Writers' Centre, 11 February 2006*, edited by Gail Hewison, 45–46. Sydney: Gay-ebooks.

———. 2006b. "Religion, Culture, and Women's Human Rights: Some General Political and Theoretical Considerations." *Women's Studies International Forum* 29, no. 4: 381–93.

———. 2007. "Pre-emptive Fridge Magnets and Other Weapons of Masculinist Destruction: The Rhetoric and Reality of 'Safeguarding Australia.'" *Signs: A Journal of Women, Culture, and Society* 33, no. 1: 25–52.

———. 2008. *Hijab and the Republic: Uncovering the French Headscarf Debate*. Syracuse, NY: Syracuse Univ. Press.

———. 2009–10. "Women and the 'Turkish Paradox': What the Headscarf Is Covering Up." *Modern Greek Studies (Australia and New Zealand)* 2009–10 (double issue): 216–39.

———. 2011a. "Guns, Money, and Justice: The 2005 Subic Rape Case." *International Feminist Journal of Politics* 13, no. 3: 371–89.

———. 2011b. "Ruin: What Happens When You Keep on Buying the Same Old Line." *Women's Studies Quarterly* 39, nos. 3–4: 270–74.

———. 2012a. "International vs Transnational? The Politics of Prefixes in Feminist International Relations." In *Woman, Body, Nation: International Efforts to Address Sexual Violence in Conflict and Post-conflict Zones*, edited by Tonia St. Germain and Susan Dewey, 15–32. West Hartford, CT: Kumarian Press.

———. 2012b. "Lily Pads and Leisure Meccas: The Gendered Political Economy of Post-base and Post-9/11 Philippines." In *Gender, Power, and Military Occupations in the Asia-Pacific and Middle East since 1945*, edited by Christine de Matos and Rowena Ward, 79–97. London: Routledge.

———. 2013. "Secularism and Religious Freedom: Challenging the 'Postsecular.'" In *Muslim Secular Democracy: Voices from Within*, edited by Lily Rahim, 141–64. Basingstoke, UK: Palgrave Macmillan.

———. 2014a. "Jews for Peace, 'Version Lite'? JCall between Right and Left." In "France and the Middle East," special issue of *Modern and Contemporary France* 22, no. 1. DOI: 10.1080/09639489.2013.867157.

———. 2014b. "The Ties That Bind Us: The Hidden Knots of Gay Marriage." In "Stigma," special issue of *Portal: Journal of Multidisciplinary*

International Studies 11, no. 1. DOI: http://dx.doi.org/10.5130/por
tal.v11i1.3296.

———. 2015. "The 'L' in the LGBTI 'Alphabet Soup': Issues Faced by Lesbian Asylum Seekers and Other Non-Western Lesbian Exiles in France." In "La Question de l'immigration aujourd'hui en France," special issue of *Contemporary French Civilization* 40, no. 2. DOI:10.3828/ cfc.2015.11.

———. 2016. "Women's Human Rights and Tunisian Upheavals: Is 'Democracy' Enough?" *Global Discourse* 6, no. 1. DOI:10.1080/2326999 5.2016.1155299.

———. Forthcoming a. "France." In *Worldwide Persepctives on Gays, Lesbians, and Bisexuals*, edited by Paula Gerber. Santa Barbara, CA: Praeger Press.

———. Forthcoming b. "Lesbian Human Rights." In *Worldwide Perspectives on Gays, Lesbians, and Bisexuals*, edited by Paula Gerber. Santa Barbara, CA: Praeger.

Withnall, Adam, and Danny Romero. 2015. "Isis, a Year of the Caliphate: How Powerful Is the 'Islamic State' and What Threat Does It Really Pose to [the] West?" *The Independent*, June 27. At http://www .independent.co.uk/news/world/middle-east/isis-a-year-of-the-caliphate -how-powerful-is-the-islamic-state-and-what-threat-does-it-really-pose -10349811.html. Accessed Oct. 14, 2015.

Wittig, Monique. 1992. *The Straight Mind and Other Essays.* Boston: Beacon Press.

Women Living under Muslim Laws. 2011. "The Struggle for Secularism in Europe and North America." Dossier 30–31, July. At http://www .wluml.org/resource/dossier-30-31-struggle-secularism-europe-and -north-america. Accessed Aug. 11, 2011.

Woolf, Virginia. [1938] 1977. *Three Guineas.* Harmondsworth, UK: Penguin Books.

World Conference against Racism, Racial Discrimination, Xenophobia, and Related Intolerance. 2001. "Declaration." Durban, South Africa, Sept. 8. At http://www.un.org/WCAR/durban.pdf. Accessed Nov. 24, 2013.

World Economic Forum. 2015. *The Global Gender Gap Report 2015.* Geneva: World Economic Forum.

World Health Organization. 2013. *Global and Regional Estimates of Violence against Women: Prevalence and Health Effects of Intimate Partner*

Violence and Non-partner Sexual Violence. Geneva: World Health Organization. At http://www.who.int/iris/bitstream/10665/85239/1/9789241564625_eng. Accessed Feb. 13, 2014.

World Trade Organization (WTO). 2013. *International Trade Statistics 2013: I: World Trade Developments*. Geneva: WTO. At https://www.wto.org/english/res_e/statis_e/its2013_e/its13_toc_e.htm. Accessed Mar. 31, 2014.

———. 2014. *International Trade Statistics 2014*. Geneva: WTO. At https://www.wto.org/english/res_e/statis_e/its2014_e/its2014_e.pdf. Accessed Apr. 10, 2015.

Wright-Neville, David. 2004. "US Counter-Terrorism in Southeast Asia: Problems on the Horizon." In *Regional Security in the Asia-Pacific: 9/11 and After*, edited by Marika Vicziany, David Wright-Neville, and Pete Lentini, 51–66. Cheltenham, UK: Edward Elgar.

Wroe, David. 2015. "Hearts & Minds." *Sydney Morning Herald*, Nov. 28–29.

Yavuz, M. Hakan. 2009. *Secularism and Muslim Democracy in Turkey*. Cambridge: Cambridge Univ. Press.

Young, Iris Marion. 2003. "The Logic of Masculinist Protection: Reflections on the Current Security State." *Signs: A Journal of Women, Culture, and Society* 29, no. 1: 1–25.

Yuval-Davis, Nira. 1997. *Gender and Nation*. London: Sage.

Yuval-Davis, Nira, and Floya Anthias, eds. 1989. *Woman, Nation, State*. Houndsmills, UK: Macmillan.

Yves. 2016. "Edouard Drumont, maître à penser de Mme Houria Bouteldja: Les Indigènes de la République réussissent leur examen d'entrée dans l'extrême droite gauloise." *Mondialisme.org*, Mar. 14. At http://www.mondialisme.org/spip.php?article2263. Accessed Mar. 25, 2016.

Zalewski, Marysia. 2013. *Feminist International Relations: Exquisite Corpse*. London: Routledge.

Zalewski, Marysia, and Jane Parpart, eds. 1998. *The "Man" Question in International Relations*. Boulder, CO: Westview Press.

Zimmerman, Augusto. 2013. "The Postmodern Underpinnings of Religious Vilification Laws: Implications for Democracy and Freedom of Speech." *Western Australian Jurist* 4:85–114.

Zubrzycki, Genevieve. 2006. *The Crosses of Auschwitz: Nationalism and Religion in Post-Communist Poland*. Chicago: Univ. of Chicago Press.

Index

Mays, Trent, 131–32

M'Barek, Sonia, 237

Médecins du monde (Doctors of the World), 276

Mellakh, Habib, 238–39

men. *See* male domination; masculinist ideology

MENA (Middle East and North Africa): Arab Spring terminology in, 213; authoritarianism in, 229; economic factors and, 230–32; emergence of Islamist movements in, 213, 214–23; enduring imperialism in, 176, 215; France and, 229–30; global economic power structures and, 34; Muslim Brotherhood's influence in, 219; in post-9/11 world, 36; religious politics in, 214, 222–23; transnational feminism and, 174–76; unemployment in, 231–32; UN geopolitical groupings and, 31

Merabet, Ahmed, 254

Merah, Mohamed, 255

Mercosur, 52, 55, 56

Mernissi, Fatima, 96

Mexico, 34, 55, 109, 134–35

micronations, 28

Middle East and North Africa. *See* MENA

MILF (Jabhat Tahrir Moro al-'Islamiyyah) (Moro Islamic Liberation Front), 294–95

militarism: antimilitarism movement against, 49–50; as hard currency of international politics, 78; Hurricane Katrina and, 138; money and, 83, 86; neoliberalism and, 134; security and, 16–17; state, 11; Subic Bay rape case and, 138

militarization: Global Firepower Index of, 280; of history, x–xi, xii; Hurricane Katrina and, 166–67; nationalism and, 280–81; in the Philippines, 138–46; post-9/11ism and, xii, 7; prostitution and, 138; spending on, 141–42, 147–50, 162, 166; Subic Bay rape case and, 136–38, 160–62, 166–67; *le treize novembre* attacks and, 279–81; Turkey and, 45, 48–49, 50; violence against women and, 119–20, 160–62; women and, 64

military bases: in Djibouti, 40–41, 44; in the Philippines, 45, 139–41, 157–58, 160; prostitution levels and, 44–45, 138; in TBA, 55; toxic waste from, 56–57; in Turkey, 49, 50

Military Bases Agreement (Philippines, 1947), 139

military exercises, in the Philippines, 6, 138, 139, 140–41, 159, 160

military-industrial complex, 147–48, 150–54

military interventions. *See* armed conflicts; war

military security, 113

military spending, 141–42, 147–54, 162, 166

Millennium Development Goals, 115

Mindanao Autonomous Region, 140, 143, 146, 293–94, 295, 297–300, 301

Mindanao People's Peace Movement (Tri-People's Peace Movement), 297–300

Misr Bank, 217

Miss France beauty contest, 262

Mizrahim women, 177–78, 187, 192

oppression and, 203; Hurricane Katrina and, 138; Islamist movements and, 230–32; in Israel, 211; marginalization of women by, 133–34; in the Philippines, 145, 299; racialized minorities and, 268–69; security talk/chatter on, 112–16; in Tunisia, 230–32; Women in Black and, 177–78

socioeconomic marginalization, 133–34, 230, 249–50, 257, 299

solidarity: cartoons of, 256; divides that separate us and, 292; between Israeli and Palestine women, 179, 186, 193; "Je suis Charlie" demonstrations of, 256–57, 278, 281; with lesbians, 188, 189, 193–202; nation and, 74; postsecularism and, 226; terrorist attacks and, 274, 281–82; transnational feminist, 17, 105, 169, 171–72, 174, 176, 190, 202

Solidarność (Solidarity), 214, 227

Soral, Alain, 271

Soumission (Houellebecq), 266

Sousse terrorist attacks (2015), 229, 231

South Africa, 31–32, 133

South America, 32, 33

South China Sea, 35

Southeastern Louisiana Flood Control Project, 162–66

Southern Poverty Law Center, 210

southern theory, 32, 36, 174

South Korea, 34, 145

South Sudan, 24

Sovereign Military Hospitaller Order of St. John of Jerusalem of Rhodes and of Malta, 24

sovereign states. *See* state sovereignty

Soviet Union, 9, 97, 214

Spivak, Gayatri, 93

Standard and Poor's, 71

state(s): constitutive, 22–23, 24–25, 27, 28; declarative, 23, 24, 25, 27, 28, 38, 76; definition of, 67; failing, 88, 91; global governance and, 15; militarism of, 11; neutrality toward religions by, 226–27; sexual hierarchies in, 205–6; transnational feminism and, 300. *See also* nation-states

state security, 115–16

states of emergency, 13–14, 243, 278–79

state sovereignty: corporate capitalism and, 70; description of, 67; failing states and, 91; global financial crisis (2008) and, 70–71; global governance and, 67–73, 86, 91; history of, 67–68, 78–80; need for, 77; R2P doctrine and, 90; types of, 67–68; women's rights and, 86–87

stereotypes, 271, 286–87

Steubenville rape (2012), 131–32

Stockholm International Peace Research Institute (SIPRI), 147, 151–52

Stop VFA! 161

Strolovitch, Dara, 164

St. Vincent de Paul Society, 130

Subic Bay rape case, 16, 136–38, 160–62, 166–67

Subic Naval Base (Philippines), 139, 141, 157–58, 160

subnational (transnational) regions, 25–26, 38, 76

substates, 25, 295

Sudan, 24

suicide bombers, 10, 21, 242, 287